# Chinese Economic Diplomacy

Economic diplomacy was declared in 2013 by Beijing as a priority in its 'comprehensive' strategy for diplomacy. The political elite undertook to further invest in economic diplomacy as an instrument for economic growth and development. Globally, Chinese cooperation in multilateral economic processes has become critical to achieving meaningful outcomes. However, little understanding exists in current literature of the factors and mechanisms which shape the processes behind China's economic diplomacy decision-making.

*Chinese Economic Diplomacy* provides an understanding of the processes and practices of China's economic diplomacy, with multilateral economic negotiations as the primary basis of analysis, specifically the UN climate change talks and the WTO Doha Round trade negotiations. It examines how early economic diplomacy in global governance contributed to the varied and evolving nature of its present-day decision-making structures and processes. Demonstrating how China's negotiation preferences are driven by networks of political actors in formal and informal domestic and systemic environments, it also highlights the capacity of international negotiation practices to alter and re-shape China's approach to multilateral economic negotiations. As a consequence, the book presents a framework for understanding China's economic diplomacy decision-making processes that is systemically constructed by domestic and international agencies.

Offering a Chinese perspective on the notion of economic diplomacy, this book will be of interest to any citizen, entity, or nation affected by China.

**Shuxiu Zhang** was Visiting Fellow at the International Trade Policy Unit, London School of Economics and Political Science, UK during the writing of this book. Her Research interests include economic diplomacy decision-making processes and the Chinese political economy.

# Routledge Studies in the Growth Economies of Asia

# Chinese Economic Diplomacy

Decision-making *actors* and *processes*

**Shuxiu Zhang**

LONDON AND NEW YORK

First published 2016 by Routledge

2 Park Square, Milton Park, Abingdon, Oxfordshire OX14 4RN

711 Third Avenue, New York, NY 10017

*Routledge is an imprint of the Taylor & Francis Group, an informa business*

First issued in paperback 2018

*British Library Cataloguing in Publication Data*
A catalogue record for this book is available from the British Library

*Library of Congress Cataloging-in-Publication Data*
Names: Zhang, Shuxiu, author.Title: Chinese economic diplomacy : decision-making actors and processes / Shuxiu Zhang.
Description: Abingdon, Oxon ; New York, NY : Routledge, 2017. | Series: Routledge studies in the growth economies of Asia ; 130 | Includes bibliographical references and index.
Identifiers: LCCN 2016000802| ISBN 9781138195868 (hardback) | ISBN 9781315638140 (ebook)
Subjects: LCSH: China–Foreign economic relations. | China–Economic policy–2000– | China–Foreign relations–21st century.
Classification: LCC HF1604 .Z23854 2017 | DDC 337.51–dc23
LC record available at https://lccn.loc.gov/2016000802

ISBN: 978-1-138-19586-8 (hbk)
ISBN: 978-1-138-58068-8 (pbk)

Typeset in Times New Roman
by Wearset Ltd, Boldon, Tyne and Wear

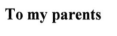
To my parents

# Contents

# Figures

# Tables

# Part I

# Chinese economic diplomacy

The fundamentals

# 1 Chinese *economic* diplomacy

## An introduction

It was the summer of 1997. Most of the Southeast Asia region fell into a contagious currency crisis. Its fatal contagion effect alarmed the Chinese political elites. On 23 September, the then Chinese Premier, Zhu Rongji, urged the National People's Congress (NPC) to exercise caution in the opening of domestic markets and state-owned enterprises (SOEs) to the global economy.[1] On the very same day, the then Minister of Finance, Liu Jibin, was reported in *China Daily* as having backed away from full convertibility of the Renminbi (RMB) to the dollar. Liu cautioned that the Southeast Asian financial crises had sent "a warning signal" to other developing countries about the dangers of surrendering control of their currencies to speculators and investors (Sanger, 1999).

While Beijing urged the injection of a stronger dose of immunity from the regional flu, the then President, Jiang Zemin, journeyed to the United States (US) as part of the continued efforts to negotiate the terms of China's accession to the World Trade Organization (WTO).[2] Despite this being the first state visit by a Chinese leader to Washington, DC in a dozen years, the two Presidents achieved little progress (*New York Times*, 1997). During the press conference at the conclusion of the visit, the two leaders twice touched on the Southeast Asian financial turmoil (Broder, 1997). Regional events had clearly sensitised China to adopting bolder trade policies.

On a bitterly cold Beijing day in January 1999, Zhu Rongji delivered an unexpected message to Alan Greenspan, the then Chairman of the US Federal Reserve. Zhu said China was ready to liberalise its agricultural, banking, insurance, and telecommunication markets in exchange for WTO membership (Sanger, 1999). This new position culminated to an early March visit to Beijing by the then US Trade Representative, Charlene Barshefsky. Following her meetings with Premier Zhu, Barshefsky stated "The Chinese Government has exhibited a very serious attitude and strength of purpose that has helped to make this week particularly productive."

The political elites in Beijing, in the grip of a new optimism, began planning next steps including an April visit to Washington, DC. According to a senior researcher for the central government's Development and Research Center, Ji Chongwei, Beijing recognised that "if China doesn't become a member [of the WTO] before the Seattle meeting later this year [1999], the issue will drag on for years" (cited in Rosenthal, 1999). With this purview, Beijing had hoped to advance the prospect of concluding its bilateral negotiations with the US in April. However, their optimism was dampened by the American business communities' criticism of China's "predatory" trade practices (Seelye, 1999). The domestic debate ultimately persuaded the then President Bill Clinton to back away from receiving a visit by Premier Zhu. This decision soured the bilateral relationship, and the trade negotiations were put on a reluctant hold.

The deadlock was seen as a significant step back in China's broader efforts to 'go global', a development strategy launched in 1978. When Deng Xiaoping succeeded Mao Zedong as the Chairman of the People's Republic of China (PRC, or China), he saw the need to de-cuff the country from the centrally planned economy in order to resource domestic needs, alleviate poverty, and to extract it out of international isolation. China began its global integration strategy with negotiations for economic assistance with the Bretton Woods institutions (i.e. the World Bank and the International Monetary Fund (IMF)), followed by the resumption of its membership of the United Nations (UN), and the subsequent negotiations to accede the WTO.

Throughout the various economic negotiations since the late 1970s, economic diplomacy has featured prominently in China's outreach. It has serviced as an instrument of the national development strategy, and an extension of domestic politics. On account of its capacity to widen China's access to global opportunities, President Xi Jinping underscored economic diplomacy as a priority in China's "comprehensive international endeavours" in December 2013, and announced new commitments to invest in economic diplomacy as a centrepiece of its foreign policy (*China Daily*, 2013).

Even though economic diplomacy sits prominently in China's foreign policy and development strategy, and as the country is expected to shape and reshape our world with its rising influence, we continue to work with less-than-satisfactory understandings about China's economic diplomacy, as a concept and a process. What is economic diplomacy in the Chinese context? Which policy instruments drive the formulation of China's economic diplomacy and what influences their negotiation preferences and approaches? How does China's economic diplomacy decision-making come about? Given that most of China's economic diplomacy occurs under the auspice of international agencies, what role and impact do these agencies and processes have on the development of China's negotiation positions? Are there factors (internal and external alike) which propel or undermine the role and impact of international agencies and processes? And to what extent can an understanding of China's economic diplomacy serve as an analytical tool for understanding the country's engagement with the world?

To date, we do not have any general books devoted to China's economic diplomacy. The influx of literature on China has commonly rushed to analyse the significance of China's rising economic and political power vis-à-vis its international relations (i.e. how it could implicate the world order) and the global economy. This is problematic because we cannot understand the global political economy without a better grasp of China's economic diplomacy and the associated decision-making processes. The central idea of this book, in a nutshell, is that variations of the processes and agencies, domestic and international alike, make significant differences to policy outcomes, and we can certainly understand the processes and agencies involved better than we do at present. Current political economy knowledge on China emphasises structure and impact. Sounder understanding of agencies and processes would be valuable to any citizen, entity, or nation affected by China. For these reasons, the contribution of this book is timely.

## Economic diplomacy … in the general sense…

Economic diplomacy was traditionally rooted in the broad and elastic notion of *diplomacy*.[3] The classical definition of *diplomacy* is "the conduct of relations between states and other entities with standing in world politics by official agents and by peaceful means" (Bull, 1995, p. 156) and "the means by which States pursue their foreign policies" (Berridge, 2002, p. 3). By the turn of the century, Barston (2006, p. 1) simplified *diplomacy* as concerning "the management of relations between states and between states and other actors".

If diplomacy is tied to state interests and actors, then *economic diplomacy* could be conceived as the use of traditional diplomatic tools to achieve economic goals and interests of the state. This is a state-centric conception, where economic diplomacy is the inter-governmental pursuit of economic security within an anarchic international system, conducted by officials of the Foreign Service, to advance economic interests of the state in foreign territories (Barston, 1997; Gardner, 1969; Marshall, 1997; Watson, 1982). On the flipside, realists believe economic diplomacy is often deployed as a tool of 'economic statecraft', which is the strategic use of positive and negative economic sanctions, including trade embargoes and aid programmes – by state and non-state actors (e.g. the United Nations) – to coerce states to cooperate (Baldwin, 1985; Davis, 1999; Hogan, 1987; Kunz, 1997; Zimmerman, 1993). Thus, economic diplomacy through the realist lens distinguishes the economic agenda from the political one (see Berridge and James, 2003, p. 91).

Yet, in the words of a former Ambassador of the United Kingdom:

> it is increasingly difficult to distinguish between what is political in diplomacy and what is economic, and indeed, whether there is a dividing line between the two which has any validity at all.[4]

Studies have shown the very origins of diplomacy lie in the development of cordial cross-border relations for the purpose of facilitating international trade (e.g. Lee and Hudson, 2004). The Foreign Ministry of Thailand's account of its historical development emphasises how trade interests in China drove Thai diplomacy of the thirteenth century, and its relations with Europe in the seventeenth century.[5] History therefore would indicate that economic diplomacy cannot be compartmentalised into separate economic and political activity or purposes. Many countries would find such a separation unrealistic in practice.

In the twenty-first century, economic diplomacy is generally a strand of diplomatic strategy – regardless of the country concerned. As Berridge and James (2003, p. 81) put it, economic diplomacy "includes diplomacy which employs economic resources, either as rewards or sanctions, in pursuit of a particular foreign policy objective", and is "concerned with economic policy questions, including the work of delegations to conferences sponsored by bodies such as the WTO". In a similar vein, Rana (2007, p. 201) defines economic diplomacy as

> the process through which countries tackle the outside world, to maximise their national gain in all the fields of activity including trade, investment and other forms of economically beneficial exchanges, where they enjoy comparative advantage; it has bilateral, regional and multilateral dimensions, each of which is important.

According to these interpretations, economic diplomacy is therefore necessary for the development of an integrated and coordinated diplomacy that congregates the essence of both politics and economics. This coordinated diplomacy involves a multiplicity of actors and individuals built around policy networks drawn from a myriad of government departments (typically led by the Foreign Ministry), as well as the private and civil sector actors across the national, regional, and international levels (Hocking, 2004).

A good encapsulation of the complex nature of coordinated diplomacy is Hocking's (2007) concept of the 'national diplomatic system' (NDS). According to this concept, economic diplomacy may be driven by the Foreign Ministry, but it involves those with economic responsibilities and interests inside and outside the government across all levels. In the NDS, by guiding the diplomatic structures and processes, the Foreign Ministry becomes the integrator or coordinator of diplomacy: that is, working with 'partners' (i.e. other government departments, international organisations or regimes, businesses, and civil groups) to deliver diplomatic goals. Some countries have developed new institutional structures within the government as a way of formalising this coordinating role. Australia, Canada, Fiji, Japan, Mauritius, and New Zealand, for example, have merged their trade and foreign ministries into one department as a bureaucratic way of integrating the *economic* dimension into foreign diplomacy. Others, such as the Czech Republic, the People's Republic of China, and the UK, have kept the two ministries distinct, and have created new joint bodies to coordinate and facilitate integrated diplomacy.

### The characteristics of economic diplomacy

The concept of *economic diplomacy* was first proposed by the government of Japan. Following its defeat in the Second World War (WWII), the government was in search of an effective instrument to channel its political influence abroad. By the mid-1950s, Japan's economy was growing at rapid speed, which stimulated a concurrent growth in domestic demand for resources and foreign markets.

In response, the Nobusuke Kishi government formulated the concept of economic diplomacy to address domestic economic needs, and actively tested this instrument with Southeast Asian economies. For instance, Japan attempted to liberalise the Southeast Asian markets through the provision of economic assistance, and other forms of support to improve national infrastructure and investment environments. In the 1970s and 1980s, Japanese academia fashioned one of the first waves of scholarly research into economic diplomacy.[7]

America's fascination with economic diplomacy began in the 1980s. Early works on this subject include David Kaiser's (1981) publication, *Economic Diplomacy and the Origins of the Second World War: Germany, Britain, France, and Eastern Europe 1930–1939* and the 1985 volume by M.S. Daoudi and M.S. Dajani, *Economic Diplomacy: Embargo Leverage and World Politics*. These works explored the American history of economic diplomacy practices. For instance, President William Howard Taft, in the early twentieth century, encouraged and supported American banks in international expansions and foreign investments in order to 'substitute dollars for bullets'. The late 1940s and early 1950s then introduced the famous Marshall Plan, which promoted American economic diplomacy within Europe. Since then, American foreign policy has often involved a 'carrot and stick' strategy, which indicates the centrality of economic interests in US diplomacy; that is, the US invests in efforts to attract foreign countries to conform to the 'carrot' of US assistance, and suppresses those that do not with the 'stick' of economic sanctions. In more recent times, the US's campaigns in the Middle East – all of which have centred on oil interests – are essentially *déjà vu*.

Since the end of the Cold War, economic diplomacy has been a priority for many countries across the world, typically for enhancing national prosperity. Brazil, for instance, has prioritised economic diplomacy especially as a platform for enhancing general interchange, technical knowledge, human resource capacity, and, more importantly, the strengthening of institutions (Juma, 2013). For the US, economic diplomacy sits at the heart of its foreign policy agenda, as stated by former Secretary of State, Hillary Clinton (Economic Club of New York, 2011). Economic diplomacy is likewise vital to the Indian foreign policy. As the former Indian Foreign Secretary Lalit Mansingh stated, the mere fact that the Development Partners Administration (DPA) – the primary platform of Indian economic diplomacy – "is located in the Ministry of External Affairs shows it is in sync with our [India's] foreign policy objectives of transforming India into a global player" (Roche, 2012). For all these countries, economic diplomacy services the negotiations of cross-border economic issues between governments, on matters including trade, investment, aid, the environment, and property rights.[8]

What distinguishes economic diplomacy today from the past is the context in which governments practise this diplomatic strategy. For much of the past 50 years, the global economy has become more integrated, either through regionalisation, or a process described as *globalisation*. The process is a widely used and contested concept in the fields of International Political Economy (IPE) or

International Relations (IR). Let's put aside the debates of globalisation and refer to the most basic understanding for the present purposes: a process of intensified global economic integration as a result of new technologies, and the expansion of economic activities between markets due to heightened flows of capital, trade, services, people, ideas, and information, exchanged between states, firms, and individuals. These changes precipitated the need for integrated diplomacy in order to facilitate and manage economic development and cross-border market integration.

Economic diplomacy, in turn, was embraced with heightened significance. Globalisation has triggered disparate diplomatic practices as well as a plethora of economic forums where networks of states and non-state actors at the domestic and systemic levels pursue both public and private interests.[9] These networks operate in, influence, and are influenced by an increasingly integrated and interdependent globalised economy. Along the way, diplomats and government negotiators have become agents of globalisation due to their direct involvement in the creation, development, and regulation of markets through intergovernmental trade negotiations and other commercial activities.

Since globalisation is one of the many processes which break down the barriers between the national and international, the agendas of economic diplomacy are found more at the fading boundaries between the domestic–international relationships. Climate change is a case in point. It is an issue which transcends national boundaries, and yet has enormous economic implications in relation to low carbon economic growth strategies. The international financial crisis of 2007–2009 is another striking example. What began as an American subprime mortgage crisis impacted economies across the continents virtually overnight. Globalisation has thus made economic diplomacy more complex, bringing in more issues, and more actors.

Aside from its multifaceted character, economic diplomacy is largely concerned with what *governments* do. Beyond foreign ministries, or a closed circle of officials, all government departments with economic responsibilities and an international operation are, one way or another, engaged in economic diplomacy. This could range from the Head of State to Ministers, independent public agencies, and sub-national bodies. International organisations and regimes are also important forums for the practice of economic diplomacy in the form of intergovernmental negotiations. Even though they are not typically considered as independent actors, the presiding staff that constitute the operational arm of these bodies are proactive providers of policy advice, inter-government brokering and coordination, research and information. Moreover, a range of non-state actors have also engaged in economic diplomacy, both by shaping government policies and as independent players in their own right. In the past, business firms tend to comprise the most active interest groups. Today, non-governmental organisations (NGOs) have joined in on the effort and actively seek publicity to place pressure on governments.

In the exercise of economic diplomacy, governments use a full range of *instruments*, most of which are produced through formal/informal negotiation and voluntary cooperation. The negotiated outcomes can range from an international harmonisation of regulatory standards (i.e. codes of conduct and best practices), to the creation and enforcement of multi-party (or multilateral) negotiated binding rules. Here, *negotiation* means a sequence of actions in which two or more Parties address demands and proposals to each other for the ostensible purpose of achieving an agreeable outcome in the form of a binding or non-binding contractual agreement.[10] Negotiation processes typically require a change in behaviour of at least one actor through persuasion. As such, the process of multilateral economic negotiations refers to a multi-party group of trade ministries, government negotiators, and diplomats, sometimes joined by others, and what they do with one another to pursue a common economic interest. The process includes consideration of the internal and external contexts in which the negotiation takes place, which offensive interests to pursue (and which defensive interests to protect), which strategies government negotiators choose to apply, how global markets and government negotiators influence each other, whether they add tactics to unearth possibilities for joint gains, how much they use tactics to guard against their own biases, and how they go about forming and splitting coalitions. Finally, this process includes the way in which government negotiators' strategic moves on the chessboard shift the domestic politics of not only their own country, but all countries that are sitting in on the game.

An understanding of economic diplomacy via its instruments is only telling half the story. Economic diplomacy is also defined by the *issues*. John Odell (2000 p. 11) has articulated the scope of economic diplomacy to include "policies relating to production, movement or exchange of goods, services, investments (including official development assistance), money, information and their regulation". The wide range of issues makes it impossible to cover in a single volume. Out of necessity, this book will focus on the central issues of international trade, and climate change – two areas that are distinctive enough for study and yet have not been viewed together in this light. As will be explained in Chapter 2, these are high-profile political topics, and bring out the interplay between different domestic and international actors in China's economic diplomacy.

## Economic diplomacy ... in the Chinese sense ...

After the founding of the PRC, Chinese leaders exercised diplomacy largely to service political goals. At the time, Beijing interpreted diplomacy as "the activity of a state for maintaining sovereignty by peaceful means, generally referring to the external activities of the heads of state and government, foreign ministers and diplomatic institutions on behalf of their respective nations".[11] *Economic* diplomacy was very much blurred with the general strategy of diplomacy.

Following the launch of the 'go global' strategy, the focus of diplomacy shifted from politics to economics, as stipulated by the new economic development objectives. The transition from a politically motivated diplomacy to an economic one reformed China's economic diplomacy as interest-oriented. This was a shift from its traditional ideology-based diplomacy (for example, China would only provide aid to countries that share common ideology with the Communist Party of China (CPC)). As the government's core interest evolved to focus on economic development, diplomacy guided by ideology was considered as unsustainable and ineffective going forward. Beijing sees it as necessary to exercise a diplomatic strategy where inter-governmental ideological differences do not affect its bilateral and multilateral economic and trade cooperation with other countries. For this reason, what is identified as the practice of *economic diplomacy* was born in China, conceived by economic development incentives, and appreciated by Beijing for its flexible nature compared to traditional diplomacy.

Initially, economic diplomacy was used by an underdeveloped Chinese economy to achieve wider access to aid, trade, foreign direct investment, and technologies. Such strategy resonates with the likes of India, which has an economic diplomacy strategy primarily focused on trade and aid (Bose, 2013). Similarly, Brazil has made a concerted effort to engage in economic diplomacy for development purposes (Juma, 2013). With the strengthening of China's economy, the country faced bottlenecks of resources and energy. Soon, China's economic diplomacy was designed to support the interests of domestic firms and investors for global expansion, including farming long-term access to offshore resources, labour, and markets.

As China's economic rise continued, it began to use economic diplomacy – primarily through foreign trade – as a means to accumulate soft power. This was a part of a broader strategy enunciated by the government in the late 1990s, entitled the *new security concept*. The concept, in essence, posits that in the post-Cold War period, nations are able to increase their security through diplomatic and economic interaction, and that the Cold War mentality of competing and antagonistic blocs is outdated. The concept influenced a number of China's foreign policies of the 1990s and early twenty-first century, including better relations with ASEAN (the Association of Southeast Asian Nations), the formation of the Shanghai Cooperation Organisation, the Treaty of Good-Neighbourliness and Friendly Cooperation Between the People's Republic of China and the Russian Federation, and the joint efforts with the US to control nuclear proliferation in North Korea.

In 2002–2003, under the leadership of Hu Jintao (Zhu, 2007, pp. 228–230), the concept was merged with the foreign policy doctrine known as *China's peaceful rise*. The policy was implemented to rebut the 'China threat theory', and to assure other countries that its political and economic rise would not threaten international peace and security. Through this policy, China sought to characterise itself as a responsible world leader that emphasises soft power and commits to resolving domestic affairs before interfering with international issues. However, as the country's global economic integration deepened, China became more aware of the intricate political implications entangled with economic transactions, such as the political risks involved in cross-border financial instruments. This awareness prompted Beijing to recognise the pertinent powers of economic diplomacy as an instrument for protecting China's international interests.[12]

Following a decade of foreign policy based on economic 'carrots', China began to use economic diplomacy for political means. Following the Norwegian Nobel Committee's decision to award the 2010 Nobel Peace Prize to Chinese dissident, Liu Xiaobo, China froze its free trade agreement negotiations with Norway and imposed new veterinary inspections on imports of Norwegian salmon. This caused the volume of salmon imports from Norway to shrink by 60 per cent in 2011 (Glaser, 2012). Likewise, on 10 September, China blocked shipments of rare earth minerals to Japan during the Senkaku Islands dispute. And during a standoff between China and the Philippines over the Scarborough Shoal (a disputed territory claimed by the PRC, the Republic of China (Taiwan) and the Philippines), Chinese Navy vessels were sent in to block Philippine ships from entering Chinese ports. In addition to blocking Philippine bananas from entering Chinese ports, the inspections of Philippine papayas, mangoes, coconuts, and pineapples were slowed down. Yet, China's economic diplomacy practices are not unique. Former Secretary of State, Hillary Clinton, for instance, has stated that economic statecraft sits at the heart of America's foreign policy agenda, and that economic development and reform is inextricably linked with democratic development (Economic Club of New York, 2011).

Consequently, as in Brazil, India, and the US, economic diplomacy is at the heart of China's foreign policy. But perhaps more profoundly than other countries, China's conception of economic diplomacy is rather deeply engrained within the broader framework of foreign policy, which is influenced by, and reflective of, China's politics, history, and values. That is, China's diplomacy is characterised by the 'three-line' approach: political, economic, and cultural.[13] The respective importance attached to each of the three dimensions varies based on the policy issue, country concerned, and time in question. For this reason, China's interpretation of diplomacy is a dynamic and evolving one, illustrated by the following formula:

Chinese diplomacy$=x$(political diplomacy)$+y$(economic diplomacy)$+(1-x-y)$ (cultural diplomacy)

Coefficient $x$ represents the political and military variables, and $y$ is the effectiveness and feasibility of economic means. For example, post-WWII Japan lacked military and political capacity, and therefore China perceived its diplomacy as characterised by a weak $x$ but stronger $y$.

Accordingly, China's interpretation of economic diplomacy is depicted in the following formula:

Economic diplomacy$=x$(diplomacy servicing economics)$+(1-x)$(economics servicing diplomacy)

Coefficient $x$ represents the economic objectives of diplomacy. When the diplomatic engagement exercises economic diplomacy primarily focused on politics and ideology, that is, when $1-x$ is greater, China's economic diplomacy will focus on direct foreign assistance or expanding diplomatic influence through investment. However, when economic diplomacy is mainly aimed at securing economic interests, that is, when $x$ is greater, the main instruments include corporate foreign investment, foreign trade, and transnational cooperation and exchange between economic and financial organisations.

Importantly, this formulaic definition of economic diplomacy is dynamic in that it evolves through time and in accordance with changing international economic and political structures. The end of the Cold War brought in an era of relatively peaceful international politics, and economic competition became the primary feature of international competition. In response, China exercised diplomacy characterised by significant economic interests – namely to secure aid and attract investment – while expanding its international presence and influence. This sort of incentive was not unique to China. With rapid economic globalisation and growing interdependence between nations, bilateral and multilateral economic cooperation emerged as common priorities worldwide.

Today, the majority of China's international activities are heavily focused on the economy, and economic diplomacy is much more than just an instrument for achieving economic development.[14] With the decline of the revolutionary legitimacy of the CPC, Beijing is ever more dependent on a stellar performance legitimacy hinging on its ability to deliver sustained economic growth (Zhao and Yang, 2013; Zhu, 2011). Economic diplomacy is Beijing's rational response to both its domestic priorities and the international environment. As the world's manufacturing hub, China's growth is highly reliant on the global economy for both inputs and market access. This makes maintaining friendly relations with China's major trading partners key to the survival of the CPC. Economic diplomacy therefore services China's need to maintain good foreign relations for the purpose of sustaining domestic growth, enables China to avoid political differences in favour of mutual economic gains, and does not present overt challenges to the existing international order.

On the flipside, Beijing believes economic diplomacy helps enhance China's global influence. That is, coefficient $y$ – the effectiveness and feasibility of economic means in diplomacy – has featured prominently in modern Chinese diplomacy. The growth of China's economic power has seen an unprecedented importance attached to economic diplomacy. China's political system has often put it at odds with some of the world's most powerful nations. Discourses about democratisation and human rights will not get China's diplomats far. But a focus on concrete economic gains has enabled China to brush aside those differences in the process of fostering global economic ties, and strengthen its own international economic status.

Labelled as the world's second-largest economy with record high economic capacity, China's rapid growth has enabled the likes of the 'China threat' and 'China collapse' theories to gain currency worldwide. In response, China's diplomatic strategy seeks to reassure the world's major powers into viewing China as a partner (Goldstein, 2001). Economic diplomacy is, in this way, useful for painting an image of China as conducive to generating joint gains for both

China and partner countries without signalling overt challenges to the status quo. Put differently, China uses economic diplomacy to exert international influence, counter speculative theories, and enhance its international reputation.

In East Asia, countries such as Japan, Vietnam, and the Philippines, with territorial claims against China, have felt the need to balance their provocations of China with an attitude of prudence due to their interwoven and interdependent economic relationships. European countries mired in the Eurozone crises have, similarly, altered from a vigilant attitude towards China to one of vigilance with reliance, as a result of tightened economic engagements. South of Europe, the China–Africa Cooperation Forum is another case in point. Since its first meeting in October 2000, the forum has become a platform for bilateral dialogue and pragmatic cooperation between China and the associated African nations. Plurilateral and bilateral cooperation between China and Africa have, since then, further strengthened, and cooperation among the Parties has expanded, broadened, and risen to a higher level. Through the application of economic diplomacy, China was better able to invest in African countries, and boost its influence in the region.

In addition to serving domestic and international interests, Chinese leaders believe economic diplomacy provides countries the capacity to cooperate economically despite political differences, which is critical to ensuring the sustainability of China's economic development. Due to their interactivity, reciprocity, and the multiplicity of participants, economic activities often have a longer-term influence than traditional diplomacy with respect to deepening friendships, defusing conflicts, and turning enemies into friends – all of which contribute to ensuring a stable global environment. In this context, Beijing takes economic diplomacy as fundamental to the facilitation of inter-governmental relationship-building, and the transcendence of ideology. The China–US relationship is an obvious example. Even though the US confronts China on sensitive issues such as human rights, democracy and trade disputes, their tightened economic relationship has also reduced the space given to those contentions in order to provide the countries space to identify economic opportunities beyond political differences. In effect, Beijing considers economic diplomacy as an aid to its global economic integration by offsetting its adverse impacts on China and enhancing the nation's friendly relations with other countries.

Finally, by seizing opportunities, China believes economic diplomacy is conducive to extending strategic opportunities. Since 2008, the global financial crisis and the subsequent European and US sovereign debt crises have inspired the virulent idea of a changing global order where the West is on the decline and the East in its ascendancy, with China as the shining star that came to the rescue. Beijing took the crisis as a strategic opportunity to accelerate its economic power and exert global influence. In this way, China uses economic diplomacy for laying the strategic foundations of future engagements with the international community.

In sum, Beijing considers economic diplomacy to be crucial for national development and international endeavours. A *Chinese economic diplomacy* is therefore *the promotion of cross-border economic interests and relations in support of its national objectives.*

## Chinese economic diplomacy ... in the multilateral sense...

In the study of international relations, a distinction is usually made between international and domestic levels. In policymaking, a distinction is typically made between actors according to the hierarchy – government and non-government, national and sub-national. In economic diplomacy, there is comparable distinction between the bilateral, plurilateral, and multilateral levels of engagement.

Multilateral economic negotiations have enjoyed a prominent position on China's economic diplomacy agenda since the country decided to go global. Beijing views multilateral economic negotiations as a way of consolidating the right political climate, and grants the appropriate international political economic environment to facilitate and institute these objectives (Van Bergeij, 2009). Multilateral economic negotiations typically involve all countries that are incorporated as Member-States of an international regime institutionalised and facilitated by a specialist agency, such as the Bretton Woods institutions, the WTO, and the UN agencies.[15] Stephen Krasner (1983, p. 2) famously defines "international regimes" as having "implicit or explicit principles, norms, rules, and decision-making procedures around which actors' expectations converge in a given area of international relations". Oran Young (1989, p. 13) likewise characterises this process as involving "international regimes" with "specialised arrangements that pertain to well-defined activities, resources, or geographical areas and often involve only some subset of the members of international society". This study builds from these definitions, and refers to international regimes (or international agencies) as *specialised intergovernmental arrangements with particular focuses on economic issues, and characterised by multi-parties, multi-issues, multi-roles, and multi-values.*

In 1989, China joined 157 international regimes, including accords, treaties, conventions, and institutions. By 2011, this figure rose to approximately 300 (Zhang, 2011, p. 129). Beijing's congenial view of multilateral economic diplomacy arises from three convictions. Beijing believes the multilateral forums are particularly congenial to their national interests, and aid their resource deficiency problem (Bergsten *et al.*, 2008, pp. 13, 223). The establishment of stronger ties through multilateral negotiations of international frameworks sits comfortably with China's interest in preserving a stable international environment that is conducive to its domestic development objectives, and implicitly ensures the political legitimacy of the ruling CPC.[16] In relation to this, Elizabeth Economy (2001, p. 230) observed, "China has shifted from an insular, autarkic state into one that has assumed a prominent role in global affairs, seeking to participate in the full range of debates regarding relations among sovereign nations" by seeking to gain entrance to key accords and treaties that regulate state behaviour.

Second, multilateral economic diplomacy is useful for overcoming domestic resistance to economic reforms and aids Beijing's efforts to implement economic and political reforms across numerous sectors and institutions, including the state administration and bureaucracy, state-owned enterprises (SOEs) and private businesses, and the trade of goods and services. By aligning domestic governance with international rules, Beijing is able to justify domestic reforms as a necessary step for international market adaptation.

Third, international regimes provide member-states the option to suspend their obligations without the need to withdraw from the system altogether (Lanteigne, 2005, p. 148). This flexibility puts China at ease with adapting to, and managing, the multilateral system in the context of domestic circumstances. By 2007, China had achieved membership of almost all existing international regimes (Table 1.1) and had a participation rate well above the global average (Johnston, 2008, pp. 32–39).

In 2013, President Xi Jinping reinforced China's emphasis on multilateral economic diplomacy as central to the continuance of international welfare, ensuring China's access to global opportunities (*China Daily*, 2013). In light of the government's emphasis on multilateral economic diplomacy, the focus of this book will be on China's economic diplomacy through the lens of multilateral economic negotiations.

### China's approach to multilateral economic diplomacy

Orthodox literature has often described China's approach to the multilateral system as characterised by the "maxi-mini principle" (Kim, 1998, pp. 60–71). The principle implies the maximisation of rights and the minimisation of responsibilities. In other words, China's approach is directed at state-enhancing, not state-diminishing functionalism. Economy (2001, pp. 232–233) has argued that Beijing engages in multilateral diplomacy to enhance its economic capabilities rather than to transfer the rights of the state to an international system.

It is natural to assume that China – like any other nation – will evaluate the benefits of multilateral diplomacy before engagement. At the same time, the experience of China's accession to the WTO suggests something quite different. Beijing paid a significant admission price for membership and was

*Table 1.1* China's multilateral organisation memberships (1949–2007)

| Year | Membership |
| --- | --- |
| 1949–1970 | 7 |
| 1980 | 66 |
| 1990 | 161 |
| 2000 | 222 |
| 2007 | 298 |

Source: Ministry of Foreign Affairs of the People's Republic of China.

unable to play the game on its own terms. Even in the years following accession, China was subject to WTO surveillance. Looking further back into China's early reform years, when China had just begun to integrate with international agencies, it felt rather marginalised by major economies in many of the economic negotiation processes.[17] Chinese scholars have asked the question, 'how can China apply the maxi-mini principle if it has to compromise so much to begin with?'[18]

Some scholars (e.g. Christensen, 1996, p. 37) point to China's unresolved ambivalent approach to multilateral economic diplomacy, and the fact that Chinese leaders will continue to view international agencies with suspicion, especially those rules they did not help write. Nicholas Lardy (1999, p. 221) points out that the Chinese leaders have at times resisted reformative steps necessary for integration. But this was not done out of political spite. Rather, it was for fear of slowing economic growth and triggering inflation of the unemployment rate. This view is, unsurprisingly, shaped by their socialist principles; the Chinese leaders believe international cooperation and interdependence can, at times, be in conflict with the perceived needs of domestic stability, and with the authority of the party leaders more generally. Such is a contrast with liberal democracies, which generally view international cooperative behaviour as complementary to the domestic standards and goals.

With that said, personal observations suggest that China's participation in multilateral economic diplomacy has evolved from the reserved postures of a spectator to active participation, as reflected in its negotiation behaviours. It has frequently spoken out against trade protectionism at the WTO.[19] In 2003 alone, China submitted a total of 65 independent written submissions, and over 100 joint submissions in relation to the Doha Development Agenda (DDA) to Geneva (*Xinhua Newswire*, 2008). Although these figures are below that of the European Union (EU) and the US, they are above the global average.

At times, the Chinese delegation has demonstrated direct and blunt articulation of criticisms of other countries, such as when China highlighted the weaknesses of the economic and financial policymakers (of American origin) of the IMF (IMF, 2010). These behaviours suggest Beijing is not only motivated by a *system-maintenance* approach, but also by one of *system-reformation* as it becomes more confident and competent in dealing with international economic affairs. This is even more apparent in light of China's incentive to transform the unipolar concentration of world power towards a multi-polar system (Kent, 2002, p. 348). As a responsive strategy to the international standing of the US, multilateral economic diplomacy is therefore an important vehicle for China's international reform agenda.

With increased multilateral economic activities in the 1990s, the government elevated the use of economic diplomacy, not least for the purpose of managing the noodle pot of economic negotiations. China's economic diplomacy has since exhibited both continuities and changes in negotiation preferences and approach. While the fundamental principles of Chinese economic diplomacy have largely remained constant, more substantive policy preferences have evolved from a posture of resistance to inclinations for flexibility, pragmatism, and, in some cases, agreement. Cases in point include China's attitudes in the DDA trade negotiations, and the Conference of Parties (COP) climate change negotiations under the United Nations Framework Convention on Climate Change (UNFCCC).

Since COP (Conference of Parties) 1, China's negotiation preference on climate change issues has shown both continuity and change. The fundamental principles for negotiation have remained constant:[20] At the same time, China's preference towards the Kyoto Mechanisms (including the Joint Implementation (JI), the International Emissions Trade (IET), and the Clean Development Mechanism (CDM)) has evolved over time, from outright opposition to gradual, if muted, acceptance (Yu, 2008, p. 58). In 2000, China put forward a 'no regrets' policy and accepted the IET. Two years later, China formally accepted and ratified the CDM. Implementation followed immediately thereafter, with projects in Gansu and Shanxi provinces. Beyond the Kyoto Mechanism, China has also demonstrated growing flexibility and pragmatism towards the international binding mitigation targets. The shift in preferences was reflected in its negotiation position at the 2011 COP17 meeting in Durban.

As with climate change, China's participation in the DDA trade negotiations has entailed continuities and changes in policy preference. For the most part, China has remained consistent in its overall position as a developing nation still in the process of digesting its WTO obligations made during accession. Yet, shifts in China's policy preferences can be identified, such as in the negotiations on the trade in services. For much of the DDA negotiations, observers have criticised China for acting passively during the services negotiations and purposely marginalising itself (Sally, 2011, p. 9). The Chinese delegation arduously reasoned that it had already made comprehensive commitments during its accession and should not be subject to further obligations. China further argued that its service sectors are too underdeveloped to weather the competitive storms of foreign firms. However, in recent years, China has proactively promoted the liberalisation of trade in services and pushed for the abolishment of regulatory restrictions.

Why did China's preference in the preceding negotiations evolve over time? How did its varied negotiation preferences come about? Why do some talks yield agreements but others end in *impasse*? What characterises China's economic diplomacy decision-making processes? What is the role and impact of international agencies?

The status of economics in China today is as important as security (if the two are not considered as intertwined). Yet, as will be shown in the next chapter, there is no single general academic study devoted to the understanding of China's – one of the most influential players of the modern global political economy – economic diplomacy and the underpinning decision-making processes in multilateral economic negotiations. As China's power matures, analysts continue to engage in heated debates as to whether its foreign policies are intent on facilitating integration with the existing international order or preparing to challenge it (Johnston, 2013; Kastner and Saunders, 2012; Ikenberry, 2008).

In every sense, this is an essential topic that deserves attention. That said, to realise an accurate and meaningful answer to the debate, knowledge about the motivators and drivers of China's economic diplomacy is essential.

### Where this book fits in...

This book is a response to the existing literature gap on Chinese economic diplomacy and the decision-making processes. It introduces a holistic understanding of Chinese economic diplomacy as a concept, an instrument, and a process critical to not only domestic China, but also the welfare of the global political economy. Within this purview, the book invests in five unique dimensions:

1    an in-depth introduction to the concept behind, and policy instrument of, China's contemporary economic diplomacy;
2    an examination of China's recent participation in multilateral economic negotiations to understand how its negotiation preferences are formulated;
3    an analysis of international agencies, negotiation practices, and processes, to identify their role and impact on the formulation processes of China's negotiation approach;
4    the identification of the contingencies and instigators which have propelling or undermining effects on China decision-making process; and
5    a framework of China's overall decision-making structure and system.

This book is concerned with both China's economic diplomacy – especially with the policy and diplomatic actors, and formal and informal negotiation structures – and the broader economic diplomacy agenda as they emerge from processes of global market integration (i.e. through trade and climate change cooperation).

This book informs our understanding of the significant role policymakers, government negotiators, and international agents play in the dense, yet largely unexplored networks of actors in our global (and Chinese) political economy. Without doubt, the current economic diplomacy, involving the promotion of inward and outward investment and exports, requires the search for competitive advantage in the global economy via a plethora of domestic and international policy networks. A perspective which includes analysis of China's current economic diplomacy practices with an emphasis on agency will better expose the connection between human agency and systemic transformation (and stability) in China – and thus contribute to debates about the relationship between agency and structure in IPE. This is a much needed insight since IPE is predominately concerned with the relationship between the state and the market, and in the process, it tends to place emphasis on the structures and processes of this relationship rather than the agency *per se*. By focusing on policymakers and government negotiators as agents, the book provides insights into the political processes involved in the creation and development of not only China's preferences and approaches to economic diplomacy and economic negotiations, but also to the global political economy.

On a China-centric level, a greater understanding of China's economic diplomacy is important for three reasons. First, economic diplomacy is an extension of domestic politics, and therefore plays an important role in the domestic economic constructions that shape the nature of the Chinese approach to the global economy. In this context, a greater understanding of this phenomenon strengthens our knowledge about China's current political infrastructure and its likely future directions of development.

Second, economic diplomacy is an instrument of economic development. As the country struggle for resources, labour, and international markets, a study of China's multilateral economic diplomacy contributes to the knowledge-creation on the national interest of China, and its approach to international objectives. Last, and most importantly, as the global economy integrates at unprecedented speed, and as China's economic capacity attains a record high, a deeper understanding of Chinese economic diplomacy is, in itself, a meaningful objective, and no doubt critical to future multilateral efforts.

Looking into the future, two facts can be predicted. First, the global economy's reliance on China to play a cooperative role in the future, both at the negotiation table, and elsewhere, will not decline. Second, China's integration with world markets has, and will continue to, expose them to new forms of friction. Considering the depth and speed at which China's economic policies penetrate societies across the continents, China's approach to economic diplomacy will have a much greater impact on aspects of our world today and in the future than at any previous time. With China's liberalising economic policy trend, Beijing has constrained its abilities to decree economic and political outcomes and empowered other actors, including those who govern international agencies. These actors seem destined to be thrown together in multiple, overlapping processes of economic bargaining with their Chinese counterparts. Regardless of which structure and institution will prevail in future world affairs, economic diplomacy will illuminate how China views and utilises international structures and institutions in its foreign (economic) policy and international engagements. By the same token, we cannot understand international economic cooperation and frictions without a better grasp of the process of economic negotiation by China.

This book's primary audience include scholars with an interest in learning in depth about the motivations, drivers, and processes behind the decision-making of China's political economy, multilateral economic negotiations, and improving the analytical tools used to study them. At the same time, the book reflects dissatisfaction with the gap between academic theory and real-world policy-making. It aspires to contribute to knowledge that will be more relevant and useful to practitioners who engage with China. Thus the book hopes to also interest readers outside the academy – readers from any country who wish to understand the Chinese political economy through the lens of economic diplomacy.

The journey to realising the objective is not without its challenges. Like the rest of the social sciences, this book grapples with an enduring intellectual challenge common in the study of Chinese political and economic decision-making:

how to develop China-relevant analytical tools that are valid and empirically useful. This ultimate purpose – to develop an analytical tool that is empirically valid – gets short shrift in too much theoretical writing about IR and IPE. The practice of policymaking and negotiations typically poses obvious barriers to the outside observer; namely, what empirical research methods are capable of uncovering relevant facts about real processes of decision-making and negotiations while simultaneously strengthening generalisations and inferences across cases? This book engages with this challenge in Chapter 2 by proposing explicit claims and supporting them with focused contrasts between two sets of case-pairs selected to provide variation on the causal variable, and matched with respect to other possible causes.

The resulting book is the first general analysis, to my knowledge, of China's economic diplomacy decision-making. It reports on the internal process, including the back-and-forth among policymakers, government negotiators, diplomats, and agents of international agencies. The analysis drawn is not limited to China's behaviour. Chapter 8 offers a resource for readers with an interest in why other countries, especially the emerging market economies, behave in economic diplomacy the way that they do, and how diplomatic negotiations come about. In addition, it shows how the analytical framework might help integrate a wider range of empirical studies over the long term.

## Notes

1 The Premier of the People's Republic of China (PRC) is the leader of the State Council of China. The Premier is the highest administrative position in the Government of the PRC, and is responsible for organising and administering the Chinese civil bureaucracy, including the planning and implementation of national economic and social development and the state budget.
2 The President of the PRC is the head of state. The President's office is classified in the Constitution as an institution of the state rather than an administrative post. It is thus equivalent to organs such as the State Council rather than to offices such as that of the Premier. The President is simultaneously the General Secretary of the Communist Party of China and Chairman of the Central Military Commission.
3 Marshall (1997, pp. 7–8) distinguishes six different meanings of diplomacy; Berridge and James (2003) offer two definitions of 'economic diplomacy'.
4 Excerpt from the speech by Christopher Meyer, British Ambassador to the United States, on 24 March, 1998. The excerpt is available from the Foreign and Commonwealth Office, 'The Future of Diplomacy', available at http://britain-info.org/bistext/embassy/24mar98.stm. (accessed May 2000).
5 For more details, see the Ministry of Foreign Affairs of the Kingdom of Thailand at www.mfa.go.th.
6 See Hocking and McGuire (2002) for a detailed case study of such linkages.
7 Notable works include S. Yamamoto (1961) and M. Yamamoto (1973).
8 See also Bayne and Woolcock (2007) and Brinkman (2005).
9 See Pigman (2005) for a detailed discussion of some of the new non-state actors in economic diplomacy.
10 The *outcome* refers to the term of a government agreement or implicit settlement (or an *impasse*), and not to the effects official settlements may have later in markets or politics.

11 For more information, see *Chinese Encyclopaedia: Volume of Politics* (1992, p. 366).
12 Interview with an expert from the Chinese Academy of Social Sciences, Beijing, 8 November 2012.
13 Interview with an expert from the Chinese Academy of Social Sciences, Beijing, 8 November 2012.
14 Interview with a senior member of the Foreign Affairs Committee of the National People's Congress (NPC), People's Republic of China, Wellington, 22 September, 2015.
15 This book will interchangeably use the terms 'international regime' and 'international agency', concepts which are considered synonymous for the purpose of this book.
16 The political legitimacy of the CPC rests on nationalism, economic growth, and social development.
17 Interview with an expert from Tsinghua University, Beijing, 22 November 2012.
18 Interview with an expert from China Foreign Affairs University, Beijing, 25 October 2012; interview with an expert from Peking University, Beijing, 23 October 2012.
19 Interview with an expert from Tsinghua University, Beijing, 22 November 2012.
20 (1) the principle of "common but differentiated responsibilities"; (2) support for the UNFCCC as the only climate change regime; (3) insistence on the "no regret" principle. The "common but differentiated responsibilities" principle implies that China will share responsibilities in information communication and scientific research without incurring any economic burdens or requirements that would reduce its energy use (Yu, 2008, p. 59).

# References

Baldwin, D.A. (1985) *Economic Statecraft.* Princeton, NJ: Princeton University Press.
Barston, R.P. (2006) *Modern Diplomacy* (3rd edn). London: Pearson Longman.
Barston, R.P. (1997) *Modern Diplomacy* (2nd edn). London: Longman Group.
Bayne, N. and Woolcock, S.B. (eds) (2007) *The New Economic Diplomacy: Decision-Making and Negotiation in International Economic Relations.* Aldershot: Ashgate Publishing Limited.
Bergsten, C.F., Freeman, C., Lardy, N.R., and Mitchell, D.J. (2008) *China's Rise: Challenges and Opportunities.* Washington, DC: Peterson Institute for International Economics and Center for Strategic and International Studies.
Berridge, G.R. (2002) *Diplomacy: Theory and Practice* (2nd edn). Basingstoke, UK: Palgrave Macmillan.
Berridge, G.R. and James, A. (2003) *A Dictionary of Diplomacy* (2nd edn). Basingstoke, UK: Palgrave Macmillan.
Bose, P.R. (2013) 'Economic Diplomacy, Indian Style'. *The Hindu Business Line.* [Online] 28 March. Available from: www.thehindubusinessline.com/opinion/columns/economic-diplomacy-indian-style/article4558849.ece [Accessed: 22 September 2015].
Brinkman, H. (2005) 'International Economic Diplomacy at the United Nations'. In J.P. Muldoon Jr., J.F. Aviel, R. Reitano, and E. Sullivan (eds) *Multilateral Diplomacy and the United Nations Today* (pp. 118–135). Boulder, CO: Westview Press.
Broder, J.M. (1997) 'Summit in Washington: The Overview; U.S. and China Reach Trade Pacts but Clash on Rights'. *New York Times.* [Online] 30 October. Available from: www.nytimes.com/1997/10/30/world/summit-washington-overview-us-china-reach-trade-pacts-but-clash-rights.html?pagewanted=all [Accessed: 22 September 2015].
Bull, H. (1995) *The Anarchical Society: A Study of Order in World Politics.* New York: Columbia University Press.

*China Daily* (2013) 'China to Deepen, Broaden Economic Diplomacy.' [Online] 26 December. Available from: www.chinadaily.com.cn/business/2013-12/26/content_17199106. htm [Accessed: 5 May 2014].

Christensen, T.J. (1996) 'Chinese Realpolitik: Reading Beijing's World-View'. *Foreign Affairs.* [Online] September/October Issue. Available from: www.foreign affairs.com/articles/asia/1996-09-01/chinese-realpolitik-reading-beijings-world-view [Accessed: 7 July 2013].

Daoudi, M.S. and Dajani, M.S. (1985) *Economic Diplomacy: Embargo Leverage and World Politics.* Boulder, CO: Westview Press.

Davis, P.A. (1999) *The Art of Economic Persuasion: Positive Incentives and German Economic Diplomacy.* Ann Arbor, MI: The University of Michigan Press.

Economic Club of New York (2011) *Remarks by Secretary of State Hillary Rodham Clinton.* [Online] 14 October. Available from: www.state.gov/secretary/rm/2011/10/175552.htm [Accessed: 4 October 2013].

Economy, E. (2001) 'The Impact of International Regimes on Chinese Foreign Policy-Making: Broadening Perspectives and Policies ... But Only to a Point'. In D.M. Lampton (ed.) *The Making of Chinese Foreign and Security Policy in the Era of Reform, 1979–2000* (pp. 230–256). Stanford, CA: Stanford University Press.

Encyclopaedia of China (2012) *Chinese Encyclopaedia: Volume of Politics.* Beijing: Encyclopaedia of China Publishing House.

Gardner, R.S. (1969) *Sterling–Dollar Diplomacy.* New York: McGraw-Hill.

Glaser, B. (2012) 'China's Coercive Economic Diplomacy: A New and Worrying Trend'. *Center for Strategic and International Studies.* [Online] 6 August. Available from: http://csis.org/publication/chinas-coercive-economic-diplomacy-new-and-worrying-trend [Accessed: 22 September 2015].

Goldstein, A. (2001) 'The Diplomatic Face of China's Grand Strategy: A Rising Power's Emerging Choice'. *The China Quarterly* 168 pp. 835–864.

Hocking, B. (2007) 'What is the Foreign Ministry?'. In K. Rana and J. Kurbalija (eds) *Foreign Ministries: Managing Diplomatic Networks and Optimizing Value* (pp. 3–19). Malta and Geneva: DiploFoundation.

Hocking, B. (2004) 'Changing the Terms of Trade Policy Making: From the "Club" to the "Multistakeholder" Model'. *World Trade Review* 3(1) pp. 3–26.

Hocking, B. and McGuire, S. (2002) 'Government Business Strategies in EU–US Economic Relations: The Lessons of the Foreign Sales Corporations Issue'. *Journal of Common Market Studies* 40(3) pp. 449–470.

Hogan, M. (1987) *The Marshall Plan: America, Britain and the Reconstruction of Western Europe, 1947–1952.* Cambridge: Cambridge University Press.

Ikenberry, G.J. (2008) 'The Rise of China and the Future of the West: Can the Liberal System Survive?'. *Foreign Affairs* 87(1) pp. 23–37.

IMF (2010) *Statement by the Hon. Zhou Xiaochuan at the IMF.* 8 October. Washington, DC.

Johnston, A.I. (2013) 'Is China a Status Quo Power?'. *International Security* 27(4) pp. 5–56.

Johnston, A.I. (2008) *Social States: China in International Institutions, 1980–2000.* Princeton, NJ: Princeton University Press.

Juma, C. (2013) 'Africa and Brazil at the Dawn of New Economic Diplomacy'. [Online] 26 February. Available from: http://belfercenter.ksg.harvard.edu/publication/22793/africa_and_brazil_at_the_dawn_of_new_economic_diplomacy.html [Accessed: 22 September 2015].

Kaiser, D.E. (1981) *Economic Diplomacy and the Origins of the Second World War: Germany, Britain, France, and Eastern Europe 1930–1939*. New Jersey: Princeton Legacy Library.

Kastner, S.L. and Saunders, P.C. (2012) 'Is China a Status Quo or Revisionist State? Leadership Travel as an Empirical Indicator of Foreign Policy Priorities'. *International Studies Quarterly* 56(1) pp. 163–177.

Kent, A. (2002) 'China's International Socialization: The Role of International Organizations'. *Global Governance* 8(3) pp. 343–364.

Kim, S.S. (1998) *China and the World: Chinese Foreign Policy Faces the New Millennium*. Boulder, CO: Westview Press.

Krasner, S.D. (ed.) (1983) *International Regimes*. Ithaca, NY: Cornell University Press.

Kunz, D. (1997) *Butter and Guns: America's Cold War Economic Diplomacy*. New York: Free Press.

Lanteigne, M. (2005) *China and International Institutions: Alternate Paths to Global Power*. London and New York: Routledge.

Lardy, N.R. (1999) 'China and the International Financial System'. In E. Economy and M. Oksenberg (eds) *China Joins the World: Progress and Prospects* (pp. 206–230). New York: Council on Foreign Relations.

Lee, D. and Hudson, D. (2004) 'The Old and New Significance of Political Economy in Diplomacy'. *Review of International Studies* 30(3) pp. 343–360.

Marshall, P. (1997) *Positive Diplomacy*. Basingstoke: Macmillan Press.

Meyer, C. (1998) 'The Future of Diplomacy'. [Online] 24 March. Available from: http://britain-info.org/bistext/embassy/24mar98.stm. [Accessed: 14 September 2015].

*New York Times* (1997) *The China Summit*. [Online] Available from: www.nytimes.com/library/world/asia/index-china-summit98.html. [Accessed: 14 September 2015].

Odell, J.S. (2000) *Negotiating the World Economy*. Ithaca, NY and London: Cornell University Press.

Pigman, G.A. (2005) 'Making Room at the Negotiating Table: The Growth of Diplomacy Between Governments and Non-State Economic Entities'. *Diplomacy & Statecraft* 16(2) pp. 385–401.

Rana, S.K. (2007) *Economic Diplomacy: The Experience of Developing States*. In N. Bayne and S. Woolcock (eds) *The New Economic Diplomacy*. Hampshire, England: Ashgate Publishing.

Roche, E. (2012) 'India Goes From Aid Beneficiary to Donor'. [Online] 1 July. Available from: www.mea.gov.in/articles-in-indian media.htm?dtl/19976/India+goes+from+aid+beneficiary+to+donor [Accessed: 16 September 2015].

Rosenthal, E. (1999) 'U.S. Calls China Trade Talks "Productive"'. *New York Times*. [Online] 5 March. Available from: www.nytimes.com/1999/03/05/world/us-calls-china-trade-talks-productive.html [Accessed: 14 September 2015].

Sally, R. (2011) 'Chinese Trade Policy After (Almost) Ten Years in the WTO: A Post-Crisis Stocktake'. *ECIPE Occasional Paper* (2) pp. 1–35.

Sanger, D. (1999) 'International Business: New Economic Chief Slow March to Open China Markets'. *New York Times*. [Online] 23 September. Available from: www.nytimes.com/1997/09/23/business/international-business-new-economic-chief-sees-slow-march-to-open-china-markets.html [Accessed: 15 September 2015].

Seelye, K.Q. (1999) 'A Visit From China: The White House; China Pact Near; Clinton Outline Benefits for U.S'. *New York Times*. [Online] 8 April. Available from: www.nytimes.com/1999/04/08/world/visit-china-white-house-china-pact-near-clinton-outlines-benefits-for-us.html [Accessed: 14 September 2015].

Van Bergeij, P.A.G. (2009) *Economic Diplomacy and the Geography of International Trade*. Northampton, MA: Edward Elgar Publishing.

Watson, A. (1982) *Diplomacy. The Dialogue Between States*. London: Eyre Methuen.

*Xinhua Newswire* (2008) 'Official: China Has Always Played Active Role in WTO Talks'. [Online] 25 July. Available from: http://news.xinhuanet.com/english/2008-07/25/content_8766911.htm [Accessed: 24 July 2011].

Yamamoto, M. (1973) *Japanese Economic Diplomacy: Its Historical Trends and Turning Points*. Tokyo: Nihon Keizai Shinbun-sha.

Yamamoto, S. (1961) *Tokyo–Washington: Japan's Economic Diplomacy*. Tokyo: Nihon Keizai Shinbun-sha.

Young, O. (1989) *International Cooperation: Building Regimes for Natural Resources and the Environment*. Ithaca, NY: Cornell University Press.

Yu, H. (2008) *Global Warming and China's Environmental Diplomacy*. New York: Nova Science Publishers, Inc.

Zhang, Z. (2011) *Energy and Environmental Policy in China: Towards a Low-Carbon Economy*. New Horizons in Environmental Economics Series, Cheltenham, England and Northampton, MA: Edward Elgar.

Zhao, D. and Yang, H. (2013) 'Performance Legitimacy, State Autonomy and China's Economic Miracle'. *Journal of Contemporary China* 132 (April) pp. 1–19.

Zhu, Y. (2011) '"Performance Legitimacy" and China's Political Adaptation Strategy'. *Journal of Chinese Political Science* 16(2) pp. 123–140.

Zhu, Z. (2007). Reviewed Work: 'China's "Peaceful Rise" in the 21st Century: Domestic and International Conditions'. *The China Journal*. [Online] 58 pp. 228–230. Available from: www.jstor.org/stable/20066356?seq=1#page_scan_tab_contents. [Accessed: 22 September 2015].

Zimmerman, R.F. (1993) *Dollars, Diplomacy, and Dependency: Dilemmas of US Economic Aid*. London: Lynne Rienner.

# 2    The frames of analysis

One aim of this book is to strengthen existing analytical frameworks for understanding China's economic diplomacy so as to make them better grounded empirically, and more useful than what is available at present. An analytical framework is useful when it accurately guides our understanding about the past and present, enabling us to reduce the future's uncertainties, or to choose courses of action that are not contradicted by real events.

Sceptics may doubt that an analytical framework is feasible when it comes to the study of China. However, no one can think without the guidance of an analytical framework at some level. Stanley Hoffman (1960) provides a helpful distinction between theory as a set of questions and theory as a set of answers. Theory as questions is a set of concepts telling us how to dissect reality into fragments, about which we can then gather evidence and derive conclusions. Even reflections on the observations of a single negotiation require a theory in this modest sense – every observer employs some sort of taxonomy or conceptual framework, whether they know it or not. Theory as answers is a set of general propositions that connect cause and effect, designed to help us understand why the social world behaves as it does, and how it will probably respond if we attempt to change it.

An alternative response to the sceptics is to argue that the one who must approach every new event without any causal generalisation as guidance will be intellectually impoverished. Every day, adults make personal decisions that are reflective of atavistic theoretical knowledge. For example, speeding while driving increases the risk of a road accident; obesity is considered to increase the likelihood of having heart disease; and the better qualified a professional, the more likely they are to acquire a better-paid job. In a similar way, when we consider a past or current multilateral economic negotiation, we often reach for patterns to help us classify the event. True, generalisation is never an adequate understanding of any particular event, and analytical frameworks or theories are not everything. However, they are essential, and empirical validity is just as important inside the academy as it is outside. It is in this way that this book contributes to the effort of improving existing analytical frameworks.

**What we know so far...**

As mentioned in the previous Chapter, this book is concerned with the agents and processes which shape China's economic diplomacy. As such, it concerns the decision-making process (also referred to as preference formation), which is a complex process involving how a range of relevant policy actors (as *agents*) concerned with a policy issue work with or against one another to carry out a proposed course of action. Policy initiatives are often considered simultaneously, with each involving different sets of specialised and concerned agencies.

An investigation into China's economic diplomacy decision-making process implies a concern about agents and drivers, leading to a certain outcome that reflects their negotiation preference and approach. Crucial to this process is the effect of *influence*, which enables effective agents and drivers to affect how national preferences will be shaped. This perception is based on the assumption that decision-making processes constitute distinct and self-equilibrating national policymaking systems that consist of established definitions of policy issues, legal and fiscal frameworks, government programmes, actors and institutions (Eisener, 1994; Harris and Milkis, 1989).

The conventional wisdom on China's decision-making rests primarily within the terrain of foreign policy, and suggests that policy preferences are shaped solely by the centralised political system in Beijing (Feng, 2007; Hamrin and Zhao, 1995; Lieberthal and Lampton, 1992). Hongyi Lai (2010) describes China's preference as being determined only by the paramount leader, the formal institutions, and the growing pluralistic government agencies. Similarly, Zhu Liqun (2010) places emphasis on domestic factors as playing more decisive roles in shaping Chinese preferences. Michael Hunt (1996), and Thomas Robinson (1994) point to the primacy of domestic politics, the weight of the past, ideology and personality as the primary determinants of Chinese preferences.

Without denying the influence of domestic policy actors, one ought to recognise that political steps towards economic liberalisation have prompted an outburst of international transactions, and spawned, concomitantly, a stark increase in global externalities ranging from the standardisation of product labelling to the enforcement of copyright and patent laws. The impact of these developments on China, as with most nation-states, is a reduced capacity to manage the global externalities without multilateral policy coordination. Although economic liberalisation has not deprived China of its policymaking autonomy, it has, to an extent, circumscribed its economic policy space. Since China engages in economic diplomacy, which makes it as much an international player as a domestic political entity, there is therefore no reason to expect that it will not be influenced by external factors.

When looking at the influence of agents and processes on policy outcome, it is important to look beyond the stable internal policy process to consider the external context. After all, any diplomat, government negotiator, or policymaker operates in highly complex external and domestic environments, and will find their duties a challenging one without frequent and direct communication with agents of international regimes. These contexts offer both opportunities and constraints, and the policymakers have to respond to them constantly by making choices, all the time trying to advance their nations' interests, however they define them.

(Holsti, 1995, p. 252)

Thus it can be expected that China's actions will be determined by both the domestic and the international context. However, this reality implies that new, and sometimes extraneous, elements are introduced into the system, and the decision-making process could throw the stable internal system out of equilibrium and thus trigger unpredictable policy outcomes. Based on this logic, it is assumed that China's economic diplomacy decision-making is inevitably shaped as much by the stable internal process as it is disturbed by external agents and processes. The more interesting question is *how*?

### Systemic perspectives

Scholars of international politics and economics have a long tradition of debating about the relative impact of external forces on the domestic environment. And scholars have studied the ways in which international agencies affect the domestic politics of China (Dai, 2007; Moravcsik, 1998; Milner, 1997; Pahre and Papayoanau, 1997; Keohane and Milner, 1996; Evans *et al.*, 1993; Cowhey, 1993; Snyder, 1991; Rogowski, 1989). Classic realists have long argued that the primary goal of foreign policy, broadly speaking, is the survival of nation-states in the international system. In this sense, China's economic diplomacy preferences are shaped by the interplay of international forces. As Robinson (1994, pp. 555–602) suggests, the structure of the international system, and the Chinese decision-makers' estimation of its relative power against the international power structures, determines China's preferences.

Inspired by such logic, Peter Gourevitch's (1978) *second-image reverse* (SIR) model highlights the impact of international actors on the domestic settings. Advocates of this model have since argued that international agencies impose critical constraints onto, and frame, China's available preference options, and that national preferences are largely shaped in response to the changing dynamics within these agencies (Tow, 1994; Ross, 1986). To that effect, "the external sources of Chinese policies" are viewed as "a matter of conditioning and shaping" its policy options (Cumings, 1989, p. 220); the internal elements of Chinese politics are "not the critical determinants" of economic diplomacy preference formation (Pollack, 1984).

A second stream of systemic theorising began with the works of Karl Deutsch (1957) and Ernst Haas (1958) on the impact of Parties and interest groups in the process of European regional integration. They highlight the importance of the 'spill-over' effect and the feedback process between domestic and international developments. As such, their work gave birth to the themes of *international regimes, interdependence,* and *transnationalism.* The intellectual heirs of this tradition, namely Robert Keohane and Joseph Nye (1977), eventually reformed the school of thought into the *interdependency theory.* The theory has three primary characteristics, including the use of multiple channels and actors in the interaction between states, and between states and international regimes; the role of economic variables in changing agendas and linkages between prioritised issues; and bringing about non-military instruments of statecraft (Keohane and Nye, 1989). By focusing on international regimes, the theory promotes the greater use of soft power, diplomacy, and cooperation through the forms and procedures of international law. In this respect, agents of international regimes impact Chinese preferences through the general interactions of diplomacy, and institutional rules, norms and principles (Ruggie, 1992, pp. 561–598; Keohane and Nye, 1989, pp. 34–35).[1] Such is the assumption of Thomas Moore and Dixia Yang (2001, p. 194), whereby the international system conditions Chinese preferences by conforming them to transnational rules, structures and norms over time.

However, the systemic and liberal traditions provide few prescriptions for the way(s) agents actualise influence. Although the interdependency theory does comparatively better in this regard by paying some attention to the conduits of influence and the way in which it shapes perceptions of national interests and policy preferences, it nonetheless dismisses details of the dynamics between its proposed channels and the domestic dimensions of decision-making. What is more, both approaches can at times lack generalisability across time, settings, and policy sectors.

### *International–domestic linkages*

In an effort to understand the interaction of different levels of policy processes, Robert Putnam's (1988) 'two-level' metaphor posits that the interaction between the international and domestic levels shape national preferences. Putnam's argument crucially takes into consideration the dynamic interaction between the domestic and international levels in economic negotiations. However, his approach also suffers from a risky assumption that preferences are shaped only by the two levels and disregards the interactions between the international, domestic, and individuals who make policy decisions. Given that decisions are the generated outcome of individuals, they matter in the grand scheme of the process.

Jeffrey Alexander and Bernhard Giesen (1987) examine such relationships in the 'micro–macro linkage' approach. The approach examines the three levels of activities and the fluidity of movement between the international, domestic, and individual agencies. Because neither the macrostructure nor the decision-makers at the micro level have absolute control over the national policy, the three levels mutually influence each other in preference formation. The advantage of this approach is its encapsulation of the three dimensions of the policy macrostructure, taking into account elements of the *levels* (in a vertical way) and the *structures* (in a horizontal way). Yet, this approach also leaves questions unaccounted for. For instance, how do domestic agents' and agencies' decisions and behaviours influence, and therefore alter, the preferences of the national macrostructure? In what way(s) or through which functions do aspects of the multilevel relationship affect each other?

Building from previous studies on the reciprocal nature of the domestic–international linkage (Almond, 1989; Gourevitch, 1978; Hintze, 1975), some researchers have investigated the ways in which national policymakers are connected with the multilateral system (Coleman and Perl, 1999; Finnemore and Sikkink, 1998; Keck and Sikkink, 1998; Risse-Kappen, 1995). This strand of literature posits that the influence of the international system varies as it is often mediated by different kinds of national government agencies (Bernstein and Cashore, 2000; Walsh, 1994; Bennett, 1991). While they claim the multilateral system have fundamentally changed how nation-states make policy, they do not specify how the changes are actualised (Botcheva and Martin, 2001; Lazar, 2001). Scholars of public policy also avoid this question. The literature (e.g. Gummett, 1996; Parry, 1993; Willett, 1988) that looks at the multilateral system and public policy tend to place more attention on international public policy (i.e. analysis of cross-border interactions for solving common public policy concerns) as opposed to how national preferences are affected by multilateral processes and actors.

### Chinese (economic) diplomacy

At present, there is little, if any, published literature on Chinese diplomacy, and even less on Chinese economic diplomacy. Existing research on diplomacy has found that factors such as distance, power, ideological affinity, trade, and investments shape China's diplomatic ties (e.g. Neumayor, 2008; Leiby and Butler, 2006; Xierali and Liu, 2006). It is unclear, however, the extent to which the findings from these mostly dyadic studies can be applied for predicting and understanding China's economic diplomacy.

Other literature which touches on Chinese economic diplomacy focuses primarily on inter-state economic relationships throughout history without much in-depth analysis of the machinery of economic diplomacy as an instrument of Chinese international affairs (e.g. Mitcham, 2005; Soeya, 1998). Thus, much of the current literature on China stems out of a foreign policy paradigm based on historical narratives, and deductive reasoning, with a lack of systematic empirical evidence to arbitrate current debates.

In the broader literature, numerous studies have considered China's relationship with international organisations. For example, Elizabeth Economy (2001, p. 231) argues that the process of establishing international organisations may influence the manner in which China makes policies through the establishment of new institutions, the emergence of new policy actors (or the enhancement of others), and the development of new ideas, values, or orientations among Chinese decision-makers. Margaret Pearson (2001, p. 338) adds that international organisations affect preference formation through an international imposition of market norms in the domestic economy. Samuel Kim (1998) looks at the decision-makers' perceptions of international organisations as key to shaping preferences. Based on the theoretical assumption that a state's preferences are shaped by its national identity, Qin Yaqing (2010, pp. 47–50) demonstrates that the deeper China integrates with the multilateral system, the more its identity changes, and this gives international organisations a stronger and more positive effect on China's preference formation.

With this said, the literature commonly dismisses details about how international organisations' influences are actualised and channelled through to the national negotiation preference formation processes. In addition, there are seldom discussions about the agencies involved, and the literature does not explain the actual role of the agents of international organisations in shaping Chinese preferences, how and why their influences are either positive or negative, and the effects which arise from China's multilateral economic diplomacy.

Second, these studies take *China* for granted, viewing it as a unitary actor, while disregarding the reality that it is the umbrella for a complex and multi-leveled system with an array of political agencies and actors. Such disregard is problematic as it dismisses the fact that different agencies have different relationships with various actors within the multilateral system, therefore giving rise to different kinds of policy effects and/or acceptance of external influences. Finally, these studies do not treat their claims with sufficient empirical backing. This is perhaps due to methodological constraint (e.g. a lack of access to the relevant Chinese policy actors). As a result, their findings only establish causal inferences and certain basic rules about Chinese preference formation based on patterns of manifest actions.

## A useful framework

At present, we have some quality knowledge, but we do not have an effective analytical framework with the power to explain China's economic diplomacy. This book addresses the gap within the existing analysis and reflects the premises on which policy choices are made. It contributes a middle range analytical framework that is eclectic and built from the assumption of bounded rationality.

Robert Merton (1968, p. 39) defines middle range theories as those which "lie between the minor but necessary working hypotheses that evolve in abundance during day-to-day research and the all-inclusive systematic efforts to develop a unified theory that will explain all the observed uniformities of social behaviour, social organisation, and social change".[2] In other words, this is not a polemic *for* or *against* any of the grand 'isms' of IR or IPE. Decades of empirical research have shown conclusively that none of these grand approaches is adequate by itself. The most lasting advances come from research which concentrates on an important and relevant empirical phenomenon, shifts attention towards formulating clear causal hypotheses that are inspired by true evidence.[3]

The aim here is not to develop the simplest or most tightly integrated analytical framework. Rather, this work aims for one that is better grounded and more useful. Naturally, any analytical framework is, to some degree, a simplified version of a more complicated beast. This book is no exception; it is organised around the central dependent variable – the decision-making process of China's economic diplomacy – and limits the focus to a few feasible factors of influence over this variable, deliberately omitting many other possible factors. With that said, this book is not suggestive of an extremely simple framework – the loss from extreme simplification can be severe. Simplification is not an end in itself, and in the long run, it is not more important than empirical validity. This book does not restrict its ideas to the deduction of a single set of axioms. Instead, its propositions benefit heavily from inductive and deductive reasoning – which are loosely linked together.

### A framework for preference formation

To investigate China's economic diplomacy decision-making process, we need to understand the country's *symbolic macrostructure*. The symbolic macrostructure refers to the political motivations, incentives, and ideological beliefs that are part of the interpretive lens through which Chinese decision-makers' perceptions are formed. The symbolic macrostructure therefore drives the formation of Chinese preferences. An understanding of China's symbolic macrostructure requires an understanding of how the decisions of Chinese policymakers and government negotiators come about.

At its most basic level, the analytical framework assumes that rationality influences the macrostructure. Policymakers and government negotiators will make decisions using bounded rationality. This premise stands between two better known positions – unbounded utility maximisation and anti-rationality. The mainstream variant of rational choice – unbounded utility maximisation – assumes the actor has coherent and stable preferences; that he or she has a fixed set of alternative options; that he or she knows the probability distribution of outcomes for each alternative; and that he or she chooses the one they expect to maximise their utility subject to factorable constraints. The actor suffers from no limitation on their capacity to make complex calculations. Unbounded rational choice generates valuable contributions and Freudians were perhaps the most extreme partisans of this position.[4] However, it is difficult to believe that, in practice, Chinese decision-makers hold fixed preferences and a simple scroll down the foreign policy section of China's history of five-year-plans is suggestive of its dynamic tendencies. It is due to this sort of reality that the Freudians decamped from this thinking some time ago. More recently postmodernists and others have rejected this form of rational choice analysis.

The Siamese twin of unbounded rationality is *bounded rationality*. In Herbert Simon's (1997, p. 291) words, it means "rational choice that takes into account the cognitive limitations of the decision-maker – limitations of both knowledge and computational capacity". The actor "wishes to attain goals and uses his or her mind as well as possible to that end" (Simon, 1997, p. 293)[5] but the postulation of rational choice is modified to fit voluminous empirical findings about these systematic limits of the human mind.[6] In essence, bounded rationality is characterised by the view that preferences are not necessarily fixed, and can be influenced by the way issues are framed: for instance, those which are malleable to the negotiation process. Rather than a cost-and-benefit analysis for all conceivable alternative options, the actor conducts analyses for a few options. He or she chooses "an alternative that meets or exceeds specified criteria, but that is not guaranteed to be either unique or in any sense the best" (Simon, 1997, p. 295).

This conception of bounded rationality entails the premise that the policy-maker or government negotiator lacks complete information about situation $x$, such as how markets will trend in the future, or the negotiating counterpart's true reservation value, or how moves will affect markets and domestic politics at home and abroad. Imagine, for instance, China's Minister of Commerce deciding whether to negotiate trade bilaterally or multilaterally. Their Politburo expects them to aim at goals such as improving China's living standards while protecting political relationships with other governments and the CPC's hold on power. Science is simply inadequate to forecast with precision and confidence how a given strategy or proposal will affect the many complex variables, no matter how powerful the computer. Thus the commerce minister substitutes simplified rules of thumb for estimating consequences and puts rough values on alternative options. These subjective heuristics can, in principle, be studied, and some may prove to be widespread and predictable rather than idiosyncratic.

If the commerce minister relies on beliefs about these causal chains, one way to improve our knowledge of the dependent variable is to study their beliefs: to conjecture which types will make the most difference, gather evidence about them, and generalise about their cause and effect. Surprisingly, a number of political economists bend over backward to avoid conceding that what people think makes any independent difference. The truth of the matter is that one of the things policy-makers or government negotiators do is to change the beliefs of others – about how they will benefit from a proposal, what will happen to them if they refuse, or whether they can be trusted – when trying for an objective. A much better approach, in my view, is to replace interests with a combination of concepts, and to collect information about each.[7] This book therefore embraces both objective and subjective causes in China's economic diplomacy decision-making process.

Rationality need not entail other assumptions that often come packaged with it. Rational policymakers, government negotiators, and diplomats care about political as well as economic values, and about the short and long terms. This book does emphasise economic objectives, but does not isolate goals concerning political relationship as likely influences on its approach to economic bargaining. In addition, rational decision-making also need not mean China is unitary as a state. On the contrary, each individual or group of policymakers and government negotiators are agents for principals in the country and divisions among the principals are common. Thus, a value proposition of this book is to illuminate how domestic (and international) actors complicate the process of economic diplomacy decision-making.

• *The calculation of costs and benefit*

Based on the assumption of bounded rationality, one could conjecture that policy-makers, government negotiators, and diplomats evaluate their options in terms of costs and benefits, and choose options which are either perceived or believed to maximise China's national gains (Underdal, 1998, p. 7).[8] This is the kind of argument rational actor theorists make. The model also assumes that policymakers have a set of specified and prioritised goals and objectives, a set of perceived options and "a single estimate of the consequences that follow from each alternative" (Allison, 1971, p. 32ff.). Hans Morgenthau suggested that a useful starting point could be to put oneself in the shoes of a statesman who is required to resolve a foreign policy issue, and under the particular circumstances,

> we ask ourselves what the rational alternatives are from which a statesman may choose who must meet this problem under this circumstance (*presuming always that he acts in a rational manner*), and which of these rational alternatives this particular statesman, acting under these circumstances, is likely to choose.
>
> (Morgenthau quoted in Allison, 1971, p. 26)

The choice of policy will be based on estimates of the consequences of each available alternative, always with the overriding goal of national utility maximisation. This requires a comprehensive calculation of costs and benefits for each possible option, given national goals and objectives.

According to this framework, foreign policy behaviour is a response to a strategic problem facing the nation. The nation will be moved to act by threats and opportunities arising from the international strategic "marketplace" (Allison, 1971, p. 33). When the rational actor model is applied to a case it is assumed that it is in fact possible to calculate the costs and benefits no matter how complex the reality is. Ideally, this requires access to all necessary information about the issue, the preferences of the other actors and possible solutions (Johansen, 2002, p. 31). In practice, decision-makers (like researchers) have to opt for a much more parsimonious approach.

As a value-maximising rational actor, China values the process of weighing the benefits against possible costs for any policy alternative. For instance, the most beneficial long-term solution for the Chinese government is one where the predicaments of climate change or trade protection are avoided. Still, rationalists argue that as a rational actor, China will weigh the benefit against possible consequences of committing to the mitigation of greenhouse gas (GHG) emission, or in reforming the national monetary system for inflation control. For instance, consider the climate change 'problem', which can lead to a range of undesirable consequences for China. The potential costs of these consequences as well as expectations and pressure from the global community make it absolutely necessary to respond to it in some way or another. Here, national interests will first be narrowly defined in economic terms, considering two different aspects of economic interests at stake in relation to global warming; vulnerability to the consequences of climate change and the costs and benefits associated with emission reduction activities. Second, policymakers will consider the international circumstances in which Chinese economic diplomacy decision-making takes place and are expected to calculate the costs and benefits related to participating in climate change cooperation, hence how external factors can provide incentives for alternative negotiation behaviour (e.g. Johnston, 1998).

So far, the example illustrates an internal stable process. This internal balance, however, could be shaken when new actors are introduced to the policy subsystems (Hoberg, 1996; Howlett and Rayner, 1995; Jacobsen, 1995; Pontusson, 1995; Baumgartner and Jones, 1991). The introduction of new actors (i.e. external agents/agencies) to the process of calculating the costs and benefits implies that new imaginations of feasible options will emerge and, in effect, fracture the otherwise predictable and consistent calculated outcomes. For instance, Chinese decision-makers involved in the climate change debate often associate China's abatement costs with the potential consequences of limiting economic development.[9] However, coordination with the Conference of Parties (COP) presidencies exposes Chinese policymakers to the counter-rationale that abatement measures do not necessarily have negative costs attached. Given that GHG mitigation improves areas such as air quality, energy efficiency and security, abatement measures actually benefit China's national development (Buen, 1998). The calculations of the COP presidencies can therefore reframe the symbolic macrostructure of the Chinese decision-makers and restructure their incentive to tackle climate change.

Although the Chinese government has yet to accept international mitigation targets, its domestic efforts to reduce GHG emissions in recent years, and increased flexibility at the multilateral negotiation table indicate it is plausible that, with other variables held constant, the calculation of costs and benefits have some degree of determinative effect on China's preference formation. As rationalists would contend, the calculation of costs and benefits essentially affects the symbolic macrostructure of China's negotiation preference. Moreover, the process is not limited to domestic actors, and principled engagements with international agencies during the costs-and-benefits exercise could alter the eventual calculations.

• *The power of information*

While the rational actor model is built mainly on the assumptions of rationality, the cognitive model brings in elements from cognitive and constructivist theories, thus providing different assumptions about the nature of the policymaking process (Underdal, 1998, p. 20). This model complements and interacts with the other models by placing the focus on the role of information, discourse, and the diffusion of ideas. Constructivism views the relation between agents/states and their structural environment as an interactive process, and it is this process which formulates preferences and spawns interests (Checkel, 1997).

It is essential to recognise that the cognitive model, as it is portrayed here, cannot be seen as a purely constructivist approach. Rather, the rationalist approach brings in constructivist elements. Within the cognitive debate, a sizeable literature (e.g. True *et al.*, 1999; Campbell, 1998; Blyth, 1997) argues in a general sense that changes in policy – be they conceptual or practical – require the penetration of new ideas into the policymaking process. The basic assumption of this model is that decision-makers enter the preference formation processes with both imperfect information and tentative preferences, but both of these can be resolved with new information (Underdal, 1998, p. 21). This is because dynamic psychological processes (i.e. perception, misperception, belief systems) often evolve when new information is presented. Joseph Nye (1987, p. 378) points out, "New information alters prior beliefs about the world … Knowledge is used to redefine the content of the national interest, and eventually goes further to take effect in the whole procedure".

In post-reform China, economic expertise ran thin across many policy areas. External information was, as a result, widely sought after. Within this context, international agencies were instrumental to China's development of issue-specific policy expertise (Economy, 2001). Harold Jacobson and Michel Oksenberg (1990, p. 151), and Margaret Pearson (2001), for instance, found strong evidence that the World Bank and the International Monetary Fund (IMF) contributed not only to the deepening of the expertise among Chinese decision-makers concerned with international trade, but also to reconfiguring the balance of power among various individuals and groups of Chinese technocrat policy-makers involved in the preference formation process. Policy choices therefore evolve through a learning process, where the decision-makers' knowledge and perception of the problem are adjusted (Underdal, 1998, p. 21). Chinese decision-makers are expected to become inculcated with international values. This form of principled engagement consequently affects China's symbolic macrostructure by enabling new information to alter how Chinese decision-makers perceive and define their interests and therefore preferences.[10]

Cognitivists further argue that the impact of information dissemination goes beyond just changing ideas. It also affects domestic policy structures. In order to manage external information (i.e. synthesise information, analyse its implications for China, monitor details and outcome assessments), new policy structures are established. For example, the intellectual property rights tribunal was created within China's judicial system in order to treat the national patent, copyright, and trademark protection affairs vis-à-vis the WTO protocol. For every environmental treaty China has signed, national expert-led Leading Small Groups (LSGs) were established to coordinate the information and preference formation (Oksenberg and Economy, 1997, pp. 12–13). The LSGs typically involve various government agencies as participating policy actors in the preference formation process, either by being tapped to provide data, participate in policy discussions, and/or engage in offshoot activities. This development thereby stems a trend of pluralisation and decentralisation in the decision-making system.

The *negotiation process* itself is another focal point in the cognitive model as it is understood as a process of learning and an arena for policy diffusion (Underdal, 1998, p. 22). The assumptions of this model imply that progress can be made within a problem area even without a formal agreement, because the negotiating process itself can contribute to changing the actors' perceptions of the problem and the way it should be handled. Policies evolve through learning, adoption of new knowledge and ideas, and the formation of beliefs (Underdal, 1998, p. 21). For instance, officials from the former State Planning Commission (SPC) who were assigned to represent China at the United Nations Framework Convention on Climate Change (UNFCCC) have, over the years, become far more sympathetic to environmentally proactive measures than their colleagues with fewer engagements of this nature. Through frequent interactions, domestic decision-makers are expected to become inculcated with the values held by the international agencies and advocate for broader preference reforms (Economy, 2001, p. 237).

The process of learning is difficult to trace empirically, and its actual impact on actor behaviour in the likes of multilateral economic negotiations may be difficult to measure. When examining the impact of information and learning on China's economic diplomacy it will be important to distinguish "learning in which beliefs and values change along with policies from simple tactical learning, in which policy changes but beliefs remain the same" (Economy, 2001, p. 240), or what Johnston (1998, p. 583ff.) terms "learning versus adaptation". *Learning*, which is the focal point of the cognitive model, refers to the process of a change in internalised values, where preferences over outcomes change, and consequently policy changes. *Adaptation* refers to changes in policy that result from exogenous constraints closing off preferred options. Exogenous constraints may be rising or declining costs of non-cooperation, such as image concerns (as will be pointed out below under the contractualist model). Learning may result from new externally generated information about climate change impacts, for instance, and its economic effects which are injected into the policymaking process. Alternatively, changes in the policy process which bring in "people and groups that have already internalised alternative, more global or biocentric values" could also contribute to learning (Johnston, 1998, p. 585).

• *The reputation factor*

Contractualists believe concern for international image provides incentives for the course of one negotiation behaviour over another (e.g. Johnston, 1998). For instance, the costs of choosing a non-commitment approach in a given negotiation can come in the form of sanctions, loss of prestige or damage to a country's international image and the possibility that other states will link failure to comply with the multilateral system to retribution on other issue-areas (Underdal, 1998). And, without doubt, uncooperative behaviour does not pass unnoticed. When the US decided to withdraw from the Kyoto process in 2001, it caused loud protests from a range of state leaders worldwide. The EU warned the US that its attitude towards climate change cooperation could harm the Euro–American relationship (Johansen, 2001, p. 51).

The example of the Montreal Protocol also points out how concerns about image influenced China's behaviour, such as displaying concern about the ozone layer and promoting China as a cooperative player in the international arena. Additionally, China was motivated by the idea of retaining a leadership voice in the developing world (Zhao and Ortolano, 2003, pp. 710–711). All these factors are related to status and international image, which can be important driving forces for behaviour at the negotiation table. Thus, interests can change dramatically even when there is no shift in the economic calculations, due to concerns regarding non-monetised commodities like leadership, image, and status (Rowlands, 1995, p. 247). The rising costs or declining benefits of non-commitment due to image concerns can lead to a tactical shift along the spectrum of commitment (Johnston, 1998, p. 584).

Concerns about image should generally be expected to lead to a more proactive position, seeing as China tends to be very sensitive to criticism. One can at least assume that China will minimise negative image costs when choosing between policy alternatives. The perceived costs to its image will vary as a function of the "size and nature of the 'audience' in which China places value" (Johnston, 1998, p. 559). As a nation that values *saving face*, reputation-dressing and reputation-maintenance prevails in China's thought process. In this context, contractualists believe it is probable that self-consciousness about image could drive China's decision-making process. In fact, some argue, even in situations where there is no change in economic calculations, China's preferences can still evolve along the spectrum of commitment because of concerns regarding non-monetised commodities like reputation (Johnston, 1998, p. 584; Rowlands, 1995, p. 247). As Robert Jervis (1970, p. 6) suggests, a desired reputation can often be "of greater use than a significant increment of military or economic power".

International agencies often assess a nation-state's reputation by setting international standards of behaviour against which national performances are measured. They also do so by linking these standards to specific issues, and by providing forums where such evaluations are made (Keohane, 1984, p. 94). Thereby reputation monitoring creates "either an enabling or a disabling environment" (Foreign Policy Centre, 2002, p. 9), and enables international agencies to raise the costs associated with non-compliance. The significance of this instrument lies in the fact that reputation in politics is an instrument of power, and affects a country's international status quo (Wang, 2006, p. 91). For China, its reputation capital affects its capacity to build international alliances vital for achieving national objectives, as well as for influencing international events. As such, when public opinion is activated, the climate of opinions can limit or broaden policy choices and actions available to China. That is why foreign perceptions and opinions of China are important to the Chinese decision-makers.

• *Are they similar, or are they different?*

The preceding discussion focussed attention on three different perspectives on the policy determinant of economic diplomacy. These three determinants were discussed because economic diplomacy decision-making typically entails a process of evaluation, the accessible resources for such an evaluation, and how a country presents itself to the world. For these reasons, the calculations of costs and benefits, information, and reputation are relevant drivers of economic diplomacy decision-making. It is important to realise whether they are competing or complementary factors in the general decision-making process.

Based on the rationalist approach, one can expect that preference formation is influenced by the expected costs relating to an economic problem, on the one hand, and the costs of taking action, on the other. This implies that Chinese decision-makers face a two-fold challenge in economic diplomacy decision-making. While the Chinese decision-makers have to evaluate the costs of commitments versus the costs of non-commitment, they also have to consider the costs and benefits of participating in a multilateral cooperation. This two-fold challenge, in turn, offers international agencies the opportunity to make a relevant contribution to China's costs and benefits assessments through intervening discussions and sharing of analyses.

By comparison, the cognitive approach highlights how national interests are tentative by nature and are variable as new information is encountered. Informal dialogues, research collaborations, and other social forums are all occasions where international agencies use information to shape the perceptions of the Chinese decision-makers regarding the optimal policy preference. Contractualists move away from the socialisation process and maintain a microeconomic and game theoretic style of analysis. Advocates of this approach believe neither information nor calculus-based factors have much impact on shaping preferences. Rather, they only alter the perceived costs and benefits of pursuing those preferences (Frank 1988, p. 143). When attempting to maximise economic gains, the effects of non-monetised values such as reputation take particular prominence in the thought process of the Chinese decision-makers.

Although the three approaches embody different assumptions; they commonly assume that the Chinese government behaves in accordance with the principle of bounded rationality as the starting point (Bang, 2004, p. 17). All three approaches expect Chinese decision-makers to act in a rational manner, and participate in multilateral economic negotiations for the advancement of their national interests. Yet, the approaches differ in their assumptions about the actualised degrees of rationality, and in how negotiation preferences are formed and influenced. Rationalists believe preferences are based on rational calculations of the costs and benefits of different policy alternatives. Cognitivists, on the other hand, have a more dynamic view of rationality and assume that preferences evolve through the exposure of new information. Still, contractualists stress the importance of non-monetised incentives such as reputation, and accordingly emphasise the concerns about reputation as a driver of Chinese preferences.

The differences between the three approaches do not stop there. They also deviate in their explanatory powers on the preference formation outcome. The rationality assumption grants it stronger explanatory powers to predict causal relationships – whether these predictions are right or wrong is a different question. Yet, the rationalist approach oversimplifies reality; it is risky to assume that China's economic diplomacy preference formation can be inferred from only the process of calculating costs and benefits. Other variables, including domestic political processes, are expected to also contribute to the formation of preferences. The rationalist approach further makes the precarious assumption that the Chinese leaders enjoy complete knowledge of all alternative solutions and have a capacity to calculate the costs and benefits of the consequences for each option. This is unwarranted in practice. In addition, rationalists presuppose a unity of views within the Chinese state. But given the multiplicity and fragmentation of Chinese political processes, such a presupposition is difficult to maintain. As Haas (1980, p. 57) points out, there is simply no "optimal" choice.

Although it is widely acknowledged that very few actual preference formation processes come close to this idea, the approach nevertheless remains widespread in the study of Chinese political economy. The main advantage of this approach lies in its ability to provide plausible hypotheses on the objectives and solutions that offer themselves to Chinese decision-makers in a situation where the nature of China's political system limits the researcher's access to the preference formation processes. It goes without saying that this approach seems particularly well adapted to approximate the decisions of a political system with a comparatively higher degree of autonomy from social pressures and in which the political leaders enjoy considerable power over their subordinates.

The strengths of rationalism are areas in which the cognitive theory lacks. Whilst the cognitive theory gives valuable attention to social psychological effects and touches on socialisation variables, it offers comparatively vague assumptions, and yield hypotheses that are methodologically difficult to confirm. For instance, it is hard to empirically trace the process of internalising ideas and beliefs, and the actual influence of norms on actor behaviour is also challenging to measure. In particular, it is hard to determine if norms are used for mere public diplomacy rhetoric or if they actually constitutes a value of the national economic policy. As rationalists argue, engagement with discourse, unlike choice, is indeterminate of policy outcomes (Underdal, 1998, p. 23). As a result, it is difficult to determine whether a preference shift was the outcome of exposure to new information, or due to other exogenous constraints that arise from non-cooperation, or the result of other monetised or non-monetised incentives.

Moreover, cognitive assumptions find it difficult to explain why (or when) certain discourses are successfully transplanted in Beijing while others result in failure. For example, why has the concept of low-carbon development spread but the prohibition of GHGs has not? This goes to show that cognitivism does not give sufficient attention to agency. This is in part because the cognitivists rely more upon structural forces than agency to explain preferences, even though – ironically – an obvious central tenet of this approach is the mutual interaction of structures and agents (Checkel, 1997; Wendt, 1987). Meanwhile, the causal mechanism for the spread of discourse arguably suffers from passivity. Martha Finnemore (1996), for example, assumes that domestic institutions mimic accepted global practices without understanding the logic of those practices. At the end of the day, rationalists argue, in a strategic problem context, decision-makers are more likely to be moved by perceived threats and/or opportunities arising from the environment and other consequential incentives than by cognitive factors (Allison, 1971, p. 33).

Critiques of this nature reflects the rationalists' tendency to take for granted the fact that negotiation preferences are nothing more than mirrors of the actors' interests (Halpern, 1989). As recent studies (e.g. Béland, 2005; Lieberman, 2002) that attribute greater roles to cognitive variables have shown, by manipulating strategic representations, political actors create conditions propitious to the formation of coalitions that transcend differences due to conflicting material interests. It is through this process of strategic representation that actors come to shape their perceived interests with regard to a given issue. The social construction of problems and of the available solutions provide the raw materials that enable the concrete expression of political interests – what is desired, or can be desired. In turn, an analysis that places emphasis on the international discourse reduces the researcher's 'disposition effect' by refocusing the analysis on the actor-level intentions and preferences (Constantin, 2007). This is why the cognitive approach is a worthwhile one to test.

Finally, the functional nature of the contractualist assumptions runs the risk of all *post hoc* arguments, where institutions may be interpreted as having arisen because of the functions they must serve, when in fact, they appeared for adventitious reasons (Keohane, 1984, p. 81). In addition, the reputation instrument suffers from a similar methodological challenge to the cognitive approach. Being able to observe reputation-building behaviour means that such behaviour is probably undertaken with the likelihood that it will be observed. Certainly, there is no point engaging in it for reputational purposes unless it is observable to others. But if behaviour is designed to be observed, and both the observer and actor know this, then the observer should have doubts that it is indeed high-cost behaviour, or that concerns about reputation actually have an effect on those behaviours. This is even more so given the expectation that Beijing's reputation costs will vary across the "size and nature of the audience in which it places value" (Johnston, 1998, p. 559). What this implies is that concerns about reputation may only be effective if China perceives the costs of the alternative options to its reputation to be high. With this said, the approach has an advantage in its generalisability capacity and applicability to the China context. Given the high value the government places upon reputation in its decision-making, it is a worthwhile testing area for the purposes of this book.

The three factors sourced from three theoretical approaches make a fitting and complementary ensemble to inform the framework for preference formation. All three factors were supplemented with theoretical assumptions and introduced policy instruments with probable impact on China's *symbolic macrostructure*. And each helps inform and refine the *a priori* assumptions about the variables of influence.

• *The situational factors: the policy propellers and underminers*

It is important to recognise that within the decision-making process, there are inevitable constraints instigated by the *institutional macrostructure* of the central government. The institutional macrostructure is the established system through which policymakers must operate, and include factors such as the rules, norms, and protocols of political action, the policy instruments relevant to preference formation, and the scope and degree of participation by the relevant policy actors (including the power factor). This assumption is generated from the *structure–agency theory*. According to the theory, in the broadest terms, *agency* is the capacity of individuals to act independently and to make their own free choices, while *structure* is the recurrent pattern of arrangements which influence or limit the choices and opportunities available (Barker, 2005, pp. 448, 664). Structures (i.e. the Chinese decision-making system) and agents (i.e. Chinese decision-makers) possess different qualities. One characteristic of the structure is anteriority (i.e. the pre-existing features of China's decision-making system). Second, the structure has endurance; and third, the structure has the capacity to both propel and undermine (i.e. the existing allocation of decision-making powers that enable some policy actors and constrain others). Among the qualities of agency are self-consciousness, reflexivity and cognition (Joseph, 2008, p. 117). The features of structure and agency make them mutually complementary, and the relationship is one of "pre-existent structures, possessing causal powers and properties … result[ing] in contingent yet explicable outcomes" (Carter and New, 2004, pp. 5–6).

It is important to know at least three things when analysing decision-making processes. First, what are the characteristics of the political and social structures within which the Chinese agents and agencies work at time $t$? What are the pre-defined norms and the associated policy preferences of the Chinese decision-makers at the time of engagement with the multilateral negotiations? Second, what are some of the characteristics of the Chinese decision-makers and government negotiators at time $t$? How do these characteristics limit or enhance the influence of the aforementioned factors? Third, what is the context in which Chinese decision-makers interact with the international agencies at time $t+1$? The net effect of external factors (i.e. international agencies) is therefore a function of the characteristics of the context in which they interact with Chinese policy actors in an on-going and deeply integrated feedback relationship, mediated by the multilateral systemic process.

From these three areas, coupled with considerations for the institutional macrostructure, stem four *situational factors*: the policy *settings*, the policy *instruments*, the policy *goals*, and *national objectives* which specify the course of action intended to operationalise an abstract goal. To illustrate, the policy goal of an industrial trade programme might be to enhance the diversification of industrial trade exports. The appropriate policy instrument for this purpose may include a subsidy set at a specific rate. The policy instrument selected would be determined by the political context at the time. Finally, the national objective consists of the specific programmatic principles deployed to inject substance into the abstract policy goals. In the present context, this might be a plan to enhance national technological capacity from outsourcing by a certain percentage over a fixed period of time.

It is easy to imagine the relevance of the four situational factors. For instance, the systemic political context and bureaucratic interest pre-establish the setting in which the influence of externally disseminated information will be either enhanced or inhibited. Factors could include Beijing's policy frameworks and systems, political dynamics and power relations among/across levels of the Chinese government, and contention among the recognised interests and the resulting levels of trust and impact on working relationships. Such are the criteria of *settings*. In addition, policy settings highlight how different sources of power are allocated within China's economic policymaking community, and how they are mobilised by different groups in a struggle for decision-making control (Zhao, 1996, pp. 25–26). Policy setting determines which kinds of policy determinant are effective in generating preference change. Such is the *instrument*. The level of impact of the *instruments* rests upon the objectives of the policy problem at hand (i.e. is it of interest to the decision-makers? Are the initiatives costly? Or beneficial? Does it have political relevance?). Such are the *policy goals*. Finally, the success of the factors of impact is contingent on their compatibility with national objectives (i.e. national interest), which, in China's case, is national development.

### *A framework for negotiation approach*

China's policy preference formation is but one of two fundamental aspects of its economic diplomacy decision-making. The second aspect is China's negotiation approach. An accurate understanding of this requires a separate framework, established primarily with a focus on the decision-making that takes place during the negotiation process and which shapes China's negotiation approach. Although important, this dimension has seldom been examined by literature, which makes building an analytical framework challenging. That said, taking inspiration from rationalism, cognitivism, and contractualism, three probable negotiation practices are relevant instruments for analysis. They are: shuttle diplomacy proximity talks, the informal negotiation practices, and side-payment bargaining. Across the three schools of thought, all three instruments are mediatory by nature, which grants them a degree of influence.

Where they differ is in the degree to which the mediatory trait of each negotiation practice could alter China's negotiation approaches. Rationalists hold that actors shape their negotiation approaches and envision the desired outcome based on the available policy options and the expected outcomes produced by those available options. Although preferences for the desired outcome are assumed to be fixed, the decision-makers' prior expectations are not. Rather, their uncertainties about the accuracy of their expectations cause them to evolve as new information emerges (Walsh, 2005, p. 5). Processes of a mediatory nature, from this perspective, are most effective when international agencies – the governing body of multilateral economic negotiations – hold superior private information about some characteristics of the foreign Parties or the utility associated with each available negotiation approach that may be important to the Chinese decision-makers.

The cognitive theory focuses on how social interactions could alter the decision-makers' identities, which makes it an easy starting point for analysing mediatory instruments. Cognitive theorists argue that the negotiation process itself is a process of learning, where new ideas are adopted and beliefs formed (Underdal, 1998, pp. 21–22). Since economic negotiations typically depend on cognitive factors such as scientific knowledge, ideas, and a process of social learning (Stein, 1993), the knowledge of policymakers will endure an evolutionary process that is open to the influence of international discourse. Gradually, it develops into new ideas and beliefs, and eventually modifies negotiation approaches. Drawing on the Habermasian theory of communicative action, cognitivists hold that influence stems out of honest communications between domestic and/or international agents and agencies. Such interactions do not entail the use of material power resources to impose their views on the Chinese decision-makers, and as a result, generate more convincing arguments. This view contrasts with rationalism, which does not accommodate the possibility for mediation to change the preferences of the decision-makers for the desired negotiation outcome, how they are defined in the context of the preferred outcome, and the definitions of what is *right* (Finnemore, 2003, p. 154; Risse, 2000, p. 20).

Finally, contractualists believe mediatory instruments are nothing more and nothing less than an effort to change the decision-makers' calculation of the costs and benefits. Advocates believe these efforts often attach both positive and negative incentive structures to secure a cooperative negotiation approach. Contractualists argue against cognitivism by suggesting that mediatory influences do not change the basic beliefs of decision-makers, especially about what kind of game is being played.

Putting aside arguments about quantifying the level of impact, all three approaches share the view that the mediatory processes do have some level of impact. Between the three processes, the underlying impact derives from the fact that international agents, as intermediaries of economic negotiations, possess diverse motives for choosing a certain form of behaviour or set of values and making recommendations towards a policy they are attempting to affect. Paradoxically, the fact that they possess goals and objectives, which they seek to further through mediatory instruments, has been a neglected aspect of research. The current literature tends to assume that while the member-states possess goals and objectives that underlie the behaviour they undertake – the incompatibility of which forms the basis of disagreements and negotiation impasse – any inter-national agent is wholly or, at worst, largely, motivated by a desire to bring about a settlement (Mitchell, 1988, pp. 29–30). On this point, it is crucial to note that the goals and objectives of the international agencies should not be taken for granted and are a proper subject for academic analysis.

Furthermore, the underlying motives from which multilateral initiatives arise and are sustained are likely to have a marked influence on the way that the inter-national agents conduct the process, on the manner in which China reacts to multilateral activities, and on the eventual outcome, particularly in terms of the form any final settlement might take. As such, it is important to recognise that an assessment on the negotiation process is a study on the impact of international agencies that facilitate such processes. Therefore, it is fitting to consider the impact of international agencies on the formation of China's negotiation approach, alongside the negotiation processes themselves.

• *Shuttle diplomacy proximity talks*

The term *shuttle diplomacy* came about from an anecdote of American diplo-macy. Following the Yom Kippur War of 1973, then-US Secretary of State, Henry Kissinger, attempted to broker peace in the Middle East by 'shuttling' back-and-forth between nations in the region and with numerous leaders to produce cease-fires and peace agreements. Although the term shuttle diplomacy is often broadly used to describe situations where negotiators from one Party (be they from a nation-state or a multilateral organisation) travel across borders to meet with their negotiating counterparts, the private meetings with national leaders are called *proximity talks* (Hoffman, 2010, p. 273). The WTO Director-General, Pascal Lamy, exercised shuttle diplomacy proximity talks with Chinese leaders during visits to Beijing.[11] Former WTO Director-General, Mike Moore, also visited China to promote the Doha Development Agenda (DDA) (Jawara and Kwa, 2004, p. 198). Numerous COP Presidents (e.g. during the Mexican Presidency) have conducted shuttle diplomacy before their annual meetings (e.g. COP16) to encourage Beijing to adopt a cooperative negotiation approach. Members of the IMF have also travelled to Beijing to gather insights about China's perspective on economic issues such as its currency, how it wishes to contribute to the global economy, and how it thinks the future world economy should be managed.[12]

The micro process of proximity talks is persuasion, which involves changing the perspectives and attitudes of the decision-makers regarding the causality and effects of non-material pressures (Johnston, 2008, pp. 25–26; Walsh, 2005, p. 3). Proximity talks have two approaches to persuasion: the *central route* and the *peri-phery route*. The central route is where international agents weigh evidences and problems through counter-attitudinal arguments, and draw conclusions that are usually different from what the Chinese government had begun with. This form of mediatory persuasion is a process involving high-intensity cognition, reflection, and argumentation about the content of new information (Bar-Tal and Saxe, 1990,

p. 122). In the climate change negotiations on mitigation, the UNFCCC Secretariat and the Intergovernmental Panel on Climate Change (IPCC) have made counter-attitudinal arguments to Beijing, such as the suggestion that mitigation measures improve energy efficiency, and can therefore be considered as a 'no-regret' policy option because of its consistency with China's national development goals. Pascal Lamy applied similar strategies of persuasion when he argued that accession into the WTO's Government Procurement Agreement (GPA) would enhance China's procurement rule-making and contribute to better governance over the private regulations of procurement activities.

The peripheral route constitutes the second persuasion approach. The peripheral route is where international agents communicate on the basis of an institutionalised relationship. The conversations are therefore more personalised, private, and casual. The Chinese decision-makers will first look for clues regarding the nature of the relationship and make judgements accordingly about the legitimacy of the counter-attitudinal arguments they make. Like other countries, China often finds proximity talks with in-groups to be more effective than with out-groups. And talks with sources that are *liked* are accepted more than sources that are *dis*liked. The determining factor of liking is based on familiarity and level of exposure to that source. In addition, given the complex and fragmented nature of China's bureaucratic system, it is often necessary to not just be trusted but also liked by all the relevant government departments in order to be effective. Otherwise, it will not be possible to surpass the pre-existing beliefs held by those that do not trust the international agent doing the talking.

• *Informal negotiation practices (INPs)*

INPs are customary practices in the form of informal plenary meetings under the chairmanship of a subsidiary body of an international agency. Alternative formats include private room discussions between select Parties, corridor conversations between two or more individuals of any Party, or roundtables where member-states are divided up in smaller groups. Generally, negotiations in an open, formal plenary with all delegates tend to be cumbersome at the best of times, but become unmanageable when too many issues complicate the negotiation agenda. INPs streamline the negotiation process by allowing texts to be discussed by smaller, more specialised groups of negotiators, who then present their work to the wider body of states in the plenary for final decision-making.[13] It is not uncommon for the Director-General (and sometimes the Chair of the General Council or one of the other Councils or committees) to steer the discussions.

An example is the "services signalling conference" called in July 2008 by Pascal Lamy in his capacity as the Trade Negotiation Committee (TNC) Chairman, which discussed service negotiations and exchanged potential offers and requests on a "without prejudice" basis (Footer, 2011, p. 230). During the 2011 COP17 meeting, the South African COP President called a roundtable (or the 'huddle'), which included representative from China, the US, EU, and India, to discuss a final resolution on the mitigation issues as part of the broader 'Durban

Package'. According to personal observations in the negotiation room, the South African COP President, Maite Nkoana-Mashabane, Chair of the roundtable, placed much pressure on China, India, and the US to accept the middle-range proposal forwarded by the EU. Interviewed observers further indicated that the deputy Director-Generals of the WTO have a high tendency to exercise corridor discussions with Chinese delegates to promote their own visions of an agreement and steer INPs towards that end.[14] The UNFCCC's Secretary-General, Christiana Figueres, is also regularly sighted having corridor conversations with Chinese decision-makers.

In theory, INPs are most effective when a Party encounters negotiation dilemmas with another Party. In such a situation, INPs are useful for consensus-building (Blackhurst and Hartridge, 2004, p. 708). The objective of the informal (and sometimes private) face-to-face interactions is to convince negotiators to take cooperative actions. The outcome could have effective influence on a Party's negotiation approach. Additionally, INPs are effective for trust-building, reducing uncertainty, and raising awareness.[15] In the climate change negotiations on the Clean Development Mechanism (CDM), the COP Presidencies in the earlier negotiation rounds purportedly reiterated discussions on the Kyoto Protocol Mechanisms – which were then unfamiliar concepts to the Chinese delegation – in small group discussions. The repetition of these concepts in informal consultation meetings caught the attention of Chinese decision-makers, and prompted Beijing to look into the issue more seriously.

According to research on past experiences where individuals have been put together in small informal face-to-face situations, there tends to be a substantial increase in the levels of cooperation.[16] Among the experiments is an analysis by David Sally (1995) which showed that face-to-face communication, on average, increases the rate of cooperation by more than 45 per cent. The results also indicate that there are no alternative variables which enjoy an effect similar to that of the face-to-face exercises. For instance, in a series of public-good experiments by Jane Sell and Rick Wilson (1991, 1992), Elena Rocco and Massimo Warglien (1995), and Rob Moir (1995), researchers found far fewer levels of cooperation as a result of signalled promises to cooperate made through computer channels compared to the face-to-face method using the same research design. Therefore it is plausible that the INPs have a level of impact on the shape and form of China's negotiation approaches.

- *Side-payment bargaining*

Between the rationalist, cognitive, and contractualist approaches, the notion of *incentive* features prevalently. As such, it is argued, especially by the rationalists, that the most attractive incentives for China – a developing country – are usually material ones since China is concerned about its capacity to adapt to the impacts of the global economy (Rowlands, 1995; Sprinz and Vaahtoranta, 1994). The ability to adapt to international standards is often closely related to the level of economic resources a country has, and if this capacity is low, then the country becomes more vulnerable to the impact of the economic problem. That is why resource assistance could be an effective policy incentive.

It is imaginable that preferences can be changed due to the possibility of receiving economic and technical assistance in exchange for taking on commitments. An international agent acting as a broker at the negotiation table could argue that any policy change for taking on commitment is actually promoting China's economic development. Such was the argument made by the WTO Negotiation Committee during China's long accession negotiations. They discussed the kind of assistance China could benefit from as a result of holding a WTO membership. But in return, China was required to make a deeper set of reform commitments. Likewise, numerous COP Presidencies have postulated similar arguments to China in the carbon emission negotiations. In fact, a key reason China actively sought multilateral institution membership throughout the 1970s and 1980s was for the economic and technical benefits. It is arguable that China's interests in cooperation are triggered by the possibility of furthering its economic goals, which can be attained through economic side-payments. In this way, it is imaginable that side-payment bargaining exercises could feasibly pull significant weight in the outcome of China's negotiation approach.

• *Social instigators: policy propellers and underminers*

The strengths of the three processes lie in their ability to enhance the innate drivers of Chinese preference formation: expectation, trust, and personal reputation. According to the research interviews, a fundamental reason for China's poor cooperative behaviour is Beijing's low expectations that other negotiating Parties will reciprocate if China does take on commitments. This finding is supported by past experiments on negotiation behaviours; the expectations of mutual commitment at the negotiation table often determine negotiation outcome. This was evident at the 2011 DDA negotiations in Geneva, where numerous negotiators indicated that they did not even intend to work hard towards an agreement since they did not expect other delegations to be interested in any form of an agreement. As one senior member of the WTO Secretariat suggested, there was little political will to push through an agreement by member-states, no expectation to be pragmatic.[17] Likewise, Chinese climate change negotiators revealed the reality that they had little expectation for progress towards a post-2020 framework ahead of the COP18 meetings. But this is not surprising given that China has had a long history of having low expectations for multilateral economic negotiations, and this explains its persistent negotiating style of holding-back – it simply does not believe other negotiating Parties will actually reciprocate to any concessions they make. And such was the case when China's COP15 pledge was received by a silent audience.

Poor expectations are often the result of asymmetrical information or a problem of "adverse selection" (Hoffman, 2010, p. 279). In multilateral economic negotiations, the adverse selection problem presents itself when the negotiating Parties do not know that they have a range of possible agreements.

Negotiation theory shows that Parties often hide their bottom-line positions because of the fear that their candour will be exploited by other negotiating Parties who are not willing to be transparent on an equal level, especially with regard to their underlying interests. A classic example is illustrated by Elinor Ostrom (1998). A person with an over-abundance of oranges (but who prefers apples) proposes a trade of some of the oranges with someone who has an over-abundance of apples (but who prefers oranges). The latter agrees to a trade but feigns a lack of interest in oranges so as to secure more advantageous trading terms (such as two oranges for each apple). In this situation, the international agency can reframe the expectations of decision-makers by altering the extent to which they expect their present actions to be affected by the behaviour of others on future issues through, for example, signalling exercises. The reverse is also true. The pre-existing expectation of decision-makers can also condition the extent to which international agents inflict on China's negotiation approach.

Second to expectation, though no less important, is *trust* – a root cause of uncertainty.[18] As a senior member of the WTO Secretariat said, "You don't feel trust among negotiators in the WTO ... or in the climate change negotiations". This lack of trust is felt not just towards other countries but also towards the multilateral institutions in their agenda, and intentions.[19] And one Chinese policy advisor to the Ministry of Commerce (MOFCOM) observed, when there is distrust from individual negotiators, they can reject a proposal simply based on a personal grudge.[20] Like other countries, China has lacked trust towards the multilateral system from the outset.[21] In the CDM negotiations, a key problem in the negotiation process was China's distrust of the underlying intent and motive behind the initiative, especially with regard to where the benefits will flow to. It was only after the Global Environmental Facility (GEF) and other UN agencies had demonstrated to the Chinese government, through pilot simulations, how the benefits come about that trust was rejuvenated. In the DDA negotiations on trade in services, Beijing has a lack of trust in the capacity, and authority, of the WTO's regulatory framework to manage and govern deeper liberalisation of the world services between nations.

In the GPA example, the Chinese government has struggled to trust the WTO's protocol and governance on government procurement, arguing that it is vague and ambiguous in many aspects of the proposed framework. Clearly, trust, or the lack thereof, is a significant hindrance to the multilateral process. For the Chinese government, as for any government, trust is seen as the *bedrock* of effective negotiations, and having trust is indispensable to agreement-building. This is supported by the theoretical presupposition that in the context of a social dilemma, trust affects whether an individual is willing to initiate cooperation based on the expectation that it will be reciprocated (Ostrom, 1998, p. 12). Hence, one central variable which has hindered China from taking a cooperative approach to the negotiations is distrust over whether its negotiating counterparts will actually reciprocate concessions offered, comply with agreements, and whether they are capable process managers.

Finally, external influence and cooperation is not possible without a highly regarded personal reputation. Chinese decision-makers and negotiators have a strong culture of saving face. And after an international negotiation, Chinese decision-makers do not want the Chinese public to think that they 'caved' in some manner to foreign demands. This is even the case in situations where the stakes are relatively modest; China does not want to be the one that 'blinked' as this is a sign of weakness.

At the multilateral level, having a strong personal reputation is equally important. When Chinese negotiators gather with other delegates at the negotiation table, the social dynamic is similar to that of a high school classroom. There are clear social cliques or distinct groups of friends. No one wants to be the odd one out or be seen as obsolete. The weaker negotiators admire representatives of larger nations, and no one wants to be seen as difficult and non-cooperative. In this emotional and vulnerable mental state, Chinese negotiators and decision-makers have a relatively high desire to acquire and/or maintain a respectable reputation amongst their peers at the negotiation table. The reputation card in this situation will therefore offer an effective leverage at the negotiation table.

As one Chinese delegate to COP17 acknowledged:

> When a Chinese negotiator is in an informal situation, they are most prone to the logics of other parties and the Chair. The repeated encounter of new ideas makes one more likely to accept them because of the social pressure and dynamic. As people, we all want to be respected and feel that we fit in. At the same time, the environment often makes Chinese negotiator more sympathetic to the Secretariat's text.[22]

The logic is simple, really: if a Chinese negotiator is positively received as having a reputation that is trustworthy, then they are more likely to be cooperative. However, the reverse is true if their reputation is negatively perceived.

## Propositions and methodology

This book posits two claims. The intended argument to be tested is: *Chinese economic diplomacy preference formation is shaped by varying direct and indirect policy instruments and at different stages of decision-making. However, the level of actualised influence is contingent on a range of situational factors and social instigators.*

Informed by the *a priori* assumptions of the first framework, the *primary* claim addresses the *how* question: *how* Chinese economic diplomacy preferences are formulated. This is mainly concerned with the preference formation stage of decision-making. The claim is that: *Chinese policymakers, government negotiators, and diplomats formulate their negotiation preferences through the calculation of costs and benefits, accessible information, and considerations about national reputation.* The caveat is that the level of actual influence of the aforementioned instruments is contingent on four situational factors: national objectives, policy goals, policy settings, and policy instruments.

The *secondary* claim is informed by the assumptions of the second framework. It addresses the supplementary decision-making during the negotiation processes. As such, it holds that: *China's negotiation approach can be shaped by shuttle diplomacy, informal negotiation practices, and side-payment bargaining.* The underlying assumption for the secondary claim is that the actual influence rests on a core set of drivers for China's negotiation approach, referred to in this study as the social instigators. They are expectation, trust, and personal reputation. The three social instigators are cumulatively necessary criteria for maximising policy outcome.

### Why multilateral economic negotiations?

Why does this book choose multilateral economic negotiations as the basis for understanding China's economic diplomacy decision-making? After all, Chinese policy actors encounter a myriad of external influences from bilateral interactions with other nation-states as well as on a regional level. From a theoretical perspective, rationalists, cognitivists, and contractualists commonly assume a connection between existing normative structures within the international system and the assimilation of these norms in the preferences of nation-states. It is in the multilateral context where the interaction between agencies is most likely and where processes of internalising external influences are most concentrated. As James Muldoon Jr. (1998, p. 3) observes, it is in the international environment that economic diplomacy with an emphasis on interpersonal communication, informal discussions, and bargaining manifests. In addition, international agencies generally have features, objectives, norms, and beliefs that challenge the core assumptions and ideologies of national policy actors. So if China is to be influenced by any counter-attitudinal agencies, it ought to be from international agencies.

For the most part, when IPE scholars look for the effect of international agencies, the unit of analysis has tended to be the agency itself as an institution (Johnston, 2008, p. 27; Meyer *et al.*, 1997; Eyre and Suchman, 1996). The problem with this is that agencies are unitary actors that do not participate in the preference formation; rather, the agents who operates under the agencies do (i.e. the Secretary-General, Chairs of the negotiation committee, working group members, and so on). For this reason, this book places greater emphasis on the influence of these agents (just as it does on the Chinese policymakers and government negotiators) on China's economic diplomacy decision-making process.

But how would one know if multilateral engagements lead to cooperative policy preferences from China? First, it is necessary to show that the Chinese government and its policy actors are conducive to the hypothesised variables. Second, it is imperative to show that after some engagements with international agents, the preference of policies (as reflected through their postures and arguments) have evolved in a way that converges with the preferences of the international agency under study. Third, it is essential to show a shift in China's preferences that is consistent with the arguments of international agents. These are the areas which this study tests.

### *How do we measure impact?*

It is one thing to identify the factors of decision-making (i.e. the instances of change) and quite another to measure them, particularly since the hypothesised variables generate different kinds of change, which renders them difficult to compare with each other analytically and methodologically. For this reason, the dependent variable of this research needs to be measured in a consistent but flexible way.

The literature on 'Europeanisation' has established four indicators of impact: *inertia, absorption, transformation*, and *retrenchment* (Lenschow, 2006; Börzel and Risse, 2000, 2003; Radaelli, 2000, 2002). *Inertia* indicates a lack of impact. Under this circumstance, the variables had minimal driving force over the policy outcome; or they did not alter an existing preference or approach. Furthermore, the reflections derived from the variables are not endorsed by any domestic actor, or are only able to build weak intra-governmental coalitions with no or very little impact.

*Absorption* implies some influence, but it is only to the point of adaptation. In other words, absorption implies a situation in which China formally adopts new policies and measures derived from the hypothesised variables, but "without changing their essential features and the underlying collective understandings attached to them" (Börzel and Risse, 2000, p. 10). What it does do is allow Chinese decision-makers to acquire new capacities to address particular issues both internally and externally.

*Transformation* indicates a deeper impact, both in terms of preference formation and in shaping the negotiation approach. In both cases, it implies a paradigmatic change in "the fundamental logic of political behaviour" (Radaelli, 2002, p. 117. See also Börzel and Risse, 2000, p. 10). Such preference changes are expected to become institutionalised.

Any policy changes found with the absorption or transformation levels of influence are, by implication, likely to trigger a sizeable alteration to the distribution of power within Beijing, as well as the birth of dedicated administrative entities, working groups, committees or networks, and/or the creation of specific bureaucratic routines. A relevant increase in the competence and ability of the Chinese government to address a particular issue is subsequently expected both in terms of its internal capacities and its international "actorness" (Costa and Jorgensen, 2012).

Finally, *retrenchment* indicates a situation where the Chinese government reacts against the hypothesised variables. In contrast to inertia, the negative reaction from China is active and explicit. Therefore, China is expected to take specific measures to counteract externally disseminated information, for example.

The way that this study identifies the qualitative influences and classifies them under any of the four indicators is as follows. If a variable is found to have triggered preference changes without any constraints imposed by the situational factors, then it is considered to have *transformation* influence. If a variable stimulates new policy adaptation but is circumscribed by one or more of the situational factors, then the influence is at the *absorption* level. If it does not lead to any adaptation processes *and* is limited by one or more of the situational factors, then it has *inertia* influence. Finally, if there are indications of rebellion or lashing-out behaviour from China, then it indicates a *retrenchment* influence. On the whole, this qualitative scale covers all the possible magnitudes and directions of policy change and is comprehensive enough to include different kinds of preference changes.

### *Methodology*

This book stems from the inductive case study tradition, but also uses primary and secondary claims to link the findings to a wider enterprise. The blend of inductive and deductive analysis involves three steps. Step 1 generates the claims about the dependent variable and identifies probable factors that drive and motivate Chinese economic diplomacy decision-making (as shown in this chapter). Step 2 identifies and provisionally selects pairs of cases as candidates for deeper analysis. Within the two purposively selected negotiations, case-pairs are further chosen to demonstrate variation in the causal variable and the effect. Step 2 therefore accounts for the degrees and variations of the various factors which could influence China's preference formation. This is also an important time for testing the primary claim. Step 3 further examines the case-pairs to draw inferences on the processes which could affect China's negotiation approach. Crucial to note is that the purpose in each case is to provide not a comprehensive history but information relevant for the propositions.

Scientific investigation of China faces daunting and age-old methodological challenges. Official secrecy makes direct, uniform observation of Chinese policymakers virtually impossible. Then again, uniform observation of war was hardly a simple endeavour, and yet substantial and careful sets of data have been assembled to contribute useful theory on military conflict and its management. By comparison, we have no uniform descriptions of a representative sample of China's decision-making process either for economic diplomacy, or foreign policy more generally. We have not even begun to discuss what representativeness would look like or mean.

Faced with a lack of uniform data, Parts 2 and 3 develop and substantiate each major idea by contrasting two multilateral economic negotiations: the UNFCCC climate change and the WTO Doha Development Round negotiations. In most cases, the level of China's ultimate preference change is not necessarily in China's interests in an obvious sense. To derive optimum accuracy, each case study is dissected into more specific 'case-pair' focuses, based on two modalities within the negotiation agenda. Each 'case-pair' will be from the same negotiation process but with different outcomes. The first set of case studies concerns China's participation in the UNFCCC, and the 'case-pair' focuses on the Clean

Development Mechanism (CDM) and the international mitigation commitment negotiations. The second set is on China's participation in the WTO trade negotiations. The 'case-pair' looks at the international trade in services and the Government Procurement Agreement (GPA) negotiations. The 'case-pairs' of observations are chosen to illustrate variation in the cause of interest and the effect while holding other possible causes constant.[23] They all demonstrate China's evolving preferences, from strong resistance to either adoption and/or flexibility positions. At the same time, the case studies exhibit different degrees of preference shifts and flexibility which enable this study to analyse causes and implication of variances and draw clearer probable causalities.

The two-case method offers four appealing advantages. First, each contrasts two outcomes which pose an interesting puzzle, a sharply posed empirical question whose answer is not obvious. Second, exposure to varying case studies generates more accurate findings about the process that may or may not prove the validity of the claims. Third, the method offers strong empirical grounding for a causal claim compared with the more common single-case study or what is possible with a statistical method that observes a larger number of cases but measures only a few variables and then often using proxies. On the latter, without detailed qualitative examination of case studies, the analyst is unable to know about the many aspects of the process that are observed – which could change interpretation. Even the most comprehensive regression analysis is subject to bias due to measurement error and omitted variables.

Fourth, qualitative case study analyses report much more information about the decision-makers' and government negotiators' beliefs, tactics, context, and outcomes than would be reported if these dimensions were reduced to statistical variables. The rich case evidence may stimulate others to formulate alternative ideas, to compare and reanalyse diverse published cases, and perhaps to use them as raw material for constructing negotiation variables, especially when we have little general knowledge about China's economic diplomacy decision-making process.

Every method has inherent drawbacks as well. Developing two case study sets necessarily limits the number of propositions this book can cover. The book stops short of presenting a complete analytical picture of the process. Even the most exhaustive research on real history will probably never find two broad negotiations that are matched perfectly with respect to every possible rival hypothesis; perfection is not a realistic expectation. Even when a pair eliminates many important threats to inference, some remaining differences could be related to the effect. Also we cannot be certain these observations, selected purposively, are representative of a larger population or that the claim is valid generally until research is conducted in other domains. There is no obvious reason why these propositions are likely to be disconfirmed in other instances, but the task of testing them elsewhere remains. Finally, qualitative contrasts deny us statistical techniques that would support more precise claims about the relative magnitudes of different causes.

The other significant challenge, as already mentioned, is the access to data. Any research that involves micro-level analyses involves what Herbert Simon (1985, p. 303) calls "specification of the situation" which is "data intensive", and "time consuming". And due to the opaque nature of the Chinese political system, access to the relevant data at the micro level presents an obstacle to the empirical research of this study. Yet, it must be made clear that the present volume does not intend to open every 'black box' in Chinese economic diplomacy decision-making. Its purpose is more modest, but nonetheless valuable – namely to provide a preliminary understanding and framework within which to examine the combined impact of international and domestic environments on the multiple levels of agents involved in China's economic diplomacy decision-making. It also intends to enhance scholars' ability to analyse the choices and preferences of Chinese decision-makers when faced with concrete economic policy issues in a diplomatic context.

Out of necessity, then, data collection would need to rely on a mix of sources. The starting point was academic resources, such as books, journal articles, and conference papers. Government documents circulated by Chinese policy actors were also used. Internet sources including the online editions of Chinese newspapers and other related websites concerning climate change and international trade were useful. To ensure accuracy of information, multiple sources were gathered to ensure the reliability of events, and facts.

In addition, the analysis relies on data accumulated from over 190 interviews with key Chinese and non-Chinese decision-makers and negotiators who work in climate change and international trade-related policy issues, representatives of the UNFCCC and WTO Secretariats and related international organisations, Chinese industrial actors, and experts from the Chinese and international epistemic community. In addition, data from participant observation at the COP17 and 2011 DDA negotiations are used to complement the interview data.

The research process of this book was limited by the restricted access to the decision-making processes inside the central government of China due to the 'asymmetric transparency' (不对称的透明度) characteristic of the Chinese political system. As a result, there is reason to suspect the level of honesty interviewed policy actors have communicated in their responses. Another possibility is that interviewees can purposely exaggerate or simplify their answers. This makes the data problematic on empirical grounds and the actual intentions of Chinese decision-makers difficult to decipher. But to minimise this effect, the researcher has carefully paid attention to the professional position of the interviewee, the interpersonal dynamics during the interviews, the wording of the interview questions, and carried out follow-up interviews where necessary for clarification. In doing so, some of the aforementioned obstacles have been remedied.

Data about the events during the negotiations is based on on-site observations and reports from non-governmental organisations. To supplement the above information sources, participatory observations were conducted on-site at the UNFCCC's COP17 negotiations in Durban for the climate change case study, and at the 2011 Ministerial negotiations on the Doha Round in Geneva for the trade case study. Access into the informal negotiations between Parties of the Member States was granted during the observations, and further on-site interviews were conducted with representatives of numerous delegations as well as the multilateral economic organisations participating in the negotiations. Finally, reports from organisations such as the Earth Negotiations Bulletin (ENB) published by the International Institute for Sustainable Development (IISD) and the International Centre for Trade and Sustainable Development (ICTSD) were used. Both organisations are regarded as independent and reliable sources of information, and are widely referenced within academia as empirical observers of the various dimensions of the multilateral climate change and trade negotiations.

The product of this method, then, is intermediate – more than rich description but less comprehensive than a true test. Since the ideas were generated in part by looking at the reported cases, the analysis does not constitute a test in the statistical sense. Yet the case-pairs are not just any cases. Thorough contrasting case studies that rule out three or more rival causes provide deeper and more rigorous empirical grounding for testing claims. No previous work, to my knowledge, has provided equivalent grounding in economic negotiations for any of the propositions supported here by this method. Such research establishes a warrant for more extensive and costly testing. Only by using multiple, complementary methods can researchers collectively transcend the limits of each.

## Notes

1 The effectiveness of these instruments lies in the fact that they imply obligations, even though these obligations are not enforceable through a hierarchical legal system.
2 Merton traces this tradition to Mill and Bacon, who cited Plato.
3 Exemplary in this respect are Snyder and Diesing (1977) in international security studies, and in political economy, Keohane and Nye (1977). The latter book acknowledges the limitations of two 'isms' and attempts to show how they might complement each other in an integrated, comparative empirical analysis.
4 The authors of one of the most convincing empirical studies drawing on this tradition, George and George (1964), dropped it in subsequent work. As exceptions, Adler, Rosen and Silverstein (1998), and Kowert and Hermann (1997) explore the effects of emotions and personality types, respectively, in bargaining.
5 Decision-making studies were influential in international relations during the 1950s and 1960s, but then intellectual fashion mostly moved elsewhere. For more, see Simon (1985).
6 For introductions and references to these many findings, see Neale and Bazerman (1991), Levy (1997), and Rabin (1998).
7 Note that when it comes to concrete situations, the line between 'information' and 'rationality' can be drawn in more than one place. Presumably the unbounded rationality actor seeks out whatever information he needs. If a particular diplomat does not have all possible information, this could be modelled either as imperfect information in the hands of an unboundedly rational maximiser, or as incomplete search by a satisficer. Most mathematical theorists have preferred to blame behavioural anomalies on imperfections in information in the hands of presumed maximisers, rather than attempting to model satisficing. This is a modeller's choice, and a few, following Simon, are working to formalise the second approach. In economics see Conlisk (1996); in political science see Bendor (1995).
8 This model is inspired by Graham Allison's (1971) rational actor model used in his classic work on foreign policy decision-making, *Essence of Decision: Explaining the Cuban Missile Crisis*.

9  Other factors include uncertainties about the availability of alternative energy sources, scientific doubts, and China's own institutional, technological and financial capacity to take on mitigation measures.

10  Similar sentiments were made by Krasner (1983).

11  Interview with a senior advisor to the WTO, Beijing, 22 November 2012.

12  Interview with an expert from the Chinese Academy of Social Sciences, Beijing, 8 November 2012.

13  Depending on the stage of negotiation and the specific topic, informal groups may be known as contact groups, drafting groups, working groups, informal consultations, or other terms. The common characteristic of these settings is that they are conducted in English only, and often exclude non-governmental organisations.

14  Interview with a policy advisor to the Ministry of Commerce, Beijing, 4 September 2012.

15  Interview with a senior advisor to the Ministry of Commerce, Beijing, 22 November 2012.

16  See Ostrom *et al.* (1994) for extensive citations to studies showing a positive effect on the capacity to communicate.

17  Interview with a senior member of the WTO Secretariat, London, 2 February 2012; interview with a financial advisor from EXIM Bank, Beijing, 20 November 2012.

18  Trust is the "expectation of one person about the actions of others that affects the first person's choice, when an action must be taken before the actions of others are known" (Dasgupta, 1997, p. 5).

19  Interview with a senior member of the WTO Secretariat, London, 2 February 2012.

20  Interview with a policy advisor to the Ministry of Commerce, Beijing, 25 October 2012.

21  Interview with an expert from Peking University, Beijing, 23 November 2012.

22  Interview in Beijing, 3 December 2012.

23  This is a variant of John Stuart Mill's method of difference. For more, see Mill (1843).

# References

Adler, R.S., Rosen, B., and Silverstein, E.M. (1998) 'Emotions in Negotiation: How to Manage Fear and Anger'. *Negotiation Journal* 14(2) pp. 161–179.

Alexander, J. and Giesen, B. (1987) 'From Reduction to Linkage: The Long View of the Micro–Macro Link'. In J. Alexander, B. Giesen, R. Munch, and N. Smelser (eds) *The Micro–Macro Link* (pp. 1–44). Berkeley, CA: University of California Press.

Allison, G. (1971) *Essence of Decision: Explaining the Cuban Missile Crisis*. Boston, MA: Little, Brown and Company.

Almond, G.A. (1989) Review Article: 'The International–National Connection'. *British Journal of Political Science* 19(2) pp. 237–259.

Bang, G. (2004) 'Sources of Influence in Climate Change Policymaking: A Comparative Analysis of Norway, Germany, and the United States'. Thesis Submitted to the Department of Political Science, University of Oslo.

Barker, C. (2005) *Cultural Studies: Theory and Practice*. London: Sage.

Bar-Tal, D. and Saxe, L. (1990) 'Acquisition of Political Knowledge: A Social-Psychological Analysis'. In O. Ichilov (ed.) *Political Socialization, Citizenship Education and Democracy* (pp. 116–133). New York: Teachers College Press.

Baumgartner, F.R. and Jones, B.D. (1991) 'Agenda Dynamics and Policy Subsystems'. *Journal of Politics* 53(4) pp. 1044–1074.

Béland, D. (2005) 'Ideas and Social Policy: An Institutionalist Perspective'. *Social Policy and Administration* 39(1) pp. 1–18.

Bendor, J. (1995) 'A Model of Muddling Through'. *The American Political Science Review* 89(4) pp. 819–840.

Bennett, C.J. (1991) 'What is Policy Convergence and What Causes It?' *British Journal of Political Science* 21(2) pp. 215–233.

Bernstein, S. and Cashore, B. (2000) 'Globalization, Four Paths of Internationalization and Domestic Policy Change: The Case of EcoForestry in British Columbia, Canada'. *Canadian Journal of Political Science* 33(1) pp. 67–100.

Blackhurst, R. and Hartridge, D. (2004) 'Improving the Capacity of WTO Institutions to Fulfil Their Mandate'. *Journal of International Economic Law* 7(3) pp. 705–716.

Blyth, M.M. (1997) 'Any More Bright Ideas? The Ideational Turn of Comparative Political Economy'. *Comparative Politics* 29(2) pp. 229–250.

Börzel, T. and Risse, T. (2003) 'Conceptualizing the Domestic Impact of Europe'. In K. Featherstone and C.M. Radaelli (eds) *The Politics of Europeanization* (pp. 57–80). Oxford: Oxford University Press.

Börzel, T. and Risse, T. (2000) 'When Europe Hits Home: Europeanization and Domestic Change'. *European Integration Online Papers (EIoP)* [Online] 4(15) Available from: http://eiop.or.at/eiop/texte/2000-015a.htm [Accessed: 26 April 2011].

Botcheva, L. and Martin, L.L. (2001) 'Institutional Effects on State Behaviour: Convergence and Divergence'. *International Studies Quarterly* 45(1) pp. 1–26.

Buen, J. (1998) 'China's Energy-Environmental Dilemma: Strategies and Framework Conditions'. *Forum for Development Studies* 25(1) pp. 163–203.

Campbell, J.L. (1998) 'Institutional Analysis and the Role of Ideas in Political Economy'. *Theory and Society* 27(5) pp. 377–409.

Carter, B. and New, C. (2004) *Making Realism Work*. London and New York: Routledge.

Checkel, J.T. (1997) *Ideas and International Political Change*. New Haven, CT: Yale University Press.

Coleman, W.D. and Perl, A. (1999) 'Internationalized Policy Environments and Policy Network Analysis'. *Political Studies* 47(4) pp. 691–709.

Conlisk, J. (1996) 'Why Bounded Rationality?' *Journal of Economic Literature* 34(June) pp. 669–700.

Constantin, C. (2007) 'Understanding China's Energy Security'. *World Political Science Review* 3(3) pp. 1–30.

Costa, O. and Jorgensen, K.E. (eds) (2012) *The Influence of International Institutions on the EU*. London: Palgrave Macmillan.

Cowhey, P. (1993) 'Domestic Institutions and the Credibility of International Commitments: Japan and the United States'. *International Organization* 47(2) pp. 299–326.

Cumings, B. (1989) 'The Political Economy of China's Turn Outward'. In S.S. Kim (ed.) *China and the World* (pp. 203–236). Boulder, CO: Westview Press.

Dai, X. (2007) *International Institutions and National Policies*. Cambridge: Cambridge University Press.

Dasgupta, P.S. (1997) 'Economic Development and the Idea of Social Capital'. Working Paper, Faculty of Economics, University of Cambridge.

Deutsch, K.W. (1957) *Political Community in the North Atlantic Area: International Organization in the Light of Historical Experience*. Princeton, NJ: Princeton University Press.

Economy, E. (2001) 'The Impact of International Regimes on Chinese Foreign Policy-Making: Broadening Perspectives and Policies … But Only to a Point'. In D.M. Lampton (ed.) *The Making of Chinese Foreign and Security Policy in the Era of Reform, 1979–2000* (pp. 230–256). Stanford, CA: Stanford University Press.

Eisener, M.A. (1994) 'Discovering Patterns in Regulatory History: Continuity, Change and Regulatory Regimes'. *Journal of Policy History* 6(2) pp. 157–187.

Evans, P., Jacobson, H.K., and Putnam, R.D. (eds) (1993) *Double-Edged Diplomacy: International Bargaining and Domestic Politics.* Berkeley, CA: University of California Press.

Eyre, D. and Suchman, M. (1996) 'Status, Norms, and the Proliferation of Conventional Weapons: An Institutional Theory Approach'. In P. Katzenstein (ed.) *The Culture of National Security* (pp. 79–113). New York: Columbia University Press.

Feng, H. (2007) 'Broken China: Fixing a Fragile Regulatory Framework'. *The Financial Regulator* 12(2) pp. 43–48.

Finnemore, M. (2003) *The Purpose of Intervention.* Ithaca, NY: Cornell University Press.

Finnemore, M. (1996) 'Norms, Culture, and World Politics: Insights from Sociology's Institutionalism'. *International Organization* 50(2) pp. 324–349.

Finnemore, M. and Sikkink, K. (1998) 'International Norm Dynamics and Political Change'. *International Organization* 52(4) pp. 887–917.

Footer, M.E. (2011) 'The WTO as a "Living Instrument": The Contribution of Consensus Decision-Making and Informality to Institutional Norms and Practices'. In T. Cottier and M. Elsig (eds) *Governing the World Trade Organization: Past, Present and Beyond Doha* (pp. 217–240). Cambridge: Cambridge University Press.

Foreign Policy Centre (2002) *Public Diplomacy.* London: The Foreign Policy Centre.

Frank, R. (1988) *Passions within Reason: The Strategic Role of the Emotions.* New York: W.W. Norton.

George, A.L. and George, J.L. (1964) *Woodrow Wilson and Colonel House: A Personality Study.* Mineola, NY: Dover Publications.

Gourevitch, P. (1978) 'The Second Image Reversed: The International Sources of Domestic Politics'. *International Organization* 32(4) pp. 881–912.

Gummett, P. (ed.) (1996) *Globalisation and Public Policy.* Cheltenham: Edward Elgar.

Haas, E.B. (1958) *The Uniting of Europe: Political, Social, and Economic Forces, 1950–1957.* Stanford, CA.: Stanford University Press.

Haas, P.M. (1980) 'Why Collaborate? Issue-Linkage and International Regimes'. *World Politics* 32 pp. 357–405.

Halpern, N.P. (1989) 'Policy Communities in a Leninist State: The Case of the Chinese Economic Policy Community'. *Governance: An International Journal of Policy and Administration* 2(1) pp. 23–41.

Hamrin, C.L. and Zhao, S. (eds) (1995) *Decision-Making in Deng's China: Perspectives From Insiders.* New York: M.E. Sharpe, Inc.

Harris, R. and Milkis, S. (1989) *The Politics of Regulatory Change.* New York: Oxford University Press.

Hintze, O. (1975) 'The Formation of States and Constitutional Development: A Study in History and Politics'. In F. Gilbert (ed.) *The Historical Essays of Otto Hintze* (pp. 157–177). New York: Oxford University Press.

Hoberg, G. (1996) 'Putting Ideas in Their Place: A Response to Learning and Change in the British Columbia Forest Policy Sector'. *Canadian Journal of Political Science* 29 (March) pp. 135–144.

Hoffman, D.A. (2010) 'Mediation and the Art of Shuttle Diplomacy'. *Negotiation Journal* 27(3) pp. 263–309.

Hoffman, S. (1960) *Contemporary Theory in International Relations.* Englewood Cliffs, NJ: Prentice-Hall.

Holsti, K.J. (1995) 'War, Peace, and the State of the State'. *International Political Science Review* 16(4). pp. 319–340.

Howlett, M. and Rayner, J. (1995) 'Do Ideas Matter? Policy Network Configurations and Resistance to Policy Change in the Canadian Forest Sector'. *Canadian Public Administration* 38(3) pp. 382–410.

Hunt, M.H. (1996) *The Genesis of Chinese Communist Foreign Policy.* New York: Columbia University Press.

Jacobsen, J.K. (1995) 'Much Ado About Ideas: The Cognitive Factor in Economic Policy'. *World Politics* 47 pp. 283–310.

Jacobson, H. and Oksenberg, M. (1990) *China's Participation in the IMF, the World Bank, and GATT.* Ann Arbor, MI: University of Michigan Press.

Jawara, F. and Kwa, A. (2004) *Behind the Scenes at the WTO: The Real World of International Trade Negotiations – The Lessons of Cancun.* New York: Zed Books.

Jervis, R. (1970) *The Logic of Images in International Relations.* Princeton, NJ: Princeton University Press.

Johansen, B.E. (2002) *The Global Warming Desk Reference.* Westport, CT: Greenwood Press.

Johnston, A.I. (1998) 'China and International Environmental Institutions: A Decision Rule Analysis'. In M.B. Elroy, C.P. Nielsen, and P. Lydon (eds) *Energizing China: Reconciling Environmental Protection and Economic Growth* (pp. 555–600). Newton, MA: Harvard University Press.

Joseph, J. (2008) 'Hegemony and the Structure-Agency Problem in International Relations: A Scientific Realist Contribution'. *Review of International Studies* 34(1) pp. 109–128.

Keck, M.E. and Sikkink, K. (eds) (1998) *Activists Beyond Borders: Advocacy Networks in International Politics.* Ithaca, NY: Cornell University Press.

Keohane, R.O. (1984) *After Hegemony: Cooperation and Discord in the World Political Economy.* Princeton, NJ: Princeton University Press.

Keohane, R.O. and Milner, H.V. (1996) *Internationalization and Domestic Politics.* Cambridge: Cambridge University Press.

Keohane, R.O. and Nye, J.S. (1989) *Power and Interdependence.* New York: Harper Collins.

Keohane, R.O. and Nye, J.S. (1977) *Power and Interdependence: World Politics in Transition.* Boston, MA: Little, Brown and Company.

Kim, S.S. (1998) *China and the World: Chinese Foreign Policy Faces the New Millennium.* Boulder, CO: Westview Press.

Kowert, P.A. and Hermann, M.G. (1997) 'Who Takes Risks? Daring and Caution in Foreign Policy Making'. *Journal of Conflict Resolution* 41 pp. 611–637.

Krasner, S.D. (ed.) (1983) *International Regimes.* Ithaca, NY: Cornell University Press.

Lai, H. (2010) *The Domestic Source of China's Foreign Policy: Regimes, Leadership, Priorities and Process.* New York: Routledge.

Lazar, D. (2001) 'Regulatory Interdependence and International Governance'. *Journal of European Public Policy* 8(3) pp. 474–492.

Leiby, M.L. and Butler, C.K. (2006) 'The Determinants of Diplomatic Dyads'. Paper prepared for presentation at the Annual Meeting of the Peace Science Society in Iowa City, Iowa, 3–5 November 2005 and the Jan Tinbergen Peace Science Conference in Amsterdam, 26–28 June 2006. Available from www.unm.edu/~ckbutler/working papers/DiplomaticDyads.pdf [Accessed: 2 August 2014].

Lenschow, A. (2006) 'Europeanisation of Public Policy'. In J. Richardson (ed.) *European Union. Power and Policy-Making* (pp. 55–71). London: Routledge.

Levy, J. (1997) 'Prospect Theory, Rational Choice, and International Relations'. *International Studies Quarterly* 41 pp. 87–112.

Lieberman, R.C. (2002) 'Ideas, Institutions, and Political Order: Explaining Political Change'. *American Political Science Review* 96(4) pp. 697–712.

Lieberthal, K.G. and Lampton, D.M. (eds) (1992) *Bureaucracy, Politics, and Decision Making in Post-Mao China.* Berkeley, CA: University of California Press.

Merton, R.K. (1968) *Social Theory and Social Structure* (enlarged edn). New York: Free Press.

Meyer, J.W., Frank, D.J., Hironaka, A., Schofer, E., and Tuma, N.B. (1997) 'The Structuring of a World Environmental Regime, 1870–1990'. *International Organization* 51(4). pp. 623–651.

Mill, J.S. (1843) *A System of Logic, Ratiocinative and Inductive: Being a Connected View of the Principle of Evidence and the Methods of Scientific Investigation* (Vol. 1). London: J.W. Parker.

Milner, H.V. (1997) *Interests, Institutions, and Information: Domestic Politics and International Relations.* Princeton, NJ: Princeton University Press.

Mitcham, C.J. (2005) *China's Economic Relations with the West and Japan, 1949–79: Gain, Trade and Diplomacy.* London: Routledge.

Mitchell, C.R. (1988) 'The Motives for Mediation'. In C.R. Mitchell and K. Webb (eds) *New Approaches to International Mediation* (pp. 29–51). New York: Greenwood Press.

Moir, R. (1995) 'The Effects of Costly Monitoring and Sanctioning Upon Common Property Resource Appropriation'. Working Paper, Department of Economics, University of New Brunswick, Saint John.

Moore, T.G. and Yang, D. (2001) 'Empowered and Restrained: Chinese Foreign Policy in the Age of Economic Interdependence.' In D.M. Lampton, (ed.) *The Making of Chinese Foreign Policy in the Era of Reform 1979–2000* (pp. 191–229). Stanford, CA: Stanford University Press.

Moravcsik, A.M. (1998) *The Choice for Europe: Social Purpose and State Power from Messina to Maastricht.* Ithaca, NY: Cornell University Press.

Muldoon, Jr., J.P. (1998) 'Introduction'. In J.P. Muldoon Jr., J.F. Aviel, R. Reitano, and E. Sullivan (eds) *Multilateral Diplomacy and the United Nations Today.* Boulder, CO: Westview Press.

Neale, M.A. and Bazerman, M.H. (1991) *Cognition and Rationality in Negotiation.* New York: Free Press.

Neumayor, E. (2008) 'Distance, Power and Ideology: Diplomatic Representation in a World of Nation-States'. *Area* 40(2) pp. 228–236.

Nye, J.S. (1987) 'Nuclear Learning and U.S.-Soviet Security Regimes'. *International Organization* 41(3) pp. 371–402.

Oksenberg, M. and Economy, E. (1997) *Shaping U.S.–China Relations: A Long-Term Strategy.* New York: Council on Foreign Relations Press.

Ostrom, E. (1998) 'A Behavioral Approach to the Rational Choice Theory of Collective Action'. Presidential Address. *American Political Science Association* 92(1) pp. 1–22.

Ostrom, E., Gardner, R., and Walker, J. (1994) *Rules, Games, and Common-Pool Resources.* Ann Arbor, MI: University of Michigan Press.

Pahre, R. and Papayoanau, P. (eds) (1997) 'Modeling Domestic-International Linkages'. *Journal of Conflict Resolution* 41(1) pp. 4–11.

Parry, G. (1993) 'The Interweaving of Foreign and Domestic Policy-Making'. *Government and Opposition* 28(2) pp. 143–151.

Pearson, M.M. (2001) 'The Case of China's Accession to GATT/WTO'. In D.M. Lampton (ed.) *The Making of Chinese Foreign and Security Policy In the Era of Reform, 1978–2000* (pp. 337–370). Stanford, CA: Stanford University Press.

Pollack, J.D. (1984) 'China and the Global Strategic Balance'. In H. Harding (ed.) *China's Foreign Relations in the 1980s*. New Haven, CT: Yale University Press.

Pontusson, J. (1995). 'From Comparative Public Policy to Political Economy: Putting Political Institutions in Their Place and Taking Interests Seriously'. *Comparative Political Studies* 28(1) pp. 117–147.

Putnam, R.D. (1988) 'Diplomacy and Domestic Politics: The Logic of Two-Level Games'. *International Organization* 42(3) pp. 427–460.

Qin, Y. (2010) 'International Factors and China's External Behaviour: Power, Interdependence, and Institutions'. In P. Kerr, S. Harris, and Y. Qin (eds) *China's 'New' Diplomacy*. New York: Palgrave Macmillan.

Rabin, M. (1998) 'Psychology and Economics'. *Journal of Economic Literature* 36 pp. 11–46.

Radaelli, C.M. (2002) 'The Domestic Impact of European Union Public Policy: Notes on Concepts, Methods, and the Challenge of Empirical Research'. *Politique Européenne* 5(1) pp. 105–136.

Radaelli, C.M. (2000) 'Whither Europeanization? Concept Stretching and Substantive Change'. *European Integration Online Papers (EIoP)* 4(8). [Online] Available from: http://eiop.or.at/eiop/pdf/2000-008.pdf [Accessed: 26 April 2011].

Risse, T. (2000) 'Let's Argue!' *International Organization* 54(1) pp. 1–39.

Risse-Kappen, T. (1995) *Bringing Transnational Relations Back in: Non-State Actors, Domestic Structures and International Institutions*. Cambridge: Cambridge University Press.

Robinson, T.W. (1994) 'China's Foreign Policy from the 1940s to the 1990s'. In T.W. Robinson and D. Shamburg (eds) *Chinese Foreign Policy: Theory and Practice* (pp. 555–602). Oxford: Clarendon Press.

Rocco, E. and Warglien, M. (1995) 'Computer Mediated Communication and the Emergence of "Electronic Opportunitism"'. Working Paper RCC13659, Universita degli Studi di Venezia.

Rogowski, R. (1989) *Commerce and Coalitions*. Princeton, NJ: Princeton University Press.

Ross, R.S. (1986) 'International Bargaining and Domestic Politics: Conflict in U.S.–China Relations Since 1972'. *World Politics* 38(2), pp. 255–287.

Rowlands, I.H. (1995) 'Explaining National Climate Change Policies'. *Global Environmental Change* 5(3) pp. 235–249.

Ruggie, J.G. (1992) 'Multilateralism: the Anatomy of an Institution'. *International Organization* 46(3) pp. 561–598.

Sally, D. (1995) 'Conservation and Cooperation in Social Dilemmas: A Meta-Analysis of Experiments From 1958 to 1992'. *Rationality and Society* 7 pp. 58–92.

Sell, J. and Wilson, R. (1992) 'Liar, Liar, Pants on Fire: Cheap Talk and Signalling in Repeated Public Goods Settings'. Working Paper, Department of Political Science, Rice University.

Sell, J. and Wilson, R. (1991) 'Levels of Information and Contribution to Public Goods'. *Social Forces* 70(1) pp. 107–124.

Simon, H.A. (1997) *Models of Bounded Rationality (Vol. 3): Empirically Grounded Economic Reason*. Cambridge, MA: MIT Press.

Simon, H.A. (1985) 'Human Nature in Politics: The Dialogue of Psychology with Political Science'. *American Political Science Review* 79(2) pp. 293–304.

Soeya, Y. (1998) *Japan's Economic Diplomacy with China, 1945–1978*. Oxford: Clarendon Press.

Snyder, G. and Diesing, P. (1977) *Conflict Among Nations: Bargaining, Decision Making, and System Structure in International Crises*. Princeton, NJ: Princeton University Press.

Snyder, J. (1991) *Myths of Empire: Domestic Politics and International Ambition*. Ithaca, NY: Cornell University Press.

Sprinz, D.F. and Vaahtoranta, T. (1994) 'The Interest-based Explanation of International Environmental Policy'. *International Organization* 4(1) pp. 77–105.

Stein, A. (1993) 'Cooperation and Collaboration: Regimes in an Anarchic World'. In D.A. Baldwin (ed.) *Neorealism and Neoliberalism: The Contemporary Debate*. New York: Columbia University Press.

Tow, W. (1994) 'China and the International Strategic System'. In T. Robinson and D. Shambaugh (eds) *Chinese Foreign Policy: Theory and Practice* (pp. 115–157). Oxford: Oxford University Press.

True, J.L., Jones, B.D., and Baumgartner, F.R. (1999) 'Punctuated-Equilibrium Theory: Explaining Stability and Change in American Policymaking'. In P.A. Sabatier (ed.) *Theories of the Policy Process* (pp. 97–115). Boulder, CO: Westview Press.

Underdal, A. (1998) 'Explaining Compliance and Defection: Three Models'. *European Journal of International Relations* 4(5) pp. 5–30.

Wang, J. (2006) 'Managing National Reputation and International Relations in the Global Era: Public Diplomacy Revisited'. *Public Relations Review* 32(2) pp. 91–96.

Walsh, J.I. (2005) 'Persuasion in International Politics: A Rationalist Account'. *Politics & Policy* 33(4) pp. 1–30.

Walsh, J.I. (1994) 'Institutional Constraints and Domestic Choices: Economic Convergence and Exchange Rate Policy in France and Italy'. *Political Studies* 42(1) pp. 243–258.

Wendt, A. (1987) 'The Agent-Structure Problem in International Relations Theory'. *International Organization* 41(3) pp. 335–370.

Willett, T.D. (1988) 'National Macroeconomic Policy Preferences and International Coordination Issues'. *Journal of Public Policy* 8(3/4) pp. 235–263.

Xierali, I.M. and Liu, L. (2006) 'Explaining Foreign Diplomatic Presence in the U.S. with Spatial Models: A Liberal Spatial Perspective'. *GeoJournal* 67 pp. 85–101.

Zhao, J. and Ortolano, L. (2003) 'The Chinese Government's Role in Implementing Multilateral Environmental Agreements: The Case of the Montreal Protocol'. *The China Quarterly* 175 pp. 708–725.

Zhao, Q. (1996) *Interpreting Chinese Foreign Policy*. Oxford: Oxford University Press.

Zhu, L. (2010) 'The Domestic Sources of China's Foreign Policy and Diplomacy'. In P. Kerr, S. Harris, and Y. Qin (eds) *China's 'New' Diplomacy*. New York: Palgrave Macmillan.

# 3 The *actors* and *processes* of economic policy-making

A study on Chinese economic diplomacy preference formation cannot begin without first understanding the intrinsic nature of the decision-making structure of the central government. In modern Chinese political history, the brutal and scarring century of humiliation – which featured the Opium War of 1840, the collapse of the imperial system in 1911, the subsequent decades of war against Japan, an intermittent conflict between the Nationalist Party (国民党) and the Communist Party of China (CPC, 中国共产党), followed in 1949 by the establishment of the People's Republic of China (PRC, 中华人民共和国) led by the CPC (Collins and Cottey, 2012, pp. 5–6; Clegg, 2009, p. 50) – constitutes a revolutionary period of great significance. The entrenchment of the communist regime not only re-established an independent and functioning Chinese state, but also inaugurated a new political, economic, and social order with features that have defined Chinese politics for the last six decades.

From the macroscopic perspective, China's state structure is a centralised one characterised by a single, cohesive decision-making body unencumbered by the need to achieve agreement from other decision-making bodies.[1] Yet, Chinese politics and processes have also evolved, especially after the death of Mao Zedong – the founding leader of the communist revolution – in 1976. The collective authority that characterises the Chinese government today at the microscopic level of interagency relations within the economic bureaucracy reveals that China's decision-making structure is, in reality, somewhat decentralised. There are multiple decision points and no single actor acts independently. State actions require the overcoming of potential domestic veto points, which are not limited to formalised institutional arrangements, and decision-making actors may even include enterprises whose active support is essential to policy success. Therefore, the centralisation characteristic of Chinese decision-making – particularly concerning economic issues – is not a fixed and absolute one.

Without challenging the fundamental principle of one-party communist rule, China has undergone a significant liberalisation of the state governance since the late 1970s. One important aspect of the liberalisation was a policy to re-engage with the multilateral system. China's growing involvement with and dependence on the world economic system heads the list of reasons for its deepened involvement in international regimes. In turn, membership has provided numerous material benefits to China's development, and active participation in these structures ensured China of an important role in the decisions that affect the world economy on which its development depends (Sutter, 2008, pp. 112–113).

Yet, who decides the approach of China's multilateral economic diplomacy? What does the domestic process look like? The purpose of this chapter is to introduce the relevant policy actors and government departments integral to Beijing's economic diplomacy decision-making process. Given the multilateral context we are working with, it is fitting and pertinent to thereafter explore possible implications of the dynamic relationship between China and international agencies for the decision-making process and structure in Beijing.

## The Chinese political structure

At the Plenary Session of the First Chinese People's Political Consultative Conference (10–31 January 1946), the Common Programme – which established the country's political system – was adopted. According to the Common Programme, the core governance structure of the Chinese political system is as follows: at the apex of the regime is the Political Bureau (or Politburo) of the CPC, which is crystallised in the form of a leadership core (领导合心) that is either a single person (e.g. Mao Zedong) or a group (e.g. as during and after the Deng era). The Politburo oversees the governing regime of the PRC which consists of three major vertical systems (系统): the CPC, the government, and the military. The three major systems operate on five levels: centre (中央); province (圣) (for the Party and the government); prefecture (地); county (线); and township (乡).

In order to effectively control the operations of the political system, this structure is further divided into six major functional sectors (系统 or 口)[2] – a management system known as *guikouguanli* (归口管理) (Lu, 2001, pp. 39–40). Each sector is supervised by a member of the Politburo Standing Committee, and the direct sectoral supervision is conducted through an institutionalised body such as a committee or a non-standing entity such as a Leading Small Group (LSG; 领导小组). The LSGs (consisting of the principals from various government agencies) coordinate between the state bureaucracy and the Party leadership and have the important task of facilitating consensus-building and coordinating decision-making among key political stakeholders.

According to the Constitution of the PRC, the National People's Congress (NPC; 中国共产党全国代表大会) is formally the highest organ of state power (Article 57 of the 1982 PRC Constitution). Among its wide-ranging functions and authority, the NPC has powers to examine and approve the plan for national economic and social development, and examine and approve the State budget (Bo, 2013, p. 18). Next to the NPC is the State Council (de facto cabinet), the executive organ of state administration. According to Article 89(1) of the Constitution, the State Council can "adopt administrative measures, enact Administrative Rules and Regulations, and issue decisions and orders". Led by the Premier, the State Council directs 27 ministries and commissions.

Compared with the NPC, the State Council plays a more important role in economic decision-making for two reasons. First, a majority of economic policies come out of the State Council in the form of State Council administrative rules or departmental regulations. Second, the 1984 NPC Standing Committee resolution requires the NPC working groups to collaborate with the State Council in the research and drafting of legislation for the implementation of economic policies. As such, a majority (80 per cent) of policies adopted by the NPC are proposed by the State Council in the first place.

To be sure, the NPC does play a policy role – its Standing Committee, which convenes in full every two months, is required to deliberate a draft policy in full session at least three times before a vote for release. But this only happens after a consensus has been reached within the State Council and a final draft has been passed to the NPC's Standing Committee Legislative Affairs Commission. Therefore, policies are typically drafted within the State Council and officially approved by the NPC (Table 3.1).

Working in parallel to the State Council is the Party Politburo, headed by the General Secretary of the CPC. The Politburo is the principal administrative mechanism of the CPC, and its Standing Committee is the most powerful body in practice (Collins and Cottey, 2012, p. 41). The Politburo in general consists of members resident in provinces and cities other than Beijing, and is a relatively large institution. Due to its size, the Politburo has often found it too cumbersome to make policy decisions that demand immediate attention. So, in accordance with the Party Constitution adopted at the 12th Party Congress, *de facto* decision-making power rests with the Politburo's Standing Committee.[3] The Standing Committee has traditionally appointed nine of the most powerful CPC leaders to occupy, *ex officio*, China's principal real or formal power loci (Lu, 2001, pp. 39–60), but membership was reduced to seven at the 18th Party Congress.[4]

The Standing Committee meets weekly to endorse a wide range of decisions, and one Committee member in particular takes charge of the foreign affairs sector (外事口). This person also acts as the head of the Central Committee's Foreign Affairs Work Leading Small Group (FAWLSG; 中国中央外事工作领导小组). Though the Politburo Standing Committee wields substantial decision-making power, it does not deny the relevance of the preeminent leader of the

*Table 3.1* Policy type and associated policy actors

| Policy type | Level issued | Approval authority |
| --- | --- | --- |
| Law (法律) | Drafted by Ministry or Commission/Coordinated by State Council Legislative Affairs Office/Passed to NPC | National People's Congress |
| State Council Regulation (行政法规) | Drafted by Ministry or Commission/Coordinated by State Council Legislative Affairs Office | State Council Executive Committee |

PRC. Former Presidents of the PRC Jiang Zemin and Hu Jintao have both exerted a significant role in economic diplomacy decision-making on the basis of the 'three-in-one' (三比一) principle. The formula seeks to better coordinate policy by permitting the government's 'Number One' to be appointed commander-in-chief on the one hand, and, as President, to be received abroad with the protocol reserved for heads of state on the other (Cabestan, 2009, p. 69).[5] However, owing to the opacity of the CPC-led political system, the preeminent leader's powers are much harder to delineate than those of the President of the United States, for instance.

### *The bureaucracy*

Mapping the constellation of bureaucratic agencies in economic diplomacy decision-making is a challenging task for two reasons. First, the governance of economic diplomacy in the PRC is often blurred with general diplomacy and foreign economic policy, which makes it difficult to distinguish a specific selection of agencies solely responsible for economic diplomacy. Second, every economic issue is interrelated to a series of different issue-areas, which implies the need to coordinate with a range of different domestic agencies, although these may vary between different economic issues. This makes it challenging to identify just one set of actors. For the purpose of this study, an indicative list (rather than an absolute list) of actors relevant to climate change and international trade is considered.

Before we do so, however, it is useful to briefly explain the structure inside a typical Chinese ministry or commission.[6] According to *Article 90* of the Constitution, the ministries and commissions under the State Council can "issue orders, directives, and regulations within the jurisdiction of their respective departments". These are generally referred to as "department regulations" (部门规章). Structurally, each ministry or commission consists of a division of labour among the Vice Ministers and Assistant Ministers, with each taking charge of a number of regional and functional departments (司) or bureaux (居) in an arrangement similar to the practice of sectoral control by the Politburo Standing Committee. Each department or bureau has one chief officer in charge of the overall work of the department and also the work of one or two divisions (除). They are assisted by two deputy chiefs, each of whom takes charge of a number of divisions. Further down the chain of command, a division chief is assisted by two deputy chiefs, with each in charge of a particular aspect of the division's responsibility.

In a number of bureaucracies there is another layer of power structure defined by sections (科).[7] According to the internal regulations, department officials have the power to oversee day-to-day operations within their respective jurisdictions under established rules. The proposed action is often referred to the responsible ministerial leader for ratification. In the case of matters that have no rules or precedents to follow, it is usually up to the ministerial leadership (and above) to make the final call (Lu, 2001, pp. 55–57). Since the ministerial officials' futures rest on the level of their professional effectiveness as administrators, government agencies are generally very protective of their ministerial interests and object-ives. With this said, ministers are still answerable to the Politburo and the State Council, and are required to regularly discuss with the Secretaries of the minis-terial Party Committees before they carry out policy deliberation. Depending on the nature of the policy in question, the minister will usually direct the relevant departments and oversee implementation.

### Climate change policy actors

Political debates on climate change began in the 1980s, initially led by the China Meteorological Administration (CMA), although it was still subject to the State Council (Ye *et al.*, 2007, p. 9). The CMA's expertise shortage soon promoted the National Environmental Protection Administration (NEPA, renamed the Ministry of Environmental Protection or MEP in 2008) to lead the climate change policy development. The NEPA/MEP was primarily responsible for environmental decision-making and the implementation of regulations. Addi-tionally, it took charge of the overall coordination, supervision and management of key environmental issues.

By the mid-1990s, the Department of Treaty and Law under the Ministry of Foreign Affairs (MFA; 中华人民共和国外交部) was allocated the responsib-ility to supervise works related to the international climate change organisations and agreements, and to ensure that China's political and economic interests were served at multilateral negotiations. The MFA is an executive agency responsible for day-to-day economic diplomacy decision-making. In addition, it plays a deci-sive role in the *tactical* aspect of the process. That is, when *strategic* policy deci-sions are made by the central leadership, they often consist of no more than a vague concept, basic policy orientation, broad policy guideline, or long-term policy goal – just the 'bones' of policy. So it is generally up to the MFA to make *tactical* policy choices and work out detailed plans for the realisation of the lead-ership's policy goals, and add the 'flesh and blood' to China's international eco-nomic policy. Acting as the primary spokespersons of China, the MFA's input in decision-making (knowledge, assessments, and professional experience) should not be underestimated.

However, the Ministry is only one of a diverse array of bureaucracies influen-cing the preferences of China's economic diplomacy. Major foreign policy deci-sions are made at a higher level, in power loci such as the Central Finance and Economics Leading Small Group (CFELSG; 中国财经领导小组). And yet, as a provider of processed information to central decision-makers, the MFA has the capacity to significantly shape policy outcomes. And among the Chinese bureau-cracies, the central leadership regards the MFA as a more reliable provider of information than other sources (Lu, 2001, pp. 50–52).[8] For these reasons, the MFA's inputs often play a significant role in shaping the central leadership's perceptions; and the MFA's policy recommendations usually prevail over other bureaucratic agencies in the battle for the leadership's attention.

When the senior leaders began to recognise the effects of climate change on China's energy security, economic development, and quality of life, various institutional arrangements were made to address climate change. One such arrangement was the establishment of the National Coordination Committee on Climate Change (NCCCC) in 1998. The NCCCC comprises 15 government agencies, chaired by the former State Development Planning Commission (SDPC, reformed into the National Development and Reform Commission or NDRC in 2003) and represents the highest climate change decision-making body in Beijing.[9] It facilitates the formulation of China's preferences and multilateral climate change negotiation positions.

By 2003, the NDRC (国家发展和改革委员) took over all climate change policy coordination responsibilities, including undertakings on the coordination of energy-saving and emissions reduction policies.[10] Moreover, the NDRC was charged with leading the Chinese delegation to the Conference of Parties (COPs) negotiations and ensuring that China fulfils its obligations under the United Nations Framework Convention on Climate Change (UNFCCC). The move indicates a shift in the relative value that the CPC attaches to the climate change issue as well as a transformed governmental conceptualisation of the issue from a purely scientific issue to a predominantly developmental one (Bang *et al.*, 2005). The move also reflected the clear need to coordinate climate change policy with energy decisions.

In 2007, the State Council created a working group tasked to ensure climate change responses and the reduction of gas emissions. The working group is called the National Working Group for Addressing Climate Change and Energy Savings (国家应对气候变化和捷能剑派工作小组), and it is headed by the Premier (formerly this was Wen Jiabao; at the time of writing it is Li Keqiang). The Office of this working group was launched within the NDRC (NDRC, 2007). The MFA had also established its own LSG in charge of international works on climate change, headed by its then Minister, Yang Jiechi (Le, 2007). However, its scope of action is narrower and its coordination power relatively weak. To be sure, the LSG is not, by definition, a decision-making organ. However, its preferences are likely to influence the final outcome. The ratification of these decisions by the central leadership is sometimes simply a formality, while at other times decisions are made by the central leadership in accordance with the suggestions of the LSG with minor modifications. Since decisions at this level often involve cross-ministerial jurisdiction or interest, the LSGs therefore play a pivotal role in the decision-making processes.

The Ministry of Finance (MOF) plays a crucial role as an operational focal point for the Global Environmental Facility (GEF) projects in China. The MOF's Department of International Cooperation acts as a window-agency through which much of the international funding for climate change projects from development banks, such as the World Bank and the Asian Development Bank, are transferred. Other periphery actors include the Ministry of Agriculture (MOA), the Ministry of Science and Technology (MOST), the Ministry of Water Resources, the Ministry of Land and Natural Resources, and the State Forestry Administration.

Beyond government agencies, the epistemic communities play a crucial advocacy role in climate change decision-making. Such institutions include the Chinese Academy of Sciences, the National Climate Center, and Chinese Academy of Social Sciences (CASS), among others. Academic institutions, including Tsinghua University, Peking University, and Nanjing University, make similar contributions to climate change research in China. Meanwhile, many professional associations within China have produced work relating to climate change issues. Among the associations are the China Association for Science and Technology, the Chinese Society of Forestry, and the Ecological Society of China. The epistemic communities actively organise occasions where they promote the exchange of ideas and findings on climate change issues. Additionally, international agencies have, in recent years, further established local committees in China, and have made positive contributions to China's climate change efforts (Ye *et al.*, 2007, p. 9). Particular examples include the International Geo-Biosphere Program (IGBP), the World Climate Research Program (WCRP), and the Earth System Science Partnership (ESSP).

### International trade policy actors

The organisational structure that governs China's international trade decision-making is a complex matrix which requires extensive bargaining and coordination. Once the Politburo's Standing Committee has established the basic strategic decisions,[11] the bulk of the policy decisions rest within the State Council structure that consist of a nucleus core – where most of the official decision-making authorities are concentrated – and a set of orbiting agencies (Pearson, 2001, p. 346). At the centre of the nucleus are the President and the Premier. Deng Xiaoping sanctioned the decision to seek membership of the General Agreement on Trade and Tariffs (GATT) in the mid-1980s. Jiang Zemin and Hu Jintao have since kept that commitment. Often the President defers to the opinion of the Premier as to what constitutes an acceptable package, and the Premier will in turn receive inputs from interested Parties, such as reports from the Ministry of Commerce (MOFCOM; 商务部), the World Trade Organization Leading Small Group (WTOLSG), the FAWLSG, and the CFELSG.[12] Chaired by the Premier, the CFELSG coordinates activities within the MOFCOM and the MFA, resolves friction, when necessary, between these two ministries (Ding, 2008); and supervises the activities of the China Investment Corporation (CIC) – an agency that oversees China's US$200 billion sovereign wealth fund (Weisman, 2008). The LSGs sanction most of the formal negotiation positions to the WTO.

Since China commenced serious negotiations to join the WTO, MOFCOM (successor of the Ministry of Foreign Trade and Economic Cooperation (MOFTEC, 对外贸易经济合作部)) has become an integral part of the multilateral trade negotiations decision-making process. It is an executive agency under the State Council, primarily responsible for formulating Chinese policies on foreign trade, export and import regulations, foreign direct investments, consumer protection, market competition, and negotiating bilateral and multilateral trade agreements. MOFCOM claims the largest number of WTO-related economic and legal experts among its ranks, and it supervises economic missions abroad including foreign aid programmes. In addition, it plays an important role in identifying potential sources of access to energy products and other raw materials, as well as new market and investment opportunities for Chinese companies (in particular, but not exclusively, state-owned enterprises (SOEs)).

Since decisions on China's foreign trade and economic relations are considered less sensitive politically than other foreign policy issues, the MOFCOM often has a higher degree of policy authority than the MFA, though many issues within its purview are run through the CFELSG (Lu, 2001, p. 52). Despite MOFCOM's large role in the WTO affairs, its authority is limited due to the distinctively divided responsibilities among different ministries. For example, the People's Bank of China (PBOC) has the primary responsibility to negotiate on finance (i.e. currency convertibility, banking, and securities); the Ministry of Information Industries (MOID) take the lead in telecommunications negotiations; the MOF on accounting and insurance services; the MOA on market access for agricultural products; and the Ministry of Internal Trade on distribution. Moreover, the MOFCOM does not actually have an official capacity to authorise package deals negotiated at the multilateral level; instead, it must report back to the LSGs and the State Council for the final approval. For these reasons, the MOFCOM's direct authority on negotiations becomes watered down.

The MOFCOM's WTO Division is responsible for the day-to-day WTO affairs. Although the WTO division is formally under the International Trade and Economic Affairs Department of the MOFCOM, it reports directly to the Vice Minister due to the importance of its work. It works under the guidance of senior officials, determines the implications of their assigned tasks, accumulates and assimilates policy reports and analyses crafted by research institutes, participates in negotiations, and reports back to its superiors on the negotiation outcomes. Additionally, the WTO division coordinates China's negotiation positions with relevant and interested bureaus and industries (i.e. responds to external interests on any aspect of the negotiations and integrates them into the overall position). Any interagency disputes that cannot be resolved between the divisions are then referred to the minster of MOFCOM for coordination, usually through a process of bargaining.

Two additional economic agencies under the State Council that matter in economic decision-making include the MOF and the PBOC. The MOF is charged with managing the state budget, financial and tax policies, and hard currency reserves, among other duties. It also plays a primarily macro-level role in the reform of the financial management systems of SOEs and other public institutions, by monitoring the local budgetary and construction fund spending, for instance. Meanwhile, the PBOC is China's central bank and a core agency for the making of monetary policies. Among its duties are monetary policy research, monetary policy formulation and implementation, and target setting (Liew, 2004, p. 28). In addition, it maintains payment and settlement systems, supervises financial institutions, and oversees the State Administration of Foreign Exchange (SAFE).

An agency that works closely with the MOF and the SAFE is the State Administration of Taxation (SAT). Its responsibilities include formulating and administering China's tax regime, which includes tax incentives for investors. Meanwhile, the China Securities Regulatory Commission (CSRC) and the China Banking Regulatory Commission (CBRC) work hand-in-hand with the PBOC. The former regulates bonds, stocks, and mutual fund markets, while the latter oversees the banking system of China. Both the MOF and the PBOC participate in the policy processes for international trade and financial negotiations, not just as domestic interest players but also representing their interest abroad as representatives of the Chinese delegation.

Beyond the core structure are peripheral actors that, at times, impose influence on policy outcomes. These actors include the economic commissions and cross-functional bureaus of the central government. They are responsible for ensuring that China's overall economic interests are integrated in both the negotiations and the coordination meetings. Other actors include the local governments and industries, which have grown more active in the negotiations in recent years. Overall, China's international trade decision-making power remains concentrated with the elite few, though the decision-making process has evolved; the constellation of organisations involved varies, depending on the issue of concern.

## The evolution of China's economic diplomacy decision-making

Since the establishment of the PRC, Beijing's decision-making has evolved through three key stages. The first stage is the *exclusionist* era (1949–1971) where China was isolated from the multilateral system, in part due to its own decision and in part because of the decisions of others. The second stage is the *transition* era (1972–2002), which was a period of rapid integration with the multilateral system, albeit with China often projecting itself through modest capacities. Since 2003, China has transitioned to the *revisionist* era, which constitutes the third stage. Not only has it become a more active international political and economic actor, it has also begun to question some of the structures and norms of the multilateral system.

Numerous studies have often been fascinated with questions of whether Beijing's active and sceptical orientation poses a fundamental challenge to the international economic order (e.g. Harding, 2011; Clegg, 2009; Sutter, 2008) and whether China can be accommodated through relatively modest and evolutionary changes in the structure and norms of the international economic system (e.g. Guo 2013; Chan *et al.*, 2012; Schlichting, 2008). However, few scholars have looked at the nexus of China's political reforms and its evolving relationship with the multilateral system. In contrast to the prevalent literature that assumes a static decision-making process in China (e.g. Lai, 2010; Lu, 2001; Lieberthal and Oksenberg, 1988) this section illustrates a dynamic decision-making process shaped by its deepening integration with the multilateral system. This effect is noted in the concept of "institutional adaptation" which refers to the "long-term substitution of existing practices and structures with new ones" not just in response to multilateral commitments and the demands of international agencies, but also as a proactive attempt to mediate those forces and maximise the ability of the state to manoeuvre effectively in the remaining or residual policy space (Zhao, 1996, p. 25).

### The exclusion era: 1949–1971

Immediately after the establishment of the new Chinese government, Beijing attempted to re-establish its international recognition and legitimation in the international community by making efforts to regain its seat in the UN. At the time, China's attitude towards multilateral organisations was generally positive. But this quest proved elusive, largely because the US refused to recognise the PRC, causing China to become increasingly critical of the multilateral order.[13] In turn, the PRC adopted a unilateralist diplomatic strategy and an isolationist attitude towards all western-led international agencies, viewing them as imperialist mechanisms designed to undermine national sovereignty and hamper the development of international socialism (Lanteigne, 2005, p. 145). At the same time, China refused to join international agencies established by the Soviet Union. Beijing did, of course, enter a bilateral military alliance with the Soviet Union in 1950, and accepted Soviet aid and advice on central planning in the mid-1950s. But Beijing refused to join the Council for Mutual Economic Assistance (CMEA) (Harding, 2011, p. 26). Instead, the Chinese leaders preferred to conduct their ties with the Third World on a bilateral basis, only to attenuate most of these relationships during the Cultural Revolution (1966–1976). During this period, China's foreign policy focused on national security issues. Foreign trade and economic aid were but instruments for the realisation of China's international political and security objectives. Hence, the concept of economic diplomacy was absent from its foreign policy agenda.

As a result, decision-making was considered as a sensitive area, and always it was officially claimed 'there is no trivial matter in foreign affairs' (外事无小事). Hitherto, Beijing's general diplomacy decision-making process under Mao was a classic socialist model. The state operated in a hierarchical system characterised by a one-person domination (Mao Zedong) over a single vertical command system (Zhang, 1996, pp. 80–81). Major decision-making was determined by Mao Zedong, with a limited degree of top leadership involved in some key decision-making. Premier Zhou Enlai and a few top leaders were mainly implementers of Mao's ideological visions in foreign policy strategies and policies (Barnett, 1985, p. 7). The rest of the political institutions and government agencies participated in a demand system of decision-making.

### The transition era: 1972–2002

In the 1970s, two developments triggered a renewed interest in Beijing in gravitating towards multilateralism. The first was the 1971 decision by the UN

General Assembly to pass *Resolution 1758*, which legitimately restored the PRC's rights in the institution. The US realised that China's communist regime was not a passing phenomenon and the prospects of the Nationalist government of Taiwan recovering the mainland were becoming remote. And given its large population, its economic resources, and strategic location, China would most likely become a major power in Asia. For these reasons, the US concluded that continuing to isolate China from the international system would be a mistake (Harding, 2011, p. 27). Consequently, Washington supported the restoration of the PRC's seat within the UN.

Regaining membership at the UN motivated Beijing to join other international regimes, although it also kept its involvement at a relatively modest level, by initially joining only a small number of UN agencies (Gill, 2010).[14] Their prudence stemmed from the Maoist suspicion that the multilateral system is dominated by foreign powers pursuing selfish interests at odds with China's. The other reason was the lack of experience within the MFA and the greater Chinese government apparatus with respect to engaging with international agencies, following the chaos of the Cultural Revolution (Sutter, 2008, p. 114). With this said, Beijing believed that joining the international economic order could provide China with concrete economic benefits which the country desperately needed.[15] The members of the international financial and trading systems appeared eager to make direct investments in China and to buy Chinese exports if they were inexpensive and well made. Chinese leaders recognised that the encouragement of inward foreign investment – tentatively at first, and then increasingly enthusiastically – could provide not only the capital and technology, but also the designs, brands, and marketing channels, all of which could greatly enhance China's export potential (Harding, 2011, p. 28).

China realised it would benefit from supporting the international financial institutions it had once scorned, including the IMF and, to an even greater extent, the World Bank. This support was not primarily financial, even though China later accepted loans from the World Bank.[16] What was more useful to China was the technical policy advice relating to economic reform and modernisation, all of which Beijing studied carefully and effectively implemented. Having put aside the Maoist practices, Chinese officials accumulated more experience engaging with international agencies, and the perceived benefits of integration overshadowed the earlier approach of restricting multilateral engagements throughout the 1980s and 1990s.

This brings us to the second development. By the late 1970s, the growing international economic interdependence coupled with China's desperate need for hard capital – in order to pull itself out of the economic despair – required the Chinese leadership, led by Deng Xiaoping, to place economic issues within the foreign policy context. Deng ensured Mao's zero-sum thinking gave way to a gradualist approach by joining the Western economic system – a strategy he characterised as "crossing a river by feeling the stones" (Lanteigne, 2005, pp. 60–61).[17] In 1978 during the third plenary session of the 11th Central Committee of the CPC, the government decided to shift its foreign policy focus from national security to economic modernisation. Rhetoric such as 'keeping in line with the international track' (与国际接轨), 'behaving according to international norms' (按照国际管理办事), and 'engaging in the international society' (参与国际社会) became part of the popular discourse within the political apparatus. Deng Xiaoping famously said, "The colour of the cat does not matter, as long as the mice are caught."

As opening up gathered further momentum in the 1980s and 1990s, and as Beijing sought to shift its national strategy from system-transformation to system-reformation, it became evident that 'politics in command' gave way to the idea that politics should serve the economy. In 1980, Beijing restored its membership of the Bretton Woods institutions (Kim, 1999, pp. 46–47). Soon it became the World Bank's largest country borrower, and worked closely with the IMF on economic development policies and other related technical training. After that, China's multilateral memberships nearly doubled between 1984 and 1996 (from 29 to 51) (Sutter, 2008, pp. 114, 117). By this time, the Chinese government appeared to truly have accepted multilateralism as a platform for promoting itself as an attractive economic opportunity (Pearson, 2006).

Towards the late 1990s, Beijing recognised its economic and diplomatic success placed it in a more prominent position to operate more actively within world affairs. Equally important was Beijing's growing concern with the so-called American unilateralism and 'hegemony'. Promoting multilateralism was, in turn, considered a useful fall-back position for guarding against US unilateralism. This also helped China build international coalitions in favour of a more 'democratic' world economic order that would not be dominated by US leadership (Carlson, 2006).

However, having been largely isolated from the multilateral system for much of the twentieth century, China was ill-equipped to handle interactions with it (Jacobson and Oksenberg, 1990). To address domestic inadequacies, Beijing strengthened ministerial staff training, and set up a UN Small Group in the Bank of China.[18] This group facilitated and assisted in the costs-and-benefits analysis of acceding to UN financial agencies. To ensure effective engagements with multilateral economic activities, Beijing implemented major administrative reforms from the individual to collective decision-making. Deng realised that this form of decentralisation was necessary, as the country's integration with the multilateral system had made its foreign relations more complex. For this reason, retaining the same high level of concentration in decision-making power as Mao became impossible.[19] These sentiments were expressed in a speech by Deng entitled 'On the Reform of the System of Party and State Leadership' addressed to the enlarged meeting of the Political Bureau of the Central Committee of the Party on 18 August 1980 (Zhou, 2012, p. 27).[20] The preponderant role of the paramount leader was subsequently reduced for the advancement of the power of the nuclear circle in economic diplomacy decision-making (Lampton, 2001). There is no longer a chairman of the CPC Central Committee, just a Secretary-General, who is responsible for convening the meetings of the Politburo and its Standing Committee and presiding over the work of the Secretariat (Zhou, 2012, p. 30).[21]

Lessening Mao's model of one-person domination, Deng retreated from active involvement in policy decisions on key economic issues such as the normalisation of economic relations with the US, and allowed Zhao Ziyang (third Premier) and Hu Yaobang (Party General Secretary), for instance, to make key economic decisions. This change gave birth to new power centres on a par with the paramount leader (Zhao, 1996, pp. 83–84). These power centres are not institutionalised, but based on personal prestige and connections; moreover, the power centres often had conflicting policy opinions. For instance, Chen Yun (senior revolutionary leader) famously clashed with Deng over China's economic development policy directions. While Deng favoured rapid growth at the expense of stability, Chen stressed stability over growth (稳定压倒一切) (Dittmer and Wu, 1995, p. 493).

By the turn of the third generation of leadership, economic affairs became so prominent that Deng and his colleagues felt it was necessary to promote technocrats such as Jiang Zemin, Li Peng, and Zhu Rongji up the political ladder, all of whom successfully arrived at the centre of political power in the 1990s. Because these technocrats individually lacked absolute authority, collective decision-making replaced earlier vertical authoritarianism. As Jiang explained in his political report to the 16th Party Congress in 2002, attention has been paid to the horizontal division of decision-making power whereby it has been rationally divided, legalised and institutionalised according to the different functions of the ruling Party and state organs (Zhou, 2012, p. 29).

In order to manage the dismantling of the planned economy, and the complex issues being negotiated at the multilateral level, the leaders felt the need to reform its administrative structure and operations in order to serve their fast-developing economy as well as the needs of its multilateral memberships. The restructuring in 1982 aimed to reduce the unusually large numbers of ministries and commissions under the State Council, which had soared to 100 in 1981. These were reduced to 61.[22] In addition, State Councillors and State Council Executive Meetings were created to aid the work of the Premier (head of the State Council). Older officials were replaced with younger cadres that had the right political and professional credentials (Lee, 1991; Whyte, 1989). The 1993 restructuring reduced the number of employees of agencies under the State Council by 20 per cent and that of the local government (administration) by 25 per cent (Lai, 2013, p. 49).

To ensure an international level of professionalism in its domestic decision-making processes, Beijing established a supra-ministerial coordination body to replace existing agencies, including the SDPC. As a leading agency in the planning of China's economic and industrial developments during the planned economy era, the SDPC was effective in aggregating interests and coordinating decision-making because the lacklustre formal market regulation provided it adequate autonomy to plan and project authority, and it had specialised sections that would directly interact with its counterpart (对口) sector.[23] Since acquiring international memberships, the need to treat the market in a liberal manner implied that indirect economic levers of economic policies had replaced the old administrative tools of central planning as the standard instrument of short-term macroeconomic management (Liew, 2004, p. 35).

As a result, the continuing use of the SDPC would be problematic for two reasons. First, the SDPC had a predisposition for central planning and therefore had vested interests in the perpetuation of the status quo. This essentially implies the SDPC's inability to act with impartiality.[24] Second, a move to market regulation *via* legislation (usually required by protocols of international regimes) meant that a body with legal expertise was better suited to act in a coordination capacity (Becker, 2006, pp. 148–149). Other organs such as the Central and State Council LSGs were also found inappropriate to play a coordination role due to partisan interests, inadequate professional staff, and their overloaded responsibilities.

One solution was to convert the CFELSG into the supreme decision-making organ following a process of decentralisation in 1993 (Liew, 2004, p. 25). The leaders expanded the role of the various departments (办公室) under the CFELSG to perform tasks including coordinating various subgroups, supervising the CFELSG's research office (研究室), and commissioning external research projects. In addition, they assist the CFELSG and the Standing Committee of the Politburo in their policy deliberation and supervision by producing reports and position papers. Given the nature of its work, the Director of the departments is therefore highly influential in decision-making. Arguably, at times their influence surpasses the Politburo members of the non-standing committee as they work directly under the top leadership. For example, when the departments decided to devalue the RMB in 1994, this was taken straight to the Politburo's Standing Committee before informing other members of the State Council of their decision. The remaining members of the Politburo were unaware of this decision until it was announced by the State Council (Liew, 2004, p. 28).

The multiplying volume of policy concerns dealt with at the multilateral level also prompted China to urgently expand the roles and capacities of its ministries/commissions. In 1998, when China was preparing to push for WTO entry, the government was restructured to better regulate the emerging market economy. Several new ministries were created to manage increasingly important aspects or sectors of the economy. These include the Ministry of Human Resources and Social Security, the Ministry of Land and Resources, the Ministry of Industry and Information Technology, and the National Drug Administration. A number of ministries that oversaw SOEs and heavy industry were abolished, reducing the institutional leverage of the SOEs. Instead, the former State Economic and Trade Commission (SETC) was empowered to supervise SOEs and assumed a new and prominent role concerning macroeconomic management. Other prominent regulatory commissions include the China Securities Regulatory Commission, formed in 1992 for overseeing securities, and the China Insurance Regulatory Commission, set up in late 1998 to supervise the insurance industry. The number of departments under the State Council shrank significantly from 40 to 29 (Lai, 2013, pp. 49–50).

In January 2000, the State Council Legislative Affairs Office (SCLAO) held a meeting to discuss the rule of law revisions necessitated by multilateral membership. The meeting was reportedly attended by the heads of the legal departments of all relevant ministries and commissions. During the meeting, the departments were instructed to clean up their own rules and regulations in order to comply with international rules (Jin and Zhang, 2001). On 19 September 2001, the CPC Party Central Committee General Office and the State Council General Office announced that various ministries and commissions had sorted out more than 2,200 laws, rules and regulations, two-thirds of which were in the foreign economic and trade system. Approximately 116 items needed to be revised, 573 needed to be abolished, and 26 new items needed to be drawn up (Becker, 2006, p. 159).

This era saw increasing numbers of government agencies marshal differentiated information in support of their preferences and interests, which were often in conflict with other agencies. Government departments were encouraged to be more self-supporting and the capacity among and within the government bureaucracy to work vigorously in protection of their interests throughout the decision-making processes was strengthened. At the same time, there was a general decline in the heavy inclination for ideological instruments, and the trend towards decentralisation in personnel management enabled many government agencies to become policy entrepreneurs. Collectively, these systemic and structural changes reduced the extent to which government agencies respond to the orders from higher levels as they have done in the past (Lieberthal, 1992, pp. 8–9). Hence, there were numerous reporting lines throughout the system, functional as well as territorial organs with resultant problems of governance. One territorial level organisation contains within it several bureaucratic ranks. A unit cannot issue binding orders to another unit at the same bureaucratic rank, not even if it is at a higher territorial level. Each territorial unit still has considerable power to control the unit one level down; therefore, bureaucrats at every level spend volumes of time negotiating for more flexibility (Yu, 2008, p. 33).

At each level of the organisational hierarchy, government representatives make decisions by a rule of consensus. If they all agree, the decision is automatically ratified by the higher hierarchy. If the bureaucrats cannot reach consensus, then the decision is referred to the senior officials, and if they fail to reach an agreement, then either nothing happens or the CPC intervenes with a solution (Shirk, 1992, p. 68). Due to the 'selfish departmentalism' nature of government departments, each seeking to advance their own interests, the consequences of this system mean that, first, the speed of the decision-making process is generally slow, and the consensus-building process tends to be protracted. Second, it is relatively difficult to identify when a decision has actually been made (Lampton, 1992, pp. 57–58).

In these contexts, the process of decision-making transitioned from vertical authoritarianism to a collective decisions-making system. The first stage is the framing of opinions by the relevant heads of divisions. They discuss their opinions with the division chiefs for an agreement. Selected others, or the whole division, may join the discussion if necessary. A draft proposal is worked out at this level before the issue goes to the department directors. The pooling of wisdom guarantees that in most cases the suggestions of the division are accepted. The directors of the department then sign the document with some technical amendments or alterations and hand it over to the minister or vice minister. If the issue is of a routine or less important nature and within the ministerial competence, then the proposal is ratified directly and enters the implementation stage so long as other Ministers turn on their green lights. Otherwise, it travels to the top leadership for a final decision.[25] At any given level from the department up, the co-signature of at least two leading persons in charge is required for most cases before the issue advances further. When a significant difference of opinion occurs, the matter is handed back down with the views of the higher body for reconsideration. On such occasions or on critical and urgent issues, a top leader or a minister may directly consult his or her subordinates or call a meeting of relevant persons in the hierarchy (Yang, 1995, pp. 95–96).

When an issue falls into the jurisdiction of more than one department in a ministry or ministries, the primary department responsible for the case is obliged to initiate interdepartmental or inter-ministerial consultations and take up the drafting of the proposal. The process also starts at the division level and goes up step-by-step, following the same procedure, as described above. Inter-department consultations are coordinated among the corresponding divisions or departments when necessary. The document must be co-signed by all the departments involved before it is delivered to the proper authority for final ruling. Disagreement by any Party indicates inadequate consultation among the participants, and renegotiation is required until a consensus is reached.

### The revisionist era: 2003–2012

Since 2003, signals have indicated a new round of political transformations aimed at more sophisticated, constructive and confident approaches to international economic affairs. This has embraced the constellation of international agencies, their rules and norms, as a means to promote the national interest. China has insisted on being treated as a shareholder, and not just as a stakeholder – in other words, as an actor that has the right to participate in the making of decisions, not just one that is affected by their outcomes. At the IMF and the World Bank, China sought for expanded shares of the capital – and thus a greater share of the votes.[26] China also began to question some of the norms that underlie the multilateral system, as seen in its activities within the WTO. What is more, China further proposed the formation of new multilateral regimes to fill in the gaps within the existing institutional structure, and use them to either replace or complement regimes which are not performing well. For instance, China played a major role in creating the Shanghai Cooperation Organisation (SCO), and its more cautious endorsement of the East Asian Summit (or ASEAN+6) reflect the widespread disappointment with the accomplishments of APEC. By organising the Boao Forum, China endeavoured to create an Asian equivalent of the World Economic Forum in Davos. In 2011, a Chinese citizen became a deputy managing director of the IMF. Likewise, in June 2008, Justin Yifu Lin, a Chinese national, became the World Bank's chief economist. These developments reflect China's rising influence in the multilateral system.

Beijing's proactive approach towards international agencies led the leadership's new appreciation of the notion of economic diplomacy as an important instrument for dealing with international economic affairs. As in previous years, Chinese leaders argued that a proactive approach to multilateral economic negotiations is not possible without an efficient and professional administrative system. Therefore, a sequence of restructuring took place in 2003, after China entered the WTO. The government was reformed in order to serve a highly internationalised and marketised economy. The SDPC was renamed the NDRC, and the SETC was reorganised into the MOFCOM. In light of the new issues, the National Drug Administration was restructured into the National Food and Drug Administration, and additionally the National Administration of Work Safety was set up. In order to supervise the performance of SOEs and state banks, the State Asset Supervision and Administration Commission (SASAC) and the China Banking Regulatory Commission, respectively, were established (Zou, 2008, pp. 153–162). Finally, the National Electricity Regulatory Commission was formed in 2003 to oversee the electricity sector (Lai, 2013, p. 50).

In general, economic diplomacy decision-making became less personalised and more institutionalised. In particular, Hu Jintao paid greater attention to formal institutions in decision-making, laid a greater emphasis on proactive and pragmatic diplomacy, and, compared with his predecessors, he collaborated more closely with Premier Wen Jiabao in administering foreign economic affairs, as Xi Jinping continues to do today with Premier Li Keqiang. Because Wen relied on the State Council and, especially, the MFA, his close working relationship with Hu elevated the relevant departments along with the process, and granted them a greater role in external economic affairs than previously (Lai, 2010, p. 37, 154).

But the bureaucratic influence does not stop at the MFA threshold. Central decision-makers today are much more susceptible to bureaucratic influence, particularly by ministerial perspectives, than previous leaders. Although the Politburo Standing Committee remains the most important general body in economic diplomacy decision-making, the MFA and the MOFCOM now have the capacity to execute economic policies. Meanwhile, top functional agencies like the CFELSG and the FAWLSG continue to specialise in managing day-to-day affairs, and drafting proposals for foreign economic policies. As in the previous era, competing inter-ministerial interests are still apparent within this apparatus, making bargaining equally important in inter-agency coordination.

In general, the top leaders deal with the key policies and oversee the wider and larger political future (e.g. the maintenance of social stability) and leave the ministries to set the policies of foreign economic affairs (due to a lack of time and expertise).[27] This implies that ministerial-level actors now enjoy increased authority to execute policy decisions and day-to-day affairs. Similarly, while

China has divided economic decision-making authority among its sprawling CPC apparatus and government departments, interest group politics, idiosyncratic preferences of individual top leaders, factional considerations, provincial governments' lobbying, think tank advocacy, and business actors' lobbying of their interests in the early stages of decision-making all contribute to the functioning of preference formation.[28] Of course, the central body retains the utmost decision-making power,[29] and the key departments, technocratic expertise and coordination mechanisms (i.e. regular top-level meetings) manage the process (Pei, 2011).

In terms of process, the decision-making of multilateral economic policies today are as follows. Once the SCLAO has compiled the legislative plans (立法 工作安排), a State Council Secretary-General Conference is convened, which reviews the draft plans, and make amendments where necessary.[30] A review of recent legislative plans indicates that multilateral commitments and timelines dominate the PRC's economic legislative agenda. Upon the approval of the plans, the relevant ministries and commissions are designated assignments, marking the beginning of the policy design process. Policy drafting occurs internally, and if the policy involves more than one ministry or commission, a joint drafting team may be set up to begin the process of research and writing. The ministry or commission in charge of coordinating the process typically invites experts in to give advice at this point.

Select ministries and commissions, thereafter, bargain between themselves in an effort to coordinate a policy consensus. It is at this point that the policy pathologies have an opportunity to wreak havoc with the policy process. In the absence of a strong policy coordination body, policies can easily get bogged down in endless rounds of negotiations, abandoned altogether in the face of bureaucratic refusals to come to a consensus, or pushed up to a higher level for possible resolution in an 'escalation of coordination'. As a result of the demands of being a participant of the multilateral processes, there exists today a much more extensive process of consultation and bargaining aimed at not only crafting a domestic consensus in a timely manner, but also reconciling domestic interests to the greatest extent possible with international pressures and commitments.

Once the policy has been drafted and an agreement has been reached among the ministries and commissions, one of several things can happen depending on the type of policy being created. If the policy is routine in nature and falls logically under an existing NPC law or State Council regulation, then, after drafting the departmental regulation internally, the ministry or commission will pass the policy independently, and no higher approval is needed. If, however, the SCLAO finds the policy to be in contradiction of existing international agreements, the policy will be returned to the ministry or commission for amendment. This latter process is critical as it ensures China's ability to comply with the terms of its international agreements and maintain credibility (Figure 3.1).

The process is a bit more complex if the issue affects more than one ministry or commission. Generally speaking, this is the case with most economic policies

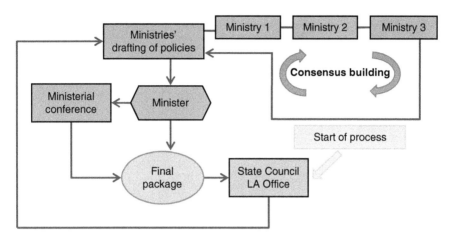

*Figure 3.1* Departmental decision-making processes.

today. For example, the MOFCOM, which has the office that handles WTO issues, is often a second Party on many policies, as is the State Tax Administration. In cases such as this, the initiating ministry drafts the departmental regulation internally, as discussed above, and it is then circulated for comments and consideration to the other relevant ministries or bodies. Alternatively, a joint drafting committee might be formed to facilitate the coordination process. If consensus is hard to reach or if the matter is more important, then it is raised to the Director-Generals (司长) of the ministries. If no consensus is reached at the Director-General level, the matter is raised to the Vice Minister. In most cases, problems are fixed at this level. However, in cases where consensus cannot be reached, then the SCLAO will be asked to coordinate consensus. Once a consensus is reached, the departmental policy will be circulated to each minister for signature (Figure 3.2).

On the whole, China's present day economic diplomacy decision-making has evolved from vertical authoritarianism to one characterised by both "macro-authoritarianism" and "micro-democracy" (Pei, 2011). At the macro level, China is a one-party state in which the CPC enjoys an unchallenged political monopoly. At the micro level, agencies, officials, government departments, and interest groups (e.g. SOEs and local governments) vigorously compete for power and influence to defend their policy turfs and interests tenaciously.[31]

## Changes and implications

Modern Chinese decision-making for economic diplomacy has evolved from 'vertical' to 'horizontal' authoritarianism, thanks largely to the growing perplexities of the negotiating issues involved. Yet, it must be made clear that this trend

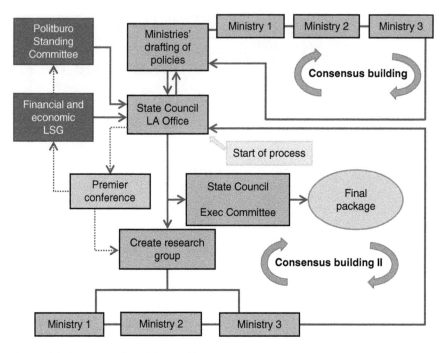

*Figure 3.2* State council decision-making processes.


towards pluralisation and decentralisation is by no means an indication that the top leadership is suffering from an erosion of decision-making powers. The core nucleus group of leaders remain utterly important in Chinese policy. What has changed is the *process*.

China's decision-making system reforms are a gradual process; and this demonstrates that in order to adapt to its role in multilateral processes, it has to change its own processes. In turn, the following transformations occurred. First, to manage the wide-ranging and technical multilateral issues, there has been a domestic shift from power-based decision-making to professionalised and specialised processes.[32] The most important feature of traditional decision-making is that it is power-based. But since Deng's 'open-up' policy, decision-making has evolved from the old impulsive style based on experience and personal judgement to more professionalised and specialised approaches. Tools, analytical methods, and procedures have since been introduced into the policy process, with intellectual, technical, and methodological support. Therefore, decision-making is no longer the undertaking of a monopoly of leaders. Experts, academics, and policy advisory bodies have become an integral part of the policy assessment and evaluation processes. More broadly, this change has also transcended Chinese decision-making from non-institutionalised to institutionalised processes. During the exclusionist era,

China's decision-making system was far from complete and robust, and one of its outstanding problems was low institutionalisation. Since China opened up to the international system, its decision-making has focused on system strengthening and institution-building. As a result, the institutionalisation of decision-making has significantly improved.

The second change, closely relates to the first, is the shift from individual to collective decision-making. As the agendas of multilateral economic negotiation tend to be cross-cutting in policy issues, this diversified interests within the Chinese government, and expanded the actors' relevance to the policy processes. As a result, there was a gradual transition, in post-Mao China, from a 'strong man' system to an elitist structure in which any key decision-making is still made by the top leadership, but collectively by a small group of top leaders at the CPC Politburo Standing Committee, aided by bureaucratic institutions and government departments, by means of providing top leaders information, intelligence, policy consultation, analysis, and recommendation.

To be sure, the decision-making structure and processes remain characterised by a centralised, elitist, and closed-door model, which is defined, constrained, or determined by the party-state political system, as long as such a system remains fundamentally unchanged (Guo, 2013, p. 280). But as Lucian Pye (1966, p. 47) rightly points out, the differentiation of highly centralised decision-making structures is an important indicator of political development because it causes "specialised functions of various political roles in the system to increase". The positive implication is that it increases the stability and predictability of China's foreign economic policy. In the words of one senior policy advisor from the MOFCOM, "China's decision-making structure has significantly evolved as it tries to converge with the international economic system, ideologies, norms, and standards".[33]

The third concerns the impact of the multilateral processes on the redistribution of bureaucratic power and authority in China's foreign economic decision-making processes. This was plainly seen within the State Council in terms of the transformation of the ministerial-level government departments such as the MFA, MOF, and MOFCOM. As a consequence, bureaucrats from those departments had their decision-making power and authority significantly elevated from previous levels. The CFELSG is another case in point, whereby entrance into the multilateral economic system took centre stage, and in order to serve China's economic interests the CFELSG became an important locus for the making of China's foreign economic policies.

But was bureaucratic power and authority really redistributed? After all, the empowerment of these actors does not in and of itself imply a redistribution of bureaucratic power and authority.[34] One apparent factor of change is the context – multilateral membership and negotiating international economic agreements imply that legislation became much more important in a relatively short period of time. For example, in the energy sector, between 1978 and 1995, only one piece of legislation was passed. By contrast, between 1996 and 2005, three major pieces of legislation were promulgated. As a result, this puts government departments like the SCLAO in a more central position with regard to economic policy. But if the SCLAO's power increased simply because legislation became more important (i.e. it became more relevant as an organisation), this would not necessarily constitute an institutional adaptation engineered by the leadership in order to enhance policy coordination and thus respond more effectively to the challenges of internationalisation. It is therefore important to note that context was not the only thing that changed. The SCLAO became more powerful and had more authority due to proactive actions by the CPC *prior to* significant shifts in the policy environment. By empowering the SCLAO through upgrades in bureaucratic rank, bestowing additional resources and personnel on the office, and taking away the ability of the ministries and commissions to rely on internal documents (e.g. through acts such as the Administrative Permissions Law), the SCLAO was put firmly in the driver's seat on legislative issues.

From the preceding discussion, one more conclusion is drawn with regard to the institutional adaptation effect arising from participation in multilateral economic processes: in an implicit way, international agencies have established themselves as interested Parties to China's decision-making process. Their interests and agendas are indirectly integrated and seriously discussed in Beijing, and their requirements, in turn, have the capacity to reconfigure national processes. This makes international agencies (or at least their agents) integrative policy actors with an active participation in China's decision-making process. Significantly, this implies that China's economic diplomacy decision-making in the twenty-first century is not necessarily a stand-alone internal process. Although, on the surface, China's preference formation is determined by its national interests and domestic factors, a deeper examination of the inner workings reveals a different story. The multilateral process plays a critical behind-the-scenes roles that indirectly shape Chinese economic diplomacy. Chapters 6 and 8 will explore this finding further. In sum, China's economic diplomacy is today shaped by a *collective* system involving domestic and international agencies.

## Notes

1 On issues that touch the 'hard politics' territory, China's decision-making is still a top-down approach; if a Ministry disagrees with the suggestions made by senior leaders, the leaders will find ways to make them agree (e.g. through compensation). But the same-level ranking agencies will need coordination. Interview with an expert from China University of Foreign Affairs, Beijing, 25 October 2012.
2 The six sectors are military affairs; legal affairs; administrative affairs, which is responsible for industrial and agricultural production, finance and commerce, foreign affairs, and so on; propaganda; United Front; and mass organisation affairs.
3 The most important policy decisions, such as major shifts in policy orientation, are generally still subject to deliberation by the full Politburo, although most Politburo members are only marginally involved in the actual consideration of policies. The members of the Standing Committee include the General Secretary of the CPC, the Chairman of the Central Military Commission, the Premier of the State Council, the

State President, the Chairman of the Standing Committee of the National People's Congress, the Chairman of the Chinese People's Political Consultative Conference, the General Secretary, the Director of the Central Advisory Commission, and the First Secretary of the Central Disciplinary Commission.

4 At the time of writing, the current members (in order) are: Xi Jinping, Li Keqiang, Zhang Dejiang, Yu Zhengsheng, Liu Yunshan, Wang Qishan, and Zhang Gaoli.

5 The role of the leader was further clarified in March 2004 in an amendment to Article 81 of the state constitution that declared "the President conducts state affairs" (国家主席进行国事).

6 Although commissions generally hold slightly more authority in decision-making than ministries, this study will classify both as both ministerial-level agencies.

7 The exact number of vice ministers, assistant ministers, deputy directors of departments, and deputy division chiefs varies by bureaucracy.

8 Much of the information provided by the MFA is processed, as opposed to the raw material generated by the Xinhua News Agency. And the MFA's diplomatic missions abroad frequently send cables directly to the central leaders. The MFA's internal publications also provide a constant flow of up-to-date, concise, readable information.

9 The NCCCC was the successor of the Climate Change Coordination Leading Small Group (CCCLSG) established in 1990.

10 The NDRC is a macroeconomic management agency under the State Council, charged to study and formulate policies for economic and social development, maintain the balance of economic development, and to guide restructuring of China's economic system.

11 Interview with an expert from the Chinese Academy of Social Sciences, Beijing, 8 November 2012.

12 Interview with a policy advisor to the WTO Division of the Ministry of Commerce, Shanghai, 25 April 2012.

13 The US recognised the Republic of China (ROC) led by the Nationalist Party in Taiwan, as the official government of China, and hence supported the ROC's bid for a seat in the UN instead of the PRC. For Mao Zedong, the PRC could not join the UN or other institutions with a ROC presence, as doing so would imply the recognition of two Chinas.

14 The multilateral groups China did join involved little actual cost to its sovereignty and ability to avoid constraints or costly commitments, while the symbolic benefits of membership (prestige, recognition, standing out as a leader for developing world interests, and having a voice in world affairs) were enhanced.

15 Following the Cultural Revolution, China's economy was in a complete shambles. Industrial production decreased by 14 per cent and agricultural production essentially ceased.

16 Combined with loans and assistance from the Asian Development Bank, which China joined in the mid-1980s, China became the largest international recipient of foreign assistance in the 1980s and much of the 1990s.

17 For instance, in 1979, Beijing reversed its opposition to receiving overseas development assistance (ODA), before it engaged with the IMF and World Bank in the early 1980s. The result was a steady influx of capital.

18 Interview with an expert from Peking University, Beijing, 21 September 2011.

19 Zhang (1996, p. 81) also points out that a domestic stimulus to the administrative reforms was in relation to the lessons from the Cultural Revolution and the constant domestic instabilities (which led to the 1989 Tiananmen incident) which created an unprecedented challenge to the CCP regime's legitimacy, such that decentralisation was seen as a necessity.

20 On 31 July 1986, then Vice Premier, Wan Li, pointed out in his speech entitled 'Democratic and Scientific Decision-making is an Important Topic of Political Reform', that the basic objective of reform of the decision-making system was to

realise democratic and scientific decision-making. (Recalled by an interviewee during a personal interview).

21 It is prescribed that the Secretariat does not have a decision-making function, but is just an administrative office of the Politburo and its Standing Committee.

22 The number of agencies under the State Council went back up to 72 in 1988, although restructuring in that year reduced it down to 68, with those related to economic reform being the focus of merger and reduction.

23 For example, the SDPC's finance bureau controlled the banks; and its bureau for rural and agricultural policies discussed and approved every stage of the rural reform (Hamrin and Zhao, 1995, p. xxxviii).

24 The problem was so severe that calls within the State Council were made to resurrect the old State Council Office for Restructuring the Economic System (SCORES) (国务院经济体制改革办公室) so that a more independent body could conduct reform planning.

25 Depending on their importance, major decisions concerning national development normally go through to the Politburo's Standing Committee, the Central Working Conference or the plenary session of the Central Committee, and/or the Party Congress. Decisions on major issues falling within the responsibilities of the State Council must be discussed by plenary meetings or executive meetings of the State Council; work rules, procedural rules, and a Democratic Life Meeting system have been established in the Politburo and its Standing Committee to institutionalise collective decision-making; a system has been established of soliciting opinions concerning major policy decisions; that is, before any major decision is collectively made, intra-party democracy must first be given full play, in-depth investigations and research must be undertaken, and the opinions of all localities, departments and democratic Parties must be listened to (Zhou, 2012, pp. 30–31). A Democratic Life Meeting (民主生活会) is a periodic gathering of cadres of the CPC who engage in organisational reviews. They are held in all levels of the Communist Party organisation from the 'grassroots' to the central leadership).

26 China's voting rights in the IMF have increased over the decades, from 2.58 per cent in 1980 (the ninth largest among single member states) to 2.95 per cent in 2001 and 3.82 per cent in 2011 (the sixth largest). In contrast, the voting power of China within the World Bank seems to have declined. In 1988 China's voting power was 3.19 per cent in the World Bank, with a share of US$3000 million, and 2.01 per cent in the International Development Association (IDA) (Jacobson and Oksenberg, 1990, pp. 65–66, 74–80). By 2011, its voting power in the World Bank was reduced to 2.72 per cent and in the IDA it grew very slightly to 2.05 per cent.

27 Interview with a member from the Department of Treaty and Law of the Ministry of Commerce, Beijing, 23 November 2012.

28 In fact, the government often invites large business organisations for consultation. It is important to note that this only applies to the larger and often state-owned enterprises rather than smaller private ones.

29 If an issue can be considered by the top leaders, then it has a much better chance of being addressed than issues that are not of the interest of the leaders.

30 The attendees at the State Council Secretary General Conference are the Secretary General of the State Council General Office, his Vice Secretary Generals, and the Director and Vice Directors of the SCLAO.

31 Based on a conversation with a government official in Beijing, 15 September 2011.

32 'Specialised' implies decisions made on a rational choice basis.

33 Interview with a senior policy advisor to the Ministry of Commerce, Beijing, 22 November 2012.

34 In order to make such claims, there needs to be a corresponding loss of power or authority in other government bodies.

# References

Bang, G., Heggelund, G., and Vevatne, J. (2005) *Shifting Strategies in the Global Climate Negotiations*. Joint Report by FNI and CICERO, FNI Report 6/2005/CICERO Report (8).

Barnett, A.D. (1985) *The Making of Foreign Policy in China: Structure and Process*. London: I.B. Tauris & Co. Ltd. Publishers.

Becker, T.S. (2006) 'Managing the Challenges of Openness: Domestic Institutional Responses to Internationalization in the PRC'. PhD Dissertation, University of North Carolina, North Carolina.

Bo, Z. (2013) 'State Power and Governance Structures'. In C. Ogden (ed.) *Handbook of China's Governance and Domestic Politics* (pp. 12–26). New York: Routledge.

Cabestan, J. (2009) 'China's Foreign- and Security-Policy Decision-Making Processes Under Hu Jintao'. *Journal of Current Chinese Affairs* 38(3) pp. 63–97.

Carlson, A. (2006). 'More Than Just Saying No: China's Evolving Approach to Sovereignty and Intervention'. In A.I. Johnston and R. Ross (eds) *New Directions in the Study of China's Foreign Policy* (pp. 217–241). Stanford, CA: Stanford University Press.

Chan, G. Lee, P.K., and Chan, L. (eds) (2012) *China Engages Global Governance: A New World Order in the Making?* London: Routledge.

Clegg, J. (2009) *China's Global Strategy: Towards a Multipolar World*. New York: Pluto Books.

Collins, N. and Cottey, A. (2012) *Understanding Chinese Politics: An Introduction to Government in the People's Republic of China*. Manchester and New York: Manchester University Press.

Ding, W. (2008) 'Five Member Taiwan Small Group: (Wang) Qishan and (Ling) Jihua Join)'. *Xinbao* (Hong Kong Economic Journal).

Dittmer, L. and Wu, Y. (1995) 'The Modernization of Factionalism in Chinese Politics'. *World Politics* 47(4) pp. 467–494.

Gill, B. (2010) *Rising Star: China's New Security Diplomacy and Its Challenges and Opportunities for the United States* (revised edn). Washington, DC: Brookings Institution Press.

Guo, S. (2013) *Chinese Politics and Government: Power, Ideology, and Organization*. London and New York: Routledge.

Hamrin, C.L. and Zhao, S. (eds) (1995) *Decision-Making in Deng's China: Perspectives From Insiders*. New York: M.E. Sharpe, Inc.

Harding, H. (2011) 'China and International Institutions'. In X. Huang (ed.) *The Institutional Dynamics of China's Great Transformation* (pp. 25–35). New York: Routledge.

Jacobson, H. and Oksenberg, M. (1990) *China's Participation in the IMF, the World Bank, and GATT*. Ann Arbor, MI: University of Michigan Press.

Jin, L. and Zhang, W. (2001) 'China's Law Reform'. *Beijing Caijing* 5.

Kim, S.S. (1999) 'China and the United Nations'. In E. Economy and M. Oksenberg (eds) *China Joins the World: Progress and Prospects* (pp. 42–89). New York: Council on Foreign Relations.

Lai, H. (2013). 'Economics'. In C. Ogden (ed.) *Handbook of China's Governance and Domestic Politics* (pp. 41–52). New York: Routledge.

Lai, H. (2010) *The Domestic Source of China's Foreign Policy: Regimes, Leadership, Priorities and Process*. New York: Routledge.

Lampton, D.M. (2001) 'China's Foreign and National Security Policy-making Process: Is It Changing, and Does it Matter?'. In D.M. Lampton (ed.) *The Making of Chinese Foreign and Security Policy in the Era of Reform, 1979–2000* (pp. 1–138). Stanford, CA: Stanford University Press.

Lampton, D.M. (1992) 'A Plum for a Peach: Bargaining, Interest, and Bureaucratic Politics in China'. In K.G. Lieberthal and D.M. Lampton *Bureaucracy, Politics, and Decision-Making in Post-Mao China*. Berkeley, CA: University of California Press.

Lanteigne, M. (2005) *China and International Institutions: Alternate Paths to Global Power*. London and New York: Routledge.

Le, T. (2007) 'West has "Key Role" on Climate Change'. *China Daily*. [Online] 22 September. Available from: www.chinadaily.com.cn/china/2007-09/22/content_6126343. htm [Accessed: 6 August 2011].

Lee, H.Y. (1991) *From Revolutionary Cadres to Party Technocrats in Socialist China*. Berkeley, CA: University of California Press.

Lieberthal, K. (1992) 'Introduction'. In K.G. Lieberthal and D.M. Lampton (eds) *Bureaucracy, Politics, and Decision Making in Post-Mao China* (pp. 1–30). Berkeley, CA: University of California Press.

Lieberthal, K. and Oksenberg, M. (1988) *Policy Making in China Leaders, Structures, and Processes*. Princeton, NJ: Princeton University Press.

Liew, L.H. (2004) 'Policy Elites in the Political Economy of China's Exchange Rate Policymaking'. *Journal of Contemporary China* 13(38) pp. 21–51.

Lu, N. (2001) 'The Central Leadership, Supraministry Coordinating Bodies, State Council Ministries, and Party Departments'. In D.M. Lampton (ed.) *The Making of Chinese Foreign and Security Policy In the Era of Reform, 1978–2000* (pp. 39–60). Stanford, CA: Stanford University Press.

NDRC (2007) *National Climate Change Program*. [Online] June. Available from: www. china.org.cn/english/environment/213624.htm [Accessed: 4 June 2011].

Pearson, M. (2006) 'China in Geneva: Lessons from China's Early Years in the World Trade Organization'. In A.I. Johnston and R. Ross (eds) *New Directions in the Study of China's Foreign Policy* (pp. 587–644). Stanford, CA: Stanford University Press.

Pearson, M.M. (2001) 'The Case of China's Accession to GATT/WTO'. In D.M. Lampton (ed.) *The Making of Chinese Foreign and Security Policy In the Era of Reform, 1978–2000* (pp. 337–370). Stanford, CA: Stanford University Press.

Pei, M. (2011) 'The China Diviner: Inside the Black Box'. *The Asia Specialist*. Received via email, 17 May.

Pye, L.W. (1966) 'Coming Dilemmas for China's Leaders'. *Foreign Affairs* 44(3) pp. 387–402.

Schlichting, S. (2008) *Internationalising China's Financial Markets*. New York: Palgrave Macmillan.

Shirk, S. (1992) 'The Chinese Political System and the Political Strategy of Economic Reform'. In K.G. Lieberthal and D.M. Lampton (eds) *Bureaucracy, Politics, and Decision Making in Post-Mao China* (pp. 59–91). Berkeley, CA: University of California Press.

Sutter, R.G. (2008) *Chinese Foreign Relations: Power and Policy Since the Cold War*. United Kingdom: Rowman & Littlefield Publishers, Inc.

Weisman, S.R. (2008) 'China Tries to Reassure US About Its Investing Plan'. *New York Times*, 1 February.

Whyte, M.K. (1989) 'Who Hates Bureaucracy? A Chinese Puzzle'. In V. Nee and V. Stark (eds) *Remaking the Economic Institutions of Socialism: China and Eastern Europe* (pp. 233–254). Stanford, CA: Stanford University Press.

Yang, G. (1995) 'Mechanisms of Foreign Policy-Making and Implementation in the Ministry of Foreign Affairs'. In C.L. Hamrin and S. Zhao (eds) *Decision-Making in Deng's China: Perspectives from Insiders* (pp. 91–100). Armonk, NY: M.E. Sharpe.

Ye, Q., Ma, L., and Zhang, L. (2007) 'Climate Change Governance in China: A Case Study'. *China Population, Resources and Environment* 17(2) pp. 8–12.

Yu, H. (2008) *Global Warming and China's Environmental Diplomacy*. New York: Nova Science Publishers, Inc.

Zhang, Z. (1996) 'Macroeconomic Effects of CO2 Emission Limits Computable General Equilibrium Analysis'. Paper presented at the 7th Annual Conference of the European Association of Environment and Resource Economists, Lisbon.

Zhao, Q. (1996) *Interpreting Chinese Foreign Policy*. Oxford: Oxford University Press.

Zhou, G. (2012) 'The Reform and Development of the Decision-making System in Contemporary China'. *Social Sciences in China* 33(2) pp. 25–45.

Zou, D. (2008) *Zhongguo gaige kaifang 30 nian* [Three Decades of China's Reform and Opening]. Beijing: Shehui kexue wenxian chubanshe.

# Part II

# Chinese economic diplomacy

## National preferences

# 4 Case one
## Negotiating climate change

Suppose policymakers vary their decision-making across economic negotiations, then it would be useful to know what determines those policy choices, assuming that policymakers do make deliberate choices over policies (notwithstanding policymakers that stumble into a process without any careful assessment of policy choices). Since the United Nations Framework Convention on Climate Change (UNFCCC) negotiations began, China's negotiation positions over the years reflect both continuities and changes. What have remained constant are China's core principles.[1] What has changed is the newfound flexibility and pragmatism in China's policy preferences on the substance of negotiations, particularly concerning issues such as the Clean Development Mechanism (CDM or 'the mechanism') and international mitigation commitments (or 'mitigation'). What triggered changes in China's policy preferences? And what effect do UNFCCC bodies have in the process?

Chapter 2 offered an objective clue, the claim that China's decision-making is driven by the calculation of costs and benefits, information and reputation. How probable is this claim in a world of bounded rationality? Consider two climate change negotiation examples in which China's position evolved differently over time.

## Negotiating the Clean Development Mechanism

Proposed in 1998 at the third Conference of the Parties (COP3) in Kyoto, the CDM was designed for two purposes. First, to assist non-Annex I Parties in tackling climate change through sustainable development.[2] And second, to assist Annex I Parties in their compliance with the quantified emission limitation and reduction commitments (greenhouse gas (GHG) emission caps) through the investment of certified emissions reductions (CERs) generated from CDM projects in non-Annex I countries (Carbon Trust, 2009, p. 14.; Grubb, 2003, p. 159).

During the inaugural CDM negotiations, China sat in the room poker faced. With little understanding about the initiative, the then lead government department on climate change, the China Meteorological Administration (CMA), was confronted with quite the undertaking – evaluating the costs and benefits of the initiative and its impact on China.[3] Other departments, such as the National

Environmental Protection Agency (NEPA, reformed into the Ministry of Environmental Protection or MEP in 2008) and the State Science and Technology Commission (SSTC, reformed into the Ministry of Science and Technology or MOST) contributed policy reports on the initiative. However, their messaging was largely inconsistent, with some reports acknowledging the merits of the CDM, and others recommending caution. The murky domestic analyses communicated mixed messages to the political elites, and, as a result, Beijing issued a cautious mandate for COP3.

At the COP3 plenary meeting, the Chinese Lead Negotiator had reiterated during China's national statement that $CO_2$ emissions should be unilaterally resolved rather than shared by all member-states. This position was substantiated at the CDM working group negotiations by their CDM Chapter Lead Negotiator. He argued that the CDM only benefits countries with an existing carbon trading regime, and those with an established climate change science and technology sector. By comparison, countries (including China) without existing infrastructure are disadvantaged as a global competitor.[4] Sitting at the heart of this issue is the fear that the CDM initiative is a political scheme (政治阴谋) designed to help Annex I countries escape their climate change commitments.[5] China subsequently submitted a request to the Chair at COP3 to delete the initiative from the negotiation agenda.[6]

To rescue the process from China's request, the Committee of the Whole facilitated an informal contact group session in November 1998, involving the US, members of the 'G77 plus China' (Group of Seventy-Seven Plus China), under the chairmanship of Brazil. Participants of the meeting recalled it as a relatively productive engagement that laid the initial building blocks of the CDM chapter negotiations (Cole, 2012, p. 44).

In order to manage the CDM process, Beijing established the National Climate Change Coordination Committee (NCCCC), a new window-agency for managing UNFCCC affairs. The establishment of the NCCCC stimulated a new wave of engagements between Beijing and the UNFCCC bodies.[7] In 1999, scientists commissioned by the UNFCCC worked together with officials from MOST and NEPA on a report which alluded to the cross-border transmittable effect of $CO_2$ emissions and the tangible benefits of CDM projects (e.g. access to clean energy technologies) for reducing emissions (Economy, 2001, pp. 246–248). The report was particularly effective at shaping the general view within MOST and NEPA that China will "miss out on significant opportunities by not agreeing to a CDM Chapter" and that a "more proactive policy was needed to gain access to new technologies from abroad through the initiative".[8] Although their policy suggestions did not wholly transform China's COP4 and COP5 negotiation positions, they did deter the delegation from further objections to partaking in the CDM negotiations (Zhang, 2003, p. 69).

In the last hours of COP5, the UNFCCC Secretariat linked China's cautious approach with a lack of familiarity with the science behind the CDM initiative.[9] And it was no coincidence that the Global Environmental Facility (GEF) was subsequently delegated to sponsor CDM pilot programmes in regions across

China.[10] In 2001, China received US$173 million in GEF grants – 17 per cent of the GEF's climate change reserves – for seven CDM pilot programmes in the Gansu Province (Yu, 2008, p. 84). In the same year, the GEF and the United Nations Development Programme (UNDP) jointly allocated US$50.7 million to pilot CDM simulations in China. In 2002, the GEF committed US$840 million to assist the Chinese government in building a CDM market. Most of the simulations were carried out jointly with various government departments, such as the simulation on renewable power energy with the Ministry of Power.

Efforts were also made to attract participation from state and private enterprises, which then led to the development of CER-trading consultancy firms.[11] For instance, the Centre for Socio-Eco-Nomic Development based in Geneva was assigned by the UNFCCC to carry out a simulation exercise – 'Can we make a CDM deal?' – in China to deepen the understanding of CDM deal making among government officials and industries to assist them in attracting foreign investment (Yiu *et al.*, 2002). Technical assistance (e.g. information sharing and training) was widely provided by the GEF throughout the process.[12]

Participants of the pilot programmes noted the increased awareness and interest in the CDM initiative among domestic industries. What they found particularly appealing was the CDM's potential to improve energy efficiency, increase access to new technologies, international funding, and technical expertise.[13] The domestic industries further saw potential in the CDM to create new market sectors that were good for generating new business and employment opportunities without hampering China's economic development.[14] The local authorities – from the provincial level to the county and community stratum – similarly emerged with new interests in the potential material benefits derived from the CDM initiative (Ye *et al.*, 2007, p. 9).

Together with the domestic industries and the science community, they voiced dissatisfaction with the Ministry of Foreign Affairs's (MFA's) hard stance on the CDM at the multilateral negotiation table, and argued that China was missing out on important prospects in technological advancements and business opportunities.[15] Having seen actual benefits arise out of the CDM pilot projects and due to domestic pressures, the State Development Planning Commission (SDPC, reformed into the National Development and Reform Commission or NDRC in 2003) asked the NCCCC to conduct CDM market analyses, and evaluate China's competitiveness against the international markets.[16]

In late 2001, a joint study on Clean Energy Ministerial (CEM) was launched by the NCCCC, the World Bank, Germany and Switzerland (published in 2004). The study projected that China had the potential to take around 50 per cent of the global CDM market (World Bank, 2006). This finding served as an encouraging signal to the political elites. Following numerous rounds of inter-ministerial coordination and consultations with the support of the UNFCCC Secretariat, the NDRC – designated authority to approve the CDM initiative – reached a consensus to adopt the mechanism on the grounds that it would serve China's domestic and international development objectives (i.e. the mechanism would improve energy efficiency, combat pollution, grant new access to international funding and technologies, and offer an economic opportunity to establish new sectors). The outputs included job creation and the dissemination of technical know-how – all of which supported China's development.[17] Additionally, the CDM – being a market-driven mechanism – serves the government's interest in economic reform to the free market, whilst planting the green and low carbon concepts in market practices and within Chinese firms.[18]

Internationally, the CDM negotiations were, at the time, confronted with a deadlock. Developed countries, especially from Europe, were challenged in their ability to integrate the CDM initiative within their existing climate change policy.[19] By comparison, China, as a freshman to the game, did not face the same constraints. Against the background of stale negotiations, Beijing saw this as an opportunity to kill two birds with one stone: with its agreement, it would inject new momentum to the negotiation stalemate, and enhance its international reputation as a cooperative player.[20] At COP6, the Chinese delegation favourably spoke about the CDM, and called it a "win-win" initiative with likely benefits for both developed and developing countries (Yu, 2008, p. 58). To the surprise of some Parties, the Chinese delegation proactively participated in the debates around the guiding principles and implementation procedures in the CDM working group.

Even though, by this stage, China was an interested Party of the CDM initiative, questions continued to linger. During the COP7 meetings in Marrakech, China questioned how to ensure that developing countries are void of binding commitments (Harris and Yu, 2005, p. 53). Chinese negotiators argued that any adoption of the CDM should not impose any binding obligations on developing countries. In addition, China fought for CDM initiatives (including nuclear energy projects) to cover all technologies, with the exception of sink activities (Tangen *et al.*, 2001, p. 242).[21]

If that were not enough, China became concerned with the political risks of committing to the CDM initiative in light of an unratified Kyoto Protocol: America's decision to opt out of the framework undermined China's impetus to sign onto the CDM. China further stressed the technical risks and challenges faced by developing countries in light of their limited access to the essential resources to ensure complex CDM procedures. China noted the UNFCCC Secretariat's lack of capacity-building assistance to help developing countries tackle the technical bottlenecks, such as baseline identification, the development of monitoring plans, and the conduct of validation and verification. Another concern related to the high transaction costs of CDM projects, as a result of charges on registration, validation, monitoring, and verification – all of which brought with them financial risks which could cause the margins to shrink to the extent that the deal simply became less attractive to the industries. Finally, Chinese negotiators pointed to the lack of details proposed for the CER price, due to China's internal fears that it could sell their CERs too cheaply.[22]

In response, the COP7 President (1) pushed for greater funding from the Annex I group and the UN Funds for developing countries; (2) signalled the possibilities for technical assistance and training opportunities to enhance developing countries' professional competence in CDM dealings; (3) assured the inclusion of

Chinese representatives in the CDM governance;[23] and (4) achieved consensus on the voluntary basis of CDM participation. However, these concessions were granted on the condition that China submit to the international monitoring, validation, and verification systems, which is something the MFA have strongly resisted in the past. One Chinese negotiator interviewed went so far to suggest the COP7 President had played the reputation card and urged China to accept the packaged deal for the sake of its international reputation as a cooperative, compliant, and responsible player.[24]

China eventually agreed to this condition and confirmed its commitment by establishing the CDM Monitoring and Management Centre (监督管理中心), which reports directly to the UNFCCC's CDM Executive Board regarding its CDM performance.[25] Other establishments include the China CDM Fund under the Ministry of Finance (MOF), CDM monitoring and research departments under the Ministry of Science and Technology (MOST) and the MEP, and new institutional structures and streamlined transparent CDM procedures to facilitate the implementation of CDM projects.[26] In early 2002, China called for an accelerated launch of the CDMs, and in August that year, the government formally signed onto the initiative (Zhang, 2003, p. 69) – an outcome that is evidence of a significant policy shift from absolute resistance to adoption.

## Negotiating internationally binding commitments on mitigation

The concept of *mitigation* in the present context refers to the action of reducing the intensity of radiative force (i.e. GHGs) for reducing the likely impacts of climate change (Molina *et al.*, 2009, pp. 616–621).[27] From the outset, the Chinese government viewed climate change as the outcome of the industrial economies' high consumption patterns and luxurious lifestyles. For this reason, they believed developed countries should take on mitigation commitments first. As a proclaimed developing country, China believed it should only monitor, as opposed to participate in, the mission to tackle climate change.[28] China was strongly opposed to any internationally binding commitments on mitigation on the premise that it would threaten its economic development.

Back then, government departments in Beijing, including the CMA, relied on outdated methodologies (e.g. paleoclimatology) for their analyses, and conservative findings were often derived regarding the impact of climate change. Other domestic government departments such as the Energy Research Institute (ERI) under the SDPC/NDRC, the NEPA/MEP and the SSTC/MOST had no track record in climate research at all. As a result, serious differences in approach and understanding about climate change and mitigation emerged between China and other countries.

It was therefore rather timely that, in 1992, the GEF initiated a research programme in China, entitled the 'GHG emissions strategy study', with US$2 million technical assistance, designed for raising awareness about climate change and mitigation (Yu, 2008, p. 90). The UNFCCC Secretariat then partnered with the World Bank, the Asian Development Bank (ADB), the United Nations Environment Programme (UNEP), and the UNDP to provide monitoring equipment for GHG emissions in China, share computer modelling techniques with officials from the NEPA/MEP and the SSTC/MOST, and provided technological assistance in developing response measures. Interviews with members of the aforementioned government departments revealed that the NEPA/MEP and SSTC/MOST thereafter were noted for their more proactive policy recommendations on mitigation compared to other departments. One SSTC/MOST policymaker recalled that his basic knowledge on mitigation was largely acquired through his engagements with experts from international agencies; and he noticed radical reorientation of policy preferences among his colleagues.[29]

By the late 1990s, as policymakers advanced their understanding on the issue, government departments emerged with divergent views regarding the extent to which China should contribute to the international mitigation efforts. At one end of the spectrum, officials from NEPA/MEP and SSTC/MOST stressed that China had a responsibility to participate in international mitigation because it was a major contributor to climate change – the country was the third largest emitter in the world at the time. At the other end, members of the SDPC/NDRC and the MFA were less enthusiastic and argued that economic development and sovereignty concerns necessitated a limited Chinese response. The internal incoherence quickly earned China an international reputation as one of the most recalcitrant participants in the mitigation negotiations by consistently advocating the weakest reporting obligations without any concrete measures or timetables for reducing GHG emissions.

In 1996, the Chinese Academy of Science (CAS) hosted a major conference on climate change and its effects on China. The resulting 560-page report, *Studies on Climate Change and Its Effects*, included a number of articles that pointed to the potential wreckage and devastation emissions can cause. But instead of advocating mitigation, the report recommended adaptation as the best way of addressing climate change.[30] This recommendation reinforced support for the conservative position that China should refuse international binding commitments on emissions reduction.

But such a position was short-lived. By the 2000s, the impacts of climate change knocked on China's door in heightening amplitude year-on-year, with natural disasters disrupting 200–400 million lives annually, and economic losses of more than 200 billion RMB per annum (Ma, 2006). In the summer of 2011 alone, a series of floods in central and southern China affected 36 million people, destroyed 432,000 hectares of crops – reducing vegetable output by 20 per cent from a year earlier – and caused an economic loss of US$6.5 billion (*News One*, 2011; Press TV, 2011; Yap, 2011). The high frequency of extreme weather events stipulated a growing recognition among senior officials that climate change is a major threat to the well-being of the Chinese people (Christoff, 2010, p. 646).

These events triggered the NDRC to implement a series of pilot projects in partnership with the GEF and the UNDP to test the abatement costs of mitigation.[31] One notable pilot was the 'Energy Conservation and GHG Emissions

Reduction in Chinese Township and Village Enterprises (TVEs)-Phase II' (2000–2007) project. The GEF and the UNDP jointly contributed US$7,992,000 to this project, which attempted to (1) reduce GHG emissions in the TVEs sector by increasing the utilisation of energy efficient technologies and products in the brick, cement, metal casting, and coking sectors; (2) build technical capacity for energy efficiency and product quality improvement in TVEs; (3) create access to commercial financing; and (4) expand the application of best practices for local and national regulatory reform. At the completion of the pilots, the project revealed that a green and low-carbon economy does not hinder, but enhances, economic development.[32]

Even so, Beijing's economic advisors, known for their conservative values, criticised the results and continued to advocate development needs over mitigation. They emphasised that with per capita income in urban China at only US$1,702 per annum (as of 2005),[33] and with over 135 million people still under the poverty line, mitigation commitments could hamper efforts to fulfil the social and industrial needs of the Chinese people (Economist Intelligence Unit, 2006; World Bank, 2006).[34] The two-sided debate eventually prompted the political elites to remain firm on economic growth and implement a domestic environmental regulatory response to the threat of climate change under the framework of its development objectives.

In 2007, the release of the Intergovernmental Panel on Climate Change's (IPCC's) fourth assessment report was widely distributed within Beijing, not least because 28 of its own experts participated in the authoring of the report.[35] Numerous Chinese negotiators claimed that this report played an important part in raising the leaders' awareness about the implications of GHG emissions on the country's development and a recognition that mitigation was as much a moral responsibility as a scientific and economic one. At the same time, Beijing felt intense pressures from the COP Presidencies and other countries to recognise and acknowledge that committing to mitigation was the responsible thing to do given that China was about to overtake the US as the world's largest emitting country. All the while, the international media subjected China's 'quietism' on tackling climate change to heavy scrutiny, portraying it as a negligent player.[36]

Amidst international scrutiny, China attended COP12 in 2007 with new pragmatism and submitted its first *National Climate Change Programme and Communication* to the UNFCCC Secretariat. The Chinese delegation diminished their resistance to engaging in dialogue concerning mitigation, which was a drastic contrast to the Kyoto negotiations in 1997 where China indicated a disinterest in mitigation discussions until it had achieved "medium-level" development (measured usually by a per capita income of US$5,000) (Pan, 2005). Arguments of this nature seldom emerge at the negotiation table today.[37]

The government also invited Chinese experts that had co-authored the IPCC fourth assessment report to join the Chinese delegation at the subsequent COPs. According to one delegate, their expertise was highly sought after by negotiators during the negotiations.[38] These experts stressed that $CO_2$ emissions are a risk to all countries including China and acknowledged that a cut in emissions is essential for safeguarding China's environment (Zhu, 2010, p. 38). It is no coincidence that during the Bali negotiations in 2007, the Chinese stance on mitigation negotiations no longer ruled out the possibility for China to play a more active role in the global climate protection efforts which would include mitigation commitments.[39] This was a significant step forward even though the Parties did not reach an agreement on the quantitative figures (Oberheitman and Sternfeld, 2009, p. 141).

At the 2008 COP14 negotiations in Poznan, China submitted two proposals for a post-2012 global climate agreement. One was the 'Cumulative per capita Emissions Convergence Proposal', where China demanded an ultimate "equity" – the merging of cumulative per capita emissions by 2100. Additionally, the proposal suggests that by 2050, global total GHG emissions should be reduced by 25 per cent compared to the 1990 levels, or halved if Annex I countries' emissions turn negative by 2040 (Hallding *et al.*, 2009, p. 97). The other proposal was the 'Carbon Budget Proposal' (CBP) drafted by the Chinese Academy of Social Sciences (CASS).

The CBP proposed an overall framework to halve international emissions by 2050, also referred to as the '450 ppm/2°C target'. The proposal allows China's emissions to peak by 2030, with 45 per cent higher emissions compared to the 2005 level. In addition, it proposes reducing emissions to 55 per cent below the 2005 level by 2050 (Pan and Chen, 2008). The CBP had set up rather ambitious targets for China. By comparison, America's plan entailed a reduction to 1990 levels by 2020 and 80 per cent below 1990 levels by 2050, which would equate to around 15 per cent below 2005 levels by 2020, and about 85 per cent below those levels by 2050 (Stern, 2006). Beijing's shift along the proactivity scale was further indicated by its COP15 pledge in Copenhagen (2009) to cut domestic emissions by 40–45 per cent per unit of GDP by 2020.[40] To achieve this pledge, China's 12th Five Year Plan (2011–2015) set domestic targets to reduce GDP per unit of energy use by 16 per cent, and reduce GDP per unit of $CO_2$ emissions by 17 per cent (NDRC, MOST and MOA, 2011, p. 5).

At COP15, China actively pushed members of the 'G77 plus China' to focus on making concrete mitigation arrangements. As Hu Jintao's brief statement to the UN Climate Summit in September 2009 emphasised, "Fulfilling our respective responsibilities should be at the core of our efforts".[41] In 2011, during the final hours of the COP17 negotiations in Durban, the Chinese delegation expressed their support for a legally binding treaty for the post-2020 period. The 2020 earmark was agreed because its pilot projects for mitigation required at least a decade to generate results, equating to the year 2020. The government would ideally want to wait until then to make a decision on the next step. As for its agreement for the 2015 deadline to negotiate a new framework, this was largely based on the date of publication for the fifth assessment report of the IPCC on the scientific review of the climate change effects and works to measure the effectiveness of emission pledges by individual countries.[42] This position very much signalled the potential for China to make post-2020 climate action commitments.

On 30 June 2015, Premier Li Keqiang announced China's new 'Intended Nationally Determined Contribution' (INDC) during an official visit to Paris. The key targets contained in China's INDC include (1) to peak its $CO_2$ emissions by 2030; (2) to cut $CO_2$ emissions per unit of GDP by 60–65 per cent from 2005 levels by 2030; (3) to increase non-fossil fuel sources for primary energy consumption to approximately 20 per cent by 2030 (which will require China to deploy some 800–1000 gigawatts in non-fossil capacity, close to the US's total current electricity capacity); and (4) to increase forest stock volume by around 4.5 billion cubic meters over the 2005 level by the same year. The country also built on these commitments with additional announcements on carbon intensity, forests, and adaptation. China's plan was considered as a "serious and credible contribution to tackle climate change" by the international community, and welcomed as a significant step forward to a decarbonised economy (World Resources Institute, 2015).

Although the INDCs are helpful vehicles to address the ambition gap between what China has already committed to and what it is further required to do, the country's approach to the negotiations on mitigation has not evolved significantly since COP1. During Beijing's preparation for COP21 in Paris (December 2015), some 20 years later, interviews with senior members of the Chinese delegation revealed that the country remain in alignment with the G77 view that while every country has a responsibility to help bridge the gap between the commitments made so far to addressing climate change and the necessary levels of mitigation, the important principles of 'common but differentiated responsibility' (CBDR), equity and respective capabilities must serve as a guideline for any new mechanism agreed to. This is not to discount China's acceptance of the new expression of the CBDR principle – 'in light of different national circumstances' – as reflective of a compromise on the part of developing countries, and a departure from China's traditional position. That said, Beijing remains firm in the view that even though some developed countries may argue the CBDR concept is now out of date, they have the expectation that it would have to be a part of the final agreement in Paris. At COP21, together with all other Parties, China agreed to the definition of a collective mitigation goal that seeks to reach global peaking of GHG emissions as soon as possible, and undertaking rapid reductions thereafter – with some recognition of developing countries' need for greater time, and the context of sustainable development and poverty eradication.

## Calculating the costs and benefits

Whenever a Chinese decision-maker begins a policy process for the purpose of economic negotiations, they will refer to a calculation of the costs and benefits first and foremost. In the preceding examples, it was clear to see that a conservative analysis of the costs and benefits yielded China's early view that climate change measures are incompatible with growth generation, and any quantified binding GHG commitments would be detrimental to China's national development (Tangen *et al.*, 2001, p. 243). This calculation derived from the fact that: (1)

China's rapidly developing economy embodies energy-intensive sectors sensitive to energy consumption cuts; (2) the available energy-efficient technologies are considered as backward and the prospect of quick improvements even with technological, and financial transfers is not perceived as probable; and (3) China's coal-dominated energy structure generally complicates efforts in $CO_2$ reductions without further reductions in its energy supply (Ye *et al.*, 2007, p. 9). For these reasons, curbing emissions was perceived as a political threat, with costs outweighing the benefits, and therefore Chinese decision-makers arrived at the negotiation preference of non-commitment to climate change measures.

The UNFCCC's IPCC, together with the UNDP, countered Beijing's pessimism by demonstrating an overall consistency between climate change action and sustainable development. In most cases, they highlighted the fact that a drop in $CO_2$ emissions can actually improve energy efficiency and conservation. In addition, the report showed a rise in living standards (e.g. through air quality improvements and pollution level controls), and climate change action can lead to new industrial development opportunities in the low-carbon technology sector, and job creation. The costs of non-commitment, however, include devastating impacts on development including the climate-sensitive sectors in agriculture and China's already scarce water resources (IPCC, 2001, 2007; UNDP, 2009/2010; Stern, 2006).

The exposure to external analyses was, according to interviews, an impetus to Beijing's revision of the costs and benefits, especially with regard to China's vulnerability to climate change. In the past, China's preference was to deflect emission reduction obligations, and its case was strong given that Chinese assertions were not dependent on emission reductions by other countries. It could thus achieve its goal in the absence of any deal. However, the new perspectives on the costs analysis altered the calculations. For the first time, the direct implications for long-term economic growth and social stability entered the political debate, on the one hand, and China realised it has a stake in other countries' emission reductions, on the other.

Here, the rationalist argument would posit that the high expected damage costs would drive greater proactivity in Beijing because national interests were threatened. Yet, as we saw in the examples, round after round, China was not ready to commit to any levels of internationally binding mitigation targets, and it was an arduous process getting China to sign on to the CDM initiative. This is because in the context of a bargaining game where one's ability to achieve one's own interest is partly in the hands of others, as is the case of multilateral climate change negotiations, one has to be prepared to give in order to gain. And it was obvious that China was unprepared to pledge to such levels of reciprocity. Thus, China's negotiation preference often reflected a sense of hesitation over the years.

So perhaps the calculation of costs and benefits is not a sole driver of China's negotiation preference formulation process. What are the factors that constrain and/or enhance this factor in the overall decision-making process?

One intervening variable is the decision-makers' *perception of political threat* resulting from (non-)action.[43] In general, Chinese decision-makers accept that climate change consequences are profound.[44] But they also perceive the threats to have stemmed out of the abatement costs on China's short-term development goals to be even more devastating than the threats of not tackling climate change. According to Chinese Officials, the commitment China has made with respect to mitigation targets has significant implications for China's economy. China's Lead Negotiator for the international climate change talks, Xie Zhenhua, estimates that the cost to China of meeting the emission reduction goals as indicated in the Intended Nationally Determined Contributions (INDC) will exceed US$6.6 trillion (41 trillion RMB). A senior official of the NDRC, who worked closely on setting the INDC targets, alluded to the NDRC's concerns over balancing economic growth and environmental objectives. The NDRC's economic modelling suggested that achieving the carbon intensity target had the potential to reduce China's GDP by approximately 3 per cent, compared to a business-as-usual trajectory by 2030. NDRC was, she explained, unwilling to therefore accept the hit to China's GDP growth rate and consequent job losses for the purpose of fulfilling a more ambitious commitment on mitigation. The consequence of not fulfilling the short-term economic objectives of growth and poverty reduction for the purpose of addressing the long-term threats of climate change could put the political legitimacy of the Communist Party of China (CPC) in peril. By comparison, the CDM initiative was considered to be less of a threat; rather, an enhancer of China's short- and long-term priorities. In this sense, costs-and-benefits calculations determine policy outcome only if the issue under assessment inflicts low (political) threats to the Chinese government.

But does this mean that the same can be said for the UNFCCC Secretariat's guidance on the costs and benefits for Beijing? It is easy and convenient to assume the answer is 'yes'. However, one ought to be prudent when jumping to such conclusions, as any policy shift as a result of exogenous calculations could be no more than tactical politics. For instance, Chinese negotiators frequently point to the IPCC's reference to China as one of the most vulnerable countries to the consequences of climate change, in order to promote China as a victim of global warming and to argue that the industrialised nations should therefore make the first move in tackling the global problem. And by claiming that it is a victim, China legitimises demands for compensation and validates purported concerns over the climate change issue (Zhang, 2003, p. 79). If increased Chinese rhetoric on vulnerability is mere tactical play, then it is not necessarily an indication that any transfer of exogenous calculations on the costs and benefits by the UNFCCC Secretariat impacted Chinese decision-making.

Yet, such sentiment can be rebutted by pointing to Beijing's prioritisation of adaptation activities, for instance, as a primary response to fears over high damage costs – as highlighted by the IPCC, which is in itself indicative of UNFCCC impact. Then again, China's new priorities around climate change are often linked to international funding and technologies. For instance, Beijing stressed in its *Initial National Communication* (National Communication, 2004, p. 18)

> China is relatively sensitive and vulnerable to climate change in areas including agriculture, natural ecology and forestry, water resources, sea level and

coastal belts, desertification and natural disasters. Technical support and funds are therefore needed for mitigating or adapting to the aforementioned areas.

More recently, Chinese officials have signalled that a COP21 agreement would need to be balanced: that is, it needs to include not only mitigation elements, but also give full attention to adaptation, financing, capacity building, and technology transfer. In addition, China emphasised the importance of developed countries to faithfully carry out their commitments under the UNFCCC, Kyoto Protocol, and the Cancun Agreement, including the promise of US$100 billion a year before 2020 in addition to Official Development Assistance (ODA), with further scaling of these financial commitments in the post-2020 period. These sentiments are indicative of the reality that China's negotiation preferences are formulated beyond a simple costs-and-benefits calculus.

## The power of information

Amongst the Chinese climate change policymakers interviewed, 69 per cent believed that China's prudent negotiation preferences in the pre-COP7 years were due to a lack of information and understanding about climate change science. One Chinese negotiator said, "Unlike the large quantities of available information today, Chinese decision-makers in the 1990s lacked resources and competent experts on climate change science".[45] Although scientific research started in the late 1980s, large-scale policy-related research programmes did not launch for another 10 years. The government therefore had capacity constraints in climate change science, and a shortage of relevant information essential for the formulation of negotiation preferences – what foreign delegations interpret as acts of "passivity".[46]

This situation changed after the establishment of the NCCCC, where information sharing with the UNFCCC Secretariat became common throughout the policy development process.[47] Over time, the high frequency of interactions with the Secretariat reoriented the negotiation preferences of Chinese decision-makers. This view is supported by 92 per cent of the interviewees. In addition, an internal study by the NDRC found that policymakers with less interaction with external actors generally had a lower level of understanding and interest with regard to climate change issues, whereas those with greater interest and capacity had comparatively more engagement with outside actors.[48]

Interviewees further indicated that the way the IPCC framed issues in the early stages of the expert review very much shaped China's policy options in the longer term.[49] An obvious example is the IPCC's identification of the environmental issues as a global problem and the coinage of the 'global climate' concept. In line with cognitive theory, the transmission of ideas can, in essence, influence perception and issue-framing. In the process, it enables external actors (e.g. the UNFCCC Secretariat) to influence policy through its particularly effective role in issue-framing and awareness-raising.

However, this reality was not realised in the case of the CDM negotiations. From the outset, there was no evidence to suggest that exogenous information triggered any preference shifts and Chinese negotiators remained quiet on the issue throughout COP4 and COP5. Interviews alluded to the fact that China's preference formation process was circumscribed by the domestic political power structure. That is, even though the CMA was, in theory, the lead department for the CDM policy coordination, the actual policy outcome was shaped by the interests of other key departments such as the SDPC and the MFA. Even though the CMA led the scientific and research stages of policymaking, it gave way to the SDPC and the MFA when it came to the political discussions (Economy, 1997, p. 30). Since the CMA, MOST, and Centre for Policy Studies (SEPA) were considered the government's window-agencies for UNFCCC-related affairs, the international discourse disseminated to them would not have reached the officials who stamp the final seal of approval. As one official from MOST recalled, on numerous occasions prior to COP4, they highlighted to SDPC/NDRC officials the environmental benefits the CDM initiative creates. But their marginal influence meant they had limited capacity to shape the final preferences. This is why, in spite of the new influx of information from the UNFCCC Secretariat, China maintained its cautious position throughout COP3–5.

From COP5, the Secretariat began to disseminate CDM-related information to ministries and commissions and the related industries beyond the traditional window-agencies. This occurred just as the GEF-sponsored CDM simulations took off. What resulted was a higher degree of absorption of the international discourse. Such influence is identified through the general reformation in attitude amongst the ministerial and industrial actors, from resistance to gradual favouritism towards the CDM initiative. The awareness-raising impact was so profound that it even triggered domestic industries to lobby the government to adopt the initiative. This was verified by numerous Chinese decision-makers, one of which claims during an interview that, "China's attitude shift in the CDM was to a large extent driven by the forces of the domestic industries". He further suggested that the degree of influence exogenous information has over preference formation is dependent on the extent to which the Chinese industries support the discourse.[50] Because Chinese industries wield the power to affect the country's economic growth, support from these actors adds substantial political weight to the source of the information.[51]

The mitigation case similarly paints a mixed picture. Even though information was frequently fed to Beijing – primarily through research efforts – the impact was relatively small. An example of this is the GEF's 1992 research programme.[52] Likewise, the NEPA/MEP and the UNEP had jointly set up a series of UN-sponsored projects, including the Joint Centre for an Environmental Information Network intended to assess China's environmental situation. However, the reaction from key decision-makers was lukewarm (Yu, 2008, p. 90), and there were no negotiation preference changes identified at the subsequent COPs. The issue here is that most research efforts were scientific by nature, and there was little analysis on the potential benefits that could come out of mitigation efforts. This, coupled with China's comparatively low per capita emission level at the time, failed to stir momentum among the decision-makers.

Some officials even argued that such studies were inappropriate for the China context due to the perceived 'Eurocentric' issue-framing.[53]

With this said, significant numbers of interviewed negotiators believe that exogenous information does play a role in framing and guiding Beijing's preference formation on mitigation. An obvious example is the shift in the Chinese decision-makers' framing of mitigation from a scientific problem to an economic concern that is imperative to 'sustainable development' – a European notion that the Chinese delegation rejected in 1992, accusing it of being an attempt to impose 'alien values' on China. Another indication would be the findings of the IPCC's fourth assessment report (2007) which triggered a sense of urgency in China to address the side-effects of climate change. The report prompted China's first *National Climate Change Programme*, released in 2007, which includes detailed domestic commitments to reduce national emissions, the 2008 Climate Change White Paper; and its COP15 pledge to cut emissions by 40–45 per cent by 2020. A further indication is Beijing's determination of its bottom line for a post-2020 mitigation framework based on the publication of the IPCC's fifth assessment report (released in 2014).[54] These indications are all suggestive of the fact that information dissemination does have an impact on China's mitigation policy preferences; the international community recognises that China places particular emphasis on knowledge-sharing.[55] But the extent to which information dissemination *influences* preference formation is perhaps reduced to one of policy guidance rather than policy outcome.

The exposure to new information has clearly generated mixed influences on China's preference formation process. Information dissemination, though weak to begin with, did eventually have an impact on China's CDM preference formation in the later years. However, the picture is less bright for mitigation, as information dissemination imposed only marginal influence. What explains the variances?

One contingency is the *nature of support* international discourse has. As discussed above, it is not sufficient to merely obtain the support of second-tier government departments such as MOST and MEP. Instead, support from the government's real power-wielding departments, together with its vital constituents (notably the industries) is imperative in order to enhance the political weight of international discourse in Beijing. The logic behind this is that such support increases the government's political risk of non-action. The availability of support from domestic industries for the CDM case, and the lack of it in mitigation is a key explanation for the deviant impact shown between the cases.

To be sure, the importance of industries in the current context lies in their power with regard to China's economic growth and therefore the legitimacy of the current leadership.[56] While the government pushed the industries forward in the past, today, the domestic industries pushes the government. Again, industries, state-owned and private alike, do not formally participate in preference formation.[57] But they do lobby their interests in government, and more often than not, their interests manage to climb onto the political agenda.[58] As one policy officer points out, "Information is a contribution to the shift in China's position, but it alone is an insufficient influence".[59] The acquisition of support from key stakeholders is fundamental.

The second contingency is the *cost to China's economic structure*. Over the years, China's economic structure has been largely characterised by emission-intensive sectors such as manufacturing, which constitutes 42 per cent of its GHG emissions (Rong, 2010, p. 4586). A meaningful response to climate change via mitigation would require a complete reorientation of China's energy structure and substantial investment in new energy-efficient technologies. For example, during the Copenhagen Climate Summit, Xie Zhenhua said that, in order to realise China's goal of reducing the carbon intensity by 40–50 per cent, at least two trillion RMB of investment will be required during the 12th Five-Year-Plan period (*Shanghai Morning Post*, 2009). The McKinsey Research Report (McKinsey & Co., 2015) stated that it will take 40 trillion RMB for China to build a "green economy" from 2010 to 2030, or an investment of 1.8 trillion RMB every year will be needed to effectively realise a "green economy".

The Chinese government acknowledges that a replacement of coal with natural gas could cut emissions by two-thirds. But unlike countries such as Brazil, which gets 90 per cent of its energy from hydropower, China only has a limited amount of alternative energy sources apart from coal, and an over-reliance on imports is unrealistic and unsustainable in the long-run (Xu and Zhang, 2013). This means that moving to clean energy is a massive challenge and requires a rapid economic restructuring that could affect China's sustainable growth in the future as well as its ability to meet other social objectives such as employment. It was a similar concern that was partially responsible for the US Senate's baulking at the Kyoto agreement. When the economic cost is high, information dissemination is thus only useful as technical guidance (e.g. statistical surveys to measure certain aspects of mitigation) and less of an influence on preference formation.[60]

This situation, however, can be overlooked by decision-makers if the large abatement costs contribute to China's economic development. This was evident in more recent mitigation negotiations, where the government recognised the challenges of remaining with the traditional economic model – based on high-volume consumption of energy and raw materials – to its national development (Zang, 2009, p. 209). The government also recognised that the long-term viability of China's economic success hinges on transforming its low-key manu-facturing and export-led growth to a more balanced strategy that is synonymous with a low-carbon economy (*Beijing Review*, 2012).[61] The 'change of China's economic development pattern' (转变经济发展方式) stood at the very top of China's political agenda, and as such, lowered the previously high economic costs of abatement.

As highlighted by a report published in 2009 by the Task Force on China's Pathway towards a Low Carbon Economy, "Central to the vision of a low carbon economy is the recognition of its potential economic, social and political bene-fits, rather than just the associated costs" (CCICED, 2009). For instance, the green economy brings with it great investment potential in new energy automobiles, energy conservation markets in industrial fields, and potential for investment in low carbon buildings. Furthermore, relevant UN reports have shown that in the coming decades, low carbon economy will generate new jobs in many new fields and sectors, such as clean energy, sustainable transport, water supply, environmental sanitation, and waste treatment. By 2030, nearly 8.5 million people will work in the field of wind and solar power. Such economic potential and reduced economic costs were therefore associated with an increased level of seriousness among Chinese decision-makers in the formulation of international discourse, as observed in recent years of mitigation policymaking.

Likewise, based on UNFCCC data and analyses[62] of the trajectory of GDP and $CO_2$ emissions per capita of major economies, China recognised that, as a country starting late in its development, it has the potential to achieve an innovative development pathway that is less carbon-intensive and will peak lower and earlier with lower income levels than other developed countries.[63] According to China's INDC targets, it is possible that China's $CO_2$ emissions per capita will peak at around eight tons when China's GDP per capita reaches around US\$14,000.[64] The CDM example presents evidence which further supports this finding. As China had not yet established a market infrastructure that would require altering after a CDM adoption, the economic costs associated with the initiative were comparatively lower in all respects, and increased the perceived feasibility of the system in China.

Following the release of China's 2015 INDC, the China National Center for Climate Change Strategy and International Cooperation (NCSC) acknowledged the findings of the IPCC Fifth Assessment Report as one "based on science and observed facts", and accordingly, advocated the low-carbon development as a "necessary condition to achieving sustainable development", which constituted the basis and motivation for China's INDCs. It recognised that while China's foremost strategic priority remains poverty reduction, raising incomes, increasing the level of social security, increasing the coverage of public services including basic infrastructure, and raising standards of living, the traditional growth model – high reliance on inputs – is no longer sustainable. As China faces growing risks of falling into the 'middle-income trap', constrained by resources and environmental conditions, it needs to innovate its development pathways and upgrade its economic growth model towards a 'new normal', in order to move from an economic growth driven by large quantity to one of high efficiency (and therefore, a reduction in the reliance on energy, resources and environmental inputs) – an environment viewed as suitable for development.[65] It is clear to see, therefore, that the third contingency has to do with the level of compatibility between international discourse and China's policy interests.

As a further note, the UNFCCC Secretariat's role as provider of operational advice can sometimes fall prey to concerns relating to the legitimacy or credibility of the output that are unrelated to the quality of the science as such. While broad membership subsidiary bodies lend well to legitimacy in providing the expert advice required for achieving a treaty's governance goals, in practice they have often failed to deliver salient and timely information to China. For example,

China has complained that the Committee on Science and Technology (CST) is inefficient and ineffective, in part because of its large size and composition (ENB, 2001). Even at the first meeting of the COP, participants at the United Nations Convention to Combat Desertification (UNCCD) process worried that the CST would be dominated by "politically-oriented members" and never get down to "scientific business" (ENB, 1997), a problem they felt also existed in the UNFCCC and the Convention on Biological Diversity (CBD) subsidiary bodies. Indeed, the CST did not agree to any impact indicators until 2009 and it will take more time to develop the accompanying methodology and data collection strategy. Many believe, however, that in addition to its size, the politicisation and lack of necessary expertise within the CST is at least in part to blame.

## The impact of reputation

Contractual theorists argue that China's reputation is a significant driver of negotiation preference.[66] As a country that aspires to be well perceived, reputation matter much to China. As a matter of fact, China's initial decision to participate in the UNFCCC in the early 1990s was largely driven by a desire to present itself as a responsible player on the international stage. The global condemnation of the 1989 Tiananmen crackdown caused much concern about international isolation and the related negative effects on China's export-oriented economy. As a result, China, in comparison with other countries, can be easily influenced by considerations of reputation, given its sensitivity to external criticism, and would make much effort to prevent international censure (Johnston, 1998, p. 519). In the words of Zhang and Zheng (2008, p. 8), from the beginning, China's "wish to be seen as a respected member of the international community [has been] one important factor behind its climate change policymaking". Likewise, Deborah Seligsohn *et al.* (2009) and Hallding *et al.* (2009) observed that China's climate change policies mesh with concerns about its international reputation and an ambition to be perceived both domestically and internationally as a 'responsible' nation-state. Such preferences are in line with China's traditional objective to redefine its position in global politics. The notion of China's emergence as a responsible big country and its stated ambition to develop its "comprehensive national power" were key sources of national strength (Zheng, 1998, pp. 192–193).

At the multilateral climate change negotiations, China is reminded of the importance of reputation by the UNFCCC Secretariat and its negotiation positions are measured against international protocols. The UNFCCC Secretary-General has pointed to China's rising income, in terms of purchasing power parity (PPP) and increased per capita emissions, which also inflates the government's actual responsibility to take on mitigation commitments.[67] Numerous indications suggest that the outcome of this reinforcement prompted a shift in China's general outlook towards the need for mitigation. When the negotiations on the Kyoto Protocol took place in 1997, China made clear that it did not wish to discuss internationally binding commitments on mitigation until its economy had reached a 'medium-level' development. This kind of argument is seldom heard today even though it continues to reinforce China's developing country status. The use of softer rhetoric could be considered as an indication of China's effort to build a benign and cooperative international image. The second indication is China's objective to improve its international reputation as one of three core objectives going into the COP15 and COP16 negotiations (Conrad, 2012, p. 442). A part of this objective was the COP15 pledge to cut carbon-intensity by 40–45 per cent by 2025, and China displayed significant domestic mitigation efforts at the COP16 conference in Cancun.

Yet a concern for reputation does not necessarily constitute a driver of negotiation preference. For instance, if reputation mattered to the extent of driving policy outcome, then one would observe an active and cooperative China at the negotiation table. However, the examples have illustrated the lacklustre changes to China's negotiation preferences since COP1. Then, at the 2006 COP in Nairobi, China took a step back by preoccupying itself with wording details and legal aspects of the negotiated text. When announcing its COP16 objective on international reputation, the Chinese delegation also implied that such an objective would not be integrated into an internationally cooperative framework (Conrad, 2012, p. 454). So on the one hand, reputation seems to be effective in reorienting China's negotiation preferences: on the other, this method of influence did not actually catalyse any positive shift in China's position.

What is more, intergovernmental politics can undermine the importance of the reputation factor. For instance, the lack of US leadership, and the mild pressure coming from China's key trading partners, have helped keep the costs of non-commitment to China's reputation relatively low (Economy, 1997, p. 39). Therefore, China feels less need to succumb to arguments of image by domestic or international agencies. Even though Beijing is concerned about its reputation, and especially whether it is seen as a major power, the intergovernmental politics have not pushed the costs of low-commitment to its reputation high enough to induce a change in negotiation preference. Therefore, the significance of reputation was undermined in the broader policy process. The united non-commitment position of the 'G77 plus China' members also helps keep China's reputation costs low. This united front enables China to hide slightly away from the limelight at the multilateral forums. The finger-pointing exercises with regard to America's inactive position, together with the support of China's position by the G77 members jointly undermine the impact of reputation as a driver of policy.

As for the CDM case, there was little data to indicate a real correlation between reputation and the country's adoption of the CDM. With this said, Chinese negotiators interviewed did suggest that one of the considerations for its eventual adoption was that it would make China look good internationally to push the mechanism forward at a time when it was stuck in deadlock (around COP6 and COP7). Again, one cannot deny the change in China's negotiating rhetoric – from blunt resistance to benign and softer tones – as well as the domestic efforts addressing climate change. Did the reputation factor lead to these changes? One interviewee implied that China's reputation for consistently promoting a non-commitment approach is today being increasingly challenged after it was placed as the world's largest emitter.[68]

One key lesson learned from the COP15 is a need for China to improve its international 'actorness' – which is to know how to conduct oneself more diplomatically and strategically. By speaking and behaving in a way that is conducive to perceptions of compliance and activism, the Chinese government believes that it could improve its international reputation without having to make real commitments. In the words of the Minister of the MEP, China's softer tone on the issue of mitigation was executed largely to prevent China from being taken as a scapegoat again and being blamed for the failures of future talks.

The Chinese government believes the UNFCCC is a useful space for achieving greater international 'actorness' since it has a large global media exposure. The government has certainly become more aware and careful with public opinion and the international media, and it has learnt to use these mediums to its advantage. During the Tianjin mini-ministerial meeting before the COP16, China used a media blitz to promote its energy initiatives, took aim at developed countries for inadequate emission cuts, and showcased its model environmental technologies. According to Barbara Finnamore, China programme director for the US-based Natural Resources Defense Council, "China is looking to rehabilitate its reputation" and the Tianjin conference was "an opportunity to not only show they're responsible and proactive, but also to raise and frame the issues" (cited in Tran, 2010). Likewise, a report by the China National Center for Climate Change Strategy and International Cooperation (NCSC) on China's 2015 INDC acknowledged that the country's proposed commitments will act as a demonstration model for other developing countries to follow in pursuit of sustainable development. As the report states, "China provides [a] demonstration and reference for future developing countries, and will transfer experience and provide support for developing countries through means such as south-south cooperation" (Fu *et al.*, 2015). Nonetheless, it is important to note that reputation does not necessarily influence negotiation preferences. It may only induce preference changes for the purpose of improving diplomatic actorness. Meanwhile, the extent to which reputation can actually be effective depends on the level of intergovernmental pressure and behaviours.

## Further remarks

This chapter tested the primary claim of this book against the case of China's involvement in the UNFCCC climate change negotiations. Three policy instruments were assessed, and each were found with mixed levels of significance in China's negotiation preference formation. Rationalists assumed calculations of the costs and benefits of tackling climate change were fundamental aspects of China's climate change policymaking, and in the context of the CDM and mitigation negotiations, this factor had some level of impact on policy outcome. However, its capacity to fully drive policy process is challenged by a *tug-of-war* effect in light of other considerations, such as the expected abatement costs (especially relating to the debate on mitigation).

Moreover, Beijing has, to an extent, used its vulnerabilities to the consequences of climate change to its advantage by pushing off commitments while pursuing international funding and resources essential for coping with the effects of climate change. In particular, the prospect of funding and technology, obtained through economic side-payments, can strengthen China's incentives to take action more than a costs-and-benefits calculation. This is because the prospective future economic gains are considered to be more definite than the costs of future damages surrounded by the senses of uncertainty. Thus, prospective gains will be much more effective in shaping the decision-making processes even if the prospective losses are likely to be large.

The likelihood of acquiring foreign technologies and attract foreign investments is a key reason for China's altered preferences concerning the CDM initiative. China was originally sceptical of the idea, and the Chinese decision-makers in particular viewed it as a loophole purposely created by the developed countries to help them escape from their commitments in tackling climate change. China also feared that the CDM was part of a larger strategy to lure developing countries into making future commitments. However, this policy preference changed when the government realised that the CDM is actually a much more realistic channel for technological transfers from abroad – an area which the developed countries have failed to consider in the past – as well as means to access further funding. What is more, adopting the CDM initiative was thought to contribute to China's reputation-building – the low-cost kind of participation that brings high profile rewards. Thus, the anticipated tangible and intangible benefits spawned from adopting the CDM were primary driving forces for China's eventual ratification of the initiative. Yet, a similar conclusion cannot be made for the mitigation case, whereby the Chinese government had no desire for external technological or financial aids.

Certainly, the mitigation example illustrated that decision-makers do not submit to economic side-payments the way China eventually subjected itself to the UNFCCC's performance monitoring system in order to establish a respected international reputation. This can be seen in China's follow-up behaviour, which is reflected in its submission of the *Initial National Communication* in 2004. China's initial attitude towards reporting and monitoring was negative, as it concerned the principle of sovereignty. But China later recognised that further prolongation of the process can inflate the reputation costs. Hence, Beijing completed the first *National Communication* to show that it does care about climate change. Its submission secured much positive attention. Yet this is not a reflection of the significance of the reputation factor. True, reputation matters to Beijing, but its response comes mainly in the form of an improved international actorness as opposed to any preference change. Then there's information. It has had a certain level of impact over China's decision-making in the CDM and mitigation cases, but, like the previous two factors, it has not caused immediate and unconditional transformations in China's preferences.

On the whole, all three factors have partial and conditioned impacts on China's negotiation preference formation concerning climate change policy. While the impact is not transformative, it is also not non-existent or ineffective.

For this reason, all three factors have an *absorption*-level of influence. In other words, the three factors do shape China's policy preferences, but only to the extent of adaptation. For this reason, the primary claim of this book is *partially valid* in the context of climate change policy.

Clearly, in a world of bounded rationality, policy processes are often more complicated. This outcome verifies the assumption that policy drivers are affected by, and contingent on, national objectives, policy goals, policy settings, and policy instruments. With respect to national objectives, the degree to which the Chinese preferences on the CDM and mitigation modalities were affected by information was contingent on China's national objectives, especially with respect to its existing economic development strategies, and therefore the perceived economic costs associated with executing the discourse.

The policy setting contingency is found in all three factors. For instance, the internal power structure undermined the effect of information in both cases; and policy setting was particularly important in determining the effectiveness of reputation, which was determined by the level of perceived international pressures on China to act responsibly, or the anticipated implications of a low reputation on its future foreign economic relationships. Finally, policy instruments are particularly important in information dissemination, such as the integration of domestic constituents, like industries, to push for preference changes. In sum, Chinese preference formation in climate change diplomacy certainly provides ways to exert influence but its success is contingent on the range of situational factors.

## Notes

1 This involves four key themes. First, like other developing countries, China is a victim of the adverse effects of climate change. Second, China has consistently advocated the principle of 'common but differentiated responsibilities' between countries of varying levels of economic development, and in accordance with their respective historical per capita emissions. Third, developed countries should take on the responsibilities of technology transfers and financial provisions as measures of contributing to the global climate change challenge. Their responsibilities are justified by the current and historical emissions. Lastly, the priority for China is national development and poverty eradication. For more information, see Ida Bjorkum (2005).
2 Annex I Parties are those countries listed in Annex I of the treaty and are primarily industrialised countries. Non-Annex I Parties are developing countries.
3 Interview with a Chinese official from the Ministry of Foreign Affairs, Beijing, 15 September 2011.
4 Interview with an official from the Chinese Ministry of Foreign Affairs, Beijing, 15 September 2011; interview with a researcher from Tsinghua University, Durban, 7 December 2011.
5 Some Chinese sceptics even called the mechanism a tool of Western "environmental imperialism" (Liu, 1999).
6 This position was also in line with the government's wish to align itself with the interest and positions of other non-Annex I Parties. Interview with an official from the Chinese Ministry of Foreign Affairs, Beijing, 15 September 2011.
7 An obvious example is the MOF, which frequently interacts with the GEF – the financial mechanism of the UNFCCC – and regularly coordinates on policies concerning international financial support for various environmental preservation programmes as

well as technology transfers. The GEF will distribute information to the MOF, for instance, which will then be passed on to other ministries for policy drafting purposes. Later, the MOF will coordinate the different preferences or interests among different bureaucracies for consensus-building. Once this has been reached, it will be fed back to the. Interview with an expert from the Chinese Academy of Social Sciences, Beijing, 8 November 2012.

8 Interview with a Ministry of Science and Technology official, Brussels, 8 November 2011.

9 Interview with UNFCCC official, Vienna, 3 July 2011.

10 Another objective was to contribute to the country's capacity-building in commercialised renewable energy sector and remove barriers to the dissemination of alternative energy technologies.

11 Interview with a Professor from Beijing University, Beijing, 17 September 2011.

12 Between late 2001 and 2006, other donor agencies and countries have also carried out capacity-building exercises, each with a different focus area. For example, the UNDP supported projects on the capacity-building of industries and three specific CDM pilot simulations on renewable energy, energy efficiency, and coal bed methane. The World Bank participated in the methodological aspect of the CDM capacity-building projects, and the Asian Development Bank participated in smaller-scale energy-related CDM projects. The Canadian International Development Agency financed operational model assignments as well as other projects that studied urban transportation and renewable energy. Interview with an expert and coordinator from ESP China, 1 September 2011.

13 Interview with a researcher from Tsinghua University, Durban, 7 December 2011.

14 The government believed this was particularly useful in order for it to place focus on other policy areas and concerns. Interview with an expert from the Chinese Academy of Social Sciences, Durban, 3 December 2011.

15 Interview with Professor from Beijing University, Beijing, 17 September 2011.

16 Interview with a researcher from Tsinghua University, Durban, 7 December 2011.

17 Interview with a researcher from Renmin University, Durban, 6 December 2011; interview with a Professor from the University of Nottingham, London, 10 November 2011.

18 Interview with an official from the China Clean Development Mechanism Fund under the Ministry of Finance, at the COP 17 Durban Conference, 7 December 2011.

19 Another key reason is that the investors in Europe did not want to make CDM investments because of the underdeveloped legal structure at the UNFCCC, the vaguely defined benefits for their investments, and the other risks involved.

20 Interview with an official from the Chinese Ministry of Foreign Affairs, Beijing, 15 September 2011.

21 China argued in opposition to the inclusion of sinks on the grounds that it is difficult to ensure the consequential reductions from sink projects have permanent endurance. Arguably, this position sufficed from Beijing's desire to maximise its share of the world's CDM projects (Tangen *et al.*, 2001, p. 242).

22 Interview with an official from the China Clean Development Mechanism Fund under the Ministry of Finance, at the COP 17 Durban Conference, 7 December 2011; interview with a researcher from Renmin University, Durban, 6 December 2011.

23 For example, Maosheng Duan of China serves as Chair of the CDM Executive Board at present.

24 Interview with an official from the China Clean Development Mechanism Fund under the Ministry of Finance, at the COP 17 Durban Conference, 7 December 2011.

25 The Centre, under the guidance of the Climate Change Office in the NDRC, mainly operates at the project level and is not involved in policymaking. Interview with an official from the China CDM Fund under the Ministry of Finance, at the COP 17 Durban Conference, 7 December 2011.

26 Interview with a Professor from Beijing University, Beijing, 17 September 2011.

27 Mitigation is distinguished from adaptation to global warming, which involves acting to tolerate the effects of global warming. Examples include using fossil fuels more efficiently for industrial processes or electricity generation, switching to renewable energy (solar energy or wind power), improving building insulation, and expanding forests and other 'sinks' to remove greater amounts of $CO_2$ from the atmosphere. For more, see UNFCCC (2007).

28 Interview with a Professor from the University of Nottingham, London, 10 November 2011.

29 Interview with policy officer from the Ministry of Foreign Affairs, Beijing, 7 June 2011.

30 Adaptation means that China will take steps to adapt to the impacts of climate change as they occur. Mitigation means that China would take measures to prevent or slow climate change.

31 Interview with an official from the NDRC, Durban, 5 December 2011.

32 Interview with an official from the NDRC, Durban, 4 December 2011.

33 The per capita income in rural areas is below US$78 per annum.

34 Rather than advocating mitigation commitments, Chinese economists have promoted the Asia–Pacific Partnership on Clean Development and Climate (AP6) as an alternative solution to carbon capture and storage, and energy cooperation. AP6 was launched on 12 January 2006.

35 The participants claim that they became more supportive of the idea that mitigation was a necessity for addressing global climate change than other non-participant colleagues. This view was expressed in numerous publications such as the two-volume study, *Climate and Environment Changes in China*, edited by the CMA's Director, Qin Dahe, among others; interview with an expert from Beijing University, 17 September 2011.

36 This is based on personal observations.

37 This is based on personal observations.

38 The Chinese delegation consisted of 34 delegates to COP 12 in Nairobi (6–17 November 2006). From agencies and institutions engaged in climate change research in China, there were 16 delegates: three each from the CMA and the ERI, one from CAS, one from the Centre for Policy Studies (SEPA), two from the Chinese Academy of Agricultural Sciences, one from the Chinese Academy of Forestry, two from the Chinese Academy of Agricultural Sciences, one from Renmin University, and two from Tsinghua University.

39 China did also emphasise that such efforts should be nationally appropriate and subject to the country's respective capacities and specific national circumstances. For more, see Hallding *et al.* (2009), p. 89.

40 Chinese Premier Wen Jiabao forwarded the letter to UN Secretary-General Ban-Ki Moon on 30 January 2010, reconfirming Beijing's announcement on 17 November 2009, about its pledge to cut emissions.

41 Personal observation.

42 Interview with researcher from Renmin University, Durban, 6 December 2011.

43 Interview with a member of the UNFCCC Secretariat, Durban, 1 December 2011; interview with an expert from the ESP China Ltd., Beijing, 1 September 2011; interview with an official from the China CDM Fund under the Ministry of Finance, Beijing, 17 February 2012; interview with an official from the Chinese Ministry of Foreign Affairs at the COP 17 Durban Conference, 9 December 2011; interview with a researcher from Tianda Institute, Durban, 1 December 2011.

44 The former executive vice-Chairman of the NCCCC, Liu Jiang (2005) has, for instance, acknowledged China's vulnerabilities to the negative impacts of climate change, and that "[China] will continue to exert profound influence on the ecological environment and its social economic system".

45 Interview with an officer from the Department of Climate Change, NDRC, Beijing, 22 September 2011; the same sentiment was also reflected through an interview with a policymaker from the Chinese Ministry of Foreign Affairs, London, 1 July 2011.

46  Interview with a policymaker from the Chinese Ministry of Foreign Affairs, London, 1 July 2011.
47  Interview with official from the Ministry of Science and Technology to the EU in Brussels, 8 November 2011; interview with a Professor from the University of Nottingham, London, 10 November 2011.
48  Interview with policy officer from NDRC, Beijing, 27 September 2011.
49  Interview with an official from the Chinese Ministry of Foreign Affairs, Beijing, 14 February 2012; interview with an officer from the NDRC's Department of Climate Change, Beijing, 22 September 2011.
50  Interview with a Chinese delegate to COP 17 in Durban, 9 December 2011.
51  Interview with an official from the Chinese mission to the EU, Brussels, 9 November 2011.
52  Interview with an officer from the Department of Climate Change, the National Development and Reform Commission, Beijing, 22 September 2011; interviews with an expert from the ESP China Ltd., Beijing, 1 September 2011, and a policymaker from the Chinese Ministry of Foreign Affairs, in London, 1 July 2011.
53  Interview with members of the UNDP in China, Beijing, 5 March 2012.
54  Another example is the UNFCCC–World Bank research cooperation with CASS on climate change and mitigation, with their final report submitted to the NDRC for consideration. Without suggesting that this report singlehandedly dictated the ultimate policy adoption on the CDMs, the leading author of the report from CASS did indicate that it made a major contribution to raising the NDRC's awareness about the benefits of the mechanism. Interview with an expert from CASS, Durban, 3 December 2011; interview with delegate to COP17, Durban, 9 December 2011.
55  Interview with a member of the UNDP, Durban, 5 December 2011.
56  Business actors hold even greater influence at the local level. For instance, local governments are usually hungry for investment to boost their local GDP and business agreements are often established between local government and the private sector. This gives the industries an opportunity to give feedback, channel their interests, and enjoy increased influence. Interview with an expert from the Chinese Academy of Social Sciences, Durban, 3 December 2011; interview with a Professor from Beijing University, Beijing, 17 September 2011.
57  Interview with an expert from ESP China Ltd., Beijing, 1 September 2011.
58  Interview with an official from the Ministry of Science and Technology, Brussels, 8 November 2011.
59  Interview with official from the Chinese Ministry of Foreign Affairs, Beijing, 15 September 2011; a similar sentiment was expressed by a member of EMCA, Durban, 7 December 2011.
60  Interview with a Professor from the Shanghai Institute of International Studies, Shanghai, 22 August 2011.
61  The strategy entails the production of technologically advanced and globally competitive goods, the expansion of the service sector, and the development of domestic consumer markets.
62  Data after 2012 is calculated based on INDC targets for each economy.
63  This is based on the historical $CO_2$ emissions trajectory of major economies formed in accordance with a Kuznets curve (an inverted 'U' curve) correlation between economic development levels and $CO_2$ emissions per capita, i.e. along with the increased of GDP per capita, the level of $CO_2$ emissions per capita will experience continual growth until reaching a peak and then dropping. Although the level of emissions peaks varies, until today, no economy has avoided this trend of 'dropping after growing'.
64  By comparison, for major developed countries, their $CO_2$ emissions per capita peaked at around 10–22 tons when their GDP per capita reached around US$20,000–25,000 per annum (at 2010 price levels).

65 In general, China's new development pathway vision is an innovative, sustainable and low-carbon pathway that is deviant from the traditional development pathways of the US and the EU, which focused on improving technological, financial and other necessary conditions.
66 Interview with a senior member of the UNFCCC Secretariat, Vienna, 2 July 2011.
67 Personal observation.
68 Interview with an expert from the Shanghai Institute of International Studies, Shanghai, 26 August 2011.

## References

*Beijing Review* (2012) 'A Self-motivated Response'. [Online] 10 December. Available from: www.bjreview.com.cn/Cover_Stories_Series_2012/2012-12/10/content_506261.htm [Accessed: 13 December 2012].

Bjorkum, I. (2005) *China in the International Politics of Climate Change: A Foreign Policy Analysis*. Norway: The Fridtjof Nansen Institute.

Carbon Trust (2009) 'Global Carbon Mechanisms: Emerging Lessons and Implications'. (CTC748). [Online] March. Available from: www.carbontrust.co.uk/Publications/pages/publicationdetail.aspx?id=CTC748&respos=2&q=global+carbon+market&o=Rank&od=asc&pn=0&ps=10 [Accessed: 31 March 2010].

CCICED (2009) 'China's Pathway Towards a Low Carbon Economy'. *CCICED Policy Research Report 2009*. CCICED Annual General Meeting (11–13 November 2009). Available from: www.cciced.net/encciced/.../report/.../P020120529358137604609.pdf [Accessed: 15 September 2013].

Christoff, P. (2010) 'Cold Climate in Copenhagen: China and the United States at COP15'. *Environmental Politics* 19(4) pp. 637–656.

Cole, J.C. (2012) 'Genesis of the CDM: The Original Policymaking Goals of the 1997 Brazilian Proposal and Their Evolution in the Kyoto Protocol Negotiations into the CDM'. *International Environmental Agreements: Politics, Law and Economics* 12(1) pp. 41–61.

Conrad, B. (2012) 'China in Copenhagen: Reconciling the "Beijing Climate Revolution" and the "Copenhagen Climate Obstinacy"'. *The China Quarterly* 210 pp. 435–455.

Economist Intelligence Unit (2006) 'Factsheet'. London: The Economist.

Economy, E. (2001) 'The Impact of International Regimes on Chinese Foreign Policy-Making: Broadening Perspectives and Policies … But Only to a Point'. In D.M. Lampton (ed.) *The Making of Chinese Foreign and Security Policy in the Era of Reform, 1979–2000* (pp. 230–256). Stanford, CA: Stanford University Press.

Economy, E. (1997) 'Chinese Policy-making and Global Climate Change'. In M.A. Schreurs and E. Economy (eds) *The Internationalization of Environmental Protection* (pp. 19–41). Cambridge: Cambridge University Press.

ENB (2001) 'Summary of the Seventh Conference of the Parties to the UN Framework Convention on Climate Change'. 12(189).

ENB (1997) 'Summary of the Third Conference of the Parties to the UN Framework Convention on Climate Change'. 12(76).

Fu, S., Zou, J., and Liu, L. (2015) 'An Analysis of China's INDC'. A Report Provided by the China National Center for Climate Change Strategy and International Cooperation (NCSC). Available from: www.ncsc.org.cn/article/yxcg/ir/201507/20150700001490.shtml. [Accessed: 2 July 2015].

Grubb, M. (2003) 'The Economics of the Kyoto Protocol'. *World Economics* 4(3) pp. 143–189.

Hallding, K., Han, G., and Olsson, M. (2009) 'A Balancing Act: China's Role in Climate Change'. Report for the Commission on Sustainable Development, Regeringskansliet.

Harris, P.G. and Yu, H. (2005) 'Environmental Change and the Asia Pacific: China Responds to Global Warming'. *Global Change, Peace and Security* 17(1) pp. 45–58.

IPCC (2007) *Fourth Assessment Report*. Geneva: Intergovernmental Panel on Climate Change.

IPCC (2001) *Climate Change 2001: Synthesis Report*. [Online] Available: www.ipcc.ch/pub/un/syreng/spm.pdf. [Accessed: 3 April 2011].

Johnston, A.I. (1998) 'China and International Environmental Institutions: A Decision Rule Analysis'. In M.B. Elroy, C.P Nielsen, and P. Lydon (eds) *Energizing China: Reconciling Environmental Protection and Economic Growth* (pp. 555–600). Newton, MA: Harvard University Press.

Liu, J. (2005) 'The Challenge of Climate Change and China's Response Strategy'. Keynote speech at the Roundtable Meeting of Energy and Environment Ministers from Twenty Nations. [Online] 20 October. Available from: www.ccchina.gov.cn/english/source/ba/ba2005032401.htm [Accessed: 14 April 2011].

Liu, J. (1999) 'Proposal on the Working Plan for China National Coordination Committee for Climate'. Speech presented at the Second Conference of China National Coordination Committee for Climate, Beijing, 29–30 June 1999. Author's personal papers.

Ma, J. (2006) '400m Lives Disrupted by Disasters Each Year'. *South China Morning Post*. [Online] 5 July. Available from: http://china.scmp.com/chimain/ZZZYTL9P7PE.html [Accessed: 3 January 2012].

McKinsey & Co. (2015) 'China's Green Revolution: Prioritizing Technologies to Achieve Energy and Environmental Sustainability'. *McKinsey Research Report.* London: McKinsey & Co.

Molina, M., Zaelke, D., Sarmac, K.M., Andersen, S.O., Ramanathane, V., and Kaniaruf, D. (2009) 'Reducing Abrupt Climate Change Risk Using the Montreal Protocol and Other Regulatory Actions to Complement Cuts in CO2 Emissions'. *Proceedings of the National Academy of Sciences* 106(49) pp. 20616–20621.

National Communication (2004) *The People's Republic of China Initial National Communication on Climate Change: Executive Summary*. [*Zhonghua renmin gongheguo qihou bianhua chushi guojia xinxi tongbao*]. Beijing, China: Planning Publishing House.

NDRC, MOST and MOA (2011) *Climate Action: China in Action 2011*. Beijing: China Meteorological Press.

*News One* (2011) 'China Lost $6.65bn Due to Floods in 2011'. [Online] 30 June. Available from: www.inewsone.com/2011/06/30/china-lost-6-65-bn-due-to-floods-in-2011/59909 [Accessed: 3 January 2012].

Oberheitman, A. and Sternfeld, E. (2009) 'Climate Change in China – The Development of China's Climate Policy and Its Integration into a New International Post-Kyoto Climate Regime'. *Journal of Current Chinese Affairs* 38(3) pp. 135–164.

Pan, J. (2005) 'China and Climate Change: The Role of the Energy Sector'. *Science and Development Network.* [Online] Available from: www.scidev.net/dossiers/index.cfm?fuseaction=policybrief&dossier=4&policy=64. [Accessed: 3 January 2012].

Pan, J. and Chen, Y. (2008) 'Towards a Global Climate Regime'. *Chinadialogue.* [Online] 10 December. Available from: www.chinadialogue.net/ [Accessed: 3 June 2012].

Press TV (2011) 'Over 460 Dead, Missing in China Floods'. [Online] 17 July. Available from: www.presstv.ir/detail/189447.html [Accessed: 3 January 2012].

Rong, F. (2010) 'Understanding Developing Country Stances on Post-2012 Climate Change Negotiations: Comparative Analysis of Brazil, China, India, Mexico, and South Africa'. *Energy Policy* 38(8) pp. 4582–4591.

Seligsohn, D., Heilmayr, R., Tan, X., and Weischer, L. (2009) 'China, The United States, and the Climate Change Challenge'. *WRI Policy Brief* (October).

*Shanghai Morning Post* (2009) 'Xie Zhenhua, Investment Over 2 Trillion Yuan will be Required During the "Twelfth Five-Year Plan" Period for China to Meet the Emission Reduction Goal'. [Online] 15 December. Available from: www.scmp.com/frontpage/international [Accessed: 7 January 2011].

Stern, N. (2006) 'What is the Economics of Climate Change?'. *World Economics* 7(2) pp. 1–10.

Tangen, K., Heggelund, G., and Buen, J. (2001) 'China's Climate Change Positions: At a Turning Point?'. *Energy and Environment* 12(2/3) pp. 237–251.

Tran, T. (2010) 'China Highlights Climate Change Efforts'. *Associated Press*. [Online] 9 October. Available from: http://phys.org/news205821378.html [Accessed: 31 August 2011].

UNDP (2009/2010) *Human Development Report 2009/2010: Overcoming Barriers: Human Mobility and Development.* New York: UNDP.

UNFCCC (2007) *Uniting on Climate.* Bonn, Germany: United Nations Framework Convention on Climate Change.

World Bank (2006) 'World Bank's New Partnership Strategy for China Focuses on Economic Integration, Poverty, and Sustainable Development'. *News Release* (2006/416/EAP). [Online] 26 May. Available from: http://web.worldbank.org/WBSITE/EXTERNAL/COUNTRIES/EASTASIAPACIFICEXT/CHINAEXTN/0,,contentMDK:20931682~piPK:141127~theSitePK:318950,00.html [Accessed: 13 September 2011].

World Resources Institute (2015) 'Statement: WRI Calls China INDC "A Serious and Credible Contribution"'. [Online] 30 June. Available from: www.wri.org/news/2015/06/statement-wri-calls-china-indc-serious-and-credible-contribution [Accessed: 22 July 2015].

Xu, N. and Zhang, C. (2013) 'What the World is Getting Wrong About China and Climate Change'. *China Dialogue*. [Online] 18 February. Available from: www.china-dialogue.net/article/show/single/en/5711-What-the-world-is-getting-wrong-about-China-and-climate-change [Accessed: 21 February 2013].

Yap, C. (2011) 'China Floods Claim Victims, Crops'. *The Wall Street Journal*. [Online] 21 June. Available from: http://online.wsj.com/article/SB10001424052702303936704576396853768579970.html [Accessed: 3 January 2012].

Ye, Q., Ma, L., and Zhang, L. (2007) 'Climate Change Governance in China: A Case Study'. *China Population, Resources and Environment* 17(2) pp. 8–12.

Yiu, L., Niederberger, A.A., and Saner, R. (2002) 'CDM Investment: A Multi-Stakeholder Simulation Exercise, "Can We Make a CDM Deal?"'. Geneva: Centre for Socio-Eco-Nomic Development.

Yu, H. (2008) *Global Warming and China's Environmental Diplomacy.* New York: Nova Science Publishers, Inc.

Zang, D. (2009) 'Green from Above: Climate Change, New Developmental Strategy, and Regulatory Choice in China'. *Texas International Law Journal* 45(1) pp. 201–232.

Zhang, Y. and Zheng, Y. (2008) 'New Development in China's Climate Change Policy'. Discussion Paper 30, China Policy Institute, University of Nottingham.

Zhang, Z. (2003) 'The Forces Behind China's Climate Change Policy: Interests, Sovereignty, Prestige'. In P.G. Harris (ed.) *Global Warming and East Asia: The Domestic and International Politics of Climate Change* (pp. 66–85). London and New York: Routledge.

Zheng, Y. (1998) 'Comprehensive National Power: An Expression of China's New Nationalism'. *China's Political Economy* 191 pp. 192–193.

Zhu, F. (2010) 'Climate Change, Climate Politics, and the Climate Business: Domestic Variables and China's Emission Reduction Policy'. In M.J. Green, C.W. Freeman III, and A.E Searight (eds) *Green Dragons: The Politics of Climate Change in Asia*. Washington, DC: Center for Strategic and International Studies (CSIS).

# 5   Case two

## Negotiating international trade

On 11 December 2001, after 16 years of active lobbying, an ambitious set of concessions, and eight years of perpetual surveillance and monitoring over its performance, China became the 143rd member-state of the World Trade Organization (WTO), during the same session as the launch of the Doha Development Agenda (DDA). As an important economic engine, China became a cornerstone to achieving a DDA agreement. In the words of the former WTO Managing-Director, Pascal Lamy, "A multilateral trade system cannot exist without agreement from China".[1]

As with the climate change negotiations, China's national preferences across various trade issues have exhibited both continuities and changes. What have remained constant are the fundamental principles of China's position on international trade, laid out in its initial application to accede the WTO in 1986. At the same time, China's policy preferences have also grown in flexibility and pragmatism in areas such as the Government Procurement Agreement (GPA) and trade in services. What shaped these positions and their evolutions? To what extent are calculations of costs and benefits, information, and reputation drivers of negotiation preferences on international trade? Consider two WTO trade negotiation cases in which China's position evolved differently over time.

### Negotiating the accession to the Government Procurement Agreement

The WTO's Government Procurement Agreement came into force at the conclusion of the Uruguay Round as one of the *Singapore Issues*. It provides an international legal framework for the liberalisation and "transparent" governance of public procurement markets (Anderson, 2008, p. 162), with coverage ranging from pencils and paper clips to computer systems, telecommunications equipment and consultation services.[2] The GPA is, at present, only a plurilateral agreement covering 42 WTO member-states.

Although joining the GPA was a condition of China's WTO accession, it has yet to accede to the framework. Immediately following China's WTO accession, Beijing's position was that transparency in government procurement processes should be at the discretion of national governments rather than the international system. The Chinese political elites believed the GPA was the West's first step in pushing for a market access agenda. One Chinese negotiator questioned, "If this was not the case, why were they so keen on it? That this will only help the developing countries by promoting good governance has raised suspicion amongst Chinese decision-makers about the actual motive behind the GPA framework".[3] Although the Doha Declaration emphasised that the GPA negotiations should be limited only to transparency and should not restrict the scope for countries to give preferences to domestic goods and suppliers, China remained suspicious.

The distrust was not without reason. The GPA that came into force on 1 January 1996 goes beyond mere transparency issues. According to the framework, it is mandatory for member-states to apply the principle of *national treatment* on goods and services, and suppliers of other Parties to the GPA. In addition, member-states are required to abide by the *most-favoured-nation treatment* (MFN) principle, which prohibits discrimination among goods, services, and suppliers of other Parties. Thus, adhering to this version of the GPA would become a costly affair for China.

Transparency itself can have market access implications by making information available to foreign suppliers unless they are barred from the procurement bids (Evenett and Hoekman, 2004). Many interviewees argued that if transparency has little to do with market access then the transparency issue has little implication for trade. If there is no implication for trade, why should an agreement of this nature be negotiated inside the WTO, an institution established to promote trade rather than good governance?[4] As a result, China had little interest to accede the GPA. Conveniently, China was able to stall its accession on the grounds of the 'Indicative Time-Frame for Accession Negotiations and Reporting on the Progress of Work', institutionalised by the WTO Committee on Government Procurement. The timeline watered down the immediacy with which China is required to accede the GPA, from 18 months following WTO accession to no fixed deadline. Taking advantage of this ambiguous and "indicative" deadline, Beijing did not consider the GPA a priority issue.[5]

Other major economies like the US and the EU did not pay much attention to China's attempt to stall its GPA accession negotiations at the time. Rather, they were more concerned about ensuring that China had implemented its broader WTO commitments.[6] Some years later, however, as new data surfaced about the market value of government procurement in China, they began to question Beijing about its accession pledge.[7] The US in particular called on China to be more transparent in its government procurement processes.[8] Against a history of Sino–US political distrust, China responded, "If there's no trust, why should there be transparency? The US should act as a reasonable leader in order to increase China's trust before asking [China] for transparency."[9] China maintained that it was not ready to partake in GPA negotiations, and did not see the GPA as of its interests (i.e. moving away from its welfare status quo).[10]

Beijing further criticised the 1996 GPA framework (Art. XXIV: 7(b) and (c)) as outdated and insisted on the need for regulatory revisions in order to provide an appropriate basis for negotiation. China feared that the old rules did not provide enough clarity on the type of entities and actions covered – an issue of great relevance to China's complex governmental spending system.[11] Members of the GPA eventually agreed to revise the text, and new principles were added to the old text to take into account of, among others, the existing government procurement practices, and additional flexibility provisions for the tendering process (Anderson, 2008, pp. 172–173).

Thereafter, the US and EU continued to press China to begin negotiations; they argued that China wanted international investments and yet it did not open its procurement market (which, in turn, makes investors incline towards investing in their own countries).[12] But Beijing had concerns of its own. For starters, Beijing did not appreciate the mere fact that all of the existing members of the GPA were developed countries. In addition, China was unclear about the benefits of joining the GPA, which led it to the additional concerns on effectiveness. In particular, the Ministry of Commerce (MOFCOM) was worried about China's industrial competitiveness against foreign firms. For this reason, they argued that China could not commit to current proposals without special concessions.[13]

The Ministry of Finance (MOF) countered the MOFCOM's hesitations with the argument that a GPA membership would contribute to the government's industrial reform plans. They reasoned that it is better to participate in the GPA rather than let others draft the rules.[14] Both arguments captured the imagination of the political elites, and in April 2006, the then Vice-Premier, Wu Yi, announced China's agreement to commence the GPA accession negotiations by late 2007 (US Department of Commerce, 2006).[15]

The subsequent accession proposal drafting process was, unfortunately, not an easy one. The government was only just learning about its new procurement regime – established only in 2003[16] – and how to operationalise it (i.e. how to regulate the procurement regime and operationalise it to general practices). Then there was Beijing's fragmented policymaking structure, which has the MOF as the "book-keeper", the National Development and Reform Commission (NDRC) as the "investor", and the MOFCOM as the "trader".[17] Rather than coordinating between themselves on a coherent policy, they each built their own "fortress of regulation" for government procurement, and at times enacted conflicting rules for the tendering process, the approved procuring agencies, review procedures, and so on. As a result, not only was there a duplication of responsibilities and inefficient management of resources, but the situation also produced inconsistencies and jeopardised the certainty in China's evolving legal framework on government procurement.

Even though the State Council attempted to resolve these issues by establishing an inter-ministerial coordination organ for governing government procurement activities in 2005 – under the 'Interim Measure on Inter-Ministerial Coordination Mechanism on Tendering Proceedings'– the structure remained vague.[18] For instance, while the NDRC is designated as the lead department for managing government procurement affairs, the MOF leads the GPA negotiations (Wang, 2010). As a result, China's negotiating behaviours tend to be relatively ambiguous, and this was very much reflected in China's initial application for GPA membership.[19]

China submitted its first offer of accession together with its application in late 2007. Although the negotiating Parties praised this as a good start, they were unsatisfied with the proposal, viewing it as a limited offering. Other Parties felt that the initial coverage of entities was limited (i.e. only to the agencies of the central government) and excluded key sub-national bodies. Second, the proposed coverage of entities (including goods and services) were rather small, and it only included general products. Third, China had a much higher threshold compared to the average level of incumbent member-states. Finally, a number of derogations were made by China in the general notes. Some believed that China had deliberately delivered a poor proposal to lower international expectations (Tu 2011; *China Daily*, 2010).

To be fair, the GPA framework also poses significant challenges for China's domestic procurement law. For instance, GPA Article XXIV: 5(a) requires that each Party shall ensure, no later than the date of entry into force of the agreement that the conformity of not only its "laws, regulations and administrative procedures" but also the "rules, procedures and practices" are applied by the covered entities with the GPA (cited in Wang, 2010). This involves establishing the procedural rules required by the GPA, training purchasers to use them, and monitoring their application. For a country with a weak government procurement regime, the costs of adaptation are high.

In the meantime, interviews indicated that the WTO Secretariat had, in the background, provided analyses which had sought to drive up the economic gains of further liberalisation. And the presiding staff at the WTO facilitated numerous negotiations with its developed country members for further financial and technical assistance targeted for supporting the industries of developing countries. What is more, they worked to incentivise more foreign direct investments (FDIs) (especially in areas such as manufacturing) into markets including China's.[20]

On 9 July 2010, Beijing submitted a revised offer, which contained only very modest improvements from the initial coverage, especially with regard to the central entity coverage. Beijing agreed to raise the threshold over time, and made new offers on the procurement of services. But these improvements were far lower than expected. During the meetings of the Government Procurement Committee in Geneva (25–26 May, 2011), the Chinese delegation met bilaterally with a list of GPA Parties, including the US and EU countries. According to the Government Procurement Committee Chairman, Nicholas Niggli, "They had good discussions with [China], and it seems also that the bilateral cooperation – with people travelling to Beijing, for instance – has been extremely fruitful" (cited in *Inside US–China Trade*, 2011).

A second revised offer from China was submitted in November 2011. In this offer, sub-central government entities in a number of the most economically advanced regions were included for the first time. Even so, numerous GPA member-states were still unhappy with the revisions. The likes of the US, EU nations, Switzerland, Japan, Singapore, and South Korea, asked China to reduce the thresholds for increasing international competition in the bidding of its public procurement projects. Doing so would require China to scale back exemptions and align its procurement legislation with the GPA framework. As part of the streamlining, the coverage of entities needs to be expanded to include local governments and state agencies, state-owned enterprises (SOEs) and public utilities (Beattie, 2011). Niggli has stressed that, "Five years into the process of China's accession to the GPA, there is some distance to go before a meeting of minds is achieved" and "positions are still quite apart, although the process is moving in the right direction" (cited in *Geneva Watch*, 2012).

By 2014, China had advanced its negotiations to join the GPA with the submission of its sixth offer (submitted in late December). The offer was made in response to its commitment in the US–China Strategic and Economic Dialogue (S&ED) to submit a new revised offer that would be "on the whole commensurate with the coverage of GPA parties" (*Perspectives on Trade*, 2015a). In its new offer, China proposes thresholds at the central government, sub-central, and other entities thresholds – the monetary value at and above which procurement is open under the GPA – that are commensurate with the thresholds of at least some GPA Parties. Since thresholds are one of the key elements in defining covered procurement, the reductions from earlier offers constitute a significant development.

With that said, GPA Parties again emphasised that the tabled offer will need significant improvements in order to conclude China's GPA negotiations, which are now in their eighth year. At the September 2015 meeting, China reaffirmed its commitment to join the GPA. Although it did not set a date for another offer, it did suggest further improvements might be possible if internal reforms of its SOEs and military procurement were concluded and autonomous regions showed interest in being added to the offer (*Perspectives on Trade*, 2015b). Even though the accession negotiations are on-going at the time of the publication of this book, it is clear to see through the revised offers over the recent decade that China has exhibited a dynamic shift in negotiation preference, from a position of reluctance and deliberate stalling to not only a submission to accession, but also the willingness to further liberalise its accession offer time and time again.

## Negotiating trade in services

The 'General Agreement on Trade in Services' (GATS) was brought into the GATT (General Agreement on Trade and Tariffs) during the Uruguay Round, and its negotiations have continued under the DDA. The GATS embodies all measures that affect the range of sectors under the trade in services.[21] The WTO defines trade in services as "the supply of a service through one of four modes" (cited in Mattoo, 2002, pp. 2–3). Mode 1 is *cross-border supply*. It arises when a service crosses national borders (e.g. the purchase of software or insurance by a consumer from a supplier located abroad). Mode 2 is *consumption abroad*.

It arises when the consumer travels to the geographic base of the service supplier (e.g. to purchase tourism, education, or health services). Mode 3 is *commercial presence*. It involves FDI (e.g. when a foreign bank or telecommunications firm establishes a subsidiary unit in another country). Mode 4 is the *movement of individuals*. It occurs when independent service providers or employees of a multinational firm temporarily move to another country.

When China was just a freshman at the WTO, it aligned itself with the Recently Acceded Members (RAMs), and had little appetite for new commitments in light of the challenges it faced implementing the ambitious commitments made during accession.[22] In a communication with the Council for Trade in Services not long after China's WTO accession, it implied that domestic small and medium-sized enterprises (SMEs) as well as infant industries "found it difficult to develop their business against fierce competition from big foreign competitors, especially as some of China's services industries are still at [their] infancy" (cited in *TWN*, 2002).[23] There were deep internal objections to further liberalisation, particularly from the SOEs as they feared a breakdown of gains.[24] Also true was the fact that services only accounted for approximately 30 per cent of China's gross domestic product (GDP) at the time, which is much less than the 70 per cent share of GDP in the US, EU, and Japan.[25] Meanwhile, the few Chinese service suppliers that have expanded abroad (e.g. the Bank of China in London) did not do so well, and failure stories de-motivated Chinese firms from venturing into offshore markets.[26]

For these reasons, Beijing did not have any incentive to respond actively, justifying its 'quietism' as a reflection of a need to adapt to, and improve its knowledge of, the WTO's complicated services framework.[27] Of course, it can be expected that some of the protection is due to political and economic pressures from interest groups, but the government generally felt the necessity to protect its domestic suppliers from external competitions because of arguments relating to industrial infancy or the facilitation of 'orderly exits'. Thus, China's negotiation preference at the DDA negotiations in 2001 was characterised as 'big door open, small door shut'; that is, the Chinese delegation called negotiations on services to address the development gaps in services between the developed and developing countries with the latter entitled to flexibility as stipulated in the GATS.

The negotiation problems assumed a new sense of urgency in the wake of the backlash from the failed trade talks in Cancun (September 2003). At this meeting, China took advantage of the opportunity to exempt from the MFN and the National Treatment obligations under the GATS, i.e. an exemption was made for the international maritime transport sector – for cargo sharing agreements with certain countries. Joint venture or wholly-owned shipping subsidiaries were only permitted on the basis of bilateral agreements and reciprocity. Beijing did not cease the existing subsidiaries in aviation, audio-visual and medical services.

Other protective measures included: the requirement that all legal representatives should reside in China for at least six months of each year; the large majority of doctors in Joint Venture (JV) hospitals were to be of Chinese origin;

capital requirements for JV construction enterprises must be different from domestic enterprises; JV travel agencies were forbidden to supply their services to Chinese citizens travelling abroad; and foreign insurance companies were subject to a 20 per cent cession with a Chinese reinsurance company (though this was to be phased out in four years) (Mattoo, 2002). In the digital communications sector, government-sanctioned blocking of western news and entertainment websites was a routine occurrence, and in July 2004 Beijing announced the regulation and filtration of phone text messaging (Kahn, 2004, p. A3).[28]

At the 2005 Hong Kong Ministerial Meeting, developed countries expressed their dissatisfaction over China's heavy restrictions and pressed Beijing to further liberalise. China responded by reiterating the imbalanced gains from the liberalisation of trade in services, and argued that developing countries should be granted the space for policy readjustments, especially the right to administer and standardise the services market.[29] At the same time, China did begin to show new interest in Mode 4 services and joined a host of developing countries in requesting the reduction of restrictions in place for the movement of people, especially those with lower skillsets – an area where China has a comparative advantage (*TWN*, 2003). The Chinese government also showed new interest in Mode 1 services. Beijing believed Mode 1 services, such as those incidental to the production of goods, were easier to manage and generally have a lower political risk attached, including the transfer of international ideologies through trade in services, which were considered less harmful to the domestic ideational culture.[30]

At the 2006 high level meeting in Geneva, China returned to its traditional low-profile and leadership-avoiding negotiation position. Although China's official line for its 'quietism' is the need for more time to digest existing WTO obligations, critical observers believe the reality of this position is that, on the one hand, Beijing did not want to step on the toes of either the developed or developing countries; and on the other, it wanted to avoid extra international pressure to improve on existing WTO commitments.[31] In addition, China sought to prevent itself from being labelled the troublemaker (Sally, 2011; Huang, 2008, p. 26).

Without denying the validity of those observations, interviews revealed that China's 'quietism' at the time stemmed more from uncertainty (i.e. the nature of impact the liberalisation of trade in services would have on their regulatory freedom). Based on Beijing's experiences as a member-state of the WTO, it viewed the system as ill-equipped to oversee the regulatory standards of trade in services. As such, Beijing was hesitant to submit itself to the binding international framework for services and be overshadowed in its regulatory autonomy by what it perceived as a weak multilateral system (Hoekman and Vines, 2007, pp. 321–324).

Although unpopular with other countries, Beijing felt the need to maintain restrictions on foreign ownership (especially in telecommunications and life insurance) because: (1) limited foreign ownership helps balance the efficiency-enhancing and rent-appropriation elements of FDIs; (2) by inducing foreign investors to form equity JVs, local firms can learn through collaboration; (3) drastic cuts in surplus labour triggered by an immediate transfer of control can be prevented by gradual retractions in ownership; and (4) a general political reluctance to accept foreign control of the essential domestic services sectors. These domestic sensitivities made Beijing reluctant to concede to stronger GATS commitments.

Following criticism from the US, China publicly accused the US of hypocrisy for heavily subsidising its own industries while requesting other countries to expose theirs to fierce international competition. Beijing highlighted the deep reforms it has already taken as part of its accession into the WTO, and the new commitments made on Mode 1 services since it joined the DDA negotiations (Sally, 2011, p. 9). China's response had taken the negotiation arena by surprise, as it was a stark contrast to its usual modest and low-profile negotiation preference.

Following a suspension of the talks as a result of the July 2006 negotiation impasse, Pascal Lamy called an informal meeting on the morning of 16 November 2006, held under the Trade Negotiations Committee (TNC). The stated purpose was to discuss the situation of the DDA negotiations, including contentions relating to the trade in services. The decision to call an informal TNC came after a Green Room meeting on 10 November 2006, to which Lamy invited some 20 influential Members, including China. The meeting saw countries discuss, in an informal manner, ways to revive the negotiations after it broke off from deadlock-breaking offers of tariff or subsidy cuts.

Then at a Green Room meeting on 22 January 2007, Lamy agreed to a request by the services *demandeurs* (i.e. the US, EU, and Japan) to emphasise in Davos that trade in services is a critical component of the overall market access package, in which a meaningful offer in services liberalisation could unlock possible concessions by major developed countries in the agriculture and industrial goods talks (Leal-Arcas, 2007). Domestically, the 2006 negotiation impasse caused domestic business groups to voice concerns about the potential costs a failure to conclude the global agreement on the economy (World Economic Forum, 2007). And some business groups went further to highlight concerns about the potential loss of economic welfare if a treaty was not concluded, and the probability of weakening the safety net that the WTO provides against rising protectionist tendencies if an agreement was not reached (European Business for Doha, 2007).

By this time, China's business service exports had rapidly expanded, growing at 15 per cent per annum from 1995–2005 (Hoekman *et al.*, 2007, p. 369). Although the restrictions on foreign equity were pervasive, they were gradually phased out, with the exception of some elementary telecommunications and life insurance. And with the exception of retail distribution, explicit restrictions on a number of firms were gradually phased out (Hoekman *et al.*, 2007, pp. 377–381). Arguments for changes in technologies and the reform of natural monopolies in the state provision of major services sectors enabled more sectors of the services industries to be internationally contested through the mediums of international trade (i.e. Mode 1 of the GATS) and FDI (Mode 3). Policy reforms, including liberalisation and privatisation, have thus complemented technological changes in support of enlarging the trade in services.

The outcome of this included rapid growth in the international exchange of business services that were historically non-tradable and further rapid expansion in services-related FDIs. China's policy pursuit of increased contestability of the services market can be explained by several reasons. For one, in order to ensure that capital is deployed where it has the best returns, it is imperative to have an efficient and competitive financial sector. In the telecommunications services sector, it features as an immediate input, and a conduit of information. Having increased contestability in this sector would therefore generate low-cost, and quality, digitisable telecommunications products with economy-wide benefits. The transport services sector likewise positively contributes to improving the efficiency of product distribution within and between nations. Other services sectors with a commercial nature (e.g. accounting and legal services) contribute to reducing the transaction costs associated with the operation of financial markets and the enforcement of contracts. In the retail and wholesale distribution services, Beijing inserts significant influences into the sector to generate competitiveness amongst domestic and international market players and to improve the important producer–consumer relationship (Hoekman *et al.*, 2007, p. 370).

In the meantime, a World Bank report encouraged China to open up its services sector to international trade and investment. They reasoned that doing so would help introduce advanced technology and expertise, promote reforms, increase competition, and ultimately enhance the efficiency and competitiveness of China's service sector. It would also provide China with 'leverage' in international trade negotiations to aggressively push for the opening of their trading partners' services markets (Pomfret and Lim, 2012). In 2008, China positively expressed its extended interests in services trade. In reference to the 'signalling conference' held during the July 2008 mini-ministerial meeting, Ambassador Sun Zhengyu reiterated in his statement:

> [I]n spite of our very extensive commitments in our services schedules, we are going to make new efforts, we are going to give *signals* to consider, *on condition that others will reciprocate*, some new sub-sectors, and some improved offers. Eventually the level of openness of our service markets will be roughly at the same level as some developed countries. So that *will* be our contribution.
>
> (Sun, 2008)

In 2011, the Chinese government pledged to open roughly 110 trade in service sector subcategories out of 160, which will be the same as many developed countries. In addition, China intends to fully liberalise Mode 4 services. According to national statistics, services sectors (which range from transportation to retail and wholesale distribution and tourism and hospitality) accounted for 44.6 per cent of China's GDP in 2012. That is less than one point behind the growth of the traditional industries (45.3 per cent).

The services sectors are rapidly developing and their growth may reflect the ongoing government rebalancing of the development strategy from exports to consumption. Certainly, the rise of services contributes to such rebalancing efforts. For instance, services tend to be labour-intensive, which means that their expansion should encourage faster job creation, higher wages and more household spending (*The Economist*, 2013). These benefits have all stimulated the government to announce an agenda to encourage the conclusion of a multilateral framework for the trade in services. At the 10th Ministerial Meeting of the Doha Round of trade negotiations in Nairobi, China's lead negotiator stressed that trade in services should be included in the final outcome. Overall, it is clear to see that since 2001, China's policy preference on services trade has evolved from resistance to newfound, though incremental, willingness to open up previously protected areas.

## Calculating the costs and benefits

The examples showed that the decision-making process typically entails costs-and-benefits analyses. China's early negotiation preference on the GPA was an inert one because decision-makers tended to believe that the costs of accession outweighed the benefits based on the assumption that GPA membership would not enlarge their overseas market access opportunities. For instance, exporters of homogenous goods may benefit, but at the expense of a fall in the purchase of differentiated products due to a rise in the government's foreign sourcing of homogenous goods. This calculation thus constituted one of the drivers of Beijing's hesitation to accede to the GPA.

Around this time, the WTO's Committee on Government Procurement provided technical assistance around the configuration of the GPA, including analyses of the benefits of joining the framework. One highlighted benefit related to corruption. China's existing system for government procurement granted significant discretion to procurement officials, which often invited opportunities for corrupt practices. Corrupt officials in turn were found to deliberately expand their expenditures on (especially highly differentiated) projects including aviation and construction where there are few comparable reference prices within the market. And "officials with an interest in rent collection are likely to employ non-transparent procurement regimes to expand government spending on those items where the opportunities for self-enrichment are greatest" (Evenett and Hoekman, 2004, p. 276). As a result, firms will be dis-incentivised follow the standard process of procurement biding, and take the easy route of bribery instead. Moreover, the contracted firms' motivation to supply to the government's needs and do the jobs well is also reduced.

The GPA, by comparison, will raise the number of firms willing to bid for contracts as opposed to resorting to bribery. Also helpful is the fact that, by joining the GPA, there will be a drop in the demand for imported differentiated goods (and more for homogenous goods), which implies that increasing transparency need not necessarily raise foreign market access in total. What it will do is improve price efficiency. For these reasons, the Committee advised that the GPA contributes to strengthening China's procurement regime, and ensures good practice.[32]

The services case similarly illustrates Beijing's long-held conviction that the costs attached to further liberalisation commitments outweighed the benefits; a vital driver of their non-cooperative negotiation preference at the outset. The regulatory concerns halted Chinese decision-makers from taking cooperative positions. For example, the Chinese delegation frequently pointed to the intangible nature of services, which makes it hard for buyers of services to investigate or test their quality prior to purchase. The extent of asymmetric information often creates a necessity to regulate services in order to protect the consumers, on the one hand, and remedy market failures due to imperfect competition and incomplete information on the other.[33]

But the Council for Trade in Services at the WTO countered China's analysis by suggesting that since most services are themselves inputs in the production of other goods and services, a wider market access opening to foreign service providers will introduce healthy competition that is good for reducing the "cartel effect"[34] and attenuates the "cost-efficiency effect".[35] FDI is a case in point. Foreign providers import their services into the domestic market, generate competitive pressures, and in so doing, induce internal and allocative efficiency. The existing FDIs in services within China have already demonstrated that they are a valuable source of new knowledge, and have contributed to the Chinese economy's production and export of advanced and superior products. As the barriers of trade drop for producer services, imports (including those through FDIs) will increase, and the costs of imported services will decline. Even if this situation displaces some domestic firms, the improved quality of services as well as the expanded variety of available services will nonetheless spawn positive public externalities for service providers due to a rise in total factor productivity (TFP) (Markusen *et al.*, 2005).

WTO advice further argues that increased competition in service sectors through international liberalisation can boost growth.[36] For example, analyses of the effects of trade and investment openness for the financial and telecommunications sectors found that fully liberalised countries grew, on average, one percentage-point faster than other countries (Mattoo *et al.*, 2006), increasing productivity in the manufacturing sector (Francois and Hoekman, 2010), and contributing to adding valuable inputs into infrastructure development (Jensen, 2012).

Comparing the two examples, it is evident that the calculation of costs and benefits is prevalent in the preference formation process; and both internal and external calculations have evidence which is suggestive of varying degrees of impact. As a due process of policymaking, it is understandable that internal calculations by government departments will shape the policy outcome to some extent. Similarly, the examples also confirmed that exogenous analyses from WTO bodies had some level of impact on China's policy development. This finding is further verified by interviews that the WTO's guidance on the costs and benefits are typically welcomed by Chinese decision-makers.

Undoubtedly, the fact that the WTO's analyses complemented Beijing's reform agenda (although it is uncertain whether the congruency is by chance or by design) is a key reason for its wide acceptance by decision-makers. The Committee on Government Procurement, for instance, made a strong case for the GPA membership by highlighting the political benefits of controlling corruption (i.e. through its rules, MFN obligations, and offsets). The argument appealed directly to the Chinese leaders and galvanised domestic political support. Since the mid-1990s, Beijing has been vigilant about ferreting out official corruption, bribe-taking, and dereliction of duty. In his opening speech to the 18th National Party Congress, former President Hu Jintao urged the need to combat corruption[37] before it erodes public confidence[38] in the government and causes the "fall of the state" (BBC News China, 8 November 2012; Phillips, 8 November 2012). Leaders considered the GPA to be a useful external force for pushing domestic political anti-corruption efforts. Interviews suggested that this motive was a driver in China's decision to submit to the GPA accession in 2007.[39]

Likewise, the WTO's analyses were perceived to be useful supplements to the government's existing plans to reform its services sectors. As one MOFCOM policy advisor points out, China's negotiation preference shift in services over recent years has much to do with the fact that an international agreement on services would benefit the country's next round of economic reforms.[40] This is not least because the average annual rate of growth in the services sectors such as the tertiary industry is approximately 10.8 per cent of added value between 1978 and 2007. This is at least three to six percentage-points higher than the agriculture and manufacturing sectors in China (Zhang and Evenett, 2010, p. 9). In addition, the Chinese decision-makers believe that opening-up Mode 4 services will help address China's domestic unemployment problems.[41] Because opening up contributes to China's domestic objectives, the decision-makers were more willing to accept WTO advice.[42] In these ways, the calculation of costs and benefits matters and external advice can influence decision-making, especially when it serves China's national objectives.[43]

However, the examples also illuminated different levels of evolution in China's negotiation position over time. While the GPA saw China conceding to greater liberalisation over the years through its proposals, their negotiation positions on trade in services have evolved only incrementally. What explains this variance?

The qualitative data suggests that a key contingency is the *perception* of the decision-makers. For instance, decision-makers for the GPA generally perceived a strong set of benefits as a result of accession, especially to China's future political system. Conversely, the risk of not participating in the GPA was considered detrimental to the CPC's political legitimacy. By comparison, decision-makers for the trade in services chapter generally perceived liberalisation as beneficial for China's domestic economic restructuring. At the same time, however, the short- and medium-term political cost of non-action was low and open to debate. More importantly, the political elites saw that beneath each suggested benefit lay potential costs. For example, although consumers, in theory, should favour services reforms as they expand the diversity of services available to them at competitive prices, it is also possible that they will oppose such reforms due to a fear that doing so will lower consumer welfare, including the quality of services.[44]

Another concern was the notion of 'stability maintenance'. That is, a primary goal for Beijing was to maintain short-term stability in its service sectors, despite a need to improve long-term efficiency. Nowhere was this debate more critical than in the banking sector reforms. The thought process was that as long as short-term financial crises do not occur, the chance of resolving the long-term problem, including efficiency, is possible. But if China was to liberalise its services sectors, then uncontrollable events such as a global financial crisis could erode long-term certainty and short-term stability (Wu, 2012).

Furthermore, there were political fears that trade in services could undermine Beijing's right to regulate, since trade brings with it regulatory intrusion, and service suppliers are only subjected to the home market's rules. This is especially the case for Mode 1 and 4 services – if trade is permitted to occur on the basis of qualifications and certifications obtained in their home country, then it is uncertain whether foreign providers will seek to also meet Chinese norms. Thus, the regulatory concerns of excessive intrusiveness, inherent unpredictability in commitment implications, and the capacity to set up complementary measures for achieving regulatory and social objectives clouded the perceptions of the decision-makers regarding the WTO bodies' more optimistic calculus of the gains from services liberalisation. It shows that the different degrees of *perceived* benefits vis-à-vis the costs generate variances of influence, as seen in the examples.

## Exposure to information

When asked about China's passive participation in the DDA negotiations, especially in the earlier years of the negotiations, 97 per cent of Chinese and non-Chinese interviewees commonly regarded the country as at a learning stage with respect to international trade and the multilateral trade system. As a US official said, "A major problem in China is economic literacy and a lack of it among the Chinese officials; making it problematic for negotiations".[45] Where domestic supplies of information fell short, China was cushioned with international support, and policymakers were well connected to external sources of international discourse.

The GPA negotiation is a case in point. The country's accession into the GPA framework was, in the beginning, almost neglected by the political elite. Jiang Zeming and Hu Jintao have rarely mentioned the issue in public, and Wen Jiabao only occasionally acknowledged it in passing (Xinhua News Agency, 2010). For the most part, China's attitude on the issue was ambiguous. Interviews suggested that Beijing's ambivalence was primarily caused by a lack of understanding about the framework; even today, Beijing is still familiarising itself with the laws of the GPA.[46]

Then when China joined the WTO, decision-makers from the MOFCOM and MOF, among others, had expanded access to international discourse around the GPA.[47] Although some policymakers complained that the WTO failed to provide substantive policy support (due to its lack of experts in the area), they were a great channel of information.[48] Interviewees recalled that the MOFCOM and the MOF "became particularly supportive of joining the GPA after realising its purpose and benefits as a result of their engagements with the WTO".[49] The then MOFCOM Minister stressed to the State Council that becoming a GPA country could help the government promote new industrial reforms and drive the country's procurement system towards openness and transparency – sentiments which align with those of the WTO.[50] The conservative decision-makers rejected this argument, however, on the basis that it is not appropriate or necessary to depend on foreign pressures to push for domestic reforms.[51] In the end, the MOFCOM's proposal was overshadowed by more influential members of the central government. This goes to show that the policy impact of international discourse can at times be barricaded by internal politics. This is supported by 72 per cent of interviewees, who are of the view that information dissemination is effective in improving the policymakers' understanding about the technicalities around the GPA, but not necessarily in influencing negotiation preferences.

Like China's initial GPA stance, its early policy on services was characterised as ambiguous. Because of the wide range of complex and technical issues involved in the services negotiations, from finance to telecommunication and distribution, it has required a labyrinth of government agencies to participate in the marathon of knowledge catch-up, and often China behaved passively at the multilateral negotiations, as a result.[52] As Hoekman and Mattoo (2011, p. 14) point out, "Matters are already complex when negotiations revolve around traditional trade policies such as tariffs and quotas; but they are an order of magnitude more complicated when it comes to services given that there is almost invariably a regulatory dimension".[53] The interviews illuminated that the Council on Services Trade within the WTO have actively supported the relevant agencies in technical and specialist training through various forms of information dissemination on (1) the scope and size of services trade liberalisation and regulations; (2) the competitiveness of the relevant industries as well as the likely impacts of services trade liberalisation on those industries; and (3) other information relevant to its negotiation preference formulation.[54]

However, participating policymakers elucidated that even though engagement with the Council produced positive learning benefits, they also felt the constant influx of diverse information complicated the inter-departmental coordination process as different agencies received too diversified and at times contradicting information, which caused the emergence of competing ministerial interests.[55] In the words of one Chinese negotiator to the WTO,

> Information that was received were confusing as it covered so many different and varied details for different government departments, and the inter-departmental discussions therefore became difficult, especially when

different departments received different kinds and amounts of information, causing imbalances in knowledge and perception.[56]

As a result, establishing a coherent consensus becomes a challenge.[57] This finding contrasts with the cognitive assumption that international discourse is useful in guiding inter-departmental negotiations as it increases their mutual understanding about the country's negotiation objectives and priorities. A similar implication for the GPA example was not found. This could be due to the fact that the GPA Commission provided elementary support too insignificant to trigger a similar effect.

Related to this point is the perception that WTO bodies lack any robust mechanism for generating reliable information (Feketekuty, 2010). Policymakers that work on the GPA stated that sometimes the WTO provides policy guidance which does not actually enhance their understanding about various aspects related to government procurement. In fact, the WTO at one point even failed to provide a clear definition for 'government procurement', and what it implies in political and economic terms. And neither the GATT 1994 nor the GPA 2007 embody precise definitions for the notion of 'government procurement'. For instance, the GATT 1994 defines 'government procurement' as the procurement for government purposes without defining what 'government purposes' are. Similarly, the GPA 2007 defines the notion as any kind of purchases made by the covered entities rather than for other commercial purposes. The lack of a concrete definition in the WTO discourse – leaving each Party to legislate their own definition based on the scope of their government procurement activities – created difficulties for Beijing in ascertaining how they should treat the negotiations.

Inconveniently, what the disseminated information from the WTO did clearly indicate in great detail were the political costs attached to joining the GPA. For example, Beijing might lose its authority to select between government control and market forces. Since Beijing believes it is important for the government to retain control over investment and consumption in order to meet economic and social development objectives, compromising this for entry to the GPA was unacceptable. A senior member of the WTO Secretariat admitted that the regime needs to improve its supply of updated information to nation-states. In fact, it was suggested that member-states often do not even know where to find information and where to seek technical assistance within the WTO. This is one area the WTO bodies need to expand in capacity.[58]

In services, a policy advisor from the MOFCOM points out that the WTO's services norms tend to be vague and there was limited support offered to China – only on the labour issues were there some support.[59] Members from the Council on Services Trade interviewed revealed that there is limited sectoral/regulatory expertise to assist China or any other country.[60] For instance, the WTO comprises around 600 people of whom only approximately 300 are working staff. Breaking down the calculation to 20 working departments, then each technical section is only comprised of approximately 10 staff.[61] One

Chinese negotiator went one step further to claim that, in many instances, the "WTO simply is not interested in expanding their expertise due to US and EU influences; if it was interested, it would have improved its expertise and information quality".[62] Instead, other international organisations, such as the World Bank, are the actual providers of regulatory and sectoral information and assistance for a number of services sectors including transport, telecommunications, and finance (Hoekman and Mattoo, 2011, p. 15).[63]

Members of the WTO have pointed out that in the absence of such a mechanism it has actively hosted a range of training workshops which serve similar purposes. However, interviews with members of the Chinese government revealed such workshops were not usually treated seriously, and this is even more so with language barriers impeding full information absorption.[64] As a result, the influence stemmed from the workshops tends to be small. The lesson here is that exposure to information and international discourse can influence decision-making to the extent that it is contingent on (1) how detailed and precise the international discourse is; (2) the benefits of adapting to the information; (3) the variety of information disseminated across different government agencies; and perhaps the most important element is (4) the level of proficiency within the source of the information, in this case, the working bodies of the WTO.

A further factor which undermines the impact of information is Beijing's fragmented decision-making structure, characterised by the inter-departmental power struggles. As already mentioned, even though the MOFCOM is, in theory, responsible for the GPA negotiations and preference formation, the MOF also leads numerous dimensions of the negotiations due to its high-level content relevance. Meanwhile, the NDRC is the oversight agency against the GPA, although the MOF – a proponent of the GPA – has on numerous occasions implemented national positions outside the NDRC authority. However, the MOFCOM has the discretion to either accept or ignore other ministerial proposals, depending on the consensus and support from the leadership (Liang, 2003, pp. 301–304). As a result of the fragmented decision-making structure, it is difficult for the WTO bodies to identify a reliable route for channelling their discourse.[65]

The preference formation for services points to a comparable situation. Although the MOFCOM is officially the lead trade policy agency and usually represents China in the services trade negotiations, it only has the authority of a negotiator on behalf of industries and not the authority of a real coordinator (Wang, 2010). In other words, the MOFCOM needs the endorsements of the relevant industrial policy-owner ministries and commissions, which is often very difficult to attain given that its interests tend to clash with fierce contradictions from other ministries in charge of various sectors such as banking, telecommunications, and insurance dimensions of the services negotiations.

That is why domestic interest groups can at times be assertive in resisting further liberalisation beyond the WTO-accession levels, as long as the political leadership does not directly intervene in the preference formation. Moreover, as

more representatives from other ministries join the MOFCOM at the WTO negotiation table, it further undermines the MOFCOM's control over the discussions.
For instance, negotiators from other ministries blamed the MOFCOM officials
for not understanding the real situation in their sectors, and as such, there was no
reason why the MOFCOM officials should speak on their behalf (Liang, 2010,
pp. 716–717). In this context, even if international discourse was effective within
the particular ministry in which it was disseminated, the incoherence between
the ministries can easily undermine the impact of the discourse. As one Chinese
expert commented, "China's domestic politics does interfere with China's trade
policy: and the lack of coordination due to competing interest between ministries
is a key impediment".[66] Thus, the second contingency of influence through
information is the policy setting in Beijing; especially the level of cohesion in
the inter-ministerial coordination process.

The third contingency has to do with the political costs attached to the international discourse. On the GPA issue, the information disseminated to Beijing
caused concerns about the impact of joining the GPA on the government's autonomy. As the GPA rules directly regulate the government's activities, and have
a restrictive effect on state interventionist policies for market activities, membership would imply a reduced autonomy over consumption and investment. This is
problematic for China because government investments have long been thought
of as a useful and effective instrument for the stimulation of social investments.
The 2008 financial crisis is a case in point; Beijing injected a stimulus package
of 4000 billion RMB in order to stimulate social investments. Although the
Commission stressed that opening its government procurement regime would
not harm the Chinese economy, it did not lessen Beijing's concern that a GPA
accession would not only be a concern for market access but, more importantly,
imply the need to undergo major government reforms of the state sectors. These
high political costs attached to supporting the WTO discourse caused some hesitation in Beijing.

Likewise, the information disseminated to Beijing on services was ineffective
in shaping China's policy preference because its intentions clashed with the
interests of Chinese SOEs. Following the economic reforms of 1978, the SOEs
have enjoyed augmented autonomy to make market-based business decisions. At
the same time, since the deliberated reforms were only partial, they have retained
the rents that were created by the former monopolised system. Together, they
have become much more influential in Chinese policy because of their relative
importance in generating the country's revenue and employment. As of 2012,
Chinese SOEs contribute to approximately 36 per cent of the world's products.[67]
Naturally, then, Beijing is keen to remain on good terms with the interests of the
SOEs or risk domestic political and social instability. Moreover, numerous presidents of major SOEs hold an affiliation with some of the major government
departments. In a way we see a paradox: the sectors which benefited from partial
reforms have become major resistance points for future reforms. Their resistance
stems from the fact that their profits and rents under the existing system are
likely to be lost if faced with external competition and scrutiny.

With this said, the powers of the SOEs are increasingly rivalled by the rapid growth of privately-owned enterprises (POEs). In the past, POEs were generally disadvantaged in the domestic market and resource access as a result of the SOEs' monopolisation of the services sectors.[68] This caused many POEs to look to foreign investors (i.e. through the 'China–China–Foreign' or CCF JV system) in order to assert themselves within the domestic market.[69] As more POEs took on the CCF system, it created a loophole for foreign entry and undermined the coherent industrial policy protected by numerous service sectors from liberalisation (Gao and Lyytinen, 2000, p. 725). On top of this development, one interviewee points out that the size of the SOEs' workforces has been falling from 85 per cent in 1952 to 30–40 per cent today, while that of the POEs has climbed steadily. The growing significance of the POEs,[70] and their expanding relationship with foreign investors, added much pressure on the State Council to revise their trade in services negotiation preferences in order to retain control over the domestic market, and mitigate any potential undermining of the CPC's legitimacy.[71] One services trade policy advisor claims that an obvious correlation can be drawn between China's negotiation preference shifts in services and the business interests.[72] In light of a somewhat ineffective WTO information generating system, business and industrial actors seem to be controlling the steering-wheel of preference formation.

## A look at reputation

From a contractualist point of view, China's concern for its international reputation could, in theory, influence its negotiation preference. And even in the absence of material constraints, states may act certain ways or refrain from certain behaviours in order to avoid a loss of status, humiliation, and/or other social sanctions (Johnston, 2008). This is fair enough, given that China is engaged in a multilateral agency that works closely with the international media (in the name of transparency) and holds daily press briefings during each negotiation round.[73] The way the WTO Secretariat assesses China's preferences, and subsequently the way they portray China to the global media places additional policy pressure on Chinese decision-makers.

The indirect influence of this is significant for political elites. As in the case of climate change, they see cooperation through international trade as an opportunity to restore China's disrupted global reputation from the events of the past century. What is more, interviews suggested that maintaining China's reputation is also important for ensuring the kind of stable international environment necessary for achieving its national development objectives. It is these concerns which prompted China's keen interest to form a united developing country front. Yet the WTO has pressed China to do more. In November 2003, Supachai Panitchpakdi, former Director-General of the WTO, stressed that the organisation hopes China could work as a bridge between developing and developed countries to help restart the new round of trade negotiations, and stated that, "It [China] has a special status, because it is rapidly becoming a very, very powerful player in international trade" (Cited in BBC Monitoring Asia-Pacific, 2003). Clearly, the reputation factor constitutes a significant driver of policy.

And yet, the GPA and services case studies allude to contrary realities. Neither example suggested any real evidence that members of the WTO actively sought to influence or guide China's GPA or services policy preference formation by playing the reputation card. And there was little indication that reputation has the level of impact that drives negotiation preference changes. The general view (supported by 79 per cent of interviewees) is that while reputation matters (especially in the implementation phase), it is generally seen as a secondary concern amidst other priorities when formulating a negotiation position. In contrast to the climate change negotiations, which are generally framed as a moral and ethical concern, and hence intensify the reputation costs of non-commitment, the moral and ethical concerns in trade negotiations, be they on government procurement or trade in services, are comparatively less weighty and therefore the reputation costs of taking non-commitment will always be low.

Still, one should not so easily dismiss this variable. With the increase of China's global economic activities, the government does feel the pressures of scrutiny around the world, particularly on whether China will succeed in its market transition, and the WTO has been a highly visible yardstick for that measurement. Hence, the government is very careful with public opinion and media commentary.[74] A case in point is China's first WTO dispute. The US filed a complaint with the Dispute Settlement Body (DSB) with regards to China's preferential value-added tax (VAT) for domestically produced or designed semiconductors. The complaint claimed that all semiconductors sold in China were subject to a 17 per cent VAT, but domestic producers – including both Chinese and foreign-invested firms – were eligible for an 11 per cent tax rebate, rising to 14 per cent if the products were designed and made in the country. Imported semiconductors, on the other hand, did not qualify for any rebate (Liang, 2007).[75] The US argued that the tax rebate for domestic producers violated the cardinal WTO principles of non-discrimination and national treatment in the GATT.[76]

Although China claimed that it was confused by the US's actions (*People's Daily*, 2004), the dispute was soon resolved without being escalated to the panel stage – on 14 July 2004, China and the US notified the DSB that they had come to an agreement. According to the notification, China agreed to amend or revoke within a few months the measures at issue to eliminate the availability of VAT refunds on Integrated Circuits (ICs) produced and sold in China, and on ICs designed in China but manufactured abroad. The speed at which China settled the case is surprising considering that over three years of prior bilateral negotiations on the issue had failed to yield any meaningful results. The key factor that prevented China from litigation was the government's concern for potential reputation loss associated with defending its protectionist measures in the formal WTO dispute resolution system (Li, 2012, p. 1130).

Several factors reinforced this fear for reputation loss. First, the Chinese leadership often finds it difficult to disentangle legal issues from political and reputation-linked concerns, and views the initiation of legal disputes in the WTO as tantamount to setbacks in diplomatic relations with the other countries (Gao, 2007). Interviews with Chinese negotiators on the VAT issue also suggested that they were given explicit instructions from Beijing to resolve the case at the consultation level by all means.[77] This kind of aversion to litigation behaviour is in line with China's Confucian philosophy that litigation would cause irreparable harm to normal relationships and should be pursued only as a last resort (Diamant, 2000).

Moreover, in the post-Deng Xiaoping leadership, China has been documented as being highly sensitive to a negative reputation because a loss of face and reputation (e.g. being sued and perhaps losing cases) would be detrimental to the CPC's political legitimacy, both at home and abroad. Furthermore, social pressures are particularly strong on novices in an uncertain environment (Checkel, 2005). China at the time of the VAT dispute can be clearly categorised as a novice in the WTO system. Merely into its third year as a formal WTO member, after decades of negotiations and promises to abide by international rules, Beijing was keen to steer clear of any action that might cause it to be stigmatised as protectionist and tarnish its image as a 'responsible power'.

Again, this does not imply that reputation influences negotiation preferences in absolute terms. Undeniably, China cares much about its reputation, just like any other country. But the reputation factor is a relative variable in the eyes of Chinese decision-makers and its significance varies accordingly to the situation and circumstances of a given issue and at a given moment in time.[78] Generally speaking, the view of the Chinese government is that if the WTO was to portray a negative reputation to the media about China, no matter what it does, it will still be portrayed negatively.[79] Chinese decision-makers know that the Chinese public generally hold the view that any negative image depicted of China is usually created by the western media and therefore it is an external problem that has no impact domestically whatsoever. Since this does not generally affect the Chinese public, it implies a relatively low political risk attached to a less-than-satisfactory reputation abroad, and thus, Beijing does not feel the need to change its preferences in response to reputation-building.

This is a basic domestic support versus international attempts at driving China's reputation balance; when the former is stronger, then the impact of the latter is weakened.[80] The reverse is also true: if domestic support is weak, then the impact of reputation could be stronger. At the end of the day, China's national interest remains at the centre core and reputation as a factor of decision-making is contingent on whether it (1) serves China's interest; and (2) the political and economic costs associated with a non-commitment approach – if the risks, especially politically, are high, then this mechanism is more likely to be impactful.[81]

## Further remarks

This chapter has considered the fact that all three policy instruments drive policy to an extent. Perhaps reputation has the least influence, because the multilateral trade negotiations under the WTO are driven primarily by commercial interests rather than moral ones, and this lowers the political risk of adopting a non-commitments negotiation preference. With this said, the decision-makers also recognise that, given the importance of international trade as a key economic lifeline of China, maintaining a reputable global image is imperative, which means that policymakers do feel the need to consider reputation factors when forming policy preferences. Still, this is a case-dependent factor that is contingent on the perceived political costs.

By comparison, a seemingly more effective instrument is the costs-and-benefits calculus. By focusing on the benefits of cooperation, WTO advice has instigated a momentum in Beijing's preference shifts for the GPA and services modalities, though to different extents. The presence of contingencies for this instrument means that the costs-and-benefits calculus does not have a transformative degree of influence, although it also does not have an absorptive level of influence. Rather, its impact-factor sits in between transformation and absorption. Finally, information was found to be effective in reshaping policymakers' awareness and understanding about the negotiating issues, but its capacity to change policy preferences is constrained by limitations in Beijing and at the WTO.

This is illustrative of the truth behind the assumption that the level of influence each variable has is contingent on situational factors: national objectives, policy goals, policy settings, and policy instruments. For starters, the examples illustrated how the effectiveness of all policy instruments is dependent on the degree to which they service China's national objectives. The calculation of costs and benefits worked well for the GPA because it served Beijing's political reform agenda on corruption. Information dissemination worked less well for services because it did not claim much benefit for China's national objectives. China's national objective to establish itself as a peaceful and cooperative nation also heightened the influence of reputation reinforcement to an extent. The policy goal contingency was a key determinant for the effectiveness of information dissemination and the costs-and-benefits calculus. For instance, with a policy goal of tackling corruption, Beijing needed resources which the WTO bodies provided, albeit at an elementary level. Conversely, the lack of congruency between China's policy goals in services and the international discourse undermines the impact of both the instrument and the WTO.

Next, the impediment of Beijing's fragmented coordination and decision-making processes is the policy setting contingency which has hampered the WTO bodies' information dissemination efforts. Also, the extent to which China takes reputation seriously depends on the broader domestic and international settings, by means of pressure and scrutiny. Finally, policy instruments as a contingency were featured in information dissemination. For instance, the WTO's lack of professional systemic support on issues such as the GPA and services undermined its perceived credibility with the Chinese decision-makers. Overall, China's negotiation preference formation does have access points for all policy instruments, but the extent of actualised influence is circumscribed by the aforementioned situational factors.

## Notes

1 This quote is cited from Pascal Lamy's opening speech at the 2011 Ministerial Meeting.
2 Typically, this accounts for between 10 and 15 per cent of GDP for developed countries and up to 20 per cent of GDP for some developing countries (Jawara and Kwa, 2004, p. 42).
3 Interview with a Chinese negotiator to the WTO, Beijing, 11 November 2012.
4 Interview with an expert from the University of International Business and Economics, Beijing, 13 February 2012.
5 Interview with a policy advisor from the Chinese Academy of International Trade and Economic Cooperation under the Ministry of Commerce, Beijing, 19 November 2012.
6 Interview with a member of the Department of Treaty and Law, Ministry of Commerce, Beijing, 23 November 2012.
7 In its 2001 accession to the WTO, China stated its intention to "initiate negotiations for membership in the GPA by tabling an Appendix 1 offer as soon as possible". *Report of the Working Party on the Accession of China*, WT/ACC/CHN/49, para. 341.
8 Interview with an official from the Ministry of Commerce, Beijing, 21 September 2012.
9 Interview with an expert from Tsinghua University, Beijing, 22 November 2012.
10 Interview with a member from the Department of Treaty and Law, Ministry of Commerce, Beijing 23 November 2012.
11 Interview with a policy advisor to the WTO Division of the Ministry of Commerce, Shanghai, 2 March 2012.
12 Interview with an expert from Fudan University, Shanghai, 25 April 2012.
13 Interview with an expert from Peking University, Beijing, 23 September 2011.
14 Interview with an expert from the Shanghai Institute of Foreign Trade, Shanghai, 25 April 2012.
15 Interview with a policy advisor to the WTO Division of the Ministry of Commerce, Shanghai, 2 March 2012. Interview with an expert from Peking University, Beijing, 23 September 2011.
16 In 2000, the State Development Planning Commission drafted and implemented the country's first piece of primary legislation on government procurement known as the *Tendering Law*; but a more comprehensive *Government Procurement Law* was later drafted and implemented in 2003 by the MOF.
17 Interview with an expert from the Chinese Academy of Social Sciences, Beijing, 8 November 2012.
18 According to Article 4 of the Interim Measure, the main duties of this coordination mechanism include: (1) analysing the status of tendering regulations and discussing possible solutions for regulating tendering activities involving multiple government organs; (2) resolving inter-departmental conflicts regarding the administrative supervision of tendering; (3) exchange of information; (4) coordinating the promulgation of tendering regulations by different departments; (5) communicating the enforcement of tendering rules; and (6) joint survey and research. For more, see Wang (2010).
19 Interview with an expert from UBIS, Beijing, 12 March 2012.
20 Interview with an expert from Peking University, Beijing, 23 September 2011.
21 The only explicit sectoral exclusion from GATS is certain 'hard' rights in the aviation sector.
22 China's WTO accession commitments in services are as follows. For most sectors, Modes 1 and 2 are either fully open or unbound, and not subject to specific restrictions. Commitments on Mode 4, specifically horizontally rather than sector by sector, are also standard – entry is guaranteed only for managers, executives and specialists, who must either be intra-corporate transferees or employed by foreign invested enterprises, and for services salespersons on exploratory business visits (Mattoo, 2002, pp. 6–7).

23 An example of this is a communication submitted to the Council for Trade in Services not long after China's WTO accession. In the communication, China implied that its infancy services sectors such as the tertiary industry are much smaller in scale than the foreign counterparts and have generally found it challenging to compete against the larger competitors from abroad.

24 Interview with a policy advisor of the China Academy of International Trade and Economic Cooperation under the Ministry of Commerce, Beijing, 19 November 2012.

25 Interview with an expert from Fudan University, Shanghai, 24 April 2012.

26 Interview with a policy advisor from the China Academy of International Trade and Economic Cooperation under the Ministry of Commerce, Beijing, 19 November 2012.

27 Interview with a policy advisor from the WTO Division of the Ministry of Commerce, Shanghai, 2 March 2012.

28 This was seen as a response to the use of cell phones in 2003 to transmit news relating to the SARS epidemic, revealing initial attempts by Beijing to suppress the health crisis, as well as cases involving state corruption and abuses of power.

29 This was expressed in the national statement made by Chinese Minister of Commerce, Bo Xilai.

30 Interview with an expert from Fudan University, Shanghai, 24 April 2012.

31 For instance, China is viewed by the developed countries as 'the biggest beneficiary' of the multilateral system and the DDA; hence, the US and EU heavily pressed China to bear more obligations beyond their capacity, while developing countries hope China will take a lead on their behalf against the developed countries.

32 Interview with a senior member of the WTO Division of the Ministry of Commerce, Beijing, 22 November 2012.

33 Interview with a member of the Department of Treaty and Law of the Ministry of Commerce, Beijing, 15 November 2012.

34 The cartel effect is "the mark-up price over marginal cost that incumbents are able to charge owing to policies that restrict entry" (Hoekman *et al.*, 2007).

35 The cost efficiency effect is "an environment where there is limited competition the marginal costs of incumbents is likely to be higher than if entry was open" (Hoekman *et al.*, 2007).

36 Interview with a policy advisor to the Ministry of Commerce, Beijing, 25 October 2012.

37 The Chinese business magazine, *Caixin*, reported in early 2012 that China's Central Bank believes as many as 18,000 government officials and SOE employees are guilty of corruption worth an estimated US$127 billion (cited in *Today Online*, 2012).

38 Recent cases of official corruption have stoked public anger and there have been a series of high-profile mass protests focusing on land grabs and environmental issues. Personal observation.

39 Interview with an expert from China University of International Business, Beijing, 17 February 2012.

40 Services reform has already begun in June 2012 with the establishment of the 'Qianhai' project based in Shenzhen worth US$45 billion. Interview with a policy advisor to the WTO Division of the Ministry of Commerce, Tsinghua University, Beijing, 22 November 2012. Interview with a policy advisor from the Chinese Academy of International Trade and Economic Cooperation (CAITEC) of the Ministry of Commerce, Beijing, 19 November 2012.

41 Interview with a policy advisor from the China Academy of International Trade and Economic Cooperation under the Ministry of Commerce, Beijing, 19 November 2012.

42 Interview with a senior Chinese negotiator from the WTO Division of the Ministry of Commerce, Beijing, 22 November 2012.

43 Interview with a member of the Department of Treaty and Law, Ministry of Commerce, Beijing, 23 November 2012.

44 Interview with experts from the Chinese Academy of Social Sciences, Beijing, 8 November 2012.
45 Interview with an expert from the Chinese Academy of Social Sciences, Beijing, 8 November 2012.
46 Interview with an expert from the University of International Business and Economics, Beijing, 17 March 2012.
47 Interview with a Japanese negotiator to the WTO, London, 26 January 2012.
48 Interview with an expert and policy advisor from the University of International Business and Economics, Beijing, 12 March 2012; interview with a Japanese negotiator to the WTO, London, 26 January 2012.
49 Interview with a policy advisor to the WTO Division of the Ministry of Commerce, Shanghai, 3 March 2012.
50 Interview with an expert from the University of International Business and Economics, Beijing, 17 March 2012.
51 Interview with an expert from the Chinese Academy of Social Sciences, Beijing, 10 November 2012.
52 Interview with an expert from Fudan University, Shanghai, 25 April 2012.
53 There are two specific dimensions to the broad challenge of *national* regulatory cooperation and services policy reform: (1) addressing knowledge gaps – increasing information on regulatory experiences and impacts and identifying alternative options/ good practices; (2) identifying the impact of – and the options for dealing with – the political economy constraints that impede the implementation of welfare improving reforms (Hoekman and Mattoo, 2011).
54 Interview with a Japanese negotiator to the WTO, London, 26 January 2012.
55 Interview with a former member of the Department of Legal Affairs in the Ministry of Commerce, Beijing, 22 November 2012.
56 Interview with a Chinese negotiator from the Ministry of Commerce, Beijing, 17 November 2012.
57 Interview with an expert from Shanghai Institute for International Studies, Shanghai, 27 August 2011.
58 Interview with a senior member of the WTO Secretariat, London, 2 February 2012.
59 Interview with a policy advisor from the Chinese Academy of International Trade and Economic Cooperation under the Ministry of Commerce, Beijing, 19 November 2012.
60 Interview with a former member of the Department of Legal Affairs in the Ministry of Commerce, Beijing, 22 November 2012.
61 Interview with a member from the Department of Law and Treaty, Ministry of Commerce, Beijing, 23 November 2012.
62 Interview with a senior member of the WTO Division in the Ministry of Commerce, Beijing, 22 November 2012.
63 For instance, on 27 February 2012, the World Bank and the Development Research Center of the State Council released *China 2030: Building a Modern, Harmonious, and Creative High-Income Society*. The 468-page document contains six broad economic policy recommendations, including achieving the trade-related goal of "mutually beneficial relations" with the rest of the world (Pomfret and Lim, 2012).
64 Interview with a member from the Department of Law and Treaty, Ministry of Commerce, Beijing, 23 November 2012.
65 As a matter of fact, if there is a solid agreement among the leadership for a particular policy preference, their consensus has therefore already established a common target for all the relevant ministries. Hence, there is not much room for ministries to take into account their own preferences.
66 Interview with an expert from an expert from Peking University, Beijing, 1 September 2011; interview with an expert from Fudan University, Shanghai, 25 April 2012.
67 Interview with an expert from Tsinghua University, 22 November 2012.

68 Interview with an expert from the Shanghai Institute of International Studies, Shanghai, 27 April 2012.

69 The CCF allows POEs and their shareholders to establish a joint venture with foreign companies whom can hold up to 70 per cent of the ownership. China–China–Foreign (CCF) structures refer to the joint ventures created to skirt rules on the business scope of a foreign direct investment and investors into restricted sectors. Under the CCF model, a 'China–Foreign' joint venture is formed between a local company and a foreign firm, routing the funds through the joint venture into a China-owned operating company (e.g. a telecommunications network provider). The contracts give foreign investors effective control of the operating company but not the ownership.

70 The significance of the POEs is also reflected in the CPC's invitation to numerous POE CEOs (Chief Executive Officers) to become members of the Party.

71 Interview with a member from the Department of Treaty and Law, Ministry of Commerce Beijing, 23 November 2012.

72 Interview with a policy advisor from the Chinese Academy of International Trade and Economic Cooperation under the Ministry of Commerce, Beijing, 19 November 2012.

73 Interview with a senior member of the UNFCCC Secretariat, 2 July 2011.

74 It is important to note that China today wields greater leverage internationally due to its economic weight, and if it makes mistakes, this is not treated as a big deal as it was before. Interview with an expert from Fudan University, Shanghai, 25 August 2011.

75 See WTO DS309.

76 Article III ("national treatment") of the GATT requires that imports be treated no less favourably than the same or similar domestically produced goods, once they have passed customs (Wang, 2010).

77 Interview with an official from the Ministry of Commerce, Beijing, 21 September 2012.

78 Interview with an expert from the Chinese Academy of Social Sciences, Beijing, 8 November 2012.

79 Interview with a policy advisor of the Ministry of Foreign Affairs, Beijing, 25 October 2012.

80 Interview with an expert from the China Foreign Affairs University, Beijing, 25 October 2012.

81 Interview with an expert from Tsinghua University, Beijing, 22 November 2012; interview with an expert from Peking University, Beijing, 23 November 2012.

# References

Anderson, R.D. (2008) 'China's Accession to the WTO Agreement on Government Procurement: Procedural Considerations, Potential Benefits and Challenges, and Implications of the Ongoing Re-Negotiation of the Agreement'. *Public Procurement Law Review* 4 pp. 1–15.

Beattie, A. (2011) 'WTO Updates Government Procurement Agreement'. *Financial Times*. Received via email, 15 December.

BBC Monitoring Asia Pacific (2003) 'WTO Chief Says China Should Be Bridge Between Developing, Developed Nations'. 10 November p. 1.

BBC News China (2012) 'China's Hu Jintao in Corruption Warning at Leadership Summit'. [Online] 8 November. Available from: www.bbc.co.uk/news/world-asia-china020233191 [Accessed: 11 November 2012].

Checkel, J.T. (2005) 'International Institutions and Socialization in Europe: Introduction and Framework'. *International Organization* 59(4) pp. 801–826.

*China Daily* (2010) 'Don't Be Too Demanding on GPA Offer.' [Online] 6 August. Available from: www.chinadaily.com.cn/china/2010-08/06/content_11106020.htm [Accessed: 12 April, 2012].

Diamant, N.J. (2000) *Revolutionizing the Family: Politics, Love, and Divorce in Urban and Rural China, 1949–1964.* California: University of California Press.

*The Economist* (2013) 'Served in China'. [Online] 23 February. Available from: www.economist.com/news/finance-and-economics/21572236-services-are-poised-become-countrys-biggest-sector-servedchina?utm_source=Sinocism+Newsletter&utm_campaign=a3d80b65cb-Sinocism02_24_13&utm_medium=email [Accessed: 26 February 2013].

European Business for Doha (2007) 'Save the Doha Round Now'. [Online] 25 January. Available from: www.esf.be/new/wp-content/uploads/2009/02/european-business-for-doha-250107-final.pdf [Accessed: 30 May, 2011].

Evenett, S.J. and Hoekman, B. (2004) 'Government Procurement: Market Access, Transparency, and Multilateral Trade Rules'. World Bank Policy Research Working Paper (3195).

Feketekuty, G. (2010) 'Needed: A New Approach to Reduce Regulatory Barriers to Trade'. [Online] 19 June. Available from: www.voxeu.org/index.php?q=node/5208 [Accessed: 2 February 2012].

Francois, J. and Hoekman, B. (2010) 'Services Trade and Policy'. *Journal of Economic Literature* 48(3) pp. 642–692.

Gao, H. (2007) 'China's Participation in the WTO: A Lawyer's Perspective'. *Singapore Year Book of International Law and Contributors* 11 pp. 1–34.

Gao, P. and Lyytinen, K. (2000) 'Transformation of China's Telecommunications Sector: A Macro Perspective'. *Telecommunication Policy* 24(8/9) pp. 719–730.

Geneva Watch (2012) 'NAMA Chair Circulates Report; Suggests New Negotiating Approaches.' Received via email, 20 July pp. 1–2.

Hoekman, B. and Mattoo, A. (2011) 'Services Trade Liberalization and Regulatory Reform: Re-invigorating International Cooperation'. *Policy Research Working Paper* 5517.

Hoekman, B. and Vines, D. (2007) 'Multilateral Trade Cooperation: What Next?'. *Oxford Review of Economic Policy* 23(3) pp. 311–334.

Hoekman, B., Mattoo, A., and Sapir, A. (2007) 'The Political Economy of Services Trade Liberalization: A Case for International Regulatory Cooperation'. *Oxford Review of Economic Policy* 23(3) pp. 367–391.

Huang, Z. (2008) 'Doha Round and China's Multilateral Diplomacy'. *International Review* pp. 18–28.

Inside US–China Trade (2011) 'China Affirms GPA Accession Timeline, Parties Focused on Revised GPA'. Received via email, 1 June.

Jawara, F. and Kwa, A. (2004) *Behind the Scenes at the WTO: The Real World of International Trade Negotiations – The Lessons of Cancun.* New York: Zed Books.

Jensen, J.B. (2012) 'Overlooked Opportunity: Tradable Business Services, Developing Asia, and Growth'. *Asian Development Bank Working Paper Series* 12(23).

Johnston, A.I. (2008) *Social States: China in International Institutions, 1980–2000.* Princeton, NJ: Princeton University Press.

Kahn, J. (2004) 'China Is Filtering Phone Text Messages to Regulate Criticism'. *New York Times.* [Online] 3 July. p. A3. Available from: www.nytimes.com/2004/07/03/world/china-is-filtering-phone-text-messages-to-regulate-criticism.html?_r=0 [Accessed: 21 June 2012].

Leal-Arcas, R. (2007) 'Bridging the Gap in the Doha Talks: A Look at Services Trade'. *Journal of International Commercial Law and Technology* 2(4) pp. 241–249.

Li, X. (2012) 'Understanding China's Behavioral Change in the WTO Dispute Settlement System: Power, Capacity, and Normative Constraints in Trade Adjudication'. *Asian Survey* 52(6) p. 1111–1137.

Liang, W. (2010) 'China's WTO Negotiation Process and Its Implications'. *Journal of Contemporary China* 11(33), November, pp. 683–719.

Liang, W. (2007) 'Bureaucratic Politics, Interministerial Coordination and China's GATT/WTO Accession Negotiations'. In K. Zeng (ed.) *China's Foreign Trade Policy: The New Constituencies* (pp. 20–39). New York: Routledge.

Liang, W. (2003) 'Regime Type and International Negotiation: A Case Study of US/China Bilateral Negotiations for China's Accession to the WTO'. PhD Dissertation, University of Southern California.

Markusen, J., Rutherford, T.F., and Tarr, D. (2005) 'Trade and Direct Investment in Producer Services and the Domestic Market for Expertise'. *The Canadian Journal of Economics* 38(3) pp. 758–777.

Mattoo, A. (2002) 'China's Accession to the WTO: The Services Dimension'. Report Prepared for the World Bank, Washington, D.C.

Mattoo, A., Rathindran, R., and Subramanian, A. (2006) 'Measuring Services Trade Liberalization and Its Impact on Economic Growth: An Illustration'. *Journal of Economic Integration* 21(1) pp. 64–98.

*People's Daily* (2004) 'MOFCOM Spokesperson Comments on VAT Rebate'. [Online] 20 March. Available from: http://english.mofcom.gov.cn [Accessed: 31 May 2011].

Perspectives on Trade (2015a) 'WTO GPA Update #5'. [Online] 4 December. Available from: http://trade.djaghe.com/?tag=china-gpa-accession [Accessed 16 October 2015].

Perspectives on Trade (2015b) 'China's 2014 Offer Advances GPA Accession'. [Online] 12 January. Available from: http://trade.djaghe.com/?p=1161 [Accessed: 16 October 2015].

Phillips, T. (2012) 'China's Hu Jintao Warns of Danger of Corruption as He Opens 18th Communist Party Congress'. *The Telegraph* [Online] 8 November. Available from: www.telegraph.co.uk/news/worldnews/asia/china/9663182/Chinas-Hu-Jintao-warns-of-danger-of-corruption-as-he-opens-18th-Communist-Party-Congress.html [Accessed: 11 November 2012].

Pomfret, J. and Lim, B.K. (2012) 'China's Ex-President Overshadows Party Congress, Transition'. *Reuters*. [Online] 10 November. Available from: www.reuters.com/article/2012/11/10/us-china-congress-jiang-idUSBRE8A90IE20121110 [Accessed: 10 November 2012].

Sally, R. (2011) 'Chinese Trade Policy After (Almost) Ten Years in the WTO: A Post-Crisis Stocktake'. *ECIPE Occasional Paper* (2) pp. 1–35.

Sun, Z. (2008) 'Statement of HE Ambassador Sun Zhenyu at the Informal Trade Negotiations Committee Meeting'. 11 August 2008. Available from: www.mofcom.gov.cn [Accessed: 1 March 2013].

*Today Online* (2012). 'Corruption Probes in China said to Rise 13%'. [Online] 30 October. Available from: www.todayonline.com/World/China/EDC121030-0000025/Corruption-probes-in-China-said-to-rise-13 [Accessed: 30 October 2012].

Tu, X. (2011) 'Organizational Aspects of China's GPA Accession Negotiation and Their Implications'. *Indiana University Research Center for Chinese Politics and Business Working Paper* (6).

*TWN* (2003) *Daily Briefing*. [Online] 3 July. Available from: www.twn.my/ [Accessed: 3 March 2010].

*TWN* (2002) *Daily Briefing*. [Online] 18–19 December. Available from: www.twn.my/ [Accessed: 3 March 2010].

US Department of Commerce (2006). 'US–China Trade Talks Achieve "Clear Progress"'. [Online] 3 April. Available from: http://trade.gov/press/publications/newsletters/ita_0406/jcct_0406.asp [Accessed: 13 April 2012].

Wang, P. (ed.) (2010) *Chinese Public Procurement Law: An Introductory Textbook*. Prepared for the EU Asia Inter University Network for Teaching and Research in Public Procurement Regulation.

World Economic Forum (2007) 'Merkel Urges New Dialogue and Closer Atlantic Partnership'. [Online] 27 January. Available from: www.weforum.org//en/media/Latest%20Press%20Releases/AM07_Angela_Merkel [Accessed: 12 February 2007].

Wu, Q. (2012) 'Stability Achieved; Now, Efficiency'. *China Daily*. [Online] 8 October. Available from: www.chinadaily.com.cn/business/2012-10/08/content_15800370.htm [Accessed: 1 November 2013].

Xinhua News Agency (2010) 'Chinese Premier Reassures Foreign Firms on Business Environment, Government Procurement'. [Online] 29 April. Available from: http://news.xinhuanet.com/english2010/china/2010-04/29/c_13272937.htm [Accessed: 29 April 2010].

Zhang, L. and Evenett, S.J. (2010) 'The Growth of China's Services Sector and Associated Trade: Complementarities Between Structural Change and Sustainability'. Paper for the Sustainable China Trade Project, International Institute for Sustainable Development.

# 6 The impact of international agencies

So far we have explored the extent to which the calculation of costs and benefits, information, and reputation can shape China's negotiation preferences. The analyses were based on the multilateral climate change and trade negotiations. These examples were considered appropriate because of the widely held perception that there would be no substantial change in China's preferences within these areas, but changes were identified. In the context of these examples, the calculation of costs and benefits, information, and reputation were found to be both relevant and, to an extent, impactful on the formulation of negotiation preferences. They were found to have occurred between policymakers and government departments in Beijing, and between Chinese policymakers and members of international agencies, notably the UNFCCC and the WTO. This chapter is interested in the second dimension of engagement, and concentrates on an assessment of the role and impact of international agencies on China's negotiation preference decision-making.

The goal here is not to identify clear causal mechanisms between success level and the institutional makeup or type of advice being produced. Rather, several factors can be identified, which have had an impact on not only the credibility, legitimacy, and salience of advice, but also on the way advice is received and responded to by the relevant policymaking body in Beijing. Our examples demonstrate that there is no single best approach, and that flexibility and adaptability are fundamental. Moreover, China does not refuse the influence of international agencies. Rather, it absorbs and adapts to their influences within the existing domestic system. And in some cases, policymakers use the weight of international agencies to their own advantage in the domestic inter-agency bargaining process. More on this later in the chapter. First, let us consider the specific impacts of international agencies on Chinese decision-making. Chapters 4 and 5 focussed specifically on the significance of policy instruments. Within the process, it was clear that international agencies engaged proactively through these instruments. As such, it is important and fitting to consider their impact on the formation of Chinese negotiation preferences.

## Calculating the costs and benefits

The interest-based rationalist approach holds the belief that states act as unitary rational actors, whereby the decision-makers will evaluate their policy options based on a costs-and-benefits calculus, and formulate positions that are perceived to be maximising the net national gains (Bjorkum, 2005, p. 15; Underdal, 1998, p. 7). Accordingly, rationalists argue that international agencies influence Chinese economic diplomacy preference formation through an incentive restructuring process that involves assisting Beijing in determining a best outcome among different equilibria situations where more than one efficient solution exists. Usually this can be achieved through advice on the estimated costs and benefits faced by China (Costa and Jorgensen, 2012, p. 4; Scharpf, 1997, p. 39; Chayes and Antonia, 1993, p. 178). In the process of doing so, international agencies structure the political situation and leave their own imprint on China's preference formation.

As seen in the previous chapters, both case-pairs exhibited this kind of activity by the respective agencies from the UNFCCC and the WTO. The empirical data indicates that the UNFCCC bodies have, over the past 15 years, regularly provided input to costs-and-benefits analyses during the preference formation process. The Intergovernmental Panel on Climate Change (IPCC), for instance, issued repeated warnings about China's vulnerabilities to the consequences of climate change, with millions of people living by the coastlines potentially affected by sea-level rises, and severe ramifications for agricultural output and fresh water resources, all of which result in significant economic costs (IPCC, 2001, 2007).

When Beijing voiced uncertainties about how mitigation might affect national development, the presiding staff of the UNFCCC's Conference of Parties (COP) provided analyses which argued against heavy abatement costs, and illustrated how mitigation improves energy efficiency, diversifies energy sources, encourages reforestation, and improves the energy sector, all of which are consistent with China's national development objectives. In addition, mitigation can spur the development of new technological and industrial sectors with long-term commercial profits and short-term technical and financial transfers from abroad (Underdal, 1998, p. 8). These benefits ultimately outweigh the alternative, which is economic predicaments and air pollution from the combustion of coal – a cause of respiratory diseases and cancer. A consistent non-cooperative stance could also result in international sanctions and damage to China's international prestige and reputation. On the whole, the real costs to China from a non-cooperative position are 100 per cent higher than the price of the abatement, which is also beneficial to development (Saich, 2001, p. 295).

Interviews indicated that such advice had an influence over Beijing's subsequent decision to complete an *Initial National Communication on Climate Change* (National Communication, 2004), and for the first time, the government acknowledged in the report its vulnerabilities to climate change. The national leaders emphasised the need for adaptation measures to be adopted and economic support for climate change activities. What is more, interviews suggest that the UNFCCC bodies' guidance on the costs and benefits played a significant role in Beijing's newfound willingness to negotiate a legally binding mitigation framework for the post-2015 period. Taking these events as indications of effectiveness, the UNFCCC bodies surely can be credited, to an extent, for having restructured Beijing's incentives on the issue of climate change through its costs-and-benefits calculus.

A similar claim can be made based on the GPA (Government Procurement Agreement) and services trade cases. In one round of negotiations, Chinese negotiators expressed China's deep concerns about regulatory uncertainties in the governance of further services trade liberalisation. In response, the WTO's Council on Services Trade argued that further opening up to foreign services providers and competition could reduce the cartel effect and attenuate the cost efficiency effect. In addition, it can introduce the domestic market to new technical know-how, and contribute to the economy's production and export of more sophisticated and advanced products. Above all, the Council argued that the increased competition in the services sectors could boost economic growth and serve China's national development.

Similar focuses on the benefits of acceding to the GPA were made by the WTO's Committee on Government Procurement. For instance, the Committee emphasised the GPA's advantage in controlling government corruption, which has prevailed within Beijing, especially in the bidding and tendering processes. The increased transparency of the procurement system meant that officials were more likely to reduce their incentives for self-enrichment, while firms would be more willing to bid, rather than bribe, for government contracts and have the incentive to do a good job. Interviewed policymakers have indicated that these arguments were relatively convincing and could have contributed to the gradual increase in flexibility for both areas of policy preferences. Clearly, the WTO bodies were effective in shaping Chinese trade policy through their contributions to the costs-and-benefit calculations.

Nonetheless, other empirical indications also call for more prudence in drawing such a conclusion. In spite of the WTO bodies' guidance on the costs and benefits, China did not officially jump from a cautious negotiation preference to one of proactivity. Whilst the extent of China's opening up has expanded over the years, it is nonetheless incremental (instead of an all-out reform): many barriers remain intact across numerous services sectors. In comparison with the GPA, advice on the costs and benefits was much less effective in influencing actual preference change in services trade. Likewise, the case-pair relating to the UNFCCC also showed that the degree of impact via the provision of costs and benefits analyses on mitigation is comparatively milder compared to the Clean Development Mechanism (CDM). This variance was measured by the time (i.e. years) it took before a shift was identified in Beijing's preferences. While it only took two to three years for this instrument to catalyse a preference change on the CDM, it took five times as long to see a slight increase in rhetorical flexibility from the Chinese delegation on the mitigation issue.

What conditioned the impact of international agencies as a provider of costs-and-benefits analyses? One contingency of influence is the *perception* of Chinese decision-makers. For the most part, the decision-makers in Beijing did not believe that the payoff from cooperating in the long-term global effort to combat climate change through mitigation actions was significant enough to prioritise the government's limited professional and other resources in this area over other short-term demands such as economic growth and poverty alleviation. This perception in turn undermined the UNFCCC bodies' guidance on the costs and benefits of mitigation commitments.

The situation could not have been more different for the CDM example. Key decision-makers in Beijing believed that the benefits of joining the initiative would contribute to both short-term development policy goals, and long-term battles against global warming. The overlap between the UNFCCC bodies' recommendations and the perception of the decision-makers thereby granted the former stronger influence. This contingency is of equal relevance to the WTO examples. China's negotiation preference concerning the GPA was more susceptible to the Committee's inputs on the calculation of costs and benefits, compared to that of the Council concerning trade in services, because the decision-makers considered the GPA framework as having potential to aid China's political reform agenda (and, therefore, the legitimacy of the Communist Party of China (CPC)).

Where the WTO and the UNFCCC cases differ is that the former indicates the importance of not just the perception of decision-makers but also the political rank of the decision-makers. For instance, the GPA case felt more external influence from the Committee's costs-and-benefits calculation, not only because it appealed to the ministerial-level policymakers, but also because it attracted the elite members of the Politburo. Services trade, on the other hand, only appealed to the second-tier decision-makers from the Ministry of Finance (MOF). At the end of the day, the political rank of the receiver of the advice matters. This is not a surprising or unique finding. Support from senior decision-makers in any country enhances the influence of international agencies. And in a system where policy preferences often rest in the hands of a few elite leaders, as in Beijing, this factor is even more pertinent.

By comparison, the UNFCCC examples did not present much evidence that this played a key role in either enhancing or undermining external influence. This is perhaps due to the disparate inter-departmental processes. In climate change, although the power structure can at times marginalise second-tier agencies, the interests and objectives among the ministries and commissions involved are generally cohesive and the power structure clearly defined. However, decision-making for trade negotiations often involve various competing interests between government departments, with many having overlapping responsibilities; the power structure is rather ambivalent and fragmented. For example, although the Ministry of Commerce (MOFCOM) coordinates trade policies, a constellation of other departments take the lead across a range of specialised trade issues, which dampens down MOFCOM's authority and disturbs the inter-departmental policy cohesion at large.[1] In this context, it is important for the government departments involved in trade policy to have the backing and support of the elite leaders in order to have their preferred preferences promoted above others. Conversely, it is also imperative that the WTO bodies establish good relations with the elite leaders in Beijing in order to enjoy greater influence when providing input on the calculation of costs and benefits.

## Information dissemination

The preceding assessment on the costs-and-benefits calculus revealed that incomplete information creates uncertainties (regardless of scale) which ultimately undermine positive sways of Chinese preferences. Cognitivists argue that this demonstrates the important role information plays in shaping Chinese preferences. John Odell (2000, p. 189) notes the importance of studying (technical) information about a problem; designing the next plan of action according to studies of the available information is imperative for designing national negotiation positions and their success in reaching the optimal outcome. International agencies, including the UNFCCC, the WTO, and others such as the Bretton Woods institutions, have played significant roles in both information sharing and in knowledge creation (i.e. fiscal and other related research) for raising technical understanding and brokering cross-border cooperation.[2] In this context, cognitivists prescribe information dissemination as an effective way in which international agencies can influence Chinese preference formation.

In contrast to rationalists, cognitivists downplay the factor of 'interests' and claim that Chinese decision-makers hold imperfect information and tentative policy preferences when they enter political processes (Haas, 1990).[3] Therefore, international agencies have the opportunity to adjust, reframe, and/or reshape the perceptions of the Chinese decision-makers through the dissemination of ideological and professional information (Søfting, 2000, p. 24; Underdal, 1998, p. 21). In the climate change and trade cases, the UNFCCC and the WTO agencies predominantly disseminated information in the forms of informal dialogue, information sharing and exchange, joint research initiatives, and training workshops. Cognitivists believe the growing complexity and uncertainties over global economic problems will often lead policymakers to turn to new and different channels for advice, and specifically to new networks of knowledge-based experts from international agencies in order to articulate their objectives in forthcoming negotiations, realise the *real* stakes or interests of the Chinese government and the perceived appropriate policy remedies (Haas, 1992, p. 12).

For the most part, interviewees across the cases commonly agree that external information affects the perceptions of Chinese decision-makers, not least because the professional training, prestige, and reputation of the expertise embodied in international agencies are viewed with great respect in Beijing and this accords them access to the Chinese political system in a way that grants them potential for policy influence. If the shortcoming of the rationalist policy instrument was due to *perception*, then, in theory, the cognitive instrument of information dissemination should be much more impactful, given its ability to shape the perception of decision-makers and their negotiation preferences.

Yet, empirical data from the two case-pairs indicated variances in the degree of influence information dissemination actually realises. Three contingencies explain the existence of such variances. The first relates to the political and economic costs involved with implementing international discourse; the higher the political and/or economic costs, the less influential the international discourse. In the GPA negotiations, the political costs of agreeing with the discourse of WTO bodies – recommendations for accession – was conceived of as potentially undermining Beijing's autonomy, and, therefore, a political cost the Chinese were unwilling to realise. The economic costs of supporting the UNFCCC Secretariat's proposals on mitigation would imply the need to restructure China's entire energy sector, which could have dire consequences for China's energy security and social stability in the short- and immediate-term. By contrast, the mild political and economic costs imposed by the international discourse on the CDM initiative led to a much faster adoption than any other climate change modality to date. The perceived economic and political costs conveyed through the information disseminated to Beijing could therefore have substantial impacts on its actual level of influence.

Clearly, the degree of influence information dissemination achieves is tightly intertwined with, and to an extent determined by the government's costs-and-benefits assessments of adopting international discourse. Although the real political and economic costs across the cases were relatively on a par for all issues, the empirical data found that the policymakers nonetheless perceived the nominal costs to be slightly higher for the services trade and mitigation cases compared to the other issues. This might explain the slower pace in preference shifts. So the management of the government's costs-and-benefits assessments certainly conditions the influence of information dissemination.

It was previously mentioned that an advantage of information dissemination is its ability to shape the perceptions of decision-makers by tailoring information to that purpose. However, cognitive theory does not explain how information can actually reform perception other than taking it as an automatic consequence. When this assumption was applied, results from the comparative empirical analyses show that it is often challenged by the real capacity of international agencies to competently design discourse in a way that can induce perceptual changes, especially where the policymaker holds strong beliefs, and/or tailor the discourse according to actual perceptions. To begin with, Chinese decision-makers have for many decades treated international discourse with scepticism and caution, partly due to its perceived *poor quality* and incompetence to even address their questions. In trade, such inadequacies were reflected in the GPA case study, where the WTO bodies failed to provide even the most basic information such as the definition of 'government procurement'. Imprecise and vague information has given Beijing challenges in ascertaining what it should negotiate about.

A similar example can be found in climate change. When, in 2003, China asked the IPCC to develop practicable methodologies to 'factor out' direct human-induced changes in carbon stocks from those due to indirect human-induced and natural effects, the IPCC responded that "the scientific community cannot currently provide a practicable methodology" that would do so (IPCC, 2003). The problem had to be brought back to the negotiating table to be addressed with a political decision. This goes to show that while there are some questions that are simply too complex for science to answer in a manner that satisfies the Chinese decision-makers, others involving moral or ethical questions are perhaps better answered directly by the policymakers.

The Chinese decision-makers have additionally held the traditional view that most international discourse are too westernised to be relatable to the 'China' context.[4] For example, when the IPCC Working Group III attempted an economic valuation of the social costs of climate change impacts, including human life, for the Second Assessment Report, the writing team used controversial assumptions based on the available literature on the 'value of statistical life'. These assumptions were based on the economists' calculation that human life is valued differently in developed and developing countries, since the risk of death is not valued equally between countries (i.e. based on a 'willingness to pay' approach). Chinese delegates, like most of the developing world, reacted with indignation to the suggestion that human lives in their countries were somehow worth less than in rich countries.[5] The disagreement between the economists who had written the report and the Chinese policymakers was such that the Working Group III report failed to get plenary approval in July 1995, and although governments eventually accepted the chapter, they changed the 'Summary for Policymakers' in such a way that it implicitly criticised the chapter. In angry responses, the IPCC authors dissociated themselves from the summary (Brack and Grubb, 1996). Thus, a discussion on the form and function of information dissemination by international agencies must acknowledge an underlying point: for Chinese policymakers, it matters *who* produces the information that is used to inform its preference formation.

Then there is Beijing's incoherent inter-departmental process.[6] Most economic issues involve multifaceted problems which require involvement from numerous departments, each varying widely in interests, and the nature and level of activities and engagement in the overall policy process. In trade, a decision on the trade in transport services, for instance, is accompanied by complicated, lengthy and changing procedures, requirements and documentation, and concerns a labyrinth of departments, ranging from transport, customs, immigration, security, health, veterinary and phytosanitary issues, product quality, and private sector actors. When compelled to come together for consensus-building, these government departments tend to aim to assert jurisdiction over the same issue and compete with each other for scarce budget resources, power, and recognition from higher government officials. Consequently, bureaucratic competition can sometimes result in their refusal to implement each other's policies, based on the claim that they lack budget resources or man-power (Lawrence and Martin, 2012, pp. 10–11).

The implication of this for China's negotiation posture is that it will often act silently so as to buy more time to address internal conflicts. Dasgupta (1997) supports this finding by suggesting that China's defensive positions in trade negotiations is often due to institutional challenges. Although China has established coordination organs (i.e. leading small groups or LSGs), they rarely function efficiently.

What is more, the examples further show that international discourse can diversify ministerial interests and deepen the fragmentation between government departments. Such was seen in the services trade case. As one policymaker said, "The WTO does a fantastic job distributing information, but sometimes the ministries are flooded with information to the extent that it becomes difficult for ministries to manage, synthesise and establish consensus accordingly".[7] So contrary to studies (e.g. Yu, 2008) which argue that engagement with international actors can improve inter-ministerial coordination, evidence showed that too much diverse information actually cause further inter-departmental divergence, which is also why international agencies often achieve modest influence through information dissemination engagements. But, learning from the CDM example, provided international agencies are able to distribute consistent and relevant information tailored for a diverse audience, it is feasible to create inter-ministerial convergence.

Finally, it is important for the international discourse to be supported by the Chinese business and industrial actors. This empirical finding contradicts an underlying cognitive assumption that international agencies usually equip the Chinese government with information and ideas for the conduct of analyses and for the purpose of reaching policy decisions independent of direct pressures from organised groups or citizens. In other words, business actors exert *little* direct influence on the policy decisions of the government officials (Jacobs and Page, 2005, p. 108). In reality, as one China expert puts it, "Enterprises are the skeleton of Chinese decision-making today".[8]

This is not to say that Chinese enterprises today operate completely independently from the central government; China is still a top-down system. But domestic enterprises do have stronger influence over the government's policy agenda. Therefore, holding their support can immensely boost the influence of international agencies on the government's preference formation.[9] It was for this reason that the CDM case demonstrated more significant UNFCCC influence and more substantial preference shifts than mitigation. Likewise, it was the domestic enterprises which pushed the government to consider greater 'open-ups' for trade in services.[10] Meanwhile it was the clear opposition from business actors concerning the information on mitigation that kept the government's preferences on the issue at near-constant resistance throughout much of the COP negotiations. At the end of the day, without the support of domestic business actors, international ideas may not necessarily attract much attention from government agencies and officials.

## Reputation reinforcement

Moving away from processes of socialisation, contractualists assume that social interactions have little or no effect on shaping preferences. Instead, actors generally emerge from interactions with international agencies with the same perceptions and beliefs with which they entered. Moreover, contractualists believe the quality and/or quantity of prior social interaction and information provision between international agencies and the Chinese decision-makers have no effect on the basic preferences of these decision-makers in the short- or long-run. So it should be irrelevant whether China decides to cooperate or not (Frank, 1988, p. 143).

With this said, contractualists do share the cognitive assumption that international agencies can provide new information to reduce uncertainty about the credibility of others' commitment and thus help China to concentrate its expectations around some cooperative outcome (Martin and Larsen, 1999). Where they differ from cognitive theorists is in the assumption that information only affects the policy actors' perception of the strategic – rather than social – environment whereby the actor pursues a *fixed* set of policy preferences – there is no reassessment of the desirability of these preferences after the information engagement.

In addition, contractualists argue that an assumption based on the information could generate a regression problem. Unless there are prior agreements on a set of criteria about success and failure, what makes the information about success or failure conclusive? How are prior agreements on these criteria formed? In what way can actors be convinced of the reliability of the information concerning the validity of the criteria? What leads to an agreement of credibility based on the criteria about credibility? At any stage it could be suggested that policy actors received reliable information regarding an economic problem and leave it at that. But this does not escape the problem that at any given point, the criteria for establishing the credibility of new information are problematic.

More effective influence, in the view of contractualists, is achieved through an under-socialised process of motivating Chinese decision-makers on the premise of reputation. Without rehearsing too many details of the assumptions, it suffices to say that with the changing global, political, and economic landscape, the proliferation of media and communication technologies, the emergence of new multilateral players (including international agencies), the complex confluence of these facets have meant that the credibility and effectiveness of standard Chinese communication practices in public diplomacy is increasingly challenged (Wang, 2006, p. 92). Hence, the desire to maximise reputation, both domestically and internationally, can motivate the Chinese government to cooperate and avoid social sanctions (e.g. psychological anxiety from opprobrium) (Frank, 1988, p. 32).[11] It is widely accepted that a motivation for compliance is the fear of opprobrium even if this causes a suboptimal outcome for the actor. Oran Young (1992, pp. 176–177) remarks,

> Policymakers, like private individuals, are sensitive to the social opprobrium that accompanies violations of widely accepted behavioural prescriptions. They are, in short, motivated by a desire to avoid the sense of shame or social disgrace that commonly befalls those who break widely accepted rules.

These specific micro-processes where actors are compelled to act in a way that prevents opprobrium are similar to those that encourage people to pursue back-patting.

At the macro level, Beijing has an interest in maintaining a consistently good reputation and credibility so other actors will be encouraged to deal with China in other areas.[12] In this context, contractualists argue international agencies can affect Chinese preference formation by reinforcing its reputation. Just as Beijing is concerned about how foreign Parties view China, and how it projects itself abroad, international agencies which engage with Chinese officials should be interested in the impact of China's projected reputation vis-à-vis its actualised behaviour.

If reputation can affect behaviour, international agencies have the capacity to influence China's preference formation by shaping the kinds of reputation it hopes to achieve. Yet, how will one know when a strategic reputation has a causal influence on China's economic diplomacy preference formation? There are two obvious ways of identifying the causal relationship. The first is to try and identify any *direct* evidence that Chinese decision-makers have adopted a preference in order to be consistent with the strategic reputation China seeks to project. The second is to identify any *indirect* evidence that a policy preference is (not) adopted because of intervening variables such as economic side-payments that may be consistent with the hoped-for reputation. Since direct evidence is difficult to find due to the largely opaque nature of China's preference formation, this analysis relies on the indirect evidence.

According to the empirical data, a prominent aspect of China's approach to international agencies is shaped by a concern about reputation. This motivation stems out of historical experiences, and recovering China's disrupted reputation was not only a national objective but a key reason for engaging with international agencies in the first place (Hatch, 2003, p. 51; Oksenberg and Economy, 1999, p. 21). In the late 1980s when issues relating to climate change gained momentum, China saw this as an opportunity to boost its prestige and bolster support, especially from the developing countries (Zhang, 2003, p. 78). At COP15 in Copenhagen, insiders interviewed for this research revealed that the UNFCCC Secretary-General, Christiana Figueres, stressed to the Chinese delegation the costliness of their non-cooperative position to their international reputation – and similar sentiments were expressed to the global media through subsequent press briefings.

And true to Figueres' words, China's part in the eventual breakdown of the negotiations did not go unnoticed. When the Chinese leaders walked out of a leaders' informal consultation, it became the reference-point for the collapse of yet another round of negotiations and was labelled as 'immoral' and 'irresponsible' to human life.[13] The impact of this was significant for a country sensitive to external criticisms. The effect is not unique to China. A parallel can be drawn with when the United States withdrew, in 2001, from the Kyoto Protocol, and caused heavy protests from many state representatives and the wider international civil society.

In the subsequent negotiations, China carefully orchestrated its rhetoric and actions in a benign manner to avoid being taken as the scapegoat for failure. The trade negotiations similarly had the Chinese government bear the brunt of international criticisms for acting 'passively' and 'selfishly' to protect its own interest at the expense of the global economic good. Members of the Chinese delegation suggested that senior members of the WTO (e.g. Pascal Lamy) often reiterate to China the importance of its reputation as a major economy and the responsibilities that come with that. Contractualists (e.g. Kreps, 1992) believe doing so promotes pro-social behaviour and incentivises nation-states to engage in norm-conforming acts.

If reputation were a very important driving force, one might have expected a more proactive set of negotiation preferences in both trade and climate change negotiations, even if the purpose was just to impress China's domestic and international audiences. However, to date, the world has yet to see any drastic preference shifts from Beijing in areas such as the mitigation and services trade negotiations, among many others. In mitigation, despite being taken as a scapegoat for past failures, China has not, to date, made legally binding commitments under the UNFCCC beyond nationally determined targets. The best it has done is pay lip service to potential future targets. Similarly, despite the international finger-pointing towards China in the trade talks, services trade remains an unfinished business. Why did reputation not trigger policy changes?

According to research interviews, a prevalent view is that the degree of influence reputation reinforcements have depends on the level of political pressures China receives from other negotiating partners or the perceived political risks of taking a non-commitment position. Across all cases, it is clear to see that although Beijing was concerned about its international reputation in the initial years of negotiations, the costs inflicted on reputation as a result of taking a low-commitment posture were not high enough to drive the Chinese decision-makers towards more proactive positions. As Elizabeth Economy (1997, p. 39) observes, China's preferences for most economic negotiations are conditioned by how willing the US is to take on serious commitments. China "has emphasised that as long as the US does not take on commitments, it would be politically unacceptable for them [China] to do so" (Bang *et al.*, 2005, p. 26). In this context, the level of pressure placed on China, which determines the reputation cost to it, stems largely from the negotiating partners as well as the members of the 'G77 plus China' and the 'Group of Twenty' (G20) as opposed to just the international agencies *per se*. So, contrary to the contractualist assumption, reputation alone does not necessarily alter China's negotiation preference. It usually requires geopolitical factors to supplement its effectiveness.

Another point of caution, as the interviews illuminated, is that the reputation card is only effective on China if it has material incentives attached to it, including the transfer of funds and technology, usually obtained through economic side-payments. For instance, there may be resistance by other players to transfer technologies to a country that is perceived as having a *free-rider* status – a reputation perhaps shaped by past experiences. Hence, the more material and economic benefits a country receives, the more careful it will be regarding its reputation as a compliant and committed actor (Johnston, 1998, p. 559). In this sense, it is not necessarily international agencies which caused China to treat reputation with care, but other materialistic incentives. In the words of one Chinese decision-maker, "Yes, reputation does play a part in China's decision-making, especially within the economic arena. But mere pressure from the multi-lateral institutions does not usually lead to substantial preference change. There are usually other factors that come into play in conjunction".[14] The UNFCCC bodies have certainly played the reputation card with Chinese negotiators since its inception. But it was only in recent years that China demonstrated growing concerns about its reputation vis-à-vis its negotiation preferences. If the reputation instrument alone can really generate effective influence, why has it taken this long to see effects?

This leads us to the critical observation that it is often difficult to judge whether a change in negotiation preference is due to the influence of inter-national agencies or whether it is strategic play – i.e. China can establish a positive image deceptively to convince other states to cooperate, as if setting them up for the sucker's payoff in some exploitative prisoners' dilemma game. As Robert Frank (1988) points out, one should be cautious not to take reputa-tions of this nature as credible or reliable. In general, reputation-building behavi-ours are carried out under the assumption that they will be observed by a wide audience. China will see no point in engaging in reputation-building activities unless it is observable to others. But if reputation-building is carried out in order to be observed, then players within the observing audience are likely to doubt that it is actually a high-cost behaviour.

With this said, such line of argument has three drawbacks. First, as Johnston (2008) points out, if other nations find out about this instrumentality, then China's reputation as a responsible co-operator will be ruined, and in turn, it will be placed in a relatively disadvantaged position. That is why it is in China's interests to naturally seek cooperation in order to strengthen its credible reputa-tion. Second, instrumentality assumes that with a positive reputation, policy actors are able to seek more concrete and calculated benefits. This implies that a good reputation can be used as some form of leverage in some issue areas. It is also the case that concrete benefits are hard to identify or that they are rather diffuse and ambiguous (Kelley, 2004). Finally, instrumental arguments about reputation invoke external (and material) costs as the disincentive to acting in anti-social ways. That is, observed anti-social behaviour is costly because it might lead to a loss of trust and thus a loss of exchange opportunities and payoffs (mostly calculated in terms of economic welfare or political power).

## Consequences for the 'structure' of decision-making

Beyond mere influence on preference formation, what are the long-term cumula-tive effects of principled engagements with international agencies on China's overall policy structure? Some Chinese decision-makers believe international agencies have marginal long-term impact because it is the issues which drive the institution rather than the institution the issues.[15] This also implies that the trajectory and design of China's national interests and policy agendas are immune to exterior forces. Without denying this view, there is evidence to suggest that international agencies do have a degree of impact on the decision-making structure.

In Chapter 3, it was argued that engagement with international organisations and agencies has contributed to the decentralisation of the Chinese decision-making system. However, that is not all. As this section will show, *engaging with international agencies fundamentally shifts the domestic inter-departmental balance by providing opportunities or constraints to certain departments over others. As a result, it alters the distribution of power among the policy actors.* This is true to an even greater extent, given that international agencies often demand the establishment of new institutions domestically, seen in both the climate change and trade examples.

As the interactions between Chinese officials and international agencies increase, they strengthen the possibility for the latter to influence the policy structure of the former through empowering the comparatively more liberal government departments at the expense of the conservative ones. The thought process is that frequent engagements between particular government departments and international agencies will, over time, establish a natural bond synonymous with an alliance. This alliance shares a converged set of values, beliefs, and policy preferences. Such relationships are particularly useful for government departments which faces a decentralised environment like Beijing's, with numerous veto points and uncertainties about the likelihood of inter-department cooperation.

In this circumstance, international agencies become useful for persuading and changing the incentives of some (often opposing) Chinese policy actors in the internal bargaining process. For instance, an international agency and its domestic allegiance can reward opposing departments for accepting a policy proposal they had initially rejected with new resources – for instance, to offset any potential loses caused to the agency as a result of their cooperation. Conversely, the international agency and its domestic allegiance can also impose costs on others upon the exercise of domestic vetoes. For instance, departments that do not fulfil their institutional commitments and obligations will be ineligible for subsequent programmes that may benefit them. If this combination of carrots and sticks is strong enough, international agencies will have the capacity to effectively determine the process of reaching a desired preference formation outcome through an intermediary government department.

As a consequence, a spiral pattern of influence emerges when domestic actors bypass government leaders and directly search for international allies in an attempt to bring external pressure on government agencies in opposition to their preferences. Such was the case when the Ministry of Environmental Protection (MEP), the Ministry of Science and Technology (MOST), and the Ministry of Finance (MOF) invited the Global Environmental Fund (GEF) and other UN agencies to invest in pilot simulations to test the applicability of the CDM; their relationships were then used as an alliance to pressure the National Development and Reform Commission (NDRC) to be more proactive on the flexible mechanism.[16] In fact, interviews revealed that the MEP's strong support from the UNFCCC played a significant role in the ministry's promotion to Ministry-level status, because the GEF, among others, demonstrated the importance of the MEP to other governmental departments involved in the internal climate change debate. The Ministry of Commerce (MOFCOM) has similarly established alliances with agencies of the WTO, such as the Working Group on Transparency in Government Procurement on the issue of the GPA. The People's Bank of China (PBOC) and the MOF established special relations with the IMF.

The implication is an empowerment of these government departments over others without a similar bond, or access to external support and resources – all of which collectively translate into policy leverage. A case in point is when Zhu Rongji used his informational advantage regarding the WTO to tie the hands of the Politburo Standing Committee. The possibility of an adverse ruling from the WTO and the resulting sanctions were too great a cost for the Standing Committee. As a result, the Standing Committee ratified the liberalisation policy instead of vetoing it. The Chinese decision-makers can use the available support from the international agencies to promote a preference against the domestic critics, present these policies as part of an international package deal, and shift onto others the political costs of unpopular policies. The interviews indicated that this was what the MOF did in the months leading up to Beijing's decision to participate in the GPA accession negotiations. The NDRC also deployed this method when attempting to convince senior leaders in Beijing of the benefits of committing to mitigation. Thus, an intimate relationship with international agencies can empower certain government departments through the redistribution of domestic power resources and permit them to loosen internal constraints imposed by the traditional government structure.

Still, the influence of international agencies does not operate as an automatic system of power redistribution in Beijing. The ability of these agencies to systematically empower government departments can be weakened if certain conditions are not fulfilled. The re-centralisation of power is more likely to happen when: (1) government departments are already granted a measure of institutional autonomy in the conduct of economic diplomacy preference formation; (2) they enjoy privileged relations with international agencies in the sense that other domestic actors do not have a similar relationship; and (3) a permissive consensus exist in favour of the policies endorsed by the government department with close relationships with international agencies. These conditions are less readily available for *new issues*, which are more prone to the mobilisation of government departments (Moravcsik, 1994, p. 61); the existence of sizeable societal groups or publics with intense issue preferences can also decrease the likelihood of a department being empowered due to its association with international agencies.

Finally, international agencies tend to require China – like other countries – to establish a corresponding set of internal arrangements *and* institutions as part of its membership. For instance, the report on the seventh session of the UNFCCC required the setting up of a National Adaptation Programmes of Action (NAPA) team which entails a lead government department and other government stakeholders, responsible for preparing and coordinating the implementation of NAPA activities. Similar impositions from the World Bank can be identified. In this way, international agencies actually guide the creation of new domestic policymaking bodies and policy systemic plans that subsequently influence preference formation. In the process of interacting with them, Chinese decision-makers will have observed how best to organise themselves in accordance with the international agencies, which is in itself a structural change process that can engender domestic institutions, sometimes at the expense of others.

In addition, these changes will promote the establishment of new government departments in Beijing, and ultimately transform the decision-making structure that corresponds to certain international norms. This was true when entry into the UNFCCC and the WTO saw Beijing establish new inter-departmental organs such as the Climate Change Coordination Leading Small Group (CCCLSG) and the World Trade Organization Leading Small Group (WTOLSG). Likewise, the ratification of the CDM was followed by the establishment of the China CDM Monitoring and Management Centre, responsible for monitoring and feeding performance-related data to the UNFCCC, while WTO accession spawned new judicial review systems in China.[17] These organs were perceived as necessary because multilateral policies often entail ambiguous functions, vaguely defined power capacity and responsibilities, limited inter-departmental information sharing, and a prevalent mentality of administering affairs based on discretion rather than macro-interests (Yu, 2008, p. 504). Therefore, international agencies tend to promote 'horizontal government policy institutions' to assist in clarifying departmental duties. Although it remains contested as to whether these departments contribute to or undermine the inter-departmental coordination processes, it is nevertheless true that their establishment has had the effect of decentralising the national decision-making processes, increasing the level of specialisation, and reconfiguring the government's internal distribution of power.

Ultimately, the deepened relationships between Beijing and international agencies have opened China's preference formation process to the greater international forums, and provided them with the opportunities to establish themselves as interested Parties of input in the Chinese economic diplomacy decision-making process. The logic behind this is that the reiterative processes of engagement with international agencies will, over time, integrate them into the general decision-making system of China – be it implicitly or explicitly, directly or indirectly, and intentionally or unintentionally. This is to suggest that, as Chinese policy actors become used to regular exchanges with the relevant international agency throughout China's preference formation process, such activities will establish themselves as a systemic norm within the broader decision-making process. Over time, policy actors may believe it is perhaps even necessary to share policy concepts and proposals with international agencies for their professional perspective and feedback.

Put in this way, China's economic diplomacy decision-making in the twenty-first century is not necessarily a stand-alone process bounded by the boundaries of the domestic. Although, on paper, China's preference formation is determined by its national interests and other domestic political factors, a deeper examination of the agency-level activities suggests that international agencies also play critical behind-the-scenes roles that indirectly shape Chinese economic diplomacy. As such, China's economic diplomacy is today arguably shaped by a *collective* system involving domestic and international agencies.

### Stable factors

In this evolving process, it is important to note that two characteristics remain crucially stable. The first is the need for consensus in preference formation. The consensus-driven nature of China's preference formation entails much discussion and inter-departmental bargaining for the purpose of reaching mutual agreement as well as compromise. Government departments that partake in the preference formation, from the Politburo to second-tier ministries, commonly endeavour to reach some sort of real or illusionary inter-departmental consensus. Failure to do so will usually postpone the decision-making, so policy actors have more time to study the matter. In the words of a ministerial official, "Policymakers are trained from early on in their careers that the taller the tree, the more wind it attracts".[18] Even the most senior members of the government, such as the President, must seek consensus in the current collective leadership system. This is to maintain unity and loyalty within the CPC and prevent factions emerging. The 2012 leadership transition is a case in point, whereby even veteran Jiang Zemin was reportedly exercising a greater influence over the selection of the succeeding group of leaders than Hu Jintao. As a Hong Kong-based China expert Willy Lam said, "He's [Jiang's] still very much the power behind the throne" (cited in Pomfret and Lim, 2012). As a result, the economic diplomacy preference formation process can be lengthy and complicated, particularly if the issue is viewed as sensitive.

To illustrate this point, in the process of China's WTO accession preference formation, the negotiators believed that Zhu Rongji (former Premier) would not assent to a WTO package unless they consulted with and gained the consensus of most (if not all) domestic interests. Therefore, Li Langqing (former Vice Premier) would not send an accession deal up the hierarchy without accompanying documents demonstrating the agreement of key domestic interests (e.g. the assent of the grain bureau to the parts of the deal related to agriculture). If a package were to be sent upward without such signatures or with dissents, Zhu would be expected to seek some explanations. He might take on the burden of trying to hammer out a compromise with the relevant constituencies, but he would be more likely to refer to the problem back down the hierarchy, and the seemingly endless coordinating meetings would begin again. This highly bureaucratic decision-making process – a product of the need to generate agreement from many potentially hostile units – played a large part in creating the stalemate that engulfed the negotiations with the

US during the late 1990s. It is also this process that was essentially scrapped in the months of 1999 leading up to a bilateral agreement (Pearson, 2001, pp. 349–350). Within Chinese policy and scholarly discourse, the weaknesses of the present consensus-driven preference formation are candidly discussed. In the words of the former President of China, Hu Jintao, the system of "collective leadership with division of responsibilities among individuals" should be improved in order to "prevent arbitrary decision-making by an individual or a minority of people" (cited in *Xinhua News*, 2007).

This takes us to the second stable factor: informal politics and allegiances. Attempts to institutionalise preference formation have been ongoing since Deng Xiaoping inaugurated economic and political reforms in the late 1970s, within the state government and the CPC. Despite those efforts, China's preference formation is still heavily affected by informal channels of influence.[19] Many China enthusiasts have stressed the importance of using a combination of the formal and informal channels. While the formal, consensus-driven system of preference formation requires both time and the willingness from all participants involved to reach compromises, the informal decision-making system based on personal relationships, or *guanxi* (关系), necessitates an understanding and consideration of the interests held within one's own network.

In Beijing, both the formal and informal systems of preference formation need to be taken into account by policy actors vying to influence the preference formation outcome. Although a weak inter-departmental process undermines any government's preference formation processes, in China, the issue of bureaucratic rivalry is even more acute because of the lack of transparency in a vertical political regime, and where the government departments' access to economic benefits, funds, and decision-making power, are fiercely contested between themselves. As such, establishing and maintaining personal relationships have been an endemic practice in China. In sum, the characteristics of a consensus-driven preference formation process and the importance of informal politics are concrete stable factors that remain consistently immune from international influences.

## Further remarks

In this chapter, the objective was to reach some conclusions about whether and how international agencies influence China's preference formation and decision-making structure. From the discussion, it is clear to see that China does not reject international influence. This claim is made on the grounds that none of the principled engagements had an inertia or retrenchment levels of influence. Instead, Chinese decision-makers absorb the consequential effects of engaging with international agencies, and China adapts as well as integrates vis-à-vis the domestic situational factors, especially relating to the calculation of costs and benefits and information dissemination. The fact that Beijing accepts and adapts to international forces is an important finding which contrasts with the existing scholarly assumption that Chinese decision-making is an opaque and highly autonomous process immune from external impacts.

Not only do international agencies have some degrees of influence on preference formation, this also impacts on the distribution of power within the decision-making structure. By establishing close relationships with various domestic actors, the long-term effect is an empowerment of those actors against others in the internal inter-agency bargaining process. Of course, the influence of the international agencies is conditioned, as expected, by a range of situational factors and stable conditions, including consensus-driven preference formation, and informal politics.

## Notes

1 Interview with an expert from Renmin University, Beijing, 14 November 2012.
2 Interview with an expert from Chatham House, Beijing, 5 November 2012.
3 Whereas rationalists conceptualise problems as 'fixed' and 'external', cognitive theorists treat the nature of the problem as concepts that leave considerable scope for interpretation, and solutions as something that will, to a significant extent, have to be discovered through the process itself (Underdal, 1998, p. 20).
4 Interview with a policy officer from the National Development and Reform Commission, Beijing, 21 September 2012.
5 A cash value of US$1.5 million was assigned to a human life in the OECD, for example, while one in a developing country was assigned a mere US$150,000.
6 Interview with an expert from Harvard University, Boston, 11 June 2012.
7 Interview with a policy officer from the Ministry of Commerce, Beijing, 21 September 2012.
8 The enterprises' independence is indicated by many companies' convergence with international standards, and their commencement of competitive operations abroad against foreign firms; some have even entered the stock market. These indicate that many SOEs (including the oil companies) are no longer under pure government governance. Interview with an expert from the Chinese Academy of Social Sciences, Beijing, 8 November 2012.
9 Interview with a financial advisor from the Export-Import Bank, Beijing, 20 November 2012.
10 Interview with a policy advisor from the China Academy of International Trade and Economic Cooperation under the Ministry of Commerce, Beijing, 19 November 2012.
11 Conversely, conforming to group behaviour could be rewarded with psychological benefits and wellbeing from back-patting.
12 Interview with a policy advisor from the China Academy of International Trade and Economic Cooperation under the Ministry of Commerce, Beijing, 19 November 2012.
13 Personal observations.
14 Interview with a senior member of the WTO Division of the Ministry of Commerce, Beijing, 22 November 2012.
15 Interview with a senior member of the WTO Division of the Ministry of Commerce, Beijing, 22 November 2012.
16 Interview with a senior member of the China CDM Fund under the Ministry of Finance, Beijing, 3 March 2012.
17 Interview with a member of the Department of Treaty and Law of the Ministry of Commerce, Beijing, 23 November 2012.
18 Interview with a policy officer from the Policy Planning Department of the Ministry of Foreign Affairs, London, 7 June 2011.
19 Interview with a policy officer from the Department of Treaty and Law of the Ministry of Foreign Affairs, Beijing, 7 September 2011.

# References

Bang, G., Heggelund, G., and Vevatne, J. (2005) *Shifting Strategies in the Global Climate Negotiations*. Joint Report by FNI and CICERO, FNI Report 6/2005/CICERO Report (8).

Bjorkum, I. (2005) *China in the International Politics of Climate Change: A Foreign Policy Analysis*. Norway: The Fridtjof Nansen Institute.

Brack, D. and Grubb, M. (1996) 'Climate Change: A Summary of the Second Assessment Report of the IPCC'. *Royal Institute of International Affairs Briefing Papers* 32.

Chayes, A. and Antonia, H.C. (1993) 'On Compliance'. *International Organization* 47(2) pp. 177–205.

Costa, O. and Jorgensen, K.E. (eds) (2012) *The Influence of International Institutions on the EU*. London: Palgrave Macmillan.

Dasgupta, P.S. (1997) 'Economic Development and the Idea of Social Capital'. Working Paper, Faculty of Economics, University of Cambridge.

Economy, E. (1997) 'Chinese Policy-making and Global Climate Change'. In M.A. Schreurs and E. Economy (eds) *The Internationalization of Environmental Protection* (pp. 19–41). Cambridge: Cambridge University Press.

Frank, R. (1988) *Passions within Reason: The Strategic Role of the Emotions*. New York: W.W. Norton.

Haas, P.M. (1992) 'Introduction: Epistemic Communities and International Policy Coordination'. *International Organization* 46(1) pp. 1–35.

Haas, P.M. (1990) *Saving the Mediterranean: The Politics of International Environmental Cooperation*. New York: Columbia University Press.

Hatch, M.T. (2003) 'Chinese Politics, Energy Policy, and the International Climate Change Negotiations'. In P.G. Harris (ed.) *Global Warming and East Asia: the Domestic and International Politics of Climate Change* (pp. 43–65). London and New York: Routledge.

IPCC (2007) *Fourth Assessment Report*. Geneva: Intergovernmental Panel on Climate Change.

IPCC (2003) *Good Practice Guidance for Land Use, Land-Use Change and Forestry*. Geneva: Intergovernmental Panel on Climate Change.

IPCC (2001) *Climate Change 2001: Synthesis Report*. [Online] Available: www.ipcc.ch/pub/un/syreng/spm.pdf [Accessed: 3 April 2011].

Jacobs, L.R. and Page, B.I. (2005) 'Who Influences U.S. Foreign Policy'. *The American Political Science Review* 99(1) pp 107–123.

Johnston, A.I. (2008) *Social States: China in International Institutions, 1980–2000*. Princeton, NJ: Princeton University Press.

Johnston, A.I. (1998) 'China and International Environmental Institutions: A Decision Rule Analysis'. In M.B. Elroy, C.P. Nielsen, and P. Lydon (eds) *Energizing China: Reconciling Environmental Protection and Economic Growth* (pp. 555–600). Newton, MA: Harvard University Press.

Kelley, J. (2004) 'International Actors on the Domestic Scene: Membership Conditionality and Socialization by International Institutions'. *International Organization* 58(3) pp. 425–457.

Kreps, D.M. (1992) 'Corporate Culture and Economic Theory'. In J.E. Alt and K.A. Shepsle (eds) *Perspectives on Positive Political Economy* (pp. 90–143). Cambridge: Cambridge University Press.

Lawrence, S.V. and Martin, M.F. (2012) 'Understanding China's Political System. CRS Report for Congress, Washington, D.C.'. [Online] 20 March 2012. Available from: www.fas.org/sgp/crs/row/R41007.pdf [Accessed: 17 March 2014].

Martin, B. and Larsen, G. (1999) 'Taming the Tiger: Key Success Factors for Trade with China'. *Journal of Marketing Intelligence and Planning* 17(4), pp. 202–208.

Moravcsik, A. (1994) 'Why the European Union Strengthens the State: Domestic Politics and International Cooperation'. *Working Paper Series* 52. Cambridge, MA: Center for European Studies, Harvard University.

National Communication (2004) *The People's Republic of China Initial National Communication on Climate Change: Executive Summary.* [*Zhonghua renmin gongheguo qihou bianhua chushi guojia xinxi tongbao*]. Beijing, China: Planning Publishing House.

Odell, J.S. (2000) *Negotiating the World Economy.* Ithaca, NY and London: Cornell University Press.

Oksenberg, M. and Economy, E. (1997) *Shaping US–China Relations: A Long-Term Strategy.* New York: Council on Foreign Relations Press.

Pearson, M.M. (2001) 'The Case of China's Accession to GATT/WTO'. In D.M. Lampton (ed.) *The Making of Chinese Foreign and Security Policy In the Era of Reform, 1978–2000* (pp. 337–370). Stanford, CA: Stanford University Press.

Pomfret, J. and Lim, B.K. (2012) 'China's Ex-President Overshadows Party Congress, Transition'. *Reuters*. [Online] 10 November. Available from: www.reuters.com/article/2012/11/10/us-china-congress-jiang-idUSBRE8A90IE20121110 [Accessed: 10 November 2012].

Saich, T. (2001) *Governance and Politics of China.* New York: Palgrave.

Scharpf, F.W. (1997) *Games Real Actors Play. Actor-Centered Institutionalism in Policy Research.* Boulder, CO and Oxford: Westview Press.

Søfting, G.B. (2000) 'Climate Change Policymaking – Three Explanatory Models'. *CICERO Working Paper* 6.

Underdal, A. (1998) 'Explaining Compliance and Defection: Three Models'. *European Journal of International Relations* 4(5) pp. 5–30.

Wang, J. (2006) 'Managing National Reputation and International Relations in the Global Era: Public Diplomacy Revisited'. *Public Relations Review* 32(2) pp. 91–96.

*Xinhua News* (2007) 'Hu Jintao Mentions "Democracy" More Than 60 Times in Landmark Report'. [Online] 15 October. Available from: http://news.xinhuanet.com/english/2007-10/15/content_6884358.htm [Accessed: 6 November 2012].

Young, O.R. (1992) *Arctic Politics: Conflict and Cooperation in the Circumpolar North.* Hanover, NE and London: University Press of New England.

Yu, H. (2008) *Global Warming and China's Environmental Diplomacy.* New York: Nova Science Publishers, Inc.

Zhang, Z. (2003) 'The Forces Behind China's Climate Change Policy: Interests, Sovereignty, Prestige'. In P.G. Harris (ed.) *Global Warming and East Asia: The Domestic and International Politics of Climate Change* (pp. 66–85). London and New York: Routledge.

# Part III

# Chinese economic diplomacy

Negotiation approaches

# 7    A look at negotiation approaches

Economic diplomacy is typically characterised not only by the negotiation preferences formulated before a negotiation round, but also by the final decision-making at the negotiation table – such is the making of a compromise outcome. As final decision-making on negotiation approach occurs at the negotiation table, it is, therefore, conditioned by both the negotiation environment and the process management, typically run by the presiding staff of international agencies. That is why an analysis of the decision-making process for negotiation approach also requires an analysis of the role and impact of international agencies and their multilateral processes.

Rationalists, cognitivists, and contractualists commonly assume that international agencies are effective *mediators* of multilateral processes. Where they differ is in the type of cognition which is altered by mediation and the steps international agencies have to take to be effective. Rationalists assume negotiation approaches are determined by the policy options and/or action available to negotiators, alongside the likely expectations for the outcome. Although the preferences as to the desired outcome are assumed to be fixed, the nation-state's expectations are not. Rather, their uncertainties about the accuracy of their expectations cause them to perpetually inform and renew their perceptions as they encounter and get hold of new information (Walsh, 2005, p. 5). In this situation, international agencies in a mediation function can use the available private negotiation information (i.e. the utility associated with each available negotiation approach) that may be important to Chinese decision-makers in order to alter their expectations, and therefore the negotiation approach of China.

Cognitivists take a slightly different approach to rationalists. Drawing on the Habermasian theory of communicative action, cognitivists hold that from a function of mediation, international agencies and the Chinese policy actors can communicate frankly with one another in the process of building consensus about cause–effect relationships, for instance, and what are considered normatively correct behaviours. International agencies interact with the Chinese policy actors without being aided by material power resources to impose their own perspectives onto the Chinese decision-makers. In turn, the Chinese decision-makers become more open to the possibility of being persuaded by the better argument regardless of whom that argument stems from. This viewpoint contrasts with rationalism, which rejects the possibility that mediation could transform how a government defines what is *right* and what constitutes *normatively correct* behaviour (Finnemore, 2003, p. 154; Risse, 2000, p. 20).

Contractualists, in the meantime, conceive mediation as nothing more and nothing less than an effort to change the costs-and-benefit analysis of a negotiation approach with exogenously positive or negative incentives to secure cooperation. Mediation does not change a player's underlying desire to defect in a suasion game, nor does it change basic beliefs – or common knowledge – about what kind of game is being played.

Building from the preceding assumption on the function of mediation, and based on the second framework of analysis – as explained in Chapter 2 – this chapter illustrates that international agencies do affect China's negotiation approach, and do so through the capacities of a mediator in shuttle diplomacy proximity talks, of a facilitator of informal negotiation practices, and of an instigator of side-payment bargaining. However, the real impact of these instruments varies, in accordance with the context of the negotiation process (making it an arduous task to quantify generalisable results).

## Shuttle diplomacy proximity talks

*Shuttle diplomacy* is the act of meeting country representatives abroad to discuss contentious cross-border issues. The inter-personal meetings held in the course of the shuttle diplomacy are known as *proximity talks*. The micro-process of proximity is a case of persuasion and it involves changing the decision-makers' minds, opinions, and attitudes about causality, and has implications for the original condition characterised by a lack of material and/or mental coercion (Johnston, 2008, pp. 25–26; Walsh, 2005, p. 3). Some political scientists believe persuasion is the "central aim of political interaction" (Mutz *et al.*, 1996, p. 1). Others consider politics as being all about persuasion (Gibson, 1998, p. 821).

The rationalists, cognitivists and contractualists mutually agree that persuasion triggers policy impact. For instance, rationalists believe the hoped-for effect of the costs-and-benefits analysis is to use it to persuade the Chinese government of better negotiation approach equilibria. Cognitivists likewise assume the purpose of information dissemination is to persuade Chinese decision-makers that the international discourse guides a better negotiation approach. Furthermore, contractualists argue that reputation reinforcement is effective in persuading the Chinese government to be cooperative. These understandings of persuasion differ from other tactics of influence (e.g. rhetorical action or heresthetics) where one Party manipulates the context (e.g. the political environment or the rules of decision-making) to achieve an objective of their interest (Schimmelfennig, 2002). Due to the conciliatory nature of mediatory persuasion, 91 per cent of the interviews indicated that it works more effectively in China than other methods. This is because international agencies generally have better knowledge about how to engage with the Chinese decision-makers in meaningful and reasoned communicative ways.[1]

Based on the cases examined in Chapters 4 and 5, two strategies of persuasion used for proximity talks were identified as actively exercised by the agencies of the UNFCCC and the WTO: the *central* route and the *peripheral* route. The central route is where international agencies weigh evidence and problems through counter-attitudinal arguments, and come to a conclusion that is different from what the Chinese government had begun with. This form of mediatory persuasion involves a high-intensity process of cognition, reflection, and argument about the content of new information (Bar-Tal and Saxe, 1990, p. 122). In the case of mitigation, with regard to the Chinese government's view that mitigation measures are threatening to economic growth, the UNFCCC Secretariat and the Intergovernmental Panel on Climate Change (IPCC) provided calculated evidence to persuade the Chinese decision-makers that improving energy efficiency, diversifying energy sources and encouraging reforestation are all 'no-regret' policy options, and contribute to the efficiency of the energy sector.

Furthermore, these policies can stimulate the development of new commercially profitable technologies, as well as new access to technical and/or economic assistance from abroad. In the case of the Government Procurement Agreement (GPA), the GPA Committee attempted to persuade the Chinese decision-makers – who viewed entry to the GPA as having ambiguous benefits for China – that the benefits of GPA membership enhance the country's rule-making in this area and contribute to better governance over the private regulations concerning the participants in procurement activities. Membership can mitigate internal corruption and other illegal behaviours as well as strengthen the efficiency of the system. Due to the visible attitudinal changes from Beijing in both areas, Chinese decision-makers could be argued to be susceptible to the central route of persuasion which occurs in proximity talks.

Yet, empirical evidence indicates that the impact of the central route of persuasion declines if the initial attitude in Beijing was already linked to a larger internally consistent *network of beliefs*. This drawback resembles that of information dissemination; and it explains why, after years of proximity talks, the UNFCCC bodies only affected a slight reform of Beijing's attitude towards the issue of mitigation. The widely held conviction, particularly within the National Development and Reform Commission (NDRC), that mitigation efforts endanger economic growth essentially undermines the effects of persuasion of the UNFCCC bodies. Likewise, the wider belief, held by numerous government departments which regulate services (e.g. public transport and telecommunication), that China's services are still shaped by weak infrastructures prompted a consistent negotiation approach characterised by a resistance to further liberalisation in trade in services, at least in the early negotiation rounds. With this said, as long as decision-makers are open to the international agencies – which the Chinese government is – and as long as they continue to face uncertainties about the available policy options, and the approximated net benefits of each available option, the central route can still be effective. Of course, this effect will be even greater when decision-makers hold weaker prior beliefs.

The second strategy is the peripheral route. This strategy promotes the establishment of institutionalised relationships between international agencies and the Chinese decision-makers in informal and private settings. The Chinese decision-makers often search for cues about the nature of a given relationship with an international agency to judge the legitimacy of their counter-attitudinal arguments – a point that was raised in the previous chapter as a weakness of information dissemination. Like other countries, China finds proximity talks with in-groups to be more effective than with out-groups; and talks with *liked* sources are usually better-received than sources that are disliked. The determining factor of *like* is based on familiarity and the level of exposure to the agency. For example, ministries with regular engagements with the UNFCCC or the WTO not only embody deeper knowledge about the relevant issues under negotiation, but are also generally more sympathetic towards the global agenda. By comparison, ministries with little or no contact with international agencies tend to accord them less legitimacy. Thus, ministries that have established relationships with one or more international agencies often consider them as having greater credibility than other ministries that do not have similar relationships and associations.

This point is nicely encapsulated by the rationalist assumption, which posits that even though preferences over the desired outcome are fixed, the actors' beliefs are not, and their uncertainties about the accuracy of these beliefs cause them to renew their beliefs infinitely as new information is encountered (Walsh, 2005, p. 5). This assumption complements the cognitive view that the dynamism of beliefs, and the new information about the utility associated with each available policy, can alter the beliefs of the Chinese decision-makers. In 2000, the COP5 (Conference of Parties) President held proximity talks with the Chinese decision-makers in an effort to encourage China to commit to the Clean Development Mechanism (CDM) initiative. The COP5 President emphasised the net benefits (e.g. new investments, technology development, and job creation) that come with cooperation. Interestingly, Chinese decision-makers responded with enthusiasm *only* when they were convinced that the COP5 President was informed and credible.[2] Chinese decision-makers needed to be convinced that the COP5 presiding staff possessed more, and more accurate, information concerning the negotiations and the policy options available to China.

At the time, the Chinese decision-makers faced uncertainties about which of the available policies on the Kyoto Mechanisms would maximise their utility. As one member of the COP5 Presidency involved in the process interviewed for this research indicates, in order to be successful at persuasion, the Chinese decision-makers needed to face some degree of uncertainty about the relationship between policies and outcomes. When this uncertainty is low, the information from international agencies is perceived as accurate and reliable guidance for the net benefits that arise from each available policy option. It is understandable that when Chinese decision-makers faced high uncertainties about the CDMs, they searched for and evaluated new information to determine as accurately as possible the correct estimations of potential economic payoffs from each available negotiation approach. They resorted to the guidance of the COP5 presiding staff's suggestions based on the belief that they might have a better grasp of the real relationship between the available policy options and their associated outcomes than their own. In the end, the Chinese decision-makers adopted the CDMs with the conclusion that the COP5 Presidency had superior and credible information concerning the true relationship between the policy and outcome nexus.

In addition, whether the Chinese decision-makers accept the persuasion of international agencies rests on how honestly these agencies have communicated their superior information. As China's negotiation approach can affect the utility of the international agencies (i.e. by determining the likelihood of reaching an agreement and the nature of the agreement), the international agencies may not necessarily act on neutral grounds when advising and mediating the negotiations; rather, they could hold preferences over the type of negotiation policies China adopts. International agencies have an incentive to play around with their information resources so that the preferred negotiation approach is adopted by China. In this situation, Chinese decision-makers will only consider agencies credible when they share China's preferred negotiation outcome. When Chinese decision-makers have the knowledge that an international agency endeavours to lock in outcomes that are similar to their own, they trust that they will then communicate on a more honest level with regards to their information and of the true consequences of the proposed negotiation approach.

On the other hand, if China holds different preferences over the outcome compared to the international agency, then it may refuse any suggestion made by them on the grounds that it is not considered credible. In other words, the Chinese government might fear that their divergent preferences may cause the international agency to deliberately communicate incorrect information for the purpose of persuading China to adopt their desired negotiation approach. This sentiment was communicated by an interviewed Chinese negotiator on trade in services at the WTO.[3] He recalled that in the early years of the Doha Development Agenda (DDA), the WTO Secretariat envisioned a complete liberal international structure for services with minimal restrictions, and shaped his words in whatever way he thought necessary in order to have China jump on board with the imagined scenario. However, the interviewee felt that much of the arguments made were not congruent to China's domestic situation, and, therefore, he could not go along with this vision of an agreement in services. Here, past experiences and interactions with an international agency impact the degree to which their preferred approach is seen to converge with the preferences of Chinese decision-makers. And often, China's general expectation about the international environment and behaviours of others further impacts its level of alignment with international agencies.

That said, through their role as mediators, international agencies can overcome China's expectation issues by exercising proximity talks and sharing insights obtained from caucus sessions with other member-states. Of course, as mentioned earlier, the problem with this strategy is, if China knows that an agency is going to share what they learn with the other Parties, what reasons does it have to distribute its own private information that may come back to bite it? On the one hand, if the agency in question keeps its insights from the proximity talks confidential, then it has limited ability to utilise the insights for improving the negotiation outcome. When international agencies encounter this dilemma in practice, they might exercise what Brown and Ayres (1994, p. 356) refer to as "noise translation" in private dialogues – i.e. share their insights about the views of other Parties without explicitly stating any one Party's perspectives. In this way, Chinese negotiators are more likely to communicate with greater honesty with the agency, with the understanding that anything they share will not be directly relayed to other Parties.

True, even partial information is beneficial for the other side in moving towards the best possible agreement. Yet, David Hoffman (2010, pp. 16–17) makes a strong point in that even though the notion of communicating only partial information seem wrong, in practice, the principle of transparency is difficult to implement. The only feasible way for this strategy to work is if China, like other Parties, has perfect knowledge about how the agency intends to apply the insights acquired from proximity talks. As such, 'noise communication' and other non-explicit means of communication such as *signalling* are commonly used as effective tools to guide Parties towards productive negotiations.

Ample evidence was found which suggests that international agencies frequently exercised signalling in their proximity talks. Signals are actions which convey a kind of information that reduces uncertainty (Jervis, 1976). In strategic interactions, where international agencies hold private information regarding the preferences of other Parties, for instance, signalling can be effective for converging China's negotiation approach to one desired by the agencies. In the process of setting the climate change negotiation agendas and in the process of drafting the Chair's text, the Secretariat of the UNFCCC requires all signatories to send their national reports to Bonn, Germany – the UNFCCC headquarters – on an annual basis (Søfting, 2000, p. 23). The UNFCCC Secretariat, in turn, uses information to alter China's negotiation approach. Equivalent functions were identified for the WTO Secretariat. One Chinese decision-maker noted that the WTO Members were required to submit national concept papers to Geneva containing elements relating to regulatory cooperation, such as transparency disciplines and negotiation intents for the DDA. As a result, the WTO holds substantial private information it can, and often does, use for signalling.

With this said, the empirical evidence also notes that international agencies do not necessarily have as much private information in practice as cognitivists assume, especially concerning access to the 'true' versus 'revealed' preferences of the member-states. It is often difficult for international agencies to verify claims by Parties, i.e. their hands are tied by domestic constraints; and it is not obvious when a member-state is bluffing when they claim that they have attractive alternatives in hand. The situation is further exacerbated when deciphering the preferences of states through coalitions. This challenge in identifying the real preference orderings is nicely illustrated by the DDA negotiations. When faced with a coalition of states putting forth a collective demand, as is often the case at the DDA negotiations, it is difficult for the WTO to determine the intent and resistance points of the individual Parties. A coalition may claim complete commitment to a particular position, and its members may threaten to collectively block the negotiation process unless their joint demand is met. But unless the WTO has some additional information about the credibility of this position, it may assume that the members of the coalition are bluffing and could actually be bought off through individual side-deals. In the DDA negotiations, the difficulty in identifying the real preference orderings of the Parties constitute a key reason why trade-offs through the Single Undertaking have been difficult to achieve. All Parties recognise to some degree that the stated positions do not represent the bottom line of the negotiating Parties. But amidst uncertainty about the extent to which coalitions (and countries within them) are willing to stand firm over certain areas and concede on others, the zone of agreement itself remains ambiguous.

Furthermore, signalling exercised in proximity talks is expected to inform policy. This expectation naturally affects the way negotiation questions are framed and how negotiation should be approached (e.g. certain matters are attended to at the expense of others; some questions are identified as political and removed from inquiry, while others are addressed as if they were merely technical and had no political implications). However, the international agencies' signalling exercises may not reflect a state of neutrality. Instead, they are located in a context of competing national and institutional interests, and their influence tends to be either enhanced or circumscribed by this context. At times, the signalling exercises may not translate well into policy and the uncertainties arising out of shallow-detailed mediatory recommendations from international agencies can dampen their credibility. For instance, the WTO is in principle charged with the function of reporting independent and private information to China and the United States regarding each other's demands and intents.

Another case in point is the 'signalling conference' held in 2008, and the subsequent informal discussions with some 25 groups, each focused on a distinct service sector. These activities helped identify sectors and activities where liberalisation might be possible (Oxford Analytica Daily Brief Service, 2012).[4] However, the WTO is also uncertain of the costs for either the Chinese or the Americans, but does have some independent information it can pass on; it must be biased in order to have any effect on the outcome of the bargaining. The intuition is that if the WTO bodies only care about preventing a deadlock, then they will always tell China and the US the situation is resolute (regardless of whether the WTO believes it) and therefore China should moderate its demands.[5] This advice, if followed, could lead to an agreement, but most likely on either *actual* or *perceived* unfair terms. And China, seeing the WTO bodies as having an incentive to lie, will consequently discount their advice, and the WTO bodies' influence is therefore undermined; the imminent regression problem ultimately reduces its effectiveness.

In general, the level of influence proximity talks can install in shaping China's negotiation approach depends on two factors: how informative the international agencies are, and the level of perceived credibility they have in the eyes of Chinese decision-makers. It is difficult to for a trustworthy but ill-informed international agency to convince the Chinese elite to alter their negotiation approach. The same goes for the reverse situation. China certainly absorbs the mediation of international agencies, but this needs to be supplemented by superior information and credibility in order to communicate honestly. In this situation, Chinese decision-makers acknowledge that international agencies have better understandings about a negotiation environment and therefore trust in their information.

## Informal negotiation practices

Cognitivists believe that influencing negotiation approaches does not just occur at the national level. The negotiation processes itself can contribute to the actor's perceptions of how a problem should be handled (Barnett and Finnemore, 2004, pp. 3–7; Finnemore, 1996, p. 333). Hence, informal negotiation practices (INPs), often facilitated by members of international agencies during the negotiation process, can modify China's expectations, strategies, and posture, all of which underline their approach to the negotiations. Under normal circumstances, negotiations in an open, formal plenary with all the attending national delegates tend to be cumbersome at best and unmanageable when the agenda grows in complexity. In turn, INPs are strategically designed (by international actors) to streamline the negotiation proceedings by allowing the texts to be discussed by smaller and specialised groups of negotiators.

INPs come in numerous forms, one of which is known as 'informal consultations'. These are open-ended and off-the-record meetings, often steered by the figurehead of an international agency or the Chair of a general council or committee. In July 2008, the WTO's Director-General, Pascal Lamy, acted as Chairman of the Trade Negotiation Committee (TNC) and steered a services signalling conference with a small group of key economies, including China, to discuss outstanding services issues and exchange potential offers (Footer, 2011, p. 230). Lamy's predecessor, Mike Moore, was also recorded to have steered informal consultations with China, Kenya, the US, and India on agricultural tariffs in 2001. According to one witness negotiator, Moore had "firmly retorted back to any doubts and objections Chinese Minister Shi and Indian Minister Maran had" about the Chair's draft text (cited in Jawara and Kwa, 2004, p. 110).

Another form of INP is roundtable discussions. Member-states in this situation are divided into smaller groups which sit across from – rather than behind – each other. During the 2011 COP17 conference, the South African COP President called a roundtable (or the 'huddle') including representative from China, the US, the EU, and India to discuss a final resolution on mitigation issues as part of the Durban Package. Based on the author's personal observations inside the negotiation room, the South African COP President, Maite Nkoana-Mashabane, acted as Chair of the roundtable discussion and placed particular pressure on China, India, and the US to accept the middle-range proposal forwarded by the EU; the negotiators were not permitted to leave until a 'landing zone' was agreed.

Finally, INPs can come in the form of inter-personal corridor or lobby dialogue outside the main meetings. According to one Chinese delegate, these corridor conversations are very effective in guiding the negotiation proceedings and outcome, and even more so when China encounters a negotiation dilemma with other Parties.[6] In 2008, the Chair of the services signalling conference exercised signalling with members of the Chinese delegation in corridor conversations. Lamy indicated that the participating ministers may improve their services offers for an agreement on agriculture and Non-Agricultural Market Access (NAMA) from China (Hoekman and Mattoo, 2011, pp. 7–8). China apparently approached the negotiations thereafter with more flexibility and approved the 2008 Chair's draft text on trade in services.

The strength of international agencies acting as facilitators of the INPs – characterised as confidential and informal/off-the-record processes of negotiation – is the effectiveness of INPs for securing agreements and elevating the probabilities that negotiating Parties will reciprocate. The probable settlement-effect stems from the setting of the INPs, which is conducive to problem-solving. For instance, a fundamental principle of the INPs is that nations can select freely how and on what grounds they should settle. As such, it is a more comfortable environment for Chinese decision-makers to consider the best negotiation approach. The setting is particularly important because, in some negotiations, especially concerning highly contentious issues, the clash of communication styles can undermine China's willingness to cooperate. In some cases, certain delegates can communicate so abrasively that the Chinese decision-makers cannot tolerate being in the same room.[7] In one DDA joint session about how certain business interests should be valued, one Chinese delegate could not tolerate the tone of voice of the foreign delegate that was making a statement. The Chinese delegate sat uncomfortably, a pained look swept her face, and it became clear that this delegate was unable to listen to what he was saying.[8] The fact that the native spoken language between the two delegates also differed further compounded the severity of the problem. In this situation, the informal nature of the INPs is much better at easing any discomfort felt by members of the Chinese delegation, and, in turn, enables a much more effective process of honest and receptive communication.

In addition, and perhaps more important, is that INPs, as informal consultations, involve processes of rationalisation in the communications between international agencies and the Chinese negotiators. The rationalisation is itself a source of opportunity and constraint because the form of justification for a recommended set of possibilities communicated by international agencies structures how the Chinese decision-makers view the available options in terms of the negotiation approaches. Therefore, how effective an international agency is in this respect could have a deterministic impact on the outlook of Chinese decision-makers.

When Parties are stuck for options in a stalemate, international agencies facilitate INPs to brainstorm alternative solutions. Brainstorming in a formal plenary can impede thinking outside the box because *distrust* can undermine the joint sessions regardless of how skilfully the agency frames the brainstorming exercises and explains the ground rules. The Chinese delegation may fear that advancing an idea could disclose private aspects of their negotiation approach, such as the level of their flexibility to solutions; or, the spontaneity of the discussion can disclose more details about China's position than they are willing to reveal. Thus, international agencies like to encourage brainstorming through a form of INPs and explore some initial ideas in a separate and safer-feeling environment before hosting joint sessions.

In the process of brainstorming, the mediatory effects of these agencies (i.e. conveying their own ideas alongside those of nation-states) will naturally be absorbed into China's final negotiation approach. This can be considered as the agencies' attempts to level the playing field by engaging in some form of negotiation coaching. For instance, international agencies have a high tendency to encourage the Chinese delegates to explore each side's underlying interests, help decision-makers generate negotiation options, and discuss the ways that different elements of a deal might be structured. Coaching of this kind is virtually impossible to do in formal plenaries, partly because it gives the appearance of partiality, and partly because candour about bargaining strategies in joint sessions is rare (Hoffman, 2010, p. 28). The implication of these exercises is that international agencies will soften the edges of China's national position and assert their beliefs in the framing of China's negotiation approach. At the same time, international agencies implicitly and indirectly impose international norms on China to constrain the possible negotiation approaches they can adopt.

To be sure, international agencies, by design, have no capacity to make negotiation decisions; their designated roles are by definition primarily administrative. Multilateral economic agreements are, in theory, member-driven. But in reality, leading representatives can exercise powers comparable to national leaders.[9] In the WTO 2001 ministerial conference, Chairman Kamal, for instance, refused to take a backseat during the negotiation proceedings, demanding that he play a central role in the process of reaching a compromise (Jawara and Kwa, 2004, p. 84). Likewise, although Lamy remains neutral and impartial in public, he has, on numerous occasions, pointed out to the Chinese delegation what he perceives as right or wrong with China's negotiation approach, and has made recommendations accordingly behind closed doors.[10] Some interviewed Chinese delegates also revealed that the WTO facilitators sometimes request China to agree to the inclusion of certain items on the negotiation agenda despite Beijing's reluctance; senior personnel often play very active roles in the final Green Room meetings of ministerial conferences to persuade the Chinese delegates to accept draft declarations.[11] One developing country delegate observed that those who supported the Chair's text were granted the floor to speak first:

> it was arranged in this way to literally set the consensus ... People cheered and clapped after every endorsement of the text ... This made those who wanted more clarifications feel like they were the bad guys ... This is a common tactic, to make a certain viewpoint appear more dominant.
>
> (Cited in Jawara and Kwa, 2004, p. 108)

This view is supported by an interviewed Asian delegate to the WTO during the 2011 ministerial conference:

> Being Chair of a committee at the WTO gave me the opportunity to see how the Secretariat functions, and how some group of countries would subtly get what they want into draft documents. It is done in a very clever, sophistic- ated and subtle manner … If, for example, the majority of delegates don't agree with a negotiating text produced by a chairperson and thus demand changes, the chair could turn to the Secretariat for help, especially if he or she is not technically competent. The clever lawyers of the Secretariat will then redraft the text in such a way that it would lean towards what it wants, and, importantly, it would also seem that consensus was reached. The chair would then be placed with the responsibility of presenting this skewed docu- ment to the membership without further consultations.[12]

This shows the level of control the Secretariat has over the direction of the nego- tiations. The reality was echoed by an interviewed African delegate during COP17: "The Secretariat has very strong views on mitigation, and they do aggressively pursue that way of thinking. You get questions like 'Why don't China want to talk about emissions-reduction?' forgetting how much China has already achieved domestically".[13] An interviewed Central American delegate to the COPs similarly said,

> The Secretariat has biased positions, which has helped create another layer on to the COPs negotiating structure. Mission officials from the developing countries not only have to negotiate with their counterparts, they also have to negotiate with a so-called 'neutral' Secretariat.[14]

By helping the developing countries extract commitments from developed coun- tries (i.e. aid, technology transfers, market access, commodity prices, and debt relief), by helping developed countries demand economic reforms in developing countries, and/or by simply listening to the different positions and redrafting a compromise text themselves, international actors are running the show behind the scenes, with immense capacity to influence the negotiation outcomes as they see best through their facilitator function.

With this said, some Chinese negotiators have noted during interviews that Chinese policy officials do take measures to ensure the presiding staff of inter- national agencies do not go beyond their job descriptions as a 'secretary' during the negotiation process, and that they remain in a limited capacity to interfere with the member-driven decision-making system.[15] Undoubtedly, the actions and decisions of their staff are constantly under tight scrutiny by Chinese negoti- ators; but this does not deny the fact that the presiding staff do exercise strat- egies and tactics – though not on an open and prevalent basis. For instance, in the DDA negotiations, the WTO Secretariat has a tendency to host informal con- sultations in remote locations where few national embassies reside (e.g. Cancun).

This makes it difficult for many national delegates, including the Chinese, to seek decision approvals from their capital cities, and in the spur of the moment with added pressure and stress, negotiators are more likely to give in to the Chair's draft texts.[16] One negotiator also mentioned that when there is a prevalent and dominant consensus, the Chinese negotiators find it harder to keep to their bottom line and have a high tendency to give in and reach agreement due to the significant pressures and environmental influences.[17] Most Chinese negotiators generally believe that the presiding staff do interfere at times in the negotiations, and the facilitators do tend to coordinate between member-states – all of which can have consequences for China's negotiation approach.[18]

Advocates of rationalism, however, argue that how China shapes its negotiation approach should be exogenous to the social interaction dimension of the INPs (Reus-Smit, 2005, p. 192). This is because China enters negotiation processes with pre-defined interests, beliefs, and expectations. Given the strategic and rational nature of nation-states, they only participate in processes such as the INPs to maximise their pre-defined interests. As a result, it is difficult to imagine the INPs as having much influence over China's negotiation approach.

The drawback of this form of argument is that it takes China's negotiation approach as a given, without consideration for *how* such a negotiation approach developed in the first place. As the preceding discussion showed, the informal and inter-personal social element of the INPs forms a strong basis of decision-making among Chinese policy actors at the negotiation stage. The informal and unstructured setting and nature of the INPs creates normative and ideational structures which can condition the available negotiation manoeuvring space China has. It does so in three ways. First, as cognitivists argue, the non-material structures of the INPs affect what China views as the realm of possibility. That is to say, how it believes it should act in negotiations, what the perceived limitations on its actions are, and what strategies it imagines to achieve its objectives. The ideas and norms floating around in the INPs thus condition what China considers, as well as expects, as necessary and possible in practical and ethical terms.

Second, the roundtable brainstorming and coaching exercises show that the INPs constrain China's negotiation approach through an emphasis on the international norms. For instance, international agencies can seek to justify their ideas and recommendations by appealing to the established information norms of legitimate conduct. Third, the processes of rationalisation in INPs (i.e. the informal consultations) are a form of constraint in themselves. Certainly, the very language of justification provides constraints on the available actions China has in a given negotiation. In all cases, these structures would not exist without their facilitation of the INPs. Thus, the dialogical effect of brainstorming exercises, roundtable discussions, and corridor conversations define much of the Chinese perceptions regarding the appropriate negotiation approach to a given economic and/or political problem.

It is important to recognise, however, that the INPs usually occur at the later stages of decision-making for multilateral negotiations. By this time, Chinese decision-makers arrive in negotiation settings with relatively strong pre-defined postures, expectations, and beliefs. Although these elements are not fixed and can be reshaped, the task of doing so is nonetheless a tough one for external agencies via a facilitating capacity. For this reason, one can be certain that international agencies as facilitators of the INPs yield conditioned influence as a result.

## Side-payment bargaining

The third way China's approach to economic negotiations could be affected is by instigating side-payment bargaining. Rationalists believe that side-payment bargaining alters Chinese incentives by bringing material payoffs into the decision-making. Theoretically speaking, this instrument works well in the China context because a primary reason why Beijing sought memberships of multilateral institutions was to access foreign assistance (Economy, 2001, p. 232). Access to foreign economic and financial capital and technical know-how was a key motivation for China's long march to the WTO. The UNFCCC examples demonstrates how Beijing often uses its economic and social vulnerabilities to justify foreign funding and technologies. For instance, the section on the "needs for funds, technologies and capacity-building" in China's *Initial National Communication* (National Communication, 2004, p. 18) states, "China is relatively sensitive and vulnerable to climate change in the fields such as agriculture. Technical support and funds are needed for mitigating or adapting to the effects of climate change". As the head of the Chinese delegation, Xie Zhenhua, said at a COP18 news conference, the core issue blocking progress at the UN negotiations is finance – an incentive that would "create very good conditions for the settlement of other issues" (cited in Pomfret and Lim, 2012).

Technology transfer has also featured as a high incentive for the government to move some of the cost of putting its own economy on a low-carbon path onto other countries. In addition, the acquisition of advanced climate technologies would help China not only decrease the energy and carbon-intensity of its economy, but also develop its growing green technology sector as a way to move from the low-level manufacturing to a skilled labour production of high-tech goods (Conrad, 2012, pp. 498–499). In order to use the international climate regime to aid these efforts, China has spearheaded proposals for technology transfer mechanisms within the framework of the UNFCCC.[19] And when the CDM simulation exercises demonstrated the initiative as a promising way of accessing technologies and finance, this acted as a key catalyst for China's proactive approach towards the initiative.

But how can one be sure the UNFCCC bodies were the main provocateurs of side-payment rather than the driving force of national interests or acts of intergovernmental reciprocity? Since the material benefits already motivated China to adopt new positions for the CDM, to what extent can it be argued that the UNFCCC bodies were responsible for the altered negotiation approach?

Although the influence of UNFCCC bodies does not seem, on the surface, to go beyond their role as a facilitator of the climate change negotiations, a closer examination of the events reveals a somewhat more interesting story. During the earlier stages of the side-payment bargaining between China and the developed nations, any positive dynamic that could have developed was significantly dampened by the developed nations' reluctance to agree to a significant expansion of technology transfers to China. This is because the developed nations thought the transfer of advanced technologies – usually owned by private western companies – raised a spectrum of complex questions that ranged from legal issues of ownership to the protection of intellectual property rights (IPR) and the potential distortion of markets and competition. This is especially true for China, which has a questionable record in terms of the IPR protection. As a result, it failed to gain the developed countries' trust due to uncertainties over its willingness and capability to deal responsibly with IPR and the fair utilisation of innovative technologies (Conrad, 2012, pp. 498–499). It became clear that the debate on technology transfers would be treated as a sideshow at best, and the Chinese team's game plan, which might or might not have included some Chinese concessions, was stifled from the outset.

Under these circumstances, the COP presiding staff at the time believed it was necessary to subject China to surveillance measures before any side-payment bargaining success could be realised. Initially, the Chinese delegation refused such a suggestion, arguing that it is a breach of national sovereignty. But interviews revealed that after numerous informal discussions with the Negotiation Committee, and side-payment bargaining with developed nations, China agreed to submit to the international monitoring, validation, and verification systems in response to the conclusion of a 'too good to miss' package deal. As one Chinese negotiator remarked, "the UNFCCC have their own visions about the kind of agreement member states should endeavour to achieve and they certainly know how to guide China towards that end".[20] In this way, the UNFCCC bodies catalysed the proceedings and details of the side-payment agreement and subjected China to a position it was initially uncomfortable with.

By comparison, side-payment in the case of climate change mitigation was identified with minimal influence. Interviewed negotiators recalled that side-payment bargaining did occur in the earlier years of negotiations but less so later. As a leading contender in the international green technology market, China has less need to seek technologies elsewhere. Already, China has become the world's largest producer of solar cells, and the government poured US$34.6 billion into investment and financing for clean energy in 2009 – nearly double the US$18.6 billion spent by the US and about a quarter of the global total invested according to a report by the Pew Charitable Trusts (Tran, 2010). In addition, the government has announced a further investment of US$738 billion over the next decade on alternative energy (Stone, 2010). Meanwhile, as most mitigation efforts are nationally based, it is not realistic to expect to receive foreign funds, which makes the financial resources incentive irrelevant. For these reasons, material incentives were less attractive.[21]

With respect to the WTO examples, few, if any, side-payment activities were identified. In the GPA negotiations, side-payment bargaining was seldom exercised. But for the present purposes, an estimation of the potential influence of side-payment is worthwhile considering. In 2006, the Chinese government increased the utilisation of the national procurement regime for industrial, environmental, and other social policy goals. For instance, in 2007 a 'buy national' policy was implemented as part of the Ministry of Finance's (MOF's) *Measure on Government Procurement of Imported Products*. This policy suggests that only imported products with approval from the designated authorities could be procured. Approvals are usually granted based on expert assessment reviews and with the satisfaction of certain criteria. In addition, preferences are usually given to foreign suppliers who offer offsets (i.e. technology transfers). This criterion could imply that raising the material incentives through side-payment bargaining could pull some weight over China's negotiation approach on the issue.

Yet, mandated by the government's 15 year strategy for the promotion of science and technology, numerous administrative decrees and regulations were enforced between 2006 and 2007 in order to accommodate the procurement of energy-efficiency, products certified as environmentally friendly,[22] and indigenous innovation products.[23] These policies are generally incompatible with the rules of the GPA. For instance, in spite of the enforcement of transitional measures (i.e. a domestic price preference programme and offsets for assisting in the promotion of indigenous innovation products and technology transfers), they are nonetheless confined to a relatively short transitional period. In a similar fashion, even though the GPA 2007 Article X: 6 permits a Party to "prepare, adapt, or apply technical specifications to promote the conservation of natural resources or protect the environment", the existing system is nevertheless incompatible. In particular, the product lists are determined by administrative organs that give little consideration for international standards, and therefore, the Chinese system has many inconsistencies with the requirements contained in the GPA 2007 Article X: 3. These regulatory clashes reduced Beijing's enthusiasm towards the material incentives realised from side-payment bargaining, because of the political and economic costs it will have to endure in the aligning the domestic system to the international one through reforms.

Like the GPA example, few side-payment activities were found for the services negotiation except for one Green Room meeting in January 2007. Pascal Lamy provoked a side-payment bargaining between the *demandeurs* of services trade (i.e. the US, the EU, Japan) and major developing countries including China. It was suggested that if China could present a meaningful offer in services liberalisation, then it could unlock possible concessions by the major developed countries in agriculture and industrial goods (Leal-Arcas, 2007). Then, in 2011, Pascal Lamy reportedly oversaw another round of side-payment bargaining to reach an agreement on Modes 2 and 3 services – liberalisation in exchange for increased financial transfers.[24]

As China subsequently announced plans to gradually open these sectors after the 2011 negotiations, one can draw the convenient conclusion that side-payment triggered a shift in China's negotiation approach. Yet, one should be careful in suggesting that this was the doing of the WTO. Since the present work only found evidence of Lamy facilitating and overseeing side-payment bargaining rather than actively negotiating the terms and details of the end package – this was the job of the member-states – it is risky to draw correlations between the WTO and China's negotiation approach. Still, interviews with members of the Chinese delegation and the Council on Services Trade revealed that while Lamy did not negotiate the details of the package, he did lay out a vision of what an agreement would look like. Also, Lamy was suggested to have stimulated the bargaining process by presenting the worse-alternative scenarios. For instance, he emphasised to the Chinese delegation that in the absence of a multilateral agreement for services, China would have to carry out delicate economic reforms in its service sectors with less international institutional support. This was argued to be a worse situation than one in which Beijing endured varying degrees of economic dislocation as a result of entering a multilateral agreement – those compromises are less formidable than navigating openings into the international markets without an institutional platform as a guideline. Hence, Lamy was instrumental in prompting China to join the bargaining process and the framing of the bargaining from the outset.

Clearly, the influence of international agencies through side-payment is not as straightforward as anticipated, with mixed outcomes across the cases. While the CDM and the trade in services examples indicate positive influence from the UNFCCC and WTO respectively, the mitigation and GPA examples reveal minimal influence as a result of side-payment bargaining facilitation. One explanation for the variance concerns whether the economic side-payments are compatible with China's policy goals. The CDM example showed that Beijing's desire to transform its domestic economy to a low-carbon path, which requires enormous investments and efforts, provided decision-makers with a strong incentive to use the multilateral framework to solicit the necessary assistance (especially in the field of technology transfer) to achieve its goals. As a result of its needs, China has also weakened its bargaining win-set abroad and, in turn, granted the UNFCCC bodies higher influences over its negotiation approach. This outcome would be less likely if China had a stronger win-set that would usually emerge when the side-payment is less compatible with China's policy needs. This finding was supported by the interviews, which suggest a key reason China eventually agreed to submit to the international monitoring, validation, and verification systems was because Beijing needed the economic payoffs in order to support its domestic (and resource-short) efforts such as the industrial gas projects to reduce hydroflurocarbon-23 (HFC23) and nitrous oxide ($N_2O$), and other renewable energy developments.[25] Participating in the CDM would therefore help fill the resource gaps in this regard and help the government realise its goals. Likewise, the government had already planned pilot programmes to liberalise its domestic services, and for this reason, any foreign technical assistance it can get access to was seen as attractive and fitting.

In contrast, the prospective material gains from making commitments on mitigation did not appeal to Beijing because it did not have any need for technologies or finances in support of mitigation targets – it was already an internationally recognised innovator of low-carbon technologies and renewable energy. Therefore, Beijing did not take them as value-added benefits. The GPA example presents another case where the economic payoffs from side-payment bargaining were less attractive due to regulatory conflicts between China's domestic procurement regime and the plurilateral GPA framework. Notwithstanding a national price preference programme and offsets which may enable China to retain certain policies for promoting indigenous innovation products and technology transfers, these measures will nevertheless be confined to a relatively short transitional period under the GPA. Likewise, even though GPA 2007 Article X: 6 allows a Party to "prepare, adapt, or apply technical specifications to promote the conservation of natural resources or protect the environment", the existing practices are incompatible with China's product lists. These regulatory clashes undermined Beijing's enthusiasm towards the material incentives of cutting a side deal.

At the end of the day, domestic policy and politics surpass material benefits. As one American official observed, "There's no bigger influence than China's own policy agenda, which is shaped by the interest of the government and its constituents. Third Parties are mere supplemental variables".[26] Numerous interviewees further emphasised that as China prospers into a middle-income country, its reliance on international support declines, which implies the reduced feasibility of effectively influencing China through side-payment deals in the future.[27]

The second explanation for the variances has to do with *trust*. In the mitigation example, interviewed negotiators explained that, following past failures to receive technologies and funding from the industrialised countries, Beijing lost its trust in the UNFCCC Secretariat's actual ability to facilitate and mediate willingness from the Annex I countries to actually commit and follow through with any financial transfer pledge they make. One interviewee questioned, "If the major donors have not followed up on their existing technology transfer commitments under the UNFCCC framework, why should China believe in anything different for mitigation?"[28]

Although China's was in the past a direct beneficiary of international financial support, this situation has changed and it is today further down the list of potential recipients of financial climate support from donor countries. This fact was articulated by Todd Stern, head of the US delegation, well in advance of the COP15 Copenhagen conference, when he remarked that he "does not envision public funds, certainly not from the US, going to China" (cited in IISD, 2009). The Chinese team responded immediately that it had never seen itself as a 'first candidate' for climate support. This little exchange of statements highlighted the fact that China's days as a beneficiary of direct climate support are over.

China's doubts are further amplified by the reality that the UNFCCC's financial capacity is limited. Although China can benefit from the Global Environmental Facility (GEF), its resources are conditioned by the level of generosity among Annex I countries. To put things into perspective, the UNFCCC (2007) estimates that the investment needed each year for climate change mitigation and adaptation for developing countries is in the range of US$104–143 billion.

However, a rough calculation by Gareth Porter *et al.* (2008) shows that the total amount of funding from all climate funds worldwide equates to less than US$6 billion a year. It is therefore understandable that China's confidence in international funding is lacklustre, to say the least. The CDM negotiations were different in this regard because the pilot simulations allowed decision-makers to see how transactions are made and therefore build the necessary trust in the system. As Robert Powell (2002, p. 6) has criticised, "A striking feature of [this] actual [rationalist] bargaining [assumption] is that it often results in costly delays and inefficient outcomes". Even rationalists themselves have acknowledged that a nation will only revise its national approach if the expected marginal costs (i.e. damage or abatement costs) of cooperation are lower than (or at most equal to) the marginal benefits it expects to receive from such a position (Underdal, 1998, p. 8). But with distrust, even the slightest cost could be perceived on a magnified scale. Hence, as is the case for most countries and negotiators around the world, establishing *trust* is a precondition to building effective side agreements with China.

In general, international agencies as instigators of side-payment bargaining can produce partial influence at best. That is, they may be able to push China's negotiation approach towards a desired direction but this does not necessarily transform the fundamental negotiation approach – that is the game between China and other nation-states. Therefore, in measuring its level of influence, it is certain that side-payment bargaining does not have a transformative or retrenchment effect. At the same time, side-payment bargaining do not have an inertia effect because the CDM and services cases showed that it can restructure China's incentives. But the actualised success depends on how relevant the economic payoffs are to China's policy goals and trust factor.

## The social instigators

Throughout the book so far, *uncertainty* has been a common theme. When designing, framing, and eventually setting their negotiation approach, the Chinese government faces at least two different kinds of uncertainty – each with an undermining effect on international agencies' capacity to influence Chinese decision-making. It faces uncertainty about the political and economic environment in which its policies are implemented, and which can change dramatically with little notice or recognition abroad. Government members also face uncertainty about one another's preferences and intentions, which may not be fully articulated in negotiations. Hence, uncertainty is a concept that emphasises the limits of our ability to obtain accurate information, particularly about the future (Best, 2012).

In the rationalist literature, uncertainty is often seen as a product of imperfect or asymmetrical information. China, like other nations, lacks perfect information about the future since political and economic events are difficult to predict. At the same time, they must also contend with limited information, knowing more about their own intentions than about those of other Parties. Drawing on Douglass North's (1990, p. 27) work on institutional economics, liberal institutionalists argue that one of the key functions of international agencies is to reduce uncertainty (Keohane, 1984, p. 245).

Building on this line of thought, uncertainty runs unnervingly throughout China's economic diplomacy decision-making, and this is the result of low expectations for foreign reciprocity, distrust, and a concern for personal reputation. These three factors constitute the *social instigators*, contingencies which determine the impact of international agencies on China's negotiation approach.

### *Social instigator I: expectation*

According to the interviews, one fundamental reason for China's seemingly low proactivity in many multilateral economic negotiations is due to Beijing's low expectations that foreign Parties will reciprocate on any of their commitments or concessions pledged. During the 2011 DDA ministerial conference, numerous interviewed Chinese negotiators indicated that they did not intend to work hard towards reaching an agreement because they did not think other national delegations were interested in any form of an agreement. This attitude was echoed by a senior member of the WTO Secretariat, who remarked that there is no political will amongst the member-states to push through an agreement or any expectations of being pragmatic.[29] Chinese negotiators to the COPs similarly indicated low expectations that foreign Parties have any willingness to commit to a post-2020 framework at COP18 well before the conference took place.

Where there are low expectations, international agencies have the opportunity to enhance the situation through proximity talks, INPs, and side-payment bargaining. Through signalling private information on the (likely) bottom lines of other negotiating Parties, for instance, international agencies can minimise doubts about reciprocity among Chinese decision-makers and elevate their expectations. Although this study was unable to find explicit evidence of this, multiple Chinese negotiators did not deny its possibility. Moreover, based on first-hand observations, Chairs of informal plenary meetings do try to steer meetings and extract mutual commitment from member-states by going around the groups and asking each delegation to promise the other that they will follow a joint strategy. They frequently end with comments such as, "Now remember everyone that we all do much better if we all follow *X* strategy". This form of intervention should often stimulate the Chinese delegation to reframe its expectations towards others and how it should act accordingly.

In the climate change negotiations, it is well known that China closely watches the actions of the US and especially designs its negotiation approaches based on a *reactive* strategy determined by their expectations of how the US is likely to act. In light of this, senior members of the UNFCCC Secretariat, together with the Mexican and South African presidencies attempted to reshape China's expectation of a non-committal American position at COP16 and COP17 by placing stronger pressures on the US decision-makers to set an example and lead the climate change efforts. In the words of one Chinese negotiator to COP16 and COP17,

Our [China's] expectations and actions very much depend on how the Americans act. If they move, we move. If they stall, we stall. Of course, the facilitators [UNFCCC] play a crucial role in shaping our expectations by mediating with the US.[30]

Similarly, during the 2011 DDA ministerial meeting, the Chinese delegation made it clear at a press briefing that, although China is committed to the negotiations, its expectations on cooperation are dependent upon the American position. And one interviewed Chinese negotiator goes further to suggest that, "The WTO Secretariat's inability to mediate between China and the US is a key explanation for China's low expectations and the many deadlocks that exist in the negotiations today".[31] In this sense, the abilities of international agencies to mediate between China and its most important counterparts have substantial effects on the nature of China's expectations.

A broader perspective of this *cognitive* and *rationalist* argument is the extent to which international agencies' effect on Chinese negotiation approaches is dependent on their capacity to mediate and generate a situation of *reciprocity*, which is a precondition for shaping Chinese expectation on cooperation.[32] *Reciprocity* refers to a family of strategies that can be used in social dilemma situations. It involves (1) an effort to identify the actors involved; (2) an assessment of the likelihood that other actors are conditional co-operators; (3) a decision to cooperate initially with other actors if they are perceived as trusted conditional co-operators; (4) a refusal to cooperate with those who do not reciprocate; and (5) punishing those who betray the trust (Ostrom, 1998, p. 10).

If international agencies can facilitate positive actions of others, then this will also influence positive expectations from China. The reverse is also true. If international agencies are unable to mediate positive actions from others, this will not influence positive expectations from China. In this tit-for-tat situation, it is important that international agencies are willing to use retribution to some degree (i.e. punish defectors) so as to demonstrate to China that it has authoritative capacity. Doing so can boost the expectations of the Chinese decision-makers. As one Chinese trade negotiator on trade said, "In both climate change and trade governances, China cannot be assured of strong and authoritative institutional bodies at the multilateral level. This causes uncertainties for the Chinese decision-makers, but that's the member-driven system for you".[33]

There are three imaginable limitations to an argument on expectation. One possible limitation is that since reciprocity norms are learned, international agencies may have a hard time mediating with all the member-states for the purpose of raising China's expectations that an agreement is likely, given that not all nations necessarily understand the same norms of behaviour for effective reciprocity. In this way, expectation-building may be difficult to do if a universal understanding of reciprocity cannot be established. True, intangible variables such as culture and context can make it difficult to converge normative understanding between nations. But it is also not an impossible barrier to overcome. As cognitivists believe, normative understandings that are repeatedly emphasised will, over time, be unconsciously internalised between negotiators across cultures and the natural tendencies for mimicking of behaviours will eventually manifest. This was verified by interviews with Chinese negotiators.

A second potential limitation regards the reality that reciprocity-related expectations are contingent on the issues of concern. For instance, although the CDM, mitigation, and GPA issues require confident expectations of reciprocity in order to move forward with the negotiations, the services area requires comparatively less traditional reciprocity-driven market access negotiations. Instead, other considerations, rather than poor expectations of reciprocity, such as the costs of inefficient services industries and the likelihood of enduring heavier pressures for unilateral reform may cause negotiation breakdowns.

That said it is often difficult to dismiss the relevance of expectation in any economic negotiation. For instance, the pre-defined expectation that other countries will expect China to liberalise its services sector has caused much domestic disagreement and anti-reform sentiments. The consequent domestic pressures contribute immensely to the ultimate expectation, and thus the negotiation approach, of the Chinese government.[34] And since Beijing has had a long-held expectation that a policy reform in services, made at the request of a trading partner, is often automatically going to benefit other countries more than China, it has withdrawn itself from a higher bottom line at the negotiation table. In this way, China refuses to take on reciprocity. As such, the reciprocity-driven expectation does matter in Chinese decision-making.

A third possible limitation is that even when it seems as if international agencies have contributed to an enhanced expectation on the part of China, such displays of positive expectations could be mere tactical play in order to lure other negotiation Parties into a dilemma only to defect on them later. The motivation behind such tactic is access to foreign resources or to gain leverage over others. When a nation-state follows reciprocity norms (for real or tactically), the international agencies' ability to detect cheaters is undermined. If this happens, the Chinese decision-makers can take advantage of the situation while silently refusing the influence of international agencies. Hence, it is risky to be too trusting with mere displays of positive expectations, and draw quick conclusions that these equate with the action of international agencies.

Even within the Chinese delegation, there are variances among the negotiators in terms of the probability that they will adapt to the multilateral norms, and in the ways that the structural variables propel their willingness to cooperate in a given context. For some Chinese decision-makers, like those from other nations, the norms of reciprocity will only be used if they know that they are closely monitored by an international agency and therefore may face strong probabilities of retribution if they do not do so. Therefore, it is imperative that the agency knows what kind of delegate(s) it is dealing with before making efforts in expectation-building.

### *Social instigator II: trust*

Second to expectation is trust. It is often the case that a root cause of uncertainty is trust, not just from China but all countries.[35] This problem was noted by a senior member of the WTO Secretariat: "You don't feel trust among negotiators in the WTO ... or in the climate change negotiations" – not just with regard to other countries but also towards the multilateral institutions, their agenda, and intentions.[36] And one Chinese policy advisor from the Ministry of Commerce (MOFCOM) observed, when there is distrust from individual negotiators, they can simply reject a proposal based on a personal grudge.[37] China's trust in the general multilateral system is a major concern.[38]

The CDM negotiations were a case in point, where China distrusted the motivation of the CDM initiative (and the countries that will benefit the most). It was only after the GEF/UN pilot simulations that Chinese trust was rejuvenated. In the mitigation case, many interviewed Chinese negotiators and UNFCCC Secretariat staff indicated that China's lack of trust in other member-states' actual commitment towards an internationally binding agreement was a root cause of its hesitant approach to the negotiations. Again, the trust issue very much stems from China's relationship with other nation-states, especially the US. In the GPA negotiations, Beijing has struggled to trust the WTO framework at large, arguing it is too vague and ambiguous. Thus, the lack of trust undermines China's willingness to positively approach negotiations.

When it comes to multilateral economic negotiations under an international framework, Beijing sees trust as the 'bedrock' of effective negotiations, and the presence of trust is indispensable to reaching an agreement. In this context, theory presupposes that trust affects the social dilemma of whether an individual is willing to initiate cooperation with the expectation that it will be reciprocated (Ostrom, 1998, p. 12). Hence, one central variable that has hindered China from in taking a cooperative negotiation approach is trust, especially over whether its negotiating counterparts will actually comply with agreements. This is not surprising given that multilateral economic negotiations often comprise multifaceted conflicts of interests amongst a large pool of member-states, and, therefore, there is little trust between them to begin with.

A labyrinth of theories have attempted to identify methods for enhancing cooperation through trust (e.g. Axelrod, 1984; Olson, 1965). However, much of the research has focused on how international agencies can monitor and improve the enforcement of agreements or how the comparatively more significant countries can foster or coerce their way to an agreement. Yet, anything that is monitored or coerced tends to have an impeding effect on trust-building.

In theory, a more effective method of building trust is by shaping national identity, which expands the potential range of possibilities for fostering cooperative outcomes. This is for two reasons. First, past research (e.g. Ostrom, 1998) has confirmed the intuitive assumption that mutual identification with a common group is associated with trust between the members of that group. The level of trust varies, and trust may of course be misplaced or abused. But trust levels usually vary most strongly with the degree to which a *trustor* identifies with the *trustee* as members of the same group.

Second, national identity evolves over time, and new identities can be fostered with the belief that humans, by nature, crave to *belong* and seek out like-minded others with whom attachments can be formed. This argument is supported by the theory of cognitivism, which further argues that identity can influence one's interests far more than any other single factor, such as desire for wealth or power, as has been assumed by theorists of other schools such as liberal economics and mercantilism (e.g. Gilpin, 1987; Morgenthau, 1956; Oye, 1986).

Over the last 20 years of multilateral economic negotiations, there have been increased efforts by international agencies to reduce the trust barriers between China and other nations by reducing competitive behaviours and through building unity and empathy among the negotiators. As acquiring trust from China is ever more important, innovative mechanisms for trust-building have been designed by various agencies to establish common identities. The agencies believe doing so not only fosters trust but also points to any overlapping and perhaps unexpressed state interests between nations.

In climate change, the UNFCCC Secretariat have made such efforts through informal, unofficial initiatives – known as the Track II methods[39] – that take place outside the official negotiating modes, to help Chinese negotiators overcome negotiation barriers and alter their perceptions of each other, and of the issues. Given the high economic, social, environmental, and political stakes, Chinese decision-makers often view the UNFCCC negotiations with high-intensity distrust and suspicion. As part of the efforts to remedy trust issues, numerous experiments for trust-building were trialled under Track II, one of which was characterised by the *Earth Negotiations Bulletin* (*ENB*) (2005, p. 7) as the "Comfy Armchair Theory". Through INPs, organisers promoted a laid-back approach that seems to put the Chinese participants at ease. Chinese delegates explained that comfortable red armchairs (for government experts) were placed on a podium that was lowered to be more on a level with the participants to lessen the formality of the discussions. Some compared it to a "television talk show" setting, while others likened the use of "comfy chairs" and the informal approach to a "nice fireside chat".[40] According to the ENB (2005, p. 7) observers, the technique helped generate a positive atmosphere and an "open, frank and broad-ranging ... exchange of information".

The initial success of this tactic inspired other in-session seminars to adopt similar methods for reducing the formality, encouraging open exchanges and building mutual understandings. The underlying assumption is that such exercises, executed under the settings of INPs can help China build openness to and appreciation of others' positions as well as 'win-win' compromises that emerge from a positive environment conducive to agreement. Equally important is that this approach rejects notions that negotiations are zero-sum games with winners and losers. The in-session seminars and other informal discussions, commencing with the comfy chair format, helped the Chinese delegates gain a greater appreciation of each other's positions on their weighty agenda leading up to COP13 in Bali in 2007. The conference effectively finalised the *Bali Roadmap*, which set out a clear framework and deadline for reaching a hoped-for bigger agreement in Copenhagen in 2009. Although the Bali success can be attributed to many factors, including the painstaking preparations and the unprecedented high-level political, media, and public attention (ENB, 2007, p. 18), the concerted trust-building exercises, including the informal dialogues held over the previous two years, played a significant part in transforming uncertainty to a clear roadmap. One Chinese negotiator claims that the "raised level of trust" resulted in agreement on the Adaptation Fund and was brought about, at least in part, by informal discussions which helped China reach an understanding with other countries.[41]

Similar trust-building efforts fell flat at Copenhagen in December 2009. Expectations for this meeting were high, with many hoping for a legally binding treaty that would chart a clear path forward in the post-2012 period. Instead, the meeting ended acrimoniously, resulting only with a non-binding agreement known as the *Copenhagen Accords* that is "noted" (rather than adopted) by Parties (ENB, 2009). On the surface, the organisers were holding a strong hand at the start of the meeting. They had succeeded in persuading over 120 world leaders (including the then Chinese Premier Wen Jiabao) to attend, thus raising the stakes and the pressure for a strong outcome. But Chinese negotiators were unable to bring talks to a point that would allow their leaders to put their signatures to a strong outcome. Instead, Premier Wen Jiabao arrived in the final days of the meeting faced with a wide array of outstanding and immensely complex issues left on the table.

Furthermore, the sheer number of participants (40,000 in a 20,000 capacity venue) meant that it was impossible to achieve the sense of inclusiveness and openness for Chinese stakeholders that have characterised some of the negotiations in previous years. Some Chinese stakeholders were literally left out in the cold due to space limitations at the venue, while organisers miscalculated the timing for document releases, not distributing them to all players, making them appear to be 'secret' texts. These missteps left a sense of exclusion and back-room horse-trading that was in opposition to the transparency and trust-building organisers had sought to generate in the early stages, prior to the adoption of the Bali Road Map (ENB, 2009).

The UNFCCC process redeemed itself somewhat in December 2010, when a more satisfactory outcome was gained with the help of the new UNFCCC Executive-Secretary, Christiana Figueres, working in close alliance with the Mexican hosts of the Cancun climate change conference. This time, there were no 'secret' texts, but periodic 'stock-taking' briefings in the plenary hall for all participants, thus it greatly increased the *real* transparency of the process. Another innovation at Cancun was the decision to pair up key ministers to work together on some of the thornier issues. For each key topic, one developing country minister and one developed country minister were tasked with convening talks among negotiators and identifying a way forward. This approach seemed to find favour with the Chinese, and perhaps the sense of ownership it generated for Chinese officials helped move things forward. At the end of the meeting, there was a far greater sense of agreement and achievement than had existed in Copenhagen, with China supporting the consensus (ENB, 2010).

Similarly, the WTO Secretariat staff have apparently played a significant role as a mediators during China's challenging bilateral negotiations with the US as part of its WTO accession process. According to a Chinese negotiator, their ability to be effective mediators was a demonstration of the WTO's capacity as an intergovernmental broker, which generated a sense of trust for China, at least towards the multilateral trade system.[42] As a result, China took on more concessions to its WTO entry than it was initially willing to do. These examples illustrate the importance of INPs in establishing and maintaining trust. At the same time, they illustrate how a lack of trust can break a negotiation process. By acting in the capacity of a trustworthy middle-agency, international agencies are effective at brokering between governments and deal-making.

However, one can imagine that even trust has its limitations, and the possibility for international agencies to impact China's negotiation approach through trust-building is not universally befitting. China may argue that there are risks of manipulation and exploitation attached to trusting someone. In other instances, the Chinese decision-makers may wonder whether making a commitment for a multilateral trust-based relationship will undermine their rights to seek competitive advantages, even in cases where the benefits outweigh the costs. Alternatively, China's interest could be jeopardised if trust is misplaced. A third possibility is that once China decides on a trustworthy counterpart, other (weaker) qualities of that country are likely to be conceived as consistent with this favourable impression even if the reality would suggest otherwise. This is the 'halo effect' which occurs when one positive characteristic of a country dominates the way that country is viewed by others. Such calculus can pull up China's defensive immunity from international influence and undermine the trust-building exercises.

What is more, trust-building through international agencies can often result in the establishment of a deterrence-based trust centred on a consistency of behaviour (i.e. countries will follow-up on what they promised to do). Such behavioural consistency is usually maintained through threats and/or knowledge of unfavourable consequences if consistency is broken. This interpretation of *trust* seems somewhat paradoxical, with a strong *power* connotation attached. Compared to an identification-based trust – which operates at the level of intrinsic motivation, deterrence-based trust is more costly to maintain as it often requires external monitoring of national compliance in order to sustain it. Furthermore, it risks backfiring because national decision-makers can react negatively to having their policy freedoms controlled by international agencies.

If international agencies wish to mitigate these limitations, and maintain a level of influence, then identification-based trust must be established. That is, trust-building exercises based on qualities of *empathy* between member-states so that China is willing take on the values of other players as a result of the emotional connection between them. In practice, both Christiana Figueres and

Pascal Lamy have, over the years, cultivated congenial relationships with members of the Chinese government through repeated face-to-face dialogue. They have also pursued non-hostile environments for the execution of the INPs, actively diffused tensions, and used their sense of humour and humane personalities.[43] The result of such personal relationships is a more sustainable trust. On the whole, it is important for the multilateral economic negotiations to cultivate a culture of trust-building and treat this as a precondition to, as well as an objective of, reaching an agreement. For China, at least, this is a fundamental imperative and a determinant driver of its negotiation approaches.

### *Social instigator III: personal reputation*

Investing in trust is only possible if the degree of perceived personal reputation is sufficiently high. Thus, *personal reputation* is the third interrelated element on which international agencies' influence depends. Proximity talks and the INPs are especially useful for boosting the (often self-) perceived reputation of Chinese negotiators. If international agencies are effective in this regard, it is likely to motivate the Chinese negotiator to converge with their preferences. At the same time, international agencies can stigmatise personal reputation with the use of retribution against a Chinese negotiator for not keeping to their promises, for instance.

In China, an individual's reputation rests on having *mianzi* (saving face; 面子). The Chinese notion of saving face is closely related to American concepts of dignity and prestige. *Mianzi* defines a person's place in their social network; it is the most important measure of social worth. Hence, if a foreign delegate causes Chinese negotiators embarrassment or a loss of composure, even unintentionally, it can be disastrous for the negotiations. Hence, it is important that international facilitators always maintain *mianzi* for Chinese negotiators in order to increase their influence over China's negotiation approach.[44] Maintaining *mianzi* is a reason why Chinese negotiators prefer proximity talks and INPs – it saves them from embarrassment as a consequence of tensions with other negotiating Parties. The 2011 DDA negotiations demonstrated instances of upholding the reputations of Chinese negotiators when the Chair of an informal plenary meeting on the GPA raised the importance of emerging market economies.

In addition, informed by a strong tradition of Confucian values of obedience and deference to one's superiors, it is imperative that international agencies acknowledge the value of *shehuidengji* (social status; 社会等级), where officials of a higher rank must be respected by those in a lower position. At some point, multilateral economic negotiations may require a meeting of equals in the hope of stimulating more cooperation. But top-level Chinese officials will not be prepared to bargain and will definitely not be persuaded, as it is not within their professional repertoire to do so. Rather, they will evaluate the relationship during a show of *chengyi* (sincerity; 诚意) by their Western counterparts. If international agencies can embrace this value, it is anticipated that Chinese decision-makers will be more accepting of their influence.

### *The reinforcing triangle*

At the core of China's negotiation approach are a set of key drivers of decision-making. The triangular relationship between expectation, trust, and personal reputation essentially shapes China's international posture. If Chinese decision-makers see that the initial levels of cooperation from others are at least moderately high, then they will also learn to trust other players and expect themselves to adopt reciprocity norms. In a situation where China sees more countries genuinely using reciprocity norms, then it will place more importance on establishing a trustworthy reputation. Thus, trust, expectation, and personal reputation are intrinsically reinforcing (Figure 7.1). In addition, this implies that a defect in any one of the three core elements will cause a downward spiral. At times, China's negotiation approach is not just circumscribed by national policy. The decision-makers' judgments on the reinforcing triangle can be influenced by variables of structure and by past experiences, personal norms, and the individual's level of trust in others. If international agencies desire to effectively influence China's negotiation approach, it is necessary to embrace and be compatible with the core triangle to affect China's level of cooperation and perceived net benefit as a result of cooperation.

In the previous sections, it was suggested that proximity talks, INPs, and side-payment bargaining are particularly well-suited and effective instruments for this purpose. This is because in order to affect China's negotiation approach, it is necessary to start at the individual level (i.e. those that make policy). The face-to-face nature of these instruments enable Chinese decision-makers to assess whether they trust the other players (including members of international agencies) enough to alter their negotiation approach. Here, it is important that international agencies control the dialogue that goes on between Chinese negotiators and other national delegates because the nature of communication can often increase, as much decrease, their trust in the reliability of others. The international agencies also need to take greater leadership and initiate the direction of dialogue to be taken as well as control the level of symmetry in economic payoffs in side-payment bargaining, for instance, among the delegations. Otherwise any asymmetry can undermine their influence and trust-building.

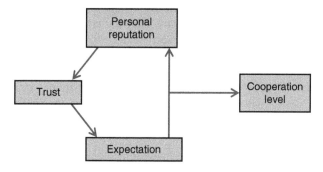

*Figure 7.1* The core triangle of social instigators.

Arguably, the Chinese decision-makers also depend on the international agencies to make a contingent agreement work. For instance, contingent agreements may deal with both cooperation and punishment for those considered as non-cooperators (Levi, 1988). Keeping in balance how to punish defectors grants Chinese decision-makers a stronger personal reputation; however, this is much more challenging in a multilateral setting than a bilateral one. In a multilateral environment, it is difficult for Chinese decision-makers to interpret outcomes that do not meet the initial expectation regardless of how much a Party may have cheated, or that a mistake was made by a country, or if a random exogenous variable undermined the expected result. The problem is even worse if there are no international agency representatives to facilitate or steer these discussions in settings like the INPs.

The counter argument is if Chinese decision-makers prefer a non-international agency-facilitated situation because China's external and internal reputation will not then be at stake, especially if no agreement is reached. Such cases mean the individual is not required to take any further action. However, once a multilateral agreement has been reached, be it verbal or in writing, it turns into the pivot of future decisions within the parameters of the agreement. This means that China's negotiation approach could be further constrained, to its dislike. At the same time, it puts China's reputation at stake if it does not reciprocate in the future. In a comparative sense, the Chinese decision-makers may therefore prefer the former outcome, which makes the international agencies' role less favourable.

Yet, interviews indicated that most Chinese decision-makers and negotiators across the trade and climate change spectrums do prefer to reach cooperation if possible, based on mutual trust. For many interviewees, this is not just beneficial to China's international integration process and the road to forming a more robust and defined international role, but also beneficial to its domestic development. One Chinese policymaker points out that, "China is not a lazy nation and if an agreement is possible within China's capacity and interest, then China is willing to participate".[45] Another Chinese negotiator commented,

> The international agencies in general needs to assert more authority in my opinion in negotiation settings. Many delegates like to observe the way these institutions have conducted themselves in negotiations and our own sense of trust in the system depends on how well and effectively they have facilitated the meetings. However, many institutions still lack this authority and need to do a better job at it.[46]

In particular, the interviewees widely shared the view that international agencies should be better at sanctioning non-conformers for not keeping their commitments. Such behaviour easily breaks China's fragile trust. Consequently, one way the international agencies can obtain trust is to first build their own credibility by improving their capacity to manage the multilateral system. Only when the Chinese decision-makers view them as credible will they believe in their capacity to help build inter-state trust.

This is why the face-to-face method of communication works more effectively than the alternative (i.e. sending computerised messages). The Chinese decision-makers like to judge the others' trustworthiness by watching facial expressions and hearing the way something is said. It is hard to establish trust in a group of strangers who will make decisions independently and privately without seeing and talking with one another. This is why the international agencies' role as facilitators is so vital. The ways in which they embrace and/or constrain the behaviour of national delegates shape the expectations of Chinese decision-makers about the others' behaviours, which are also preconditioned by their capacity to build trust in Chinese decision-makers. The norms disseminated by the international agencies and past experiences also shape Chinese decision-makers' trust levels.

Finally, how international agencies identify with, project their intentions and norms onto, and relate to the Chinese negotiators can affect the global identities of these individuals and their reputation.[47] If all three variables of the core triangle are satisfied, then the international agencies should expect to exude a higher level of influence. Of course, the reverse effect is also true. In sum, understanding how the social instigators feed into one another helps explain why the instruments of proximity talks, INPs, and side-payment bargaining are either effective, or not, in influencing China's negotiation approach.

### *What are the strengths and weaknesses?*

Between the proximity talks, the INPs, and the side-payment bargaining, the underlying impact is derived from the fact that international agencies, as the intermediaries of economic negotiations, possess diverse motives for choosing a certain form of behaviour or set of values and recommendations towards a policy they are attempting to effect. Paradoxically, the fact that they possess goals and objectives and attempt to further them through mediatory practices has been a neglected aspect of studies in economic diplomacy. The current literatures tends to assume that while the member-states possess goals and objectives that underlie the behaviour they undertake – the incompatibility of which forms the basis of disagreements and negotiation impasse – any international agency is wholly or, at worst, largely motivated by a desire to bring about a settlement. On this point, it is crucial to note that the goals and objectives of the negotiation process managers through mediatory channels should not be taken for granted and are a proper subject for scholarly analysis.

The general strengths of the three mediatory instruments in shaping Chinese negotiation approach come in three forms. First, the venue change – the endogenous shift in China's negotiation approach as a corollary of a change in the location of decision-making – provides more receptive hearings of Chinese and non-Chinese concerns. As Schattschneider (1960) puts it, this process takes the form of actors transferring the policy to another subsystem by altering the understanding of a policy with the objective of altering the resulting policy outputs in a way that suits the actors' interests. The effectiveness of the INPs lie in the fact that sensitive discussions were taken out of the formal plenary sessions and into more casual and comfortable small-group settings where negotiators feel more at ease about talking honestly and accepting counter-vantage-points, and thus help build trust, expectations, and personal reputation.

In a similar light, interviews points to the reality that shuttle diplomacy proximity talks are generally effective because Chinese leaders are able to communicate on an interpersonal level with international agency representatives and in their local vicinities whereby the *Chinese context* can be better reflected and their objectives clarified. The effect of venue change is not unique to China. Frank Baumgartner and Bryan Jones (1991) found in the American decision-making process that policy actors deploy numerous common strategies to gain access to the policymaking process and affect the policy outcome by changing the venue where decisions are made. Michael Howlett (1994) similarly points to Canada and Australia, where successful venue-shifting activities have been undertaken over the recent decades by First Nations or Aboriginal groups.

Second, the instruments have the capacity to create settlement by boosting expectation. For an interested international agency, using any one of the instruments communicates the provision of a safety net for China from a threatened negotiation *impasse*, and this often obtains influence for them. Such is the payoff that is derived from changing the patterns of interaction and/or from establishing a new relationship between the agency and Chinese decision-makers. The preceding section mentioned the importance of establishing a good relationship with Chinese decision-makers when attempting to frame the course of a negotiated outcome. Through the mediatory channels, and the change of venue, a trusting relationship can be built, and thereafter, converge differential interests between China and other Parties, clarify resoluble disagreements, and build a kind of consensus which is agreeable to their own objectives.

At the same time, the instruments provide international agencies the capacity to use their intermediary role to affect the actual course of a deadlock through a judiciously timed mediation offer. Through both shuttle diplomacy proximity talks, and INPs, international agencies can delay or alter a negotiating trend to provide a breathing space for China, for instance, to buy time to regroup, reorganise, restrategise. This way, during the actual process of negotiations, international agencies can use their various roles to increase their own influence on China through numerous bargaining/persuasion strategies such as side-payments. They may be able to buy promises of future compliance or increased sensitivity to their wishes with rewards offered to themselves or with promises of concessions to be extracted from other Parties to the negotiation, over which an interested international agency may have some considerable influence.

Third, the instruments have the advantage of deriving tangible and intangible benefits for China. For instance, side-payment bargaining yields material benefits for China, which may include the restoration or increase of previous transfers of goods and resources between the international agency and China or between other Parties and China; or in some cases, the denial of goods and resources to others. Benefits which come in the form of influence include base rights, rights to information or of passage, the promises of future support, greater sensitivity to the wishes of China, and greater openness to the goods, information and personnel of the agency for Chinese agencies. Intangible benefits include reputational rewards enhanced through the INPs, which accrue to a country that is deemed to have made a commendable attempt to bring about a negotiated agreement (Mitchell, 1988, pp. 44–45). Such benefits are of particular importance to China as it is often perceived as having some special responsibility for the maintenance and restoration of global welfare.

Of course, for each advantage, there are also disadvantages. Disadvantages can be incurred both through undertaking the processes of mediating itself and through achieving a settlement, although it seems more likely that disadvantages will accrue through an unpopular or unsuccessful settlement than for merely adopting the role of go-between or honest broker. Similarly, using the aforementioned channels to influence Chinese negotiation approach can sometimes backfire and the international agencies are left with less influence, and less opportunity to establish what they regards as a satisfactory relationship with China. Equally, instruments can damage reputation as well as enhance it. In short, although China is generally ready to approve the agencies' mediatory role, is necessary to recognise that, although somewhat asymmetric, there is always a *balance* of potential strengths and weaknesses in undertaking influence through these instruments.

## Notes

1 Interview with a policy advisor to the Ministry of Commerce, Beijing, 4 September 2012.
2 Interview with a Chinese negotiator from the Department of Law and Treaty, the Ministry of Foreign Affairs, Beijing, 11 February 2012.
3 Interview with a Chinese negotiator to the WTO, Geneva, 19 December 2011.
4 Promising areas included some air transport services (e.g. maintenance and repair), computer-related services, civil engineering, and rules on establishment of banks and other financial services institutions. Only limited opportunities were signalled for legal and architectural services, rail and road freight, education and postal services and telecommunications.
5 Andrew Kydd (2003) makes arguments along similar lines.
6 Interview with a policy advisor to the Ministry of Commerce, Beijing, 4 September 2012.
7 Personal observation.
8 Personal observation at the 2011 WTO Ministerial Meeting, Geneva, December 2011.
9 Interview with a Japanese delegate to the WTO, London, 3 February 2012.
10 Interview with a senior advisor to the WTO, Beijing, 22 November 2012.
11 Interview with an official from the Ministry of Commerce, Beijing, 17 September 2011.
12 Interview with a trade negotiator, Geneva, 6 December 2011.
13 Interview with a Tanzanian delegate to COP17, Durban, 3 December 2012.
14 Interview with a Central American delegate to COP17, Durban, 7 December 2012.
15 Interview with a former member of the Department of Legal Affairs, the Ministry of Commerce, Beijing, 22 November 2012; interview with a policy advisor to the Ministry of Commerce, Beijing, 23 November 2012.
16 Interview with a senior Chinese negotiator from the WTO Division, Ministry of Commerce, Beijing, 22 November 2012.

17 Interview with a Chinese negotiator from the Department of Treaty and Law, Ministry of Commerce, Beijing, 23 November 2012.
18 Interview with a senior Chinese negotiator from the WTO Division, Ministry of Commerce, Beijing, 22 November 2012; interview with a member from the Department of Treaty and Law, Ministry of Commerce, Beijing, 23 November 2012.
19 For an overview of current proposals on climate technology transfer see Gerstetter and Marcellino (2009).
20 Interview with a Chinese delegate, Beijing, 14 February 2012; interview with a Professor from Beijing University, Beijing, 17 September 2011.
21 Interview with an official from the Chinese Ministry of Foreign Affairs, Beijing, 14 February 2012.
22 For 'energy-efficient' products and products certified as environmentally friendly, the regulations merely require that preference be given to such products contained in listed promulgated by the competent authorities without specifying a margin or any detailed procedure.
23 Articles 13–17 of the MOF's *Measure on the Evaluation of Government Procurement of Indigenous Innovation Products* provide that indigenously innovated products shall be given preference at a margin of 5 to 10 per cent in case price is the sole determining factor and 4 to 8 per cent otherwise.
24 Interview with a member from the Department of Treaty and Law, Ministry of Commerce, Beijing, 23 November 2012. Interview with a senior advisor to the WTO, Beijing, 22 November 2012. Interview with a Chinese negotiator to the WTO, Beijing, 11 April 2012.
25 Interview with an official from the China CDM Fund under the Ministry of Finance, Beijing, 17 February 2012.
26 Interview with an official from the US Mission, Shanghai, 22 August 2011.
27 Interview with a policy advisor from China Academy of International Trade and Economic Cooperation under the Ministry of Commerce, Beijing, 19 November 2012.
28 Interview with a policy official from the Ministry of Finance, Beijing, 15 March 2012.
29 Interview with a senior member of the WTO Secretariat, London, 2 February 2012.
30 Interview with a senior advisor to the WTO, Geneva, 6 December 2011.
31 Interview with a Chinese trade negotiator from the Ministry of Commerce, Geneva, 5 December 2011.
32 Interview with a former member of the Department of Legal Affairs in the Ministry of Commerce, Beijing, 22 November 2012.
33 Interview with a Chinese negotiator, Geneva, 19 December 2011.
34 Interview with an expert from Peking University, Beijing, 24 October 2012.
35 Trust is the "expectation of one person about the actions of others that affects the first person's choice, when an action must be taken before the actions of others are known" (Dasgupta, 1997, p. 5).
36 Interview with a senior member of the WTO Secretariat, London, 2 February 2012.
37 Interview with a policy advisor to the Ministry of Commerce, Beijing, 25 October 2012.
38 Interview with an expert from Peking University, Beijing, 23 November 2012.
39 Track II methods were originally identified as such from conflict resolution approaches employed in the Middle East.
40 Interview with a trade negotiator, Geneva, 6 December 2011.
41 Interview with a Chinese trade negotiator from the Ministry of Commerce, Geneva, 5 December 2011.
42 Interview with a policy advisor to the Ministry of Commerce, Beijing, 4 September 2012.
43 Personal observations.
44 Interview with a policy advisor to the Ministry of Commerce, Beijing, 25 October 2012.

45 Interview with a policy advisor to the WTO Division under the Ministry of Commerce, Beijing, 25 November 2012.
46 Interview with a Chinese negotiator to the WTO, Beijing, 28 November 2012.
47 Coming to an initial agreement and making personal promises to with another places an individual's identity at risk. The thought process is that one who keeps to their words will increase their perceived trustworthiness, and in turn, prompt others to reciprocate.

## References

Axelrod, R. (1984) *The Evolution of Cooperation*. New York: Basic Books.

Barnett, M.N. and Finnemore, M. (2004) *Rules for the World: International Organizations in Global Politics*. Ithaca, NY: Cornell University Press.

Bar-Tal, D. and Saxe, L. (1990) 'Acquisition of Political Knowledge: A Social-Psychological Analysis'. In O. Ichilov (ed.) *Political Socialization, Citizenship Education and Democracy* (pp. 116–133). New York: Teachers College Press.

Baumgartner, F.R. and Jones, B.D. (1991) 'Agenda Dynamics and Policy Subsystems'. *Journal of Politics* 53(4) pp. 1044–1074.

Best, J. (2012) 'Ambiguity and Uncertainty in International Organizations: A History of Debating IMF Conditionality'. *International Studies Quarterly* 56(4) pp. 674–688.

Brown, J.G. and Ayres, I. (1994) 'Economic Rationales for Mediation'. *Virginia Law Review* 80(2) pp. 323–402.

Conrad, B. (2012) 'China in Copenhagen: Reconciling the "Beijing Climate Revolution" and the "Copenhagen Climate Obstinacy"'. *The China Quarterly* 210 pp. 435–455.

Dasgupta, P.S. (1997) 'Economic Development and the Idea of Social Capital'. Working Paper, Faculty of Economics, University of Cambridge.

Economy, E. (2001) 'The Impact of International Regimes on Chinese Foreign Policy-Making: Broadening Perspectives and Policies … But Only to a Point'. In D.M. Lampton (ed.) *The Making of Chinese Foreign and Security Policy in the Era of Reform, 1979–2000* (pp. 230–256). Stanford, CA: Stanford University Press.

ENB (2010) 'A Summary Report of the Development and Climate Days at COP 16'. *International Institute for Sustainable Development* 99 pp. 1–9.

ENB (2009) 'Summary of the Copenhagen Climate Change Conference'. *International Institute for Sustainable Development* 12 pp. 1–30.

ENB (2007) 'Summary of COP13'. *International Institute for Sustainable Development* 12 pp. 1–22.

ENB (2005) 'A Summary Report of the Development and Adaptation Days at COP 11'. *International Institute for Sustainable Development* 99 pp. 1–7.

Finnemore, M. (2003) *The Purpose of Intervention*. Ithaca, NY: Cornell University Press.

Finnemore, M. (1996) 'Norms, Culture, and World Politics: Insights from Sociology's Institutionalism'. *International Organization* 50(2) pp. 324–349.

Footer, M.E. (2011) 'The WTO as a "Living Instrument": The Contribution of Consensus Decision-Making and Informality to Institutional Norms and Practices'. In T. Cottier and M. Elsig (eds) *Governing the World Trade Organization: Past, Present and Beyond Doha* (pp. 217–240). Cambridge: Cambridge University Press.

Gerstetter, C. and Marcellino, D. (2009) 'The Current Proposals on the Transfer of Climate Technology in the International Climate Negotiations: An Assessment'. Washington, DC: Ecologic Institute. [Online] 16 November. Available from: www.ecologic.eu/sites/files/project/2013/8208_Ecologic_Technology_Transfer_Final.pdf [Accessed: 18 August 2011].

Gibson, J.L. (1998) 'A Sober Second Thought: An Experiment in Persuading Russians to Tolerate'. *American Journal of Political Science* 42(3) pp. 819–850.

Gilpin, R. (1987) *The Political Economy of International Relations.* Princeton, NJ: Princeton University Press.

Hoekman, B. and Mattoo, A. (2011) 'Services Trade Liberalization and Regulatory Reform: Re-invigorating International Cooperation'. *Policy Research Working Paper* 5517.

Hoffman, D.A. (2010) 'Mediation and the Art of Shuttle Diplomacy'. *Negotiation Journal* 27(3) pp. 263–309.

Howlett, M. (1994) 'Policy Paradigms and Policy Change: Lessons From the Old and New Canadian Policies Towards Aboriginal Peoples'. *Policy Studies Journal* 22(4) pp. 631–651.

IISD (2009) 'Highlights from Thursday, 10 December of the Fifteenth Conference of the Parties to the UN Framework Convention on Climate Change (UNFCCC) and the Fifth Meeting of the Parties to the Kyoto Protocol'. [Online] 10 December. Available from: www.iisd.ca/climate/cop15/10dec.html [Accessed: 10 December 2011].

Jawara, F. and Kwa, A. (2004) *Behind the Scenes at the WTO: The Real World of International Trade Negotiations – The Lessons of Cancun.* New York: Zed Books.

Jervis, R. (1976) *Perception and Misperception in International Politics.* Princeton, NJ: Princeton University Press.

Johnston, A.I. (2008) *Social States: China in International Institutions, 1980–2000.* Princeton, NJ: Princeton University Press.

Keohane, R.O. (1984) *After Hegemony: Cooperation and Discord in the World Political Economy.* Princeton, NJ: Princeton University Press.

Kydd, A. (2003) 'Which Side Are You On? Bias, Credibility, and Mediation'. *American Journal of Political Science* 47(4) pp. 597–611.

Leal-Arcas, R. (2007) 'Bridging the Gap in the Doha Talks: A Look at Services Trade'. *Journal of International Commercial Law and Technology* 2(4) pp. 241–249.

Levi, M. (1988) *Of Rules and Revenue.* Berkeley, CA: University of California Press.

Mitchell, C.R. (1988) 'The Motives for Mediation'. In C.R. Mitchell and K. Webb (eds) *New Approaches to International Mediation* (pp. 29–51). New York: Greenwood Press.

Morgenthau, H.J. (1956) 'The Decline and Fall of American Foreign Policy'. *The New Republic* 135 pp. 11–16.

Mutz, D.C., Sniderman, P.M., and Brody, R.A. (eds) (1996) *Political Persuasion and Attitude Change.* Ann Arbor, MI: University of Michigan Press.

National Communication (2004) *The People's Republic of China Initial National Communication on Climate Change: Executive Summary.* [*Zhonghua renmin gongheguo qihou bianhua chushi guojia xinxi tongbao*]. Beijing, China: Planning Publishing House.

North, D. (1990) *Institutions, Institutional Change and Economic Performance.* Cambridge: Cambridge University Press.

Ostrom, E. (1998) 'A Behavioral Approach to the Rational Choice Theory of Collective Action Presidential Address'. *American Political Science Association* 92(1) pp. 1–22.

Oxford Analytica Daily Brief Service (2012) 'INTERNATIONAL: Services Trade Deal May Gain Traction'. Received via email, 28 May.

Oye, K.A. (1986) *Cooperation Under Anarchy.* Princeton, NJ: Princeton University Press.

Pomfret, J. and Lim, B.K. (2012) 'China's Ex-President Overshadows Party Congress, Transition'. *Reuters.* [Online] 10 November. Available from: www.reuters.com/article/2012/11/10/us-china-congress-jiang-idUSBRE8A90IE20121110 [Accessed: 10 November 2012].

Porter, G., Bird, N., Kaur, N., and Peskett, L. (2008) 'New Finance for Climate Change and the Environment'. Heinrich Boll Stiftung.

Powell, R. (2002) 'Bargaining Theory and International Conflict'. *Annual Review of Political Science* 5 pp. 1–30.

Reus-Smit, C. (2005) 'Constructivism'. In S. Burchill, A. Linklater, R. Devetak, J. Donnelly, M. Paterson, C. Reus-Smit, and J. True (eds) *Theories of International Relations* (3rd edn) (pp. 188–212). New York: Palgrave Macmillan.

Risse, T. (2000) 'Let's Argue!' *International Organization* 54(1) pp. 1–39.

Schattschneider, E.E. (1960) *The Semsovereign People; A Realist's View of Democracy in America*. New York: Holt, Rinehart and Winston.

Schimmelfennig, F. (2002) 'Introduction: The Impact of International Organizations on the Central and Eastern European States – Conceptual and Theoretical Issues'. In R.H. Linden (ed.) *Norms and Nannies: The Impact of International Organizations on the Central and Eastern European States*. Lanham, MD: Rowman and Littlefield.

Søfting, G.B. (2000) 'Climate Change Policymaking – Three Explanatory Models'. *CICERO Working Paper* 6.

Stone, R. (2010) 'Severe Drought Puts Spotlight on Chinese Dams'. *Science* 327(5971) p. 1411.

Tran, T. (2010) 'China Highlights Climate Change Efforts'. *Associated Press*. [Online] 9 October. Available from: http://phys.org/news205821378.html [Accessed: 31 August 2011].

Underdal, A. (1998) 'Explaining Compliance and Defection: Three Models'. *European Journal of International Relations* 4(5) pp. 5–30.

UNFCCC (2007) *Uniting on Climate*. Bonn, Germany: United Nations Framework Convention on Climate Change.

Walsh, J.I. (2005) 'Persuasion in International Politics: A Rationalist Account'. *Politics & Policy* 33(4) pp. 1–30.

# 8 The '*dragonomic*' diplomacy decoded

The journey of this book began with the vision to explore the instruments which shape China's economic diplomacy, with particular attention to multilateral economic negotiations. Part II of the book continued the journey through the exploration of three instruments relevant to the development of negotiation *preferences*: the calculation of costs and benefits, information, and reputation. However, the formation of negotiation preferences is only half the picture. In order to fully understand Chinese economic diplomacy, it is also important to understand the development of China's negotiation *approach*. As such, Part III of this book shifted its focus to consider the decision-making that takes place during multilateral negotiation processes. As these processes are typically managed by the presiding staff of international agencies, an assessment of this nature is inevitably intertwined with an assessment of the role and impact of international actors, particularly through the instruments of shuttle diplomacy proximity talks, informal negotiation practices (INPs), and instigators of side-payment bargaining.

In this final segment of the journey, reflections are made on the vital variables identified throughout this book, and generalisable lessons are drawn about the integrated decision-making process where international agencies are integral players. The claims made here are significant and may, perhaps, shock the mainstream scholarly assumption that China's decision-making is a national process immune from external forces. To be clear, this book does not intend to suggest that the domestic variables are by any means inferior or less important. The empirical discussions certainly showed that domestic variables, in the form of situational factors and social instigators, play rather decisive roles in shaping Chinese economic diplomacy. At the same time, China's preference formation has a less definitive boundary against the participation of international agencies. There seems to be an invisible fence between the two sides and the point where international agencies can or cannot participate in China's decision-making processes is increasingly blurred depending on their relevance, function, and resources.

## What are the lessons drawn?

The book set out to test two claims. The first was a primary claim that asks the primary research question about *how* Chinese economic diplomacy preferences are formulated. It holds that *Chinese policymakers, government negotiators, and diplomats formulate their negotiation preferences through the calculation of costs and benefits, accessible information, and considerations about national reputation.* However, their actual level of influence is contingent on four situational factors: national objectives, policy goals, policy settings, and policy instruments.

The second claim addresses the supplementary decision-making during the negotiation processes and the impact of international agencies. As such, it holds that: *China's negotiation approach can be shaped by shuttle diplomacy, informal negotiation practices, and side-payment bargaining.* However the actual influence rests on a core set of social instigators. They are expectation, trust, and personal reputation. The three social instigators are cumulatively necessary criteria for maximising policy outcome.

Part II of this book assessed these claims against empirical examples relating to the UNFCCC climate change negotiations and the WTO trade talks. However, it is one thing to assess the claims and quite another to measure influence, especially as policy instruments and international agencies can generate different levels of influence on the formulation of negotiation preferences and approaches across different issues, which renders them difficult to compare with one another, and to judge accurately the comparative strength of influence through each variable. Nevertheless, the dependent variable – China's economic diplomacy preference formation – has been measured in a consistent and flexible way. And the qualitative scale has covered all the possible magnitudes and directions of preference change and it is comprehensive enough to include different sorts of change. In this way, as explained in Chapter 2, four indicators of influence are helpful for measuring influence: *inertia, absorption, transformation,* and *retrenchment.* These indicators will be the premise of analysis in the next section.

### So the validity of claim no. 1 is…

In general, the evidence suggests the primary claim is *partially valid.* None of the three policy instruments independently drive China's preference formation. At best, they have an *absorption* level of significance on China's decision-making process because all policy instruments are circumscribed by situational factors. In Chapter 2, it was assumed that the situational factors (policy settings, policy instruments, policy goals, and national objectives) circumscribe influence. The taxonomy of contingencies was informed by the structure–agency debate: that pre-defined structures can enable or constrain agency, while agents can affect structure through reflexivity and cognition, among others. In this context, it was assumed that there are four categories of contingencies which determine (either by enhancing or undermining) the effectiveness of policy instruments and international agencies alike. And the extent of their influence felt in Chinese preference formation depends on how well it complements the situational factors.

*Policy setting* refers to the policy framework (i.e. administrative and regulatory); the political dynamics and power relations within and across levels of the government; the degree of connectedness within and across existing policy networks; and the historic levels of conflict among recognised bureaucratic and sectoral interests and the resulting levels of trust and impact on working relationships. *Policy instruments* are internal and external operational instruments and tools used to deliberate policy options, and the resource conditions needed to reach a policy outcome. Here, policy instruments can be those in Beijing and/or from the international systems.

*Policy goals* are the short- to medium-term ambitions of the national government, which may include targets and aims from five-year development plans or global commitments, among others. As such, they pre-set the boundaries and parameters of preference formation. Similarly, *national objectives* concern the ultimate interest and aim of the government, which defines their (business) model of governance and justification for their political legitimacy. Like policy goals, these factors sets the general boundaries of preference formation. But unlike policy goals, these boundaries are more expansive in coverage as they concern the government's long-term ambitions. In any case, the decision-makers are concerned about whether a policy initiative is of the interest to the country; i.e. does it serve its goals or objectives? Is the proposed preference or negotiation approach costly or beneficial to its goals or objectives?

It is important to note that the situational factors are not fixed as starting conditions; rather, they are broader ulterior contexts of which external conditions (e.g. economic downturn, or newly enacted regulation) may influence the dynamics, not only at the outset but at any time during the engagements, thus opening up new possibilities or posing unanticipated challenges.

The costs-and-benefits instrument is conditioned by the situational factors of national objective and policy setting. The former is largely concerned with the *perception* of the Chinese decision-makers. For the most part, the decision-makers in Beijing did not believe the payoff from cooperating in the long-term global effort to mitigate climate change justified prioritising the government's limited professional and economic resources over pressing short-term demands such as economic growth and poverty alleviation. This perception in turn also undermined the UNFCCC Secretariat's attempts at advancing agreement on mitigation by partaking in discussions about the costs and benefits. The situation could not have been more different for the Clean Development Mechanism (CDM). Key decision-makers in Beijing believed that the benefits of joining the initiative would contribute to both the short-term development policy goals, and the long-term battles against global warming. The convergence between the UNFCCC Secretariat's assessment of the costs and benefits to that of the perceptions of Chinese decision-makers thereby enabled the advancement of the former to assert stronger influence over the preference formation process of the latter.

The second situational factor relates to the political rank of the decision-maker to whom the costs-and-benefits assessments are communicated. For instance, the Government Procurement Agreement (GPA) case felt more impact from the Committee's inputs into the costs-and-benefits discussions, not only because it appealed to the ministerial-level policymakers, but also because it attracted the elite members of the Politburo. On the other hand, the trade in services case illustrated that appealing only to second-tier decision-makers from the Ministry of Finance (MOF) achieves outcomes of little significance. So the political rank of the receiver of the costs-and-benefits analysis matters, especially in a political system characterised by hierarchy. The immediate effect of the engagement is therefore different between the cases on the basis of the decision-makers' perception and the rank of the policy actors with whom the international agency discusses costs and benefits. The fact that costs-and-benefits instruments are circumscribed by situational factors in this way means they are at best capable of conditioned influence.

Like the costs-and-benefits instrument, information has an *absorption* level of influence. Information dissemination activities from the UNFCCC and the WTO agencies were prevalent, and primarily in the form of informal dialogues, information exchanges, research collaborations, training workshops, and the like. These activities are supportive of the cognitive assumption that the growing complexity and uncertainties over global economic problems will often lead policymakers to turn to new and different channels for advice, and specifically to new networks of knowledge-based experts from international agencies in order to articulate their objectives in forthcoming negotiations and realise the *real* stakes or interests of the Chinese government and the perceived appropriate policy remedies (Haas, 1992, p. 12).

For the most part, interviewees across the cases agree that external information affects the perceptions of the Chinese decision-makers. However, the actual influence varied greatly between the cases due to three reasons. The first relates to the political and economic costs involved with aligning with the recommendations of international discourse. That is, the higher the political and/or economic costs, the less likely it is that Chinese decision-makers will adopt the thinking of international discourse. In the GPA negotiations, the political costs of supporting the accession recommendations of the Commission were considered threatening to Beijing's regulatory autonomy – a political cost they were unwilling to bear (at least initially). By contrast, the marginal political and economic costs that would be inflicted as a result of aligning with international discourse on the CDM initiative stimulated Beijing on a route to agreement. Hence, the perceived economic and political costs of following international discourse conditions the force of information as a driver of negotiation preference and the impact of international agencies.

The second explanation concerns Beijing's incoherent inter-departmental processes.[1] As seen in Chapters 4 and 5, most economic issues have implications for a host of policy issues, and hence require the engagement of a labyrinth of government departments. Each department tends to vary widely in its ministerial interests, and compete against the others for influence, recognition, and resources. At times, the fragmentation can be made even worse by the widely diversified information disseminated by international agencies, causing a divergence in ministerial interests. The result is an undermining of the actualised influence of international discourse.

The third instrument concerns reputation, which was found to have a combination of *inertia* and *absorption* levels of significance. Historically, China has valued its national and international reputation, and the experiences of the twentieth century have further highlighted the significance of this value. If reputation was an important driving force, then one would expect to see a more proactive negotiation preference on the trade and climate change issues. Yet, there were no indications to suggest that reputation considerations wholly determined the negotiation preferences; to date, Beijing has not indicated any preference shifts in mitigation or trade in services, among others, as a result of reputation considerations. In mitigation, despite being taken as a scapegoat for past failures, China did not commit to any legally binding agreements under the auspice of the UNFCCC beyond its nationally determined targets. At most, it has signalled possible future targets through media statements. Similarly, despite the many blame games in the trade talks, trade in services remains an unfinished business.

Why did reputation not trigger preference changes? A prevalent view from the interviews was that the force of the reputation instrument depends on the level of political pressures China feels from other negotiating partners or the perceived political risks of taking a non-commitment position, as opposed to the actions of international agencies *per se*. So contrary to the contractualist assumption, reputation alone does not determine China's preference formation. It requires geopolitical incentives to supplement its effectiveness.

Clearly, there is no single variable which solely drives Chinese negotiation preferences. One way or another, all instruments are circumscribed by one or more of the situational factors. This finding is consistent with the research assumption that the institutional macrostructure of the Chinese political system goes hand-in-hand with, at times external, instruments of influence in determining China's preference formation.

### ...and the impact of the principled engagements with international agencies...

In Chapters 4 and 5, it was clear to see that international agencies engaged proactively with China's decision-making process through the said instruments, through the provision of input to Beijing's calculation of costs and benefits, the provision and dissemination of information, and by acting as an overseer of China's international behaviours. In principle, such engagements imply that international agencies have some capacity to affect China's preferences, and evidence revealed that they can – at least to the extent of an absorption level of influence – alter the decision-makers' policy views. In the process, international agencies empower Chinese decision-makers with the acquisition of new capacities to manage policy issues involving a technical dimension. However, this is not to suggest that international agencies have overarching influence over

Chinese decision-makers. Indeed, decision-makers sitting in Beijing will only adapt to international influence rather than allow it to trigger a paradigm shift in their preference formation. Nor do they change the pre-defined features of the preferences or the underlying beliefs held by the decision-makers.

Within the probable parameters whereby international agencies can influence Chinese decision-makers, the comparatively more effective instruments are through engaging in the calculation of costs and benefits and the provision of information. When an international agency engages with China through the calculation of costs and benefits, it frames the way in which the pros and cons of cooperation are framed through counter-attitudinal analyses that generally skew towards the benefits over the costs. However, doing so does not necessarily guarantee full impact. Consider the WTO example. In spite of the WTO's inputs in the calculation of costs and benefits, China did not formally allow transformative shifts in its negotiation positions on trade in services. True, the extent of China's opening up has expanded over the years. But this expansion was largely incremental and many barriers remain intact across numerous services sectors. Likewise, the climate change case-pair showed that the degree of impact this instrument has on mitigation is milder compared to the CDM. While it only took two to three years for this instrument to catalyse a CDM preference change, it took five times as long to see a slight increase in rhetorical flexibility on the mitigation issue.

Then there's information dissemination. The extent of international agencies' impact through the provision of information is contingent on whether their efforts are supported by the Chinese industries. A key reason China's preference for the CDM initiative changed so quickly was because the UNFCCC discourse was supported by the local industries. In contrast, the lacklustre industrial support for mitigation contributed to China's modest profile at the multilateral mitigations negotiations. As such, while international discourse does inform Chinese preferences, their influence does not exist in a vacuum.

It makes sense then to measure influence based on the extent to which the influence of international agencies is constrained by contingencies. As was seen, substantial variances in the degrees of influence presented themselves across the policy instruments, examples, and at different levels of analysis. As expected, the capacity of international agencies to influence China's negotiation preferences is unevenly distributed, and the variation of influence needs to be accounted for. One thing that is certain is that none of the examples have shown a *retrenchment* effect. That is, the Chinese government have not reacted against any of the international agencies, at least within the time period under current focus. This means that international agencies do have *a* level of influence. If international agencies have a lack of influence, it would have been suggested by an active and explicitly negative Chinese attitude towards them. In addition, we would expect to see China take specific measures to counteract the effects of international agencies. However, the empirical research has not identified any data which corresponds to such scenario. Therefore, international agencies *do* hold a degree of influence over China's preference formation.

The more important question is *how*? In what way can international agencies channel the most significant influence? The examples showed that international agencies do not have a *transformative* level of influence over China's negotiation preference formation process, in the sense of channelling influence through one means of engagement without any contingencies. Likewise, international agencies do not exhibit a purely *inertia* level of influence. As *inertia* indicates a level of influence that is only slightly above minimal impact, if it were to be argued that international agencies exhibited such insignificant impact, then this would require evidence of the Chinese government merely acknowledging engagements by international agencies (i.e. through policy advice) while their negotiation preferences remain constant throughout. However, there was no such evidence found amongst the three variables to satisfy this criterion.

The only variable that drew close to, though it cannot be placed as wholly, having an inertia level of influence is reputation. This variable was found to have a mid-range influence of both inertia and absorption, which implies that international agencies may have triggered some momentum, but this did not catalyse actual shifts in negotiation preference. Not only is reputation constrained by situational factor contingencies, but it is also challenged by a vague distinction between the impact of the international agencies, and the influence of other factors such as the national governments of other countries. Such ambivalence cannot qualify the instrument to an absorption level of influence. And yet, the evidence which points to some level of significance in the preference formation implies that it does not have just an inertia level of influence. For this reason, reputation can be placed as somewhere in between. With this considered, international agencies do not have a transformation or an inertia level of influence on China's negotiation preference formation.

The last indicator is *absorption*. Absorption implies some influence on China, but this influence only propels the country to the point of adaptation, and any preference change is the result of both the international agencies and other intervening variables. In other words, absorption refers to a situation in which China formally adopts the features, and the underlying collective understandings attached to them, as derived from the international agencies, but may not adopt any real policies and measures derived from an international agency *unless* other factors (e.g. domestic constituents, existing interests) complement absorption. Looking at the preceding analyses, information dissemination and the costs-and-benefits calculus exhibited such a level of influence consistently across the cases. The absorption of the international agencies' policy advice, proposals, recommendations, norms and practices has allowed the Chinese government to acquire new capacities to address the relevant issues, both internally and externally. But both instruments only reformed Chinese preferences to the point of acceptance and perhaps attitudinal and rhetorical adaptation in various forms.

Given that the majority of the instruments exhibit this level of influence, international agencies have, at best, an *absorption* level of influence over China's economic diplomacy preference formation. And the calculation of costs and benefits and information dissemination are the most consistent and effective ways to channel influence over policy.

Although international agencies hold a circumscribed level of influence, they nonetheless do have impact. This impact is made possible because Chinese policy actors and agencies, under normal circumstances, *do not reject the influence of international agencies*. Instead, they are open to engagements with international agencies and absorb the consequential effects on policymaking. Evidence of this was seen in China's generally adaptive attitude towards the principled engagements of international agencies in the decision-making process, and especially through the provision of inputs to the calculation of costs and benefits, and through information dissemination.

Moreover, Chinese policy actors generally respect the analyses and viewpoints of international agencies, and take them into serious consideration during the decision-making process. This is particularly the case when Chinese decision-makers lack the necessary information to make an informed and utility-maximising decision. At times, the influence of the international agencies is also used by certain government agencies to support their own ministerial interests and/or preferred policy outcome. This was the case when the Ministry of Environmental Protection (MEP) and the Ministry of Science and Technology (MOST) pushed for the adoption of the CDM initiative, and when the MOF encouraged a revision of China's position for the GPA framework. Overall, China's reception of the international agencies' influence is generally a positive one (see Table 8.1).

What explains the variance in the levels of influence identified? Looking at the examples of this book, their qualitative data has indicated that much of the variance is due to different conformity to the aforementioned situational factors. For instance, *national objectives* played a fundamental contingency role across all examples and policy instruments. In the climate change examples, the influence of the costs-and-benefits assessments was undermined by a *perceptive* issue about the political opportunity costs that comes with advice from international agencies. On the issue of mitigation, while Chinese decision-makers do not deny the predicament of climate change, they also perceive mitigation efforts as expensive to their short-term development goals, and ultimately to the government's political legitimacy. For Beijing, the perceived cost of committing to

*Table 8.1* Levels of influence for international agencies

|  | Negotiation modality | Costs-and-benefits calculus (rationalism) | Information dissemination (cognitivism) | Reputation reinforcement (contractualism) |
|---|---|---|---|---|
| UNFCCC | CDMs | Absorption | Absorption | Inertia/absorption |
|  | Mitigation | Absorption | Absorption | Inertia/absorption |
| WTO | GPA | Absorption | Absorption | Inertia/absorption |
|  | Services | Absorption | Absorption | Inertia/absorption |

mitigation is much more detrimental than the costs of non-action. By comparison, the CDM initiative comes with lower threats, given that it does not undermine but enhances China's short-term priorities and contributes to its long-term objectives. That is why the UNFCCC Secretariat's costs-and-benefits analyses had more effectively shaped China's CDM preferences compared to mitigation.

Information dissemination was likewise affected by the contingency of national objective. Continuing with the climate change cases, it was seen that a meaningful participation in mitigation would require a complete reorientation of China's energy structure and substantial investment in new energy-efficient technologies. This implies an entire restructuring of the Chinese economy and inevitably affects the country's growth and social development, particularly in the short term. However, when the abatement cost of mitigation was later found to contribute to a rebalancing of China's future development strategy, the government did overlook the short-term costs of economic restructuring and participated in the discussions about a future multilateral mitigation framework. Similar examples can be identified in the trade cases in support of this contingency. For instance, the influence of information dissemination was undermined in the GPA preference formation when regulations of the framework clashed with the government's national objective of supporting the social development of the local indigenous population, as well as the realisation that a GPA membership could affect the government's national autonomy. Thus, national objectives are a key determinant of the international agencies' influence, especially for principled engagements through the provision of advice on costs and benefits, and information dissemination.

Related to national objectives is the *policy goal* contingency. The GPA example demonstrated that the costs-and-benefits assessments advice from the WTO's Commission on Government Procurement effectively instigated preference shifts because the consequential benefits complement the government's corruption control policy goal. The leaders were convinced that the GPA framework would be a useful external force for addressing the domestic policy goal and, as such, the Committee's analyses galvanised much support in Beijing. China's gradual flexibility in the services negotiations is a reflection of the fact that it had existing policy goals to reform the domestic services infrastructure and market. Therefore, the Council's advice on costs and benefits also had gradual influence given that its estimated outcome converged with China's policy goal in this regard.

In the CDM case study, it was found that Beijing had a policy goal to transform its domestic economy to a low-carbon framework, which required significant amounts of investments that were available through the initiative. This provided a strong incentive for Beijing to reach an agreement with the help of economic side-payments. Thus, the extent to which international agencies' efforts are compatible with China's policy goals matters much in determining their ultimate level of impact, especially for the calculation of the costs and benefits factor.

The third contingency is the *policy setting*. Across the case studies, it was seen that China's political structure and system was a major impediment to the international agencies' influence, especially through the instrument of information dissemination. In climate change, initial information dissemination efforts were overshadowed by the power structure between core ministries such as the Ministry of Foreign Affairs (MFA) and the National Development and Reform Commission (NDRC), and the periphery ones such the MOST, the Chinese Meteorological Association (CMA), and the MEP. Although the CMA the MOST and the MEP lead the policy coordination process and policy drafting, they are marginalised by the MFA and the NDRC when the political debates begin.

In trade, although the Ministry of Commerce (MOFCOM) is responsible for the GPA negotiations and policy coordination processes, the MOF also leads numerous dimensions of the negotiations due to its high-level content relevance. Meanwhile, the NDRC is the oversight government department of the GPA, although the MOF has on numerous occasions implemented national positions outside the NDRC's authority. All the while, the MOFCOM has the discretion to either accept or ignore other ministerial proposals, depending on the consensus and support of the top leaders. Decision-making for services points to a comparable situation. Although MOFCOM is formally the leading trade policy agency, and usually represents China in trade negotiations, it only has the authority of a negotiator on behalf of industries but not the authority of a real coordinator. Fragmented decision-making settings as these make it very difficult for the WTO agencies to channel information successfully, let alone produce impact.

In a similar fashion, the external setting that surrounds China's preference formation (i.e. international monitoring, foreign country observations, international scrutiny, and global media pressures) can impose much impact on China's ultimate preference as the government does care about its domestic and international reputation. And the higher the pressures, the more susceptible Beijing becomes to the influence of international agencies. In all, policy setting plays a crucial role in determining the influence of international agencies, especially through information dissemination and reputation reinforcements.

Last but not least, *policy instruments* determine much of the international agencies' influence. A particularly useful and effective policy instrument for information dissemination as identified across all case-pairs was support from the Chinese business and industrial actors – a key constituent group for the Communist Party of China (CPC). Gaining support from domestic industries, state-owned and private alike, enhances the political weight of the discourse disseminated to Beijing, because it raises the political ante of non-action. Hence, the availability of industrial support for the CDM case, and the lack of it in mitigation was a key reason for the difference in the influence level of the UNFCCC Secretariat. Similarly, the clash of the WTO bodies' discourse with the interests of the state-owned enterprises (SOEs) played a significant part in China's initial rejection of a further liberalising of services trade. Then, support from the domestic private enterprises in services prompted the government to reform their position, though incrementally.

It is worth noting that the systemic mechanisms within the UNFCCC and the WTO further constrain the impact of these agencies. The UNFCCC Secretariat's role as provider of operational advice can sometimes fall prey to concerns relating to the credibility of the output that are unrelated to the quality of the science as such. While broad membership subsidiary bodies lend well to legitimacy in providing the expert advice required for achieving a treaty's governance goals, in practice they often fail to deliver salient and timely advice to China. Likewise, interviews point out that the WTO's services norms tend to be vague, and there is limited support available to China. Within the WTO's Council on Services Trade, there is only a handful of expert staff that provides sectoral/regulatory expertise to China, among other countries. The limited support from the WTO means that China has often had to seek support from elsewhere. Hence, the international agencies' deficiencies served to undermine their own attempts at influence. In all, having effective and reliable policy instruments is important for boosting the influence of international agencies, especially through information dissemination.

### And the validity of claim no. 2 is…

The second dimension of this book considered the formulation of national approaches to economic negotiations, and the multilateral instruments – namely, shuttle diplomacy proximity talks, INPs, and side-payment bargaining – that have impact probabilities on China's decision-making. It is important to recognise that an analysis of multilateral instruments is intrinsically tied to an assessment of the role and impact of international agencies, given their role as guardians of such multilateral instruments, as well as the processes in which the instruments are utilised.

Proximity talks involve processes of interpersonal counter-attitudinal discussions and the establishment of institutionalised relationships with the Chinese decision-makers. Their influence level varies depending on the kind of information international agencies hold and its perceived credibility. If the international agency has superior information and credibility, proximity talks are likely to have an *absorptive/transformative* level of influence in shaping China's negotiation approach. If they have superior information but lack credibility, China may be unwilling to respond to their acts of mediation in fear of being manipulated. In such situation, proximity talks are likely to have an *inertia* level of influence. Where the international agency is viewed as credible but lacks superior information, Chinese decision-makers will consider the agency as trustworthy but will not necessarily allow themselves to fully absorb the mediated effects. As such, proximity talks will have an *inertia/absorption* level of influence. Finally, the combination of no superior information and a lack of credibility lead China to conclude that the international agency is dishonest and manipulative in its communications to serve its own ends. Thus, proximity talks in this situation have a *retrenchment* effect on the shape and form of China's negotiation approach (see Table 8.2).

Meanwhile, the ideational and normative structures of the informal negotiation practices (INPs) shape China's negotiation approach in three ways. First,

*Table 8.2* Scenarios of the influence of proximity talks

|  | *Credibility* | *No credibility* |
| --- | --- | --- |
| *Superior information* | Absorption/transformation | Inertia |
| *No superior information* | Inertia/absorption | Retrenchment |

the INPs affect how China believes it should act in negotiations, what the perceived limitations on its actions are, and what strategies its imagines to achieve
their objectives. The ideas and norms floated around in the INPs thus condition
what China considers and expects as necessary and possible in practical and
ethical terms. Second, the INPs constrain China's negotiation approach through
an emphasis on international norms. For instance, international agencies can
seek to justify their ideas and recommendations by appealing to the established
information norms of legitimate conduct. Third, the processes of rationalisation
through INPs are a form of constraint in itself. The very language of justification
imposes a form of constraint on the options available to China in a given
negotiation.

It is also important to recognise that INPs usually occur at the later stages of
economic diplomacy decision-making and, by the time Chinese decision-makers
arrive at the negotiation settings, they will have a relatively strong set of pre-
defined positions, attitudes, and postures. Although these pre-defined positions
are dynamic – rather than fixed – they are tough factors to undermine through a
facilitator role. Hence, it is expected that this instrument will not achieve a transformation level of influence. But given the number of probable ways they can
assert immediate impacts without being limited by contingencies INPs do have
an influence level that swings between *absorption* and *transformation*.

Side-payment bargaining has an influence level between *inertia* and *absorption*. The influence of side-payment can either be strengthened or undermined by
how complementary potential economic benefits are with China's national
objectives or policy goals. If a deal serves the government's development programmes and ambitions, for instance, then it is likely to be received relatively
well. The reverse is also true; the government will reject the influence of international agencies if the economic side-payment clashes with Beijing's policy
agenda or is perceived as irrelevant. Another contingency of this instrument has
to do with *trust*. How much China trusts international agencies as well as foreign
counterparts plays a decisive role in China's decision-making. The study finds
that the levels of trust decision-makers have are shaped by their past experiences,
and expectations on whether foreign Parties can deliver on their promises.

When considered together, a key advantage of the three roles of influence is
their ability to enhance the social instigators; that is, they are good for building
expectation, trust, and the personal reputations of the Chinese decision-makers –
the core drivers of the nature of China's negotiation approach. Often a fundamental reason for China's lack of cooperative behaviour is Beijing's low
expectations that other negotiating Parties would take on the norm of reciprocity

if China did take on commitments. Through proximity talks, INPs, and side-payment bargaining, such expectations can be raised with the use of communicative strategies (i.e. the tools of persuasion).

A second root problem with China's lack of cooperative behaviour is its ongoing uncertainties caused by problems of trust. The informal settings and smaller-group discussions in proximity talks and the INPs humanise the negotiation process, and, in turn, build both unity and empathy between the negotiators. The outcome is improved inter-personal trust. Finally, investing in trust and expectations is only possible if the initial degree of personal reputation is high. For this reason, personal reputation is an interrelated variable. Through these three capacities, international agencies can demonstrate their sincerity to Chinese negotiators and decision-makers as well as a willingness to integrate China's cultural values at the international level, as long as it is within their capacity and interest.

In the existing literature, as in the original theoretical framework of the present study, the social instigators are rarely discussed as determinants of China's economic diplomacy decision-making. This is an unfortunate dismissal because for Chinese decision-makers, the core of their negotiation behaviour depends on this triangular relationship between the level of trust decision-makers have in the counterparts, the level of investment decision-makers make in building a trustworthy reputation, and the expectation of the probability that others will cooperate. The lack of any one of these variables can lead to a downward spiral in their incentive to cooperate multilaterally. If international agencies wish to effectively influence China's negotiation approach, it is necessary to embrace and understand the fundamental nature of these elements in Chinese economic diplomacy.

### *The social instigators*

The *social instigators* constitute the second set of contingencies. They refer to the internal drivers that are behavioural and psychological by nature, and can either enhance or undermine the impact of the principled engagements, especially the influence of international agencies. The drivers include the ability of international agencies to build *trust* with the Chinese decision-makers, enhance their *expectations* on the norm of reciprocity, and promote the *personal reputation* of the Chinese decision-makers and negotiators in the multilateral arena. In an ideal world, where Chinese decision-makers have high expectations that other negotiation Parties will adopt the norm of reciprocity, there is an incentive for the Chinese negotiators and decision-makers alike to acquire positive and respectable personal reputations as promise-keeping and action-performing global actors. Thus, trustworthy individual decision-makers who trust policy-makers of other countries – who also have a reputation for being trustworthy – can engage in mutually productive negotiated exchanges, so long as they limit their dealings primarily to those with a reputation for keeping promises. As such, a personal reputation for being trustworthy becomes a valuable asset.

Similarly, developing trust in an environment where others are expected to be trustworthy is also an asset. Trust is the expectation of one person about the actions of others that affects the first person's choice, when an action must be taken before the actions of others are known (Dasgupta, 1997, p. 5). In this context, trust affects whether China is willing to initiate cooperation based on the expectation that it will be reciprocated by its negotiating counterpart nation-states. Thus, the trust in other countries, the investment in a trustworthy reputation of the individual decision-makers, and the expected probability that other countries will use reciprocity are intricately interlinked. This mutually reinforcing core is affected by structural variables as well as the past experiences of the Chinese decision-makers.

In reality, the levels of expectation and trust held by the Chinese decision-makers are typically low because of unpleasant past experiences. For this reason, individual decision-makers, when abroad, can lack confidence in their perceived reputation in the international community. Through soft mediatory instruments like proximity talks and INPs, international agencies have the capacity to improve Beijing's confidence in these three regards and produce outcomes including improved clarity on key issues and concerns; effective management of differences and negotiation conflicts; enhanced trust and mutual respect between the Parties; increased social, operational, and decision-making capacities; improved integration of relevant knowledge into deliberations and decisions; and greater perceived legitimacy within and outside the multilateral processes. Some scholars have gone a step further to combine these outcomes dynamically with engagement processes, whereby a 'virtuous cycle' is set in motion (e.g. Ansell and Gash, 2008; Imperial, 2005; Huxham, 2003). Upon achieving these outcomes, it is probable that international agencies will kindle a reformation in China's negotiation approach from prudent resistance to active cooperation.

The claims of this section are depicted in Figure 8.1. The diagram has three nested dimensions, shown as boxes, representing the general systemic context. The outermost box, depicted by solid lines, represents the surrounding *situational factors* which are the national objectives, policy goals, policy settings, and policy instruments. These situational factors generate opportunities and constraints for international agencies to exert impact. From the outset, and over time, situational factors affect the dynamics of the principled engagements, represented by the first dashed-line box within the situational factors systemic context. Within this box are the interactions and decision-making processes as depicted in Figure 8.2. From their principled engagements emerge the *social instigators*, including expectation, trust, and reputation, which either drive a paradigm shift instigated by the engagements or impede a cooperative negotiation approach from China.

So far, attention has focused on the preference formation and negotiation approach as separate decision-making processes, and rightly so for analytical purposes. But this does not mean these processes do not interact, and by no means are they incompatible or incommensurate. Rather, they are mutually complementary and reinforcing. For instance, the costs-and-benefits instrument complements, in

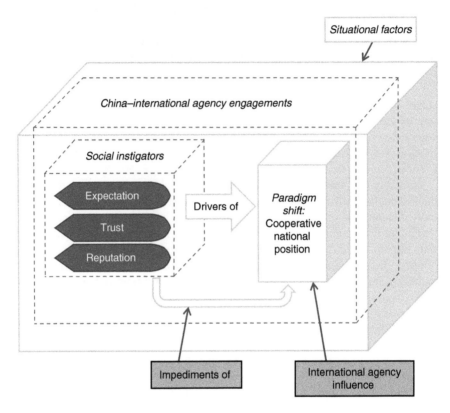

*Figure 8.1* The causal effects of contingencies.

effect, the information dissemination activities. The INPs usually sets the provocation process for side-payment bargaining. The costs-and-benefits calculus and information dissemination are the prerequisites for the shuttle diplomacy proximity talks and the INPs. Often the Chinese decision-makers have to subscribe to the same information and frame of mind and issue before they can be persuaded through the mediatory practices of proximity talks and INPs. When international actors travel to Beijing for proximity talks, it is likely that a discussion of the costs and benefits will occupy the meetings. In addition, reputation is usually assessed and reinforced in proximity talks and the INPs. These are but a few of the many possibilities in the ways that the variables reinforce each other.

## The principled engagements between China and international agencies

The preceding discussion alluded to how the principled engagement between China and international agencies implicates the growing dynamism in China's economic diplomacy. That is, international agencies *do* generally influence

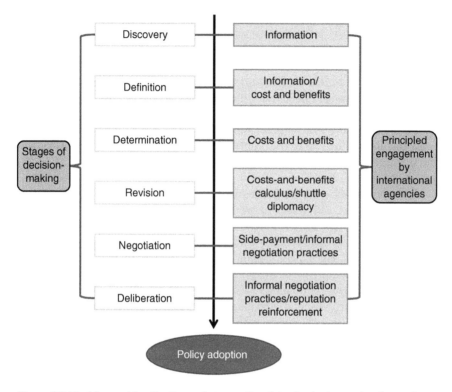

*Figure 8.2* Decision-making timeline and stages of participation by international agencies.

China's economic diplomacy preference formation and negotiation approach. Indeed, the relationship between China and international agencies is shaped by the cyclical interactions of actors that administer the two polities. The interactions occur over time, either in a face-to-face context or through virtual communication technologies. For Beijing, policy actors and decision-makers are concerned with designing preferences that serve their national interests while preventing adverse consequences on their multilateral developments. In doing so, meso-level policymakers seek to expand their share of decision-making power by forming informal allegiances within the bureaucracy. On the other side of the chessboard, international agencies seek to encourage the Chinese decision-makers to adopt preferences that complement their own visions of an international agreement and interests. International agencies strive to satisfy the pressures of their member-states and other concerned Parties, while minimising the adverse effects and costs on China. In the end, their cyclical interactions serve to solve policy and negotiation problems.

International agencies engage with China at different stages of decision-making. Possible instruments of influence at the policy drafting stage (in Beijing) include the costs-and-benefits calculus, information dissemination, and reputation reinforcement. In the later stages of decision-making that take place simultaneously with the multilateral negotiations, they may act as mediators of shuttle diplomacy proximity talks, facilitators of INPs, and instigators of side-payment bargaining to shape China's negotiation approach.

Through each of these instruments, international agencies participate in four general stages of preference formation: *discovery, definition, determination,* and *deliberation.*[2] Through this iterative process, they seek to develop a shared sense of purpose (e.g. an agreement on tackling climate change) and a shared plan of action for achieving that purpose. This shared action plan includes a common understanding of the size of the problem or challenge in need of addressing, and the scope and scale of the chosen activities or interventions (Koontz *et al.*, 2004; Leach and Pelkey, 2001).

At the policy *discovery* stage, international agencies attempt to identify shared interests, concerns, and values between China and the multilateral community. This is done through the identification and analysis of relevant and pertinent information and its implications, which is communicated through information dissemination. In the policy *definition* stage, they attempt to build shared meaning with China by articulating common purposes and objectives; agreeing on the concepts and terminologies used to describe and discuss problems and opportunities; clarifying and adjusting tasks and expectations of one another; and setting forth shared criteria with which to assess information and alternatives. These efforts are possibly carried out through the costs-and-benefits calculus and information dissemination.

International agencies play a role in the joint *determination* of the procedural decision-making process (e.g. agenda-setting, tabling a discussion, assigning a working group) and more substantive determinations (e.g. reaching agreements on action items or final recommendations). Although substantive determination can be an end product, in the interaction between international agencies and Beijing, it is also made over time and is integrated in the framework as a reiterating element of their engagement. The most likely instrument used here to transfer the influence of international agencies includes the proximity talks and the INPs.

Finally, international agencies play a role in the *deliberation* of China's negotiation policy. Through proximity talks and INPs, actors of international agencies thoughtfully examine and listen to Chinese decision-makers and their perspectives on negotiated issues, and thereafter derive judgements about what represents the *common good*, advocates the global interests, and establishes effective strategies for conflict resolution. Included in this process are international actors participating in hard conversations, constructive self-assertion, asking and answering challenging questions, and expressing honest disagreements. Here, international agencies may also constrain preference formation by reinforcing the nation-state's reputation through institutional assessments of their performance or media pressures. These stages are summarised in Figure 8.2. Figure 8.3 depicts the general inter-departmental coordination process and international agencies' respective participation.

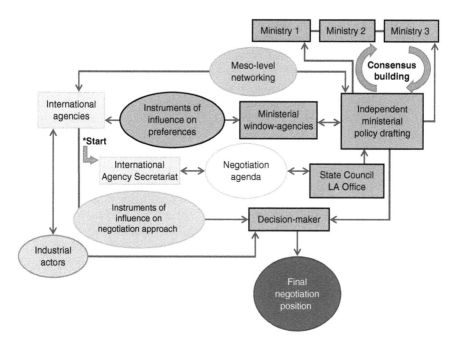

*Figure 8.3* China's economic diplomacy decision-making and the principled engagements with international agencies.

It is important to note that in between the four general stages of decision-making are probable intervening stages. An example is the semi-ministerial negotiation stage, which are the meetings with foreign delegations before the formal joint sessions. At this stage, international agencies seek to bridge a consensus regarding an agenda for negotiation, mediate inter-governmental tensions, and provide logistic support to their member-states. As such, they are likely to channel influence through a costs-and-benefits calculus and the INPs. Another probable intervening stage is *policy revision*. This usually follows the semi-ministerial meetings whereby the decision-makers would have encountered new information about the underpinnings of other Parties, their intentions and about their own posture, expectations and perceptions about the forthcoming joint session negotiations. With the new information, China is likely to revise its initial negotiation preferences and approach. At the same time, international agencies may exercise proximity talks in their continual efforts to shape Chinese economic diplomacy preference formation.

Across the stages, it is clear to see that Chinese policymakers and government departments do not reject the influences of international agencies. Instead, they are open to engagements with international agencies and absorb the consequent effects of the engagements. Evidence of this can be found in China's generally adaptive reactions to their contributions to the costs-and-benefits discussions, and provision of new information during the preference formation processes. The study finds that, under normal circumstances, Chinese policy actors generally respect the analyses and viewpoints of international agencies and take them into serious consideration during the decision-making process. At times, they are also used by select government agencies to support their interests and/or desired policy outcome. In addition, the fact that Chinese officials generally like participating in proximity talks and INPs, as this addresses their social instigator problems, is also an indication that they views the effects of international agencies as helpful to their multilateral involvement. In this sense, China's reception of international agencies' influence is generally a positive one.

Important to note is that international agencies do not necessarily, by intent, strategise how to assert influence over China's decision-making process. Nor do they necessarily assert influence across all stages of decision-making. Rather, it is believed to be a generally eclectic process executed by different international agencies across different government departments at different stages of China's decision-making process. As a result, a sustained and reiterative engagement process between Chinese policymakers and international agencies throughout the decision-making process will gradually internalise the latter in the preference formation of the former. Chinese policymakers and government departments are ultimately confronted with the challenge of maintaining a state of immunity from the influences of international agencies when forming negotiation preferences and approaches.

The resultant outcome of this constitutes the third overarching conclusion: the reiterative engagements with international agencies will, over time, integrate them into the general decision-making system of China – be it implicitly or explicitly, directly or indirectly, and intentionally or unintentionally. This is to suggest that as Chinese policy actors become used to regular communications and coordination with the related agencies throughout the preference formation, this kind of activity will eventually establish itself as a systemic norm within the decision-making process. Over time, policy actors may believe it is perhaps even necessary to bypass certain proposals to the agencies for their professional perspective and feedback.

China's economic diplomacy decision-making in the twenty-first century is no longer a stand-alone domestic process. Although, on paper, China's preference formation is determined by its national interests and other domestic political factors, a deeper examination of the bureaucracy-level of activities suggests that international agencies also play critical behind-the-scenes roles which indirectly shape Chinese economic diplomacy. As such, China's economic diplomacy at present and into the future is shaped by a *collective* system involving domestic and international agencies.

### Road blocks and the facilitating conditions

When *influence* is taken as a whole, international agencies' capacity to impose their desired outcomes on Chinese economic diplomacy decision-making can be challenged as much as it can be facilitated by the domestic political structure, processes, and actors. Earlier in the chapter, the situational factors were identified as a constraint to influence. Yet, all four situational factors are interestingly dynamic by nature, rather than fixed variables, in that they can be affected by a change in the decision-makers' beliefs, worldviews, and/or a change in the central government's strategy of governance. As such, a change in the core foundation of the state can alter abstract policy goals, or the type of policy instruments utilised for meeting the needs of those goals. According to the research interviews, the drivers of changes in the situational factors are fundamentally the emergence of new ideas and policy actors. An understanding about the relationship between the two variables – actors and ideas – can lead to new appreciations for the situational factors as determinants of China's negotiation preference formation. For example, China's policy goal can evolve when new policy actors – emerged from a leadership change, for instance, or from the introduction of new policy specialists and interested Parties – have different preferences at the same time. Alternatively, policy goals could also change as a result of the emergence of new ideas (which may include a shift in the general policy frames that emerges either from a change in the preference formation venue and/or through a policy learning process).

However, the advent of new actors and ideas into the preference formation apparatus is not an automatic one, because factors such as informal politics (i.e. path dependencies and closed networks) can weaken the possibilities of altering the existing constellations of beliefs and the related policy actors (Hansen and King, 2001; Coleman and Perl, 1999). Hence, the emergence of new actors in a path-dependent situation, for example, is only likely to cause a change in the kind of policy instrument Chinese decision-makers use in preference formation rather than any broader shifts in policy goals or national objectives. In this context, the propensity for change in the situational factors can be considered as driven by the interactive effects of stable and change processes. This implies that an assessment of the influence of international agencies in China's preference formation necessitates an analysis of how the macro-level processes impact the micro- and meso-level structures.

*Path dependency* refers to the manner in which current policy decisions are influenced by the internal institutional and behavioural legacies of past decisions made by the Chinese decision-makers (Pierson, 2000; Rose, 1990). Policy legacies affect current policymaking because of factors such as the sunk costs or institutional routines and procedures, all of which can force decision-making towards certain directions by either eliminating or distorting the range of options available to the Chinese government (Weir, 1992). Hence, a decision to alter China's core energy structure or domestic services infrastructure in which billions of RMB may already have been invested by the government is a much more difficult decision to make than a corresponding decision about a programme that has not yet started (i.e. the CDM) or is vaguely institutionalised (e.g. the government procurement regime).

*Closed networks* refer to policy stability promoted by the ability of the existing key policy actors (e.g. the NDRC) to prevent new members from entering into policy debates and discourses. This logic is in line with the works of Rhodes (1997), Schaap and van Twist (1997), and Baumgartner and Jones (1991). They share the view that all bureaucratic policy actors attempt to construct 'policy monopolies' in which the interpretation of and approach to an issue are more or less fixed. In Beijing, the uneven distribution of power within the bureaucratic system has frequently seen the NDRC, and at times, the MFA marginalise the MEP and MOST in the climate change preference formation processes, even though the latter two agencies probably have more competencies in this issue-area. This road block is even greater for the preference formation of international trade. The NDRC, keen to cling to power, often blocks the interests of the MOF and MOFCOM in preference formation even though the latter is charged with trade policy coordination responsibilities. In most sectors, the structure of the policy system provides certain actors with the ability to veto or block changes in the preference or negotiation approach for that sector; and sometimes this can be done so by establishing 'critical subsectors' with special abilities or resources vis-à-vis other subsectors (Rayner *et al.*, 2001). This was the case when the NDRC established the National Center for Climate Strategy and International Cooperation of China (NCSC), a new think tank on climate research directly under the NDRC, to increase its climate change policy capacities and resources.

In spite of these road blocks, there are also facilitating conditions that ensure the effective diffusion of impact from international agencies in the preference formation process. One facilitating condition concerns the meso-level networks. International agencies which deal with issues likely to be grasped by the meso-level networks within the Chinese government are more likely to see their asserted influence absorbed and internalised into the preference formation process. Meso-level networks develop within and among the myriad of government departments run by the specialised middle-ranking policymakers and bureaucrats. On this level, technocratic and expert rationality tends to prevail, in that decisions are approached technically even when they are of a political nature. In this context, when international agencies disseminate specialised information and/or transfer calculations of the costs and benefits to the meso-level networks, their views are more likely to be absorbed due to the reduced politicisation of the process.

A similar outcome may not be possible if the specialised information is disseminated to the highly politicised policy actors whose main concern revolves around power politics. When international agencies engage directly with the meso-level networks, they have increased capacity to frame preferences and shape the policy debates. A case in point is when the UNFCCC Secretariat communicated directly with the implicit network consisting of the MEP, MOST, and the CMA with regards to the CDM initiative. As Chapter 4 showed, there were clear indications that the UNFCCC Secretariat's viewpoints were reflected in the policy recommendations that emerged from this network. Similar effects presented themselves in the GPA example. When the Commission communicated directly with the implicit network consisting of the MOFCOM and MOF, the international influence was gradually absorbed by these government agencies.

Against the NDRC, MOFCOM and MOF eventually managed to promote entry into the GPA despite their initial opposite position. This goes to show that transnational network relations between the agencies of the Chinese government and international agencies can induce and push a dynamic which Beijing cannot escape from. An added implication of engagements in this form is that they will encourage the meso-level network agencies to act as policy entrepreneurs and promote policies in line with the preferences of international agencies. Naturally, not all issues are equally suitable for such processes. Issues as such can this be expected to be less permeable to the influence of international agencies.

A possible limitation to this facilitating condition is that not all issues are suitable for such processes, which means that they are also less open to the influence of international agencies. Highly politicised issues are a key factor of this equation. This can be so for at least two different, but complementary reasons. First, by definition, the more politicised an issue is, the less it will be dealt with in a technocratic manner, which is the way issues are framed at the meso-level of the Chinese government. The WTO's lacklustre impact in the rules concerning hormone-treated beef, Genetically Modified Organisms (GMOs), and sugar are cases in point.[3] These are unlikely cases for the influence of international norms on China precisely because they are highly politicised issues. As such, the likelihood that external pressure will prompt preference changes is reduced.

Second, in a more speculative way, issues that are framed more politically fit better with the nature of the Chinese government. And by establishing its own political platforms for policy debates, the government can control the direction of its preference formation. With these said, the fact that there is a strong agency presence in the preference formation process implies the necessity to nuance this assumed limitation. Politicisation being a debated concept, the key parameter might not (only) be where an issue is located along the continuum of high and low politics, but also whether an issue is new to China's political agenda, or has already been dealt with, for instance.

Another facilitating condition has to do with the open-ended characteristic of the Chinese government. Owing to the fact that the country is in a *developing* phase, where positions on an array of multilateral economic issues remain *in the making*, there is a range of policies within the purview of the Chinese government that is not clearly defined. In turn, international agencies can take advantage of any one of the instruments to expand the range of issues under consideration, and with it, expand the scope of China's willingness to cooperate. In their study, Farrell and Héritier (2003, p. 580) have shown how "substantive issues may be instrumentalised to establish informal institutional gains" which can create a new status quo and, therefore, changes in the formal institutions. In this sense, international agencies that promote actions for enhancing China's international capacity are expected to find more supporters in Beijing, especially among those that favour a greater degree of Chinese integration to the multilateral economic system. Once these supporters absorb the discourse of international agencies, they are expected to expand China's policy spheres with the introduction of new issues, and/or competences of government institutions.

The impacts of international agencies are anticipated to be even stronger when China faces new issues it has not previously dealt with. Such impacts were seen in the CDM and GPA examples.

A similar argument applies to the recommendations extended from international agencies, which help build the international *actorness* of the Chinese government, or which empower specific government institutions. The research of this book has identified a *quid pro quo* in the relationship between the Chinese government and international agencies. It is as if China offered openness vis-à-vis the influence of international agencies in exchange for a role, particularly a leadership role, in multilateral negotiations. Or as if it had to compensate for its *sui generis* character as an international actor and *pay the price* of a rather high degree of influence by (some) international agencies. This is of course especially so in the domains of which the *actorness* of the Chinese government is not (perhaps yet) well established.

Certainly, the influence of the WTO on China has been, in part, a function of the attempt by the latter to establish itself and exert its preferred positions on international trade governance. Martijn Groenleer (2012) advances a similar argument in the context of the EU. According to Groenleer, the EU agencies often align themselves with the goals and interests of international agencies in order to be able to act as a partner to them. In other words, on occasions the influence of international agencies seems to be, in part, a function of the attempt by China to establish itself as an actor before them. Yet, the increase in policy powers induced by the decision to adopt policies and norms derived from international agencies should not cross a certain (probably issue-specific) threshold. If the increase is perceived as too large, then (reluctant) bureaucratic polities will be more likely to oppose it.

### *Does the strength of international agencies matter?*

In the debate on institutional influence, Costa and Jorgenson (2012) point to the strength (i.e. the stringency of the constraints imposed on China and the robustness and endurance of the organisational setting) of international agencies as an indicator of the extent to which they can affect preference formation. Can institutional design affect the resilience of the influence of international agencies in light of the road blocks? Evidence suggests that a strong international agency, despite its strength, can be insignificant (e.g. the WTO); and comparatively weaker international agencies (e.g. the UNFCCC) can have an important effect. These findings accord well with the growing scholarship on the effects of international institutions, and, especially, studies that highlight the power of weak international institutions (Dai, 2007). In this context, a broad conclusion on the strength of international agencies can be made: *the comparatively stronger international agencies do not generate greater degrees of influence on China.*

Even when they seem to impact China's preference formation and negotiation approach, it is often not through their coercive power. The WTO is a strong agency with relatively robust enforcement mechanisms. Agreements through the

WTO are legally binding. States sign and ratify these treaties holding them accountable to the obligations endorsed in these agreements. If a state violates these obligations, other states may file a case against them within the WTO's dispute resolution process. With the WTO's approval, other states may legally sanction the violator. These are powerful mechanisms that give strength to the WTO. However, in the case-pair examined in Chapter 5, the evidence does not reveal any *real* apparent correlation between the *strength* of the WTO and a strong degree of influence on China's preference formation. Clearly, the WTO does not always have domestic influence, and when it does, it is not necessarily through the coercive mediums. This study certainly did not find any domestic actors that were mobilised or changed their preferences due to the WTO rulings. Just as well, the WTO did not attempt to do this in any case. So despite the strength of the WTO, the agency does not necessarily produce more significant influences.

By comparison, the degree of policy and attitude changes in the UNFCCC – a non-binding agency – negotiations were comparatively higher than those in the WTO despite the latter's more stringent legal framework. The CDM and mitigation negotiations show how some of the stronger influences are generated by international agencies that are only loosely formalised, have few (or no) substantive binding commitments, and contain no (or only toothless) compliance mechanisms. In this vein, the UNFCCC has proven to be influential even before the relevant international treaties are adopted. By comparison, the WTO's formalised and legalised rules on trade in services are a case of imposing a comparatively weaker influence on China. Moreover, interviews suggest that China is less likely to feel any constraint arising from the strength of international agencies given that it is a rule-setter.[4]

Thus, international rules embedded in strongly legalised organisations equipped with compelling compliance mechanisms (e.g. the WTO) are not actually systematically more influential on China than international agencies consisting of non-binding treaties (e.g. the UNFCCC). Obviously, the limited number of cases considered in this study makes generalisation a challenge. What the book demonstrates, however, is that the stronger agencies are not always able to have domestic influence. It also reveals the importance of domestic factors and the role of government agencies, and even industrial actors, in transferring the influence of international agencies. Without the support of domestic actors, they will find it much more difficult to impose influence.

However, Johnston (2008) lends strong support to the proposition that the institutional design of international agencies does matter, especially in relation to channelling influence through cognitive instruments such as information dissemination or sociological aspects such as proximity talks and INPs. With this said, agencies that are weakly institutionalised and make decisions by consensus (e.g. G20) can be ideal for persuasion efforts. By contrast, contracting strategies involving back-patting and opprobrium are more influential with a large audience, such as the World Bank and the UNFCCC (Johnston, 2008). This implies that it is not necessarily a case of institutional strength; rather this feature is contingent on the issue of concern. International agencies with small membership are well suited for persuasion strategies, while those with large memberships are preferred for social influence. Johnston's analysis suggests that the notions of 'efficient' institutional design employed in a rationalist sense must be complemented by analyses of the sociological processes by which institutions shape actor preferences. Consistent with his constructivist approach, he recognises that institutions vary not only according to formal design features but also in terms of the less tangible processes, internal cultures, and working philosophies. In other words, they are social environments as well as incentive structures.

Consequently, it is fair to say that the rationalist's contracting strategy is usually most effectively done by the more formal and bureaucratic organisations such as the WTO and UN, because commitments to such organisations are more explicit and difficult to reverse. Among the cognitive persuasion strategies, if the intention is only to legitimise a policy with an external endorsement, a politically independent agency with a large and diverse membership represents the best avenue for channelling its actions. On the other hand, if the purpose is to change interests or values of competing domestic agencies, then a more functionally focused institution with expertise and authority in a particular issue-area is perhaps more effective.

## Implications for policymaking structure

Generally speaking, the process of the principled engagements between China and international agencies is expected to influence a decentralisation of the decision-making structure. In the course of adapting to the multilateral processes, China will see the need to undergo institutional adaptation where domestic decision-making structures are pluralised and decentralised to ensure it meets the requirements of the multilateral system. In contrast to the existing literature that imagines the structure and process as a fixed and static one, Chapter 3 showed that China's economic diplomacy decision-making has already evolved three times in the short life-span of the People's Republic of China (PRC). The first was the exclusion era (1949–1971), in which China was largely isolated from international agencies. The second was the *transition* era (1972–2002), in which China began its integration international agencies. Since 2003, China has entered into the *proactive* period.

Here, China not only became an active international political and economic actor, but also began to question some of the structures and norms of international agencies of which it holds membership. In this way, *the more international agencies China participates in, and the deeper its engagements, the more decentralised the decision-making process becomes.* This is because engaging with international agencies prompts the introduction of new actors and issues, undermines the traditional policy structure and monopolies, and promotes new policy goals and instruments. This trend is driven either by the conditions of joining an international agency and/or Beijing's conviction that doing so would bring them a more effective and efficient management system of related affairs.

Regular interactions not only pluralise the range of policy actors and issues involved in the preference formation process, they also alter the government's inter-departmental distribution of power by empowering certain individuals and/ or bureaucratic entities over others, because regular engagements provide international agencies the opportunity to build close allegiances with the government departments of Beijing. In the meantime, with new access to resources and therefore leverage, the government departments are also empowered by their relationship with international agencies. This is because, in a decentralised policymaking environment with numerous veto points, international agencies become a useful means of empowerment to the related government departments in the broader inter-departmental bargaining process given them new access to external support, leverage and resources. As a result, the inter-ministerial distribution of power is altered. Through the process of empowerment, international agencies weaken the traditional distribution of power and elevate the departments and policymakers which are supportive of international initiatives.

This is an important consequence because it stimulates a spiral pattern of influence when domestic actors bypass government leaders to push through certain issues above others with the use of external force. In most cases, however, international agencies' capacities to assert this form of influence are only achieved if they have established robust institutional relationships with domestic policy actors and/or government departments.

Furthermore, international agencies promote shifts in domestic policies by promoting change processes, such as the advent of new political agencies, internal adaptation to the international systems, and venue change for building expectation, trust, and personal reputation, while undermining stability factors including path dependencies and closed networks. The new actors and ideas that come to dominate the policy system in this phase promote further changes by increasing the potential for new systemic spill-overs and venue changes. This outcome is augmented by the new policy processes set in motion by direct engagements with international agencies.

In this evolving process, however, two characteristics remain constant. The first is the consensus-based decision-making culture that involves inter-departmental discussion and bargaining between the ministerial actors involved. The second is informal politics, which involves the inter-bureaucratic allegiances between political actors and their interests. Thus, the suggested influence is only feasible under the following conditions: (1) when the decision-maker(s) or ministry/commission already wields a level of authority or autonomy in preference formation; (2) when a bureaucratic entity is in a privileged relation with one or more international agencies compared to other agencies; and (3) when a permissive consensus exists in favour of the policies endorsed by the decision-maker of concern.

## Is this relevant to other countries?

From the policy and methodological standpoints, the findings of this book are useful for developing a more nuanced understanding of the drivers of, and international agency impacts on, the policy processes of emerging market economies than is currently found in the literature. For instance, the United Nations Conference on Environment and Development (UNCED) has, through costs-and-benefits discussions, played a part in reforming Brazil's traditionally resistant attitude towards climate change to one of embrace. The traditional attitude in Brazil concerning climate change issues was that sovereignty is the sole defining factor for preference formation. Of course, this position was adopted by all the emerging market economies, especially in the earlier years of negotiations.

However, this attitude changed after the UNCED (Rio 92). Evidence from the meeting suggests that the Negotiation Committee emphasised that Brazil's autonomy could be strengthened if it integrated with the multilateral environmental regime – the legitimacy mainstream – rather than by repudiating the social and international pressures to cooperate (Fonseca, 2011). The political benefit was welcomed by Brazil at the time as it underwent political regime changes from the former military government. Hence, the external force was perceived as a useful leverage for tackling its domestic challenges. In turn, Brazil's former resistance evolved to one that admitted to international cooperation. It hosted the 1992 Rio Earth Summit and became a signatory of the Kyoto Protocol. Moreover, the UN discourse has significantly shaped Brazil's multilateral diplomacy outlook thereafter. This was indicated when the Brazilian government claimed the UN to be at the core of their multilateral ideology (Fonseca, 2011). While this may not be unique to Brazil, it is nevertheless a key to understanding Brazil's multilateral diplomacy. The international discourse, in this respect, has not only informed, but reformed Brazil's negotiation preferences to a willingness to accept greater responsibilities for the costs of attenuating the effects of climate change, for instance, without abandoning the need to find a balanced and just solution for developing countries.

This leads us to the point that international agencies have engaged with the emerging market economies through activities of information dissemination. For example, South Africa has had a history of resource deficiency from human to economic capitals. The South African government often struggled to retain good staff, and in June 2005, the Department of Foreign Affairs was the most understaffed agency within the government. There was a lack of capable personnel for managing global economic affairs, and due to poor information distribution, many ministerial agencies and missions abroad lacked sufficient information flow, and they often had to rely on old information when formulating policies (Landsberg, 2005). Circumstances such as this caused the South African government to face difficult challenges in the preference formation process for multilateral economic negotiations. According to an interview with a former South African diplomat, international agencies played very important, though informal, roles in this respect. The decision-makers that had personal contacts with international agencies had better access to more and new information – the quality of their work was therefore naturally better and more liberal compared to those without similar connections.[5] Moreover, the World Bank, for instance, worked closely with members of the policy unit in the presidency, and the Policy

Research and Analysis Unit in the Department of Foreign Affairs. These engage-ments were relatively effective in raising awareness among the policy actors.

The IMF also enjoyed remarkable influence in the early 1990s disseminating information and policy recommendations to Argentina following a hyperinfla-tion crisis after their transitions to democracy. The IMF succeeded in impressing upon the new government that overcoming hyperinflation required drastic macroeconomic policy corrections. This recommendation prompted the Argen-tinian President, Carlos Menem, to turn the economic portfolio over to Domingo Cavalo, a technocrat and former central banker, whom he knew held consider-ably more orthodox economic views that were more in line with the IMF's. After discussions with the IMF agencies, the country decided to opt for exchange-rate based stabilisation, which included a Convertibility Law which established a currency board regime, and fixed the peso at parity with the dollar – a short-term solution that was supported by the IMF agencies for slowing down inflation during a transition (Fang and Stone, 2012).

Brazil and South Africa both attach particular weight to reputation and each has a its own special unit in the office of the Minister of Foreign Relations to oversee reputation-related activities. Brazil's emphasis on international reputa-tion is particularly important in decision-making because of the regime change in the mid-1980s. As Gelson Fonseca (2011, pp. 387–388) observed, Brazil's "new and essential objective was to recover its international status and, to achieve this goal, an assertive multilateral attitude would be crucial". Thus, the country sought to overcome two distinct challenges. First, it sought to transform its negative image – a legacy of the authoritarian years. For many years, the Brazilian government was viewed as an enemy of the environment, and timid in commitments to multilateralism. In response, the Brazilian government began to change its internal institutions and its international conduct for the purpose of bringing itself closer to the principles of international legitimacy in environ-mental matters. Furthermore, arguments were made by members of the UN that commitments to the multilateral environmental framework would contribute to its reputation-building as it would demonstrate Brazil's awareness of environ-mental problems and show that the country was open to international cooperation in this area (Fonseca, 2011). Thus, it is conceivable that international agencies can have considerable impact on Brazil's preference formation through the repu-tation instrument.

Of course, these variables, when applied to the emerging economies, are not without contingencies. A key reason the costs-and-benefits instrument worked well in Brazil was because it served their national objectives. That is, it was per-ceived to serve Brazil's national development. In his inaugural speech, former President Lula stated that "Foreign policy would reflect the aspirations for change seen on the streets, guided by humanistic perspectives and as an instru-ment for national development" (cited in Visentini and da Silva 2010, p. 55). Similarly, the national objective contingency of South Africa was compatible with the tone of the international discourse. As a country also concerned about development, the African National Congress-led government has since 2000 placed heavy emphasis on multilateral agencies as a strategy for development due to their huge importance and positive implications for development.

Meanwhile, Argentina in the late 1990s demonstrates a case where the policy goal contingency undermined the influence of the IMF through information dissemination. By the late 1990s, the domestic economic circumstances shifted in that a policy of exchange-rate based stabilisation was no longer a necessary radical reform proposal. Elections had been waged and won on the basis of the fixed exchange rate, a policy that the IMF criticised as unsustainable in the long run. The clash of opinions triggered by these incongruent policy goals therefore saw the IMF's leverage deteriorate markedly, and its staff found it harder to convince the Argentinian policy actors to change their views (Fang and Stone, 2010).

The South African example demonstrates the significance of the policy setting contingency. While exposure to new information raised political awareness, the fragmented policymaking structure and processes in the South African system undermined the significance of such new information, nor was the international discourse evenly distributed to all the relevant and critical government agencies that wield veto power in the domestic policy processes. This goes to show that the fragmented political setting to which information flows can undermine the ultimate impact of both information as a policy variable, and of international discourse. This is also a reflection of the road blocks of path dependency and closed networks, whereby the Department of Foreign Affairs has demonstrated tendencies to monopolise the policy space, refusing to let new actors enter into the process. Of course, this kind of behaviour is the product of past political legacies which the Department of Foreign Affairs merely inherited. Other emerging market economies like India reveal similar shortcomings.

In India, institutional disharmony is a major weakness of preference formation, particularly in the shape of the turf battle between the Ministry of External Affairs and the ministries with an economic focus. For instance, the Ministry of External Affairs sometimes swaps posts abroad with the Ministry of Commerce in exchange for placements in that ministry for its officials. As a result, those holding commercial assignments abroad are answerable to both ministries. The permanent secretary that heads the Ministry of Commerce serves on the Ministry of External Affairs personnel board, which selects officials for sub-ambassador-level assignments abroad. But all issues related to international agencies such as those concerning the WTO are handled primarily by the Ministry of Commerce, which also appoints the envoy handling this subject in Geneva. The Economics Division under the Ministry of External Affairs receives less than satisfactory cooperation from the Ministries of Commerce and Industry. The Finance Ministry's Department of Economic Affairs, which handles inbound aid as well as the interface with the World Bank and the IMF, has even less to do with the Ministry of External Affairs. Hence, the Ministry of External Affairs essentially works on closed-shop policies, with no placement among the economic ministries.[6]

In corollary, India's negotiation postures at the WTO, for instance, are not often sufficiently backed with matching advocacy at the key bilateral capitals; nor is investment promotion activity sufficiently harmonised, producing the 'approved-but-not-implemented' limbo. India does not have, as yet, a diplomacy board where the foreign ministry takes the lead in suggesting cohesive actions to autonomous agencies. Instead, actors have to seek harmonisation with their sectoral interests and national priorities through reaching out. Such coordination cannot impose or dictate. Hence, the inter-ministry coordination has been uneven, and sometimes notably absent. In these circumstances, it is hard to imagine mere exposure to new information or access to international discourse to wield the capacity to influence much of the policy outcomes.

Brazil's diplomatic behaviour often also rests on the policy instrument contingency which serves its national development. The main tools for national development include the promotion of multilateral trade, the building up of capacities through advanced technologies, including alternative energy, and the search for productive investments, global and regional integration, and negotiations with other blocs and countries (Visentini and da Silva, 2010, p. 55). However, the means of the engagement with international agencies has at times caused doubts among Brazilian decision-makers. One case in point is the competence of the WTO to manage and oversee the Chair of a Doha Development Agenda (DDA) panel. Former Brazilian Ambassador Clodoaldo Hugueney Filho, secretary-general for Economic and Technological Affairs of the Ministry of Foreign Affairs and main negotiator for the country in the WTO, has criticised various Chairs of the meetings, including the Uruguayan candidature, Perez del Castillo, for steering the 2003 Cancun negotiations to their failure, and blamed the WTO Secretariat for their inabilities to drive the process with professionalism. The South African government likewise has doubts in the managerial instrument of international agencies and their capacity to adequately manage the multilateral system. These governments are further critical of their capacity to ensure the major industrial countries, especially the US, will come to respect the multilateral rules more than they have done in the past. These concerns were suggested to have prompted hesitation from the South African decision-makers to formulate cooperative negotiation preferences for numerous economic negotiations.[7]

In the meantime, evidence reveals that international agencies contribute more positively to addressing national uncertainties through their functions in proximity talks and the INPs. In December 2003, the former WTO Director-General, Supachai Panitchpakdi, travelled to Brazil as a special guest and met with Brazilian leaders and ministers. On that occasion, they held proximity talks and discussed issues such as national and international goals, namely the elimination of distorted trade and agricultural practices along with food security. The Agriculture Minister reiterated the need to preserve the whole of the DDA and emphasised that any reinterpretation or dilution of the mandate would affect the delicate balance among the various negotiation fronts, compromising the focus of the work programme. They also affirmed that an effective liberalisation and reform of agricultural trade would largely contribute to the development goals in the DDA (Visentini and da Silva, 2010, p. 59).

Evidence of the INPs was identified when the WTO Secretariat oversaw numerous technical and political consultations with the G20 group as a means to make the negotiation process more dynamic in light of the stalemate after the Cancun meeting in 2003. These consultations took place in Brasilia (December 2003), Sao Paulo (June 2004), New Delhi (March 2005), Durban (September 2005), and Geneva (October and November 2005). During these meetings, specific proposals were raised regarding the WTO negotiations on agriculture, for instance. The results include greater understandings about the intentions of other nation-states – hence, new levels of trust, expectation, and personal reputations were established – and an agreement for the way forward (Visentini and da Silva, 2010, p. 58). Using the same indicators for measuring influence, the preceding discussion shows that, in general, due to the constraint imposed by situational factors, the variables have an *absorption* level of influence on negotiation preference formation. Meanwhile, the proximity talks and the INPs measure slightly above. These outcomes therefore reinforce that of the China case.

As for the long-term consequence of the principled engagements with international agencies on national decision-making structure, the Brazil example, like that of China, produces evidence of a pluralisation of actors and a reshaping of the internal distribution of power. For instance, the Ministry of External Relations (or *Itamaraty*) had to accommodate the entry of new subjects in the international dialogue by establishing new departments (Lampreia and da Cruz, 2005, p. 108). The increasing technicality of subjects has prompted the *Itamaraty* to hand over some responsibilities to the specialists of the Ministry of Commerce and shift its economic diplomacy management to a multi-agency mode where a Trade Council based in the Presidency carries out the inter-departmental coordination process. In the Argentina case, it was also found that the IMF's insistence on the severity of the hyperinflation crisis and the need for radical policy change lent crucial credibility to the domestic policy teams' calls for economic austerity (Fang and Stone, 2010). This is a further illustration of the impact international agencies have on the national distribution of power structure.

Although the countries discussed above share a common nickname as the emerging market economies, their political regimes are nonetheless different from that of China, and their economic structures and political cultures are largely deviant. Yet, the level of applicability of the findings based on a study of China is relevant to the other emerging market economies. In the brief discussion here, all country cases showed that the various variables of decision-making have an absorption-level of influence. This is because they are constrained by a series of contingencies similar to that of the situational factor taxonomy. Meanwhile, the factors which affect negotiation approaches produced accommodating outcomes because of their ability to embrace and address the social instigators. And as the Brazil example showed, despite its different political system as a democracy – while China's is a socialist model – engagements with international agencies triggered the same consequences for the decision-making structure as was found in the China case. Therefore, the findings and theoretical assumptions yielded in this study have significant resonance and applicability to a range of emerging market economies across the continents of the world.

## Chinese economic diplomacy going forward

Although it is both tricky and risky to predict the characteristics of China's economic diplomacy in the future, it is expected that China will reinvent itself as an active governor and rule-setter of future multilateral economic negotiations. The philosophies of modernisation and nationalisation are likely to continue in the post-Hu Jintao and Wen Jiabao era. That is, any future negotiation preference and approach will be designed to serve Beijing's commitment to modernise China, and this is more than likely to remain as its first priority and national objective. Such was highlighted in the country's 12th Five Year Plan (2011–2015), and emphasised by the new generation of leaders at the 18th Party Congress in early 2013. To this end, China's international objective will remain with the pragmatic quest for the stable environment needed for effective modernisation and development, and China's economic diplomacy will remain pragmatic, economically-oriented, independent and yet generally disposed towards trying to fit in with the multilateral economic system. That is why Beijing is likely to continue experiencing institutional adaptation in order to converge with the multilateral processes by transforming its decision-making system from a vertical to a horizontal system, and ensuring that all possible political inputs and interests are considered in the formulation of China's economic diplomacy.

Worthy of note is that national reputation is likely to remain in the minds of decision-makers in the future. As William Callahan (2010) claims, there is a combination of national pride and national humiliation in the Chinese dual identity that has affected the mind-set of Chinese decision-makers and the wider public. With China's rise, the government has boosted its national pride, but national humiliation has always affected its decision-making. In this respect, China's pride and humiliation are interwoven. While China does promote a positive and proud image of itself, it also presents a very negative view of its relationship with the world based on the history of its national humiliation.

China's view of the world and approach to its neighbours present two images of itself: China as a victim state and China as a great power. Some China scholars (e.g. Guo, 2013) look at the dual identity as contradictions constraining Chinese foreign economic policymaking; i.e. China views itself as a major power and wants to play a global role accordingly, while lacking adequate power to do so. China wants to be fully integrated into the multilateral economic system, while strong concerns over sovereignty makes it difficult for Beijing to embrace some of the mainstream international values born out of Western philosophy. China agrees on a set of principles embedded in the multilateral economic negotiations, while considerations of its national interests cause Beijing to make a pragmatic compromise from time to time. Beijing has long been accustomed to dealing with foreign counterparts in bilateral settings, but the post-Cold War era is witnessing a rise of multilateralism that challenges China's traditional concepts of diplomacy. Even so, Beijing will continue to emphasise reputation-building in the future given its centrality and importance to Chinese politics and its people.

Where there are continuities lie changes. The fact that the government plans to implement administrative reforms indicate several changes that could effectively transform China's future negotiation preferences and approaches. The first concerns changes in the symbolic macrostructure (i.e. ideology) which may have a decisive impact on the decision-makers' interpretation of the internal and external environments at the micro level. Many foreign policy analysts have found a decline or irrelevance of ideology in Chinese foreign policymaking (Guo, 2013). But the qualitative data of this study finds that ideology continues to play an important role in the decision-making process of Chinese economic diplomacy, especially for setting out the principles and policy guidelines. Concepts and slogans are often symbols of ideological orientation and representation of those principles and guidelines. These concepts and slogans are also used by the government to educate the world about itself, establish its international reputation, and justify its negotiation approaches. China has traditionally declaimed to the world that its foreign policy decisions are based on the 'Five Principles of Peaceful Coexistence' (和平共处五项原则).[8]

'Peaceful development' (和平发展) and 'harmonious world' (和谐世界) were slogans religiously applied under Hu Jintao's leadership, to guide China's integration with the world. In addition, this has offered the world an alternative for a new world order in which all nation-states perceive the value of peaceful development, respect the internal affairs of other nations, and cooperate to create a harmonious relationship with one another (Guo, 2013). At the 2013 18th Party Congress, the new leader, Xi Jinping introduced further new development strategies and outlook. It is expected that under his leadership, the ideological framework will further evolve. In particular, it will bring about changes in China's foreign policy priorities. It is likely that ideas will serve as the road maps in the future design of China's economic diplomacy. As Bernard Giesen (1987, p. 351) claims, "The symbolic macrostructure can have explanatory emergence in relation to micro-social processes of interaction, whereas practical macrostructure cannot". And as Quansheng Zhao (1996) argues, major orientation changes in the symbolic macrostructure are likely to bring about fundamental and strategic changes in Chinese foreign policy, such as the shift from a 'closed' policy under Mao to an 'open' one under Deng. Under Xi Jinping, the ideas of 'proactivity' away from 'modesty and transparent social democracy' and away from 'asymmetric transparency' are ever more apparent. It is probable that these macrostructural shifts will cause a new policy focus, new negotiation preferences, and a new negotiation approach in the near future.

Second, tactical changes in Chinese economic diplomacy are likely to be governed by the dynamics of a new internal-plus-external institutional macrostructure. That is to say, external agencies such as the Secretariat bodies and Working Groups of international agencies are gradually becoming integral policy instruments for the Chinese government. This trend has a direct influence on the rules and norms of political actions and instruments of Beijing's policymaking processes. Furthermore, the institutional macrostructure is also influenced by changes at the symbolic macrostructural level. For example, the enlarged scope of participants in the formulation of China's negotiation positions is not simply an institutional arrangement, but also reflects the changes of basic beliefs in China's political system.

Third, concerns about the Communist Party of China's (CPC) political legitimacy and internal power politics will continue to be a central element in the formation of negotiation preferences. As China transitions away from 'strong man' politics to 'collective leadership', Chinese decision-making in economic diplomacy will be ever-more influenced by formal and informal channels. Bureaucratic institutions are formal channels by which officials in different sectors within the government have striven to influence the top leadership's decision-making. At the same time, other emerging actors since China's reform have also moved to influence the preference formation process through informal channels. These new actors operate outside the official realm of the decision-making establishment and include not just ministerial actors but also industrial and business actors, financial institutions, energy companies, local governments, research institutions, the media and netizens. These new actors have emerged from the process of professionalisation of the expert-based bureaucratic elite with a higher level of specialised knowledge in world economic affairs; corporate pluralisation with the proliferation of social organisations; the decentralisation of the authority to local authority and local actors in cross-border economic exchanges; and the economic and information globalisation with increased interdependence and pressure on Chinese cooperation and conformity with the international norms. All these actors seek to assert influence on decisions in international economic affairs, which increases the diversity of views and interests in the preference formation processes and makes for an increasing amount of coordination in policy implementation.

As a result, the central leadership has been forced to consult more broadly, and consider different views, which puts the formal preference formation process in a position of reacting to issues and challenges imposed by the bureaucratic elites, local governments, society, and global actors, especially when dealing with multilateral economic issues and challenges. This makes establishing robust relations and meso-level networks with Chinese decision-makers all the more important for international agencies, given that informal politics tend to affect, sometimes invisibly, the formation of China's negotiation preferences.

Finally, the intertwined picture of the three dimensions of the macro reality opens up the possibility of more alternative and different channels through which decision-makers can consider their preferences and make choices. The growing engagements with international agencies play a key role in this trend. One of the primary tasks before international economic policy specialists is therefore to explore and examine the opportunities and channels faced by the Chinese decision-makers. These available choices are situational and case contingent, and thereby creating never-ending exercises in the study of Chinese economic diplomacy.

### *The future of shuttle diplomacy and INPs*

In the long run, it is expected that shuttle diplomacy proximity talks and the INPs will facilitate much more sustainable mediums for international agencies to influence Chinese economic diplomacy. As the global nature of economic issues has forcibly entered the international arena, and debates and discussions on economic issues have reached greater and more global levels, these instruments present international agencies with the most relevant and effective roles and platforms to manage and guide future negotiation preference formation and multilateral negotiation approaches. This is for three reasons. First, future multilateral economic agreements will be determined largely by the nature of the North–South relationship. Whether agreements can be reached largely depends on whether international agencies administering the negotiations can coordinate between the polarised camps and construct a common interest. This task generally requires much mediatory effort, of which the relevant tools and settings are typically available from the practices of informal negotiation and proximity talks. In doing so, international agencies will shape the interests and policy directions of China, as they do for other countries, and the best perceived policy option for the common public good.

The second reason regards the social dilemma that characterises China's relationship with the US. The US is the most powerful and the largest developed country with a strong capacity to influence multilateral economic negotiations. Yet, the US is not immune to the changing world order and American policy-makers are now influenced by a wide array of forces external to Washington, DC. These include the rise of the emerging market economies, including China, rising requirements emanating from international treaty obligations, pressures from transnational interests groups and multinational corporations, global civil society, and so forth. In light of the changing world system, the US has begun to propose that other rising powers should also take on the burden of leadership. This kind of argument runs unfavourably in Beijing, a government that considers itself as a leader of the developing world only.

A parallel dilemma can be found in numerous economic negotiations, where the Chinese and American delegations constantly eye each other for their next move. The significance of this mutual tactic was emphasised by numerous interviewed delegates from both countries. The Sino–US prisoners dilemma has typically been at the centre of negotiation impasse across different arenas. Hence, it is imperative that international agencies play a stronger mediatory role through the instruments of proximity talks and INPs to break the ice between the world's largest and second largest economies. The potential of these instruments is concentrated on their ability to improve national expectations for reciprocity, trust, and reputation – factors that have caused negotiation stalemates.

Third, China's perception of international agencies has, for the most part, been characterised by distrust. This is not least because Beijing did not participate in the initial design of the multilateral architectures, and that it is to the present day still characterised by the values, interests, and norms of the major developed countries. Therefore, Beijing has consistently held onto its scepticism towards them despite its encouraging rhetoric. The mediatory role of international agencies in shuttle diplomacy and INPs in turn contributes to the advancement of their capacity to establish new trust and credibility with China, in addition to improving China's perception of the international system as governed by integrative and incorporated agencies that seek to support Chinese interests. In addition, these platforms enhance the perceived personal and national reputations of China and its decision-makers.

For these three reasons, proximity talks and the INPs are likely to enable stronger future impacts. Of course, costs-and-benefits analyses, new information, and reputation considerations will continue to play a part in China's thought process. However, their significance in the decision-making process is expected to be comparatively less defined than proximity talks and the INPs.

## Future research directions

The result of this study and its case studies is a clear understanding about Chinese economic diplomacy in a multilateral setting. Bearing in mind the risks of generalisation about a country with asymmetric transparency, this book keeps its claims modest. That said, the book adds value to the little understanding we had about Chinese economic diplomacy decision-making processes. Although there is growing literature on China's involvement in international institutions, there is still limited insight into China's participation in multilateral economic negotiations. Except for a small amount of research, most work on Chinese political economy focuses on China's relationships with major powers and regional blocs, or the historical perspective of China's integration with the world systems. For instance, Samuel Kim (1998) was the first to alert the field to the importance of examining China's behaviour in international institutions, and to add critical insights into Beijing's worldviews. Economy (1997) and Pearson (2001) are pioneers in providing evidence about empirical behaviour to test hypotheses and assumptions about how the international institutions may affect what China does. Undeniably, these contributions are critical parts of understanding Chinese political economy. But they are also limited semi-equilibriums in the broader studies of China in the international political economy.

This study follows on from the tremendous scholarly efforts of Kim (1998), Jacobson and Oksenberg (1990), Economy (1997), Pearson (2001), among others. But, unlike these studies, it focuses primarily on the application of a combination of convention and unorthodox analytical tools from a variety of theories to so-called hard cases, with particular interest in the impact of international agencies. Four dimensions in which the economic diplomacy field in China studies has generally lacked attention can be highlighted.

The first is the processes by which China's international economic policy's ideational base and its interests may change as a result of engagements with external actors (e.g. through discussions about costs and benefits, information dissemination, reputation reinforcement, proximity talks, INPs, and side-payment bargaining). Second, the interests that are hard to observe but appear critical for Chinese leaders when they calculate trade-offs from cooperation (e.g. national and personal reputation). Third, the internal and external motives that are contextual, instrumental, and psychological by nature and that weigh the plausibility of cooperation from the Chinese decision-makers. Fourth, the causal relationship between the principled engagement between China and international agencies, and the evolution of China's decision-making processes and the actors and issues that become integral structural assets. The hope here is that future policy actors and China enthusiasts alike can apply the thought processes and theoretical logics introduced in this book to design future strategies effective for cooperating with the Chinese government as part of the international efforts to establish new public goods critical to the development of the international economic system.

This book, of course, only looked at a relatively small part of the totality of Chinese economic diplomacy and its transformation over the recent decades and in the years ahead. Can the cases examined in this work explain anything more general about other areas of Chinese economic diplomacy, not just at the multilateral level but on a bilateral or regional level? Are the cooperative tendencies and the related contingencies examined in this study representative of China's cooperation in other areas? And how applicable and relevant is the model developed in this research to other developing and transition countries beyond the emerging market economies, such as that of the African and the Central American countries? These are pertinent topics for future research.

Further efforts should also be made into the social psychological factors that drive or undermine cooperative policy outcomes in China. Are there identifiable institutions, be they international or domestic, which could help hypothesise the influence of the social psychological factors as new definitions of interest and policy tools for economic diplomacy? Are there identifiable policy processes that allow these factors to impact China's external negotiation behaviours? Can one also identify the domestic institutions that contribute to the hypothesisation of international agencies, as agents of enhancing the social psychological factors, in shaping the attitudes of the Chinese decision-makers that might be resistant or enhancing to the policy instruments? Can one hypothesise about the kind of hybridity and/or level of resistance that these competing policy instruments produce in the Chinese economic diplomacy decision-making? These questions constitute a research agenda for future testing, and their contribution will be critical to the theorisation of Chinese economic diplomacy as well as that of other (especially developing) countries.

Finally, the integrative agenda introduced in this chapter raises future areas of theoretical research for the study of Chinese economic diplomacy. New attention should be paid to the structural and substance aspects of the model to increase its applicability to policy realities. Here, it is important to acknowledge one again the limits of this study – there is not yet sufficient access to empirical microlevel material to cover a thorough application of this model, to fully cover the interactions between different levels with regard to diplomatic policy choices, or the impact of the principled engagements between China and international agencies. In the future, it will be beneficial for China scholars to further build on this theoretical agenda through similar research.

# Notes

1 Interview with an expert from Harvard University, Boston, 11 June 2012.
2 For more information about the stages of decision-making, see Emerson *et al.* (2011).
3 For more information on the rules on the hormone-treated beef, GMOs and sugar cases, see Alasdair Young (2012).
4 Interview with an expert from the Chinese Academy of Social Sciences, Beijing, 8 November 2012.
5 Interview with a South African diplomat, Durban, 18 December 2011.
6 Interview with a retired Indian diplomat, London, 1 February 2013.
7 Interview with a South African diplomat, Durban, 18 December 2011.
8 This principle refers to mutual respect for sovereignty and territorial integrity, mutual nonaggression, non-interference in each other's internal affairs, equality and mutual benefit, and peaceful coexistence. These principles were originally adopted in 1954 in Mao's China, but have continued to serve the guiding principle of Chinese foreign policy and negotiation behaviour.

# References

Ansell, C. and Gash, A. (2008) 'Collaborative Governance in Theory and Practice'. *Journal of Public Administration Research and Theory* 18(4) pp. 543–571.

Baumgartner, F.R. and Jones, B.D. (1991) 'Agenda Dynamics and Policy Subsystems'. *Journal of Politics* 53(4) pp. 1044–1074.

Callahan, W. (2010) *China: The Pessoptimist Nation.* Oxford: Oxford University Press.

Coleman, W.D. and Perl, A. (1999) 'Internationalized Policy Environments and Policy Network Analysis'. *Political Studies* 47(4) pp. 691–709.

Costa, O. and Jorgensen, K.E. (eds) (2012) *The Influence of International Institutions on the EU.* London: Palgrave Macmillan.

Dai, X. (2007) *International Institutions and National Policies.* Cambridge: Cambridge University Press.

Dasgupta, P.S. (1997) 'Economic Development and the Idea of Social Capital'. Working Paper, Faculty of Economics, University of Cambridge.

Economy, E. (2001) 'The Impact of International Regimes on Chinese Foreign Policy-Making: Broadening Perspectives and Policies ... But Only to a Point'. In D.M. Lampton (ed.) *The Making of Chinese Foreign and Security Policy in the Era of Reform, 1979–2000* (pp. 230–256). Stanford, CA: Stanford University Press.

Economy, E. (1997) 'Chinese Policy-making and Global Climate Change'. In M.A. Schreurs and E. Economy (eds) *The Internationalization of Environmental Protection* (pp. 19–41). Cambridge: Cambridge University Press.

Emerson, K., Nabatchi, T., and Balogh, S. (2011) 'An Integrative Framework for Collaborative Governance'. *JPART* 22(1) pp. 1–29.

Fang, S. and Stone, R.W. (2012) 'International Organizations as Policy Advisors'. *International Organization* 66(4) pp. 537–569.

Farrell, H., and Héritier, A. (2003) 'Formal and Informal Institutions Under Co-decision: Continuous Constitution-Building in Europe'. *Governance: An International Journal of Policy, Administration and Institutions* 16(4) pp. 577–600.

Fonseca, G. Jr. (2011) 'Notes on the Evolution of Brazilian Multilateral Diplomacy'. *Global Governance* 17(3) pp. 375–397.

Giesen, B. (1987) 'Beyond Reductionism: Four Models Relating Micro and Macro Levels'. In J. Alexander, B. Giesen, R. Munch, and N. Smelser (eds) *The Micro–Macro Link*, Berkeley, CA: University of California Press.

Groenleer, M. (2012) 'Linking Up Levels of Governance: Agencies of the European Union and Their Interaction with International Institutions'. In O. Costa and K.E. Jorgensen (eds) *The Influence of International Institutions on the EU: When Multilateralism Hits Brussels* (pp. 135–154). London: Palgrave Macmillan.

Guo, S. (2013) *Chinese Politics and Government: Power, Ideology, and Organization.* London and New York: Routledge.

Haas, P.M. (1992) 'Introduction: Epistemic Communities and International Policy Coordination'. *International Organization* 46(1) pp. 1–35.

Hansen, R. and King, D. (2001) 'Eugenic Ideas, Political Interests, and Policy Variance: Immigration and Sterilization Policy in Britain and the U.S.'. *World Politics* 53(2) pp. 237–263.

Huxham, C. (2003) 'Theorizing Collaboration Practice'. *Public Management Review* 5(3) pp. 401–423.

Imperial, M. (2005) 'Using Collaboration as a Governance Strategy: Lessons from Six Watershed Management Programs'. *Administration & Society* 37(3) pp. 281–320.

Jacobson, H. and Oksenberg, M. (1990) *China's Participation in the IMF, the World Bank, and GATT.* Ann Arbor, MI: University of Michigan Press.

Johnston, A.I. (2008) *Social States: China in International Institutions, 1980–2000.* Princeton, NJ: Princeton University Press.

Kim, S.S. (1998) *China and the World: Chinese Foreign Policy Faces the New Millennium.* Boulder, CO: Westview Press.

Koontz, T.M., Steelman, T.A., Carmin, J., Kormacher, K.S., Moseley, C., and Thomas, C.W. (2004) *Collaborative Environmental Management: What Roles for Government?* Washington, DC: Resources for the Future Press.

Lampreia, L.F. and da Cruz, A.S. (2005) 'Brazil: Coping with Structural Constraints'. In J. Robertson and M.A. East (eds) *Diplomacy and Developing Nations* (pp. 97–113). London: Routledge.

Landsberg, C. (2005) 'Toward a Developmental Foreign Policy? Challenges for South Africa's Diplomacy in the Second Decade of Liberation'. *Social Research* 72(3) pp. 723–756.

Leach, W.D. and Pelkey, N.W. (2001) 'Making Watershed Partnerships Work: A Review of the Empirical Literature'. *Journal of Water Resources Planning and Management* 127(6) pp. 378–385.

Pearson, M.M. (2001) 'The Case of China's Accession to GATT/WTO'. In D.M. Lampton (ed.) *The Making of Chinese Foreign and Security Policy In the Era of Reform, 1978–2000* (pp. 337–370). Stanford, CA: Stanford University Press.

Pierson, P. (2000) 'Increasing Returns, Path Dependence, and the Study of Politics'. *American Political Review* 94(2) pp. 251–267.

Rayner, J., Howlett, M., Wilson, J., Cashore, B., and Hoberg, G. (2001) 'Privileging the Sub-Sector: Critical Sub-Sectors and Sectoral Relationships in Forest Policy-Making'. *Forest Policy and Economics* 2(3–4) pp. 319–332.

Rhodes, R.A.W. (1997) *Understanding Governance: Policy Networks, Governance, Reflexivity, and Accountability.* Buckingham: Open University Press.

Rose, R. (1990) 'Inheritance Before Choice in Public Policy'. *Journal of Theoretical Politics* 2(3) pp. 263–291.

Schaap, L. and van Twist, M.J.W. (1997) 'The Dynamics of Closedness in Networks'. In W.J.M. Kickert, E.H. Klijn, and J.F.M. Koppenjan (eds) *Managing Complex Networks: Strategies for the Public Sector* (pp. 62–77). London: Sage.

Visentini, P.G.F. and da Silva, A.L.R. (2010) 'Brazil and the Economic, Political, and Environmental Multilateralism: The Lula Years (2003–2010)' . *Revista Brasileira de Politica Internacional* 53 pp. 54–72.

Weir, M. (1992) 'Ideas and the Politics of Bounded Innovation'. In S. Steinmo, K. Thelen, and F. Longstreth (eds) *Structuring Politics: Historical Institutionalism in Comparative Analysis* (pp. 188–216). Cambridge: Cambridge University Press.

Young, A.R. (2012) 'Less Than You Might Think: The Impact of WTO Rules on EU Policies'. In O. Costa and K.E. Jorgensen (eds) *The Influence of International Institutions on the EU: When Multilateralism Hits Brussels* (pp. 23–41). London: Palgrave Macmillan.

Zhao, Q. (1996) *Interpreting Chinese Foreign Policy*. Oxford: Oxford University Press.

# Index

Page numbers in *italics* denote tables, those in **bold** denote figures.

 Taylor & Francis eBooks

## Helping you to choose the right eBooks for your Library

Add Routledge titles to your library's digital collection today. Taylor and Francis ebooks contains over 50,000 titles in the Humanities, Social Sciences, Behavioural Sciences, Built Environment and Law.

**Choose from a range of subject packages or create your own!**

**Benefits for you**

>> Free MARC records
>> COUNTER-compliant usage statistics
>> Flexible purchase and pricing options
>> All titles DRM-free.

 REQUEST YOUR **FREE** INSTITUTIONAL TRIAL TODAY

**Free Trials Available**
We offer free trials to qualifying academic, corporate and government customers.

**Benefits for your user**

>> Off-site, anytime access via Athens or referring URL
>> Print or copy pages or chapters
>> Full content search
>> Bookmark, highlight and annotate text
>> Access to thousands of pages of quality research at the click of a button.

## eCollections – Choose from over 30 subject eCollections, including:

| | |
|---|---|
| Archaeology | Language Learning |
| Architecture | Law |
| Asian Studies | Literature |
| Business & Management | Media & Communication |
| Classical Studies | Middle East Studies |
| Construction | Music |
| Creative & Media Arts | Philosophy |
| Criminology & Criminal Justice | Planning |
| Economics | Politics |
| Education | Psychology & Mental Health |
| Energy | Religion |
| Engineering | Security |
| English Language & Linguistics | Social Work |
| Environment & Sustainability | Sociology |
| Geography | Sport |
| Health Studies | Theatre & Performance |
| History | Tourism, Hospitality & Events |

For more information, pricing enquiries or to order a free trial, please contact your local sales team: www.tandfebooks.com/page/sales

 **Routledge** Taylor & Francis Group | The home of Routledge books

**www.tandfebooks.com**

For Product Safety Concerns and Information please contact our EU
representative GPSR@taylorandfrancis.com
Taylor & Francis Verlag GmbH, Kaufingerstraße 24, 80331 München, Germany

www.ingramcontent.com/pod-product-compliance
Ingram Content Group UK Ltd.
Pitfield, Milton Keynes, MK11 3LW, UK
UKHW021617240425
457818UK00018B/608